Kurdish Culture and Society

Kurdish Culture and Society

An Annotated Bibliography

Compiled by
Lokman I. Meho and Kelly L. Maglaughlin

Bibliographies and Indexes in Ethnic Studies, Number 9

GREENWOOD PRESS
Westport, Connecticut • London

Library of Congress Cataloging-in-Publication Data

Meho, Lokman I., 1968–
    Kurdish culture and society :   an annotated bibliography / compiled by Lokman I. Meho
and Kelly L. Maglaughlin.
        p. cm.—(Bibliographies and indexes in ethnic studies, ISSN 1046–7882 ; no. 9)
    Includes bibliographical references and indexes.
    ISBN 0–313–31543–4 (alk. paper)
    1. Kurds—Bibliography.   I. Maglaughlin, Kelly L.   II. Title.   III. Series.
Z3014.K85M43 2001
[DS59.K86]
016.305891′597—dc21   00–063654

British Library Cataloguing in Publication Data is available.

Library of Congress Catalog Card Number: 00–063654
ISBN: 0–313–31543–4
ISSN: 1046–7882

First published in 2001

Greenwood Press, 88 Post Road West, Westport, CT 06881
An imprint of Greenwood Publishing Group, Inc.
www.greenwood.com

Printed in the United States of America

The paper used in this book complies with the
Permanent Paper Standard issued by the National
Information Standards Organization (Z39.48–1984).

10 9 8 7 6 5 4 3 2 1

To the School of Information and Library Science at the University of North Carolina, Chapel Hill

Contents

Abbreviations

AI	Abstracta Iranica
HA	Historical Abstracts
IJKS	International Journal of Kurdish Studies
IPSA	International Political Science Abstracts
MEJ	Middle East Journal
PSA	Political Science Abstracts
SA	Sociological Abstracts

Preface

This is the first comprehensive annotated bibliography exclusively devoted to Kurdish culture and society. It includes entries in many areas including but not limited to anthropology, archaeology, art, communication, demography, description and travel, economy, education, ethnicity, folklore, health conditions, journalism, language, literature, migration, music, religion, social structure and organization, urbanization, and women. It also includes entries on the Kurds in Syria, Lebanon, Israel, former Soviet Union, Europe and other countries of the world. These topics have been selected for two main reasons: first, they need more attention from bibliographers and, second, locating published information on these topics is not an easy task, particularly because such information is highly diverse (e.g., in terms of language and country of publication) and very much scattered (see below). This bibliography will assist researchers and other readers to locate relevant published information very easily and efficiently. It will fill a major gap in the Kurdish, Middle Eastern, and world library.

Literature on the aforementioned topics was covered in a number of previously published comprehensive bibliographies; however, each of these bibliographies has a number of disadvantages in comparison to this project. For example, *ISK's Kurdish Bibliography*, one of the earliest and most exhaustive bibliographies on the Kurds and Kurdistan with 9,350 entries in more than twenty languages, did include material on Kurdish culture and society.[1] How-

---

[1]International Society Kurdistan, *ISK's Kurdish Bibliography*, edited by Silvio van Rooy and Kees Tamboer (Amsterdam: International Society Kurdistan, 1968), 2 vols. An earlier bibliography was published by Mohammad Mokri, entitled "Kurdologie et enseignment de la langue kurde en URSS (avec une bibliographie concernant les etudes kurdes" and published in *L'Ethnographie* N.S. 57 (1963), pp. 71-105. It lists 13 doctoral dissertations awarded between 1939 and 1955 at USSR academic institutions.

ever, none of the bibliography's entries is annotated and its only index—a subject index—is not sufficiently detailed to provide good levels of precision and recall. Also, the work is now very much in need of an update.

Another comprehensive bibliography on the Kurds and Kurdistan was compiled by Joyce Blau.[2] Her work is a collection of short reviews of books and articles on the Kurds and Kurdistan which have appeared in *Abstracta Iranica*[3] between 1977 and 1987. Many of the annotations were originally written by Blau herself. The book is considered the first comprehensive annotated bibliography to cover works on Kurdish language, history, literature and culture in all parts of Kurdistan.[4] It includes an impressive number of publications in Kurdish. It further includes works in Persian, Turkish, and some East and West European languages. Blau's bibliography, however, is weak in its coverage of Arabic, English, French, and German materials. The bibliography moreover does not cover materials published before 1977. An update to Blau's bibliography was compiled in 1996 by Gilet and Beriel,[5] yet, the problem of poor coverage of Arabic, English, French, and German materials persisted. In addition, there were very few items included in this bibliography covering the period after 1993.

More recently, I compiled a bibliography on the Kurds.[6] It was the first annotated bibliography to be published in English and cover all parts of Kurdistan.[7] The bibliography includes 814 entries covering some of the most impor-

---

It also lists 269 items in various USSR languages on Kurdish language and linguistics, literature, folklore, social anthropolgy, history, politics, religion, and sociology. Also before ISK's, an annotated bibliography, titled "Bulletin raisonne d'etudes kurdes," was published by Father Thomas Bois in *Al-Machriq* (July-October 1964), pp. 528-570. It was reprinted in a separate volume in 1964 under the same title (Beirut: Imprimerie Catholique, 1964).

[2]Joyce Blau, *Les Kurds et le Kurdistan: bibliographie critique, 1977-1986* (Paris: Institut français de recherche en Iran, 1989).

[3]*Abstracta Iranica*, Téhéran: Département d'iranologie de l'Institut français de Téhéran, 1978- .

[4]Before publishing this book, Blau compiled an annotated bibliography of more than 150 items housed in the Kurdish Institute in Paris. The bibliography, entitled "Bibliographie des ouvrages de kurdologie parus a partir de la fondation de l'Institut Kurde de Paris en 1983 jusqu'en 1986," was published in *Studia Kurdica*, no. 1-5 (1988), pp. 157-183. Items covered were those published between 1983 and 1986 in Arabic English, French, Italian, Kurdish, Russian, and some other east and west European languages dealing with Kurdish language and linguistics, literature, folklore, journalism, music, and history.

[5]M Gilet and M.-M. Beriel, *Les Kurdes et le Kurdistan: Bibliographie 1987-1996* (Paris: CNRS, 1996).

[6]Lokman I. Meho, *The Kurds and Kurdistan: A Selective and Annotated Bibliography* (Westport, CT: Greenwood Press, 1997).

[7]Wolfgang Behn had an annotated bibliography published in English, but his emphasis was, as the title suggests, on the Kurds in Iran: *The Kurds in Iran: A Selected*

tant works that were published between the early 1940s and mid-1990s. The bibliography is general in character; however, it focuses more on history, politics, and human rights literature than on other research areas. Almost 70% of the records in the bibliography are listed under history and politics. The remaining 30% are primarily divided between language, religion, and Kurdish Jews. Moreover, the materials included are overwhelmingly in English.

As far as non-English and non-French general comprehensive bibliographies on the Kurds are concerned, only two were found: (1) Dzhalile Dzhalil[8]—a 534-page long bibliography covering items in Armenian, Kurdish, and Russian; and (2) Zh. S. Musaelian[9]—a 918-page long bibliography covering items in Armenian, Kurdish, Russian, and other East European languages. Bibliographies in Arabic and German were located.[10] However, they were either dated or had no or poor coverage of Kurdish culture and society literature. Most of them also lacked annotations. It is primarily the above discussed problems of earlier bibliographies that motivated us to compile this comprehensive, up-to-date, and annotated bibliography on Kurdish culture and society. Certainly, the need for such a bibliography with particular emphasis on Arabic, English, French, and German materials was another reason. Although many general items that cover all aspects of Kurdish life and history are included in this bibliography, researchers looking for extensive materials on the history and politics of the Kurds and Kurdistan and/or for literature in Kurdish, Persian Turkish, Russian, and East European languages, are encouraged to consult the above mentioned bibliographies. Researchers are also encouraged to consult, among other sources, the indexing and abstracting services used to compile this bibliography (see below).

Students, educators, researchers, policy makers, and the general public interested in Kurdish studies will find this bibliography as an indispensable guide for any research or reading on the Kurds and Kurdistan. Over 930 items are included in this bibliography ranging from books, scholarly journal articles,

---

and Annotated Bibliography (London: Mansell, 1977). His bibliography, compiled chiefly from holdings of the Islamic Union Catalogue in Germany, includes 275 items, arranged under 13 subject headings. Most of the items are in Arabic, English, and Persian. It was intended to supplement International Society Kurdistan's *Kurdish Bibliography*, for the years 1966-1975, and to include items omitted from *Index Islamicus*.

[8]Dzhalile Dzhalil, *Kurdy Sovetskoi Armenii: Bibliografiia, 1920-1980* (Erevan: Izd-vo AN Armianskoi SSR, 1987).

[9]Zh. S. Musaelian, *Bibliografiia po kurdovedeniiu: nachinaia s XVI veka* (Sankt-Peterburg: TSentr "Peterburgskoe vostokovedenie," 1996).

[10]Examples include: 'Abd Allah Ghafur, *Bibliyughrafiyat Kurdistan* (Stockholm: Sara Distribution, 1994); Gerda Hansen, *Die Lage der Kurden: Literatur seit 1985* (Hamburg, Germany: Deutsches Ubersee-Institut, Ubersee-Dokumentation, Referat Vorderer Orient, 1991); Gerda Hansen, *Die Kurden und der Kurdenkonflikt: Literatur seit 1990: eine Auswahlbibliographie* (Hamburg, Germany: Deutsches Ubersee-Institut, 1994); and Mustafa Nariman, *Ma Asdahu al-Akrad ila al-Maktaba al-'Arabiya, 1900-1981* (Baghdad: Matba'at Husam, 1983).

and chapters in books to doctoral dissertations, conference papers, and articles in scholarly dictionaries and encyclopedias. Sixty percent of the items included are in English, 15% in Arabic, 15% in French, 5% in German, and 5% are in Italian and other European languages. The publication date of items included range from the 1700s through the year 2000. More than 70% of the items are accompanied by 50-300 words-long annotations either written by me or extracted from other sources such as book reviews and abstracting databases. These latter sources were particularly used for items that I did not have access to. Some of the annotations included are informative in nature, others are descriptive, and still others evaluative. A combination of two or more of these annotation styles has been applied to a large proportion of items. Unless an English translation was provided by the authors of the items, no attempt was made at translating foreign titles. Almost none of the Arabic sources was accompanied by an English translation. Therefore, I provided a short description and/or annotations of these titles.

Records included in this bibliography were gleaned from many print and electronic sources. Only the most important are listed here—information in parentheses refers to years covered followed by the subject matter of the source:

> *Abstracta Iranica* (1978-1996/General)
> *Anthropological Index Online* (late 1960s–mid-1990s/Anthropology)
> *Anthropological Literature* (1985-1999/Anthropology)
> *Art Abstracts* (1984-2000/Art)
> *ARTbibliographies Modern* (1974-1998/Art)
> *Arts & Humanities Citation Index* (1980-2000/Art & Humanities)
> *Avery Index to Architectural Periodicals* (1977-1999/Architecture)
> *Bulletin analytique de documentation politique, economique et sociale contemporaine* (1946-1995/General)
> *Dissertation Abstracts Online* (1861-2000/General)
> *Expanded Academic ASAP* (1980-2000/General)
> *al-Fihrist* (1981-1994/General)
> *Health Star* (1975-2000/Health, Medicine)
> *Historical Abstracts* (1960-2000/History)
> *Index Islamicus* (1665-1999/General)
> *International Index to Music Periodicals* (1874-1999/Music)
> *International Political Science Abstracts* (1951-2000/Political Science)
> *Linguistics and Language Behavior Abstracts* (1973-2000/Linguistics)
> *Medline* (1965-2000/Health, Medicine)
> *MLA International Bibliography* (1963-1999/Linguistics, Literature)
> *Muhtawayat al-Dawriyat al-'Arabiya* (1989-1995/General)
> *Periodicals Contents Index* (1770-1993/General)
> *PsychLit* (1887-2000/Psychology)
> *Religion Index* (1949-1999/Religion)

RILM Abstracts of Music Literature (1969-1999/Music)
Social Sciences Citation Index (1972-2000/Social Sciences)
Sociological Abstracts (1963-2000/Sociology)
WorldCat (1700s-2000/General)

To locate information that may not have been found in any of the above mentioned databases, I browsed the reference and circulation shelves of the libraries of the University of North Carolina at Chapel Hill, Duke University, and the American University of Beirut. I also examined previously published bibliographies and references listed in a number of books, dissertations, and journal and encyclopedia articles.

The records included in this bibliography are divided into chapters. Some chapters are further subdivided into different sections. For example, the chapter on Description and Travel has a section on travels before 1900 and another section on travels since 1900, the chapter on Language has a section on dictionaries and another on study and teaching, and so on. Items within each section are arranged alphabetically by author name. Because many titles cover more than one geographical area or topic, extensive cross references are made to track down entries from one section to the other. A comprehensive subject index is also provided at the end of the bibliography. Author and title indexes are provided too. Additionally, a list of some of the most important Kurdish World Wide Web resources is provided (see Appendix). These sources provide a lot of unpublished information and links to many other related sources. The bibliography moreover includes a 24-page long introduction providing a general background of the Kurds and Kurdistan. Because virtually nothing is published on the Kurds in Lebanon, a chapter discussing the topic in some detail is also provided.

Although this is a comprehensive bibliography, there are certain topics that are poorly represented such as Arts, Economy, Education, Health, Music, Population studies, Urban Planning, and Women's studies. This poor representation is a result of the scarcity of research conducted in these areas. Accordingly, it is suggested that any weaknesses found in the areas covered in this bibliography should be considered as a call for future research in those areas. This future research should also be theoretically informed, rich in descriptive detail, original, and objective. The reason for this is because many of the works included in this bibliography were found repetitious or marred by nationalist, ideological, and political preconceptions.

This book has been made possible thanks to the institutions which offered us the opportunity to use their resources. These institutions are the University of North Carolina at Chapel Hill, Duke University, and the American University of Beirut. We are very grateful to all of them.

Lokman I. Meho
Chapel Hill, NC

PART I
ESSAYS

The Kurds and Kurdistan: A General Background

Lokman I. Meho

GEOGRAPHY AND POPULATION[1]

Kurdistan, or the homeland of the Kurds, is a strategic area located in the geographic heart of the Middle East. Today, it comprises important parts of Turkey, Iran, Iraq, and Syria. These parts were created at two different occasions: first, in 1514 when Kurdistan was divided between the Ottoman and Persian empires following the battle of Chaldiran and, second, in 1920-1923 when Britain and France further altered the political contours of Kurdistan by dividing Ottoman Kurdistan among Iraq, Syria, and Turkey. Today, estimates of the size of the land where the Kurds constitute the dominant majority range from

---

[1]A few sources have been extensively used in this Introduction. Rather than repeatedly citing these sources, they are listed here: Martin van Bruinessen, *Agha, Shaikh and State: The Social and Political Structures of Kurdistan* (London: Zed Books Ltd., 1992); Gerard Chaliand, ed., *A People Without A Country: The Kurds and Kurdistan* (London: Zed Press, 1993); Nader Entessar, *Kurdish Ethnonationalism* (Boulder, CO: Lynne Rienner Publishers, 1992); Edmund Ghareeb, *The Kurdish Question in Iraq* (Syracuse, NY: Syracuse University Press, 1981); Michael Gunter, *The Kurds and the Future of Turkey* (New York: St. Martin's Press, 1997); Michael Gunter, *The Kurdish Predicament in Iraq: A Political Analysis* (Basingstoke: Macmillan, 1999); Amir Hassanpour, *Nationalism and Language in Kurdistan, 1918-1985* (San Francisco: Mellen Research University Press, 1992); *International Journal of Kurdish Studies* 11, nos. 1-2 (1997), pp. 251-257; Mehrdad Izady, *The Kurds: A Concise Handbook* (Washington, D.C.: Taylor & Francis, Inc., 1992); David McDowall, *A Modern History of the Kurds* (London: I. B. Tauris, 1996); David McDowall, *The Kurds.* 7th ed. (London: Minority Rights Group, 1996); Robert Olson, *The Emergence of Kurdish Nationalism and the Sheikh Said Rebellion, 1880-1925* (Austin, TX: University of Texas Press, 1988); and Robert Olson, ed. *The Kurdish Nationalist Movement in the 1990s: Its Impact on Turkey and the Middle East* (Lexington, KY: University Press of Kentucky, 1996).

230,000 to 300,000 square miles in size, divided as follows: Turkey (43% of the total area of Kurdistan), Iran (31%), Iraq (18%), Syria (6%), and former USSR (2%). The Kurds in the former USSR (mainly in Armenia and Azerbaijan) had passed into that area when territories were ceded by Persia in 1807-1820, and by the Ottomans in 1878.

As in the case with most Middle Eastern stateless nations, estimates of the total number of Kurds vary widely. Kurdish nationalists are tempted to exaggerate the number, and governments of the region to minimize it. Although there are no official censuses regarding the number of the Kurds, most sources agree that today there are more than 30 million Kurds and at least one-third of them live outside Kurdistan because of war, forced resettlements, or economic deprivation. Slightly more than half of the Kurds live in Turkey, about one-fourth in Iran, and one-sixth in Iraq. The remaining Kurds live in Syria (1.5 million), Europe (over 1 million), former Soviet Union (.5 million), and several other countries. The largest concentrations of Kurds outside Kurdistan are in the major cities of Turkey, Iran, Iraq, Syria, and former Soviet republics, and in two Kurdish enclaves in central and north-central Anatolia in Turkey and in Khurasan in northeast Iran and southern Turkmenistan. There are also large concentrations of Kurds in Germany (over 600,000),[2] Israel (over 100,000),[3] and Lebanon (75,000-100,000). Australia, Canada, England, Finland, France, Greece, Sweden, and the United States each have a Kurdish population of over 10,000 (see bibliography for relevant sources). It is important to note here that despite all efforts by Turkey, Iran, Iraq, and Syria to downsize the number of Kurds, no one can deny that the Kurds are the fourth largest ethnic group in the Middle East, after the Arabs, Persians, and Turks, and that they are one of the largest stateless nations in the world.

Anthropologically, the Kurds are now predominantly of Mediterranean racial stock, resembling southern Europeans and the Levantines in skin, general coloring and physiology. There is yet a persistent recurrence of two racial substrata: a darker aboriginal Palaeo-Caucasian element, and more localized occurrence of blondism of the Alpine type in the heartland of Kurdistan.[4]

KURDISH SOCIETY AND NATIONALISM

Kurdish society is still basically tribal. Accordingly, the loyalty of the Kurds is primarily directed towards the immediate family clan—the cornerstone of the social system—and thence to the tribe—the largest grouping within

---

[2]Eva Ostergaard-Nielsen, "Trans-state Loyalties and Politics of Turks and Kurds in Western Europe," *SAIS Review* 20, no. 1 (Winter-Spring 2000), pp. 23-38.

[3]Yona Sabar, "Jews of Kurdistan," in *Encyclopedia of World Cultures, Volume IX: Africa and the Middle East*, edited by John Middleton and Amal Rassam (Boston, MA: G.K. Hall and Co., 1995), pp. 144-147.

[4]http://kurdweb.humanrights.de/kwd/english/society/society-frame.html.

Kurdish society. The cohesion of the Kurdish tribe, in turn, is based on a mixture of blood ties and territorial allegiances associated with strong religious loyalties. Until very recently, beyond the tribe, many Kurds, especially those who live in rural areas, only occasionally showed loyalty to a nation, state, or any other entity. This state of affairs continues to be present today but it is in steady decline. The socio-economic and political changes that most Kurds have witnessed since the 1960s—such as the mechanization of agriculture, industrialization, subsequent revolts, rural-urban migration, emigration, political mobilization in party politics, the expansion of public education and mass communications—have weakened the tribal structure of the Kurdish society and provided an impetus for developing larger Kurdish nationalism.

Taking the Kurds in Turkey as an example, more than 25 percent of the total Kurdish population there lives today in Istanbul, Ankara, Izmir and other major Turkish cities, let alone the Kurds who moved into European countries. Many of these emigrants left Kurdistan either voluntarily (for social and economic purposes) or forcibly (because of political difficulties and state terror which took the forms of mass evacuations, village-razing, killings, and imprisonment). Becoming aware of the great disparity between their impoverished life in Kurdistan and their new lives in Turkish and European cities, Kurdish emigrants became more socially and politically conscious, and their awareness of their Kurdish identity and ethnic solidarity was strengthened.[5] Such improvements or developments in the social, economic, and political status of the Kurds have become a vital source for the growth of the Kurdish movement in Turkey. In summary, the social and economic negligence of Kurdistan by the local governments and the protracted cultural and political repression exercised against Kurdish populations were decisive factors in fostering Kurdish nationalism rather than suppressing it as was hoped from the governments' harsh policies.

LANGUAGE

The Kurds speak various dialects of Kurdish that can be divided into two main groups. The Kurmanji group, which is spoken by more than 75 percent of the Kurds and composed of two major branches: Bahdinani (or North Kurmanji)—the most widely spoken dialect[6]—and Sorani (or Central Kurmanji). The Pahlawani group, spoken by the rest of the Kurds, is also composed of two major branches: Dimili (or Zaza or Hawrami) and Gorani (or Kerman-

---

[5]See Martin van Bruinessen, "Kurdish Society, Ethnicity, Nationalism and Refugee Problem," in *The Kurds: A Contemporary Overview,* edited by Philip G. Kreyenbroek and Stefan Sperl (London: Routledge, 1992), pp. 48-54.

[6]Most of the Kurds in Turkey, a large portion of the Kurds in Iran and Iraq, and almost the entire Kurdish population in Syria and the former Soviet Union speak the Northern Kurmanji dialect.

shahi or South Kurmanji).[7] All of these major dialects are further divided into scores of sub-dialects as well, yet, all are members of the north-western division of the Iranic branch of the Indo-European family of languages.

In their attempts to suppress Kurdish identity and revivalism, Turkey, Iran, Iraq, Syria, and the former Soviet Union have not only used political oppression and economic exploitation, but also targeted cultural oppression as well. The forms in which cultural oppression were implemented are diverse, yet language oppression was perhaps the most important. The following are just brief summaries of state policies towards the Kurdish language.

After the creation of modern Turkey in 1923, Ataturk decided to substitute the alphabet used in Turkish from Arabic to Latin. Consequently, the Kurds of Turkey were forced to do the same and adapt a modified version of the Latin characters for their language that incidentally fitted Kurdish more but inhibited the exchange of literature between the Kurds in Turkey and Syria, on the one hand, and those in Iran and Iraq, on the other. The Kurds in Iran and Iraq continued to use a modified version of the Perso-Arabic alphabet. Less than a year later (i.e., in 1924), new measures were introduced and implemented in Turkey with the aim of suppressing the Kurdish language. These measures took the form of banning both the spoken and written use of Kurdish, and ensuring that education and information are only provided in Turkish or to those people who speak Turkish. Possession of written material in Kurdish also became a serious crime punishable by a long-term prison sentence.

Turkish repressive measures against Kurdish continued since then, with varying degrees of severity: easing during civilian rule and strengthening during military rule. The following excerpt extracted from *Otuken*, a Turkish journal, sums up the attitude of the Turkish government towards the Kurds and their language:

> If they [the Kurds] want to carry on speaking a primitive language with vocabularies of only four or five thousand words; if they want to create their own state and publish what they like, let them go and do it somewhere else. We Turks have shed rivers of blood to take possession of these lands; we had to uproot Georgians, Armenians, and Byzantine Greeks... Let them go off wherever they want, to Iran, to Pakistan, to India, or to join Barzani. Let them ask the United Nations to find them a homeland in Africa. The Turkish race is very patient, but when it is really angered it is like a roaring lion and nothing can stop it. Let them ask the Armenians who we are, and let them draw the appropriate conclusions.[8]

In Iran, speaking and writing in Kurdish are absolutely forbidden by law. Only in the 1990s did the Kurds begin to publish material in Kurdish more openly and use the language in many other cultural activities. This was thanks

---

[7]See Izady, pp. 172-182.
[8]*Otuken* (June 1967). Cited in Kendal, "Kurdistan in Turkey," p. 77.

to pressures from Kurdish revolutionaries there rather than an ease on the government part.

In Iraq, Kurdish language, literature, and some other forms of cultural expression were guaranteed by the 1932 Constitution. This situation further progressed after 1958 when the Kurdish language was officially recognized as the second language of the country and was used and studied in schools and universities. However, what the Kurds have achieved in Iraq was a result of a long struggle against official animosity rather than granted by a noble government.[9] Even though the situation in Iraq is by far better than anywhere else in Kurdistan, it is unfortunate that the cultural freedom enjoyed by the Kurds in the country is and has always been under the mercy of the regime's mood: improving when relations between the Kurdish leaders and the government are good, and deteriorating when relations are bad.

In Syria, although 90 percent of the Kurds use Kurdish in their everyday life, the use of the Kurdish language in any form is still against the law. Despite the greater tolerance the Syrian government has been showing in the 1990s towards its Kurdish minority, the government still prohibits the use of Kurdish in schools and forbids broadcasting and publishing in the language.[10]

In the former Soviet Union, the situation was relatively good before World War II when Kurdish was in steady promotion. After the war, the assimilation processes (carried out by the resettlement campaigns of Stalin), the discontinuation of the use of Kurdish as a medium of instruction in schools, the cultural isolation of the Soviet Kurds from their brethrens across the borders (a consequence of changing the alphabet into Cyrillic), and the recent plight of the Kurds in Armenia, Azerbaijan, and Georgia all denied the Kurds an effective development of their language.

Given the current conditions of Kurdish language use in Kurdistan, it is not surprising that only in countries other than those mentioned above Kurdish is used with little or no restrictions. The best example is the Kurds in Europe who use Kurdish for instruction and in printing, publication, and broadcasting, just to mention a few.

RELIGION

At least two thirds of the Kurds are Sunni Muslims of the Shafi'i school of law, in contrast to their Arab and Turkish Sunni neighbors who adhere mostly to the Hanafi school, and their Azeri and Persian neighbors who

---

[9] Kreyenbroek, p. 76.

[10] See David McDowall, *The Kurds of Syria* (London: Kurdish Human Rights Project, 1998); Middle East Watch, *Syria Unmasked: The Suppression of Human Rights by the Assad Regime* (New Haven: Yale University Press, 1991); and Ismet Cheriff Vanly, "The Kurds in Syria and Lebanon," in *The Kurds: A Contemporary Overview*, edited by Philip. G. Kreyenbroek and Stefan Sperl (London: Routledge, 1992).

are Shi'ites.[11] There are, however, many Shi'i Kurds concentrated in southern Kurdistan (Iran) and in the districts of Khanaqin and Mandali in Iraqi Kurdistan. Most of the remaining Kurds are adherents of heterodox, syncretistic sects "with beliefs and rituals that are clearly influenced by Islam but owe more to other religions, notably old Iranian religion."[12] Such sects include the Alevis (or the Qizilbash) with an estimate of more than three millions, the Ahl-i Haqq ('People of Truth' or the Kaka'is) and the Yezidis. There are also several thousands of Christian Kurds and more than 150,000 Jewish Kurds most of whom are today residing in Israel. These Christians and Jews became Kurdish by culture and language.

Until the mid-twentieth century, religion among the Kurds played a prominent role in the Kurdish nationalist movement. In fact, most of the Kurdish rebellions which broke out in the period between the 1880s and the 1930s were led by *Sheikhs*. These rebellions, however, were intensely influenced by the religious diversity of the Kurds. Sunnis, for example, divided into two *tariqas* or mystical orders—the Naqshbandi and the Qadiri—never cooperated effectively with each other in any of the rebellions instigated by either side's leaders.[13] The Shi'ite Kurds of Iran, on the other hand, never took part in the Kurdish national movement. The Alevi Kurds, fearing Sunni fanaticism, did not support the rebellion of Sheikh Sa'id in 1925; the Alevis, conversely, received no support from Sunni Kurds in their rebellions of 1921 and 1937-1938.[14]

OTHER CULTURAL ASPECTS

Often disregarded by many writers, Kurdish national identity is not only manifested in tribe, kinship, language, religion, or history. Other cultural traits, such as literature and folklore and art and music have important primary roles in fostering Kurdish nationalism.[15] For example, despite the supremacy of Arabic, Turkish, and Persian, Kurdish literature have retained its originality, developed, and contributed to the consolidation of national feeling. Kurdish literature, be it romantic or realist, written or oral, contemporary or old, was, and still is, a mirror for the Kurdish people through which they recognize the

---

[11]Martin van Bruinessen, "Religion in Kurdistan," *Kurdish Times* 4 (Summer-Fall 1991), p. 7.

[12]Ibid, p. 8.

[13]For example, the Naqshbandis did not participate in any of Sheikh Mahmud's revolts in Iraq in the 1920s. Cited in Sami Shurash, "Tanawwu' Akrad al-'Iraq: Madkhal ila al-Siyasa," *Abwab* [London], no 3 (Winter 1995), p. 49.

[14]Van Bruinessen, "Religion in Kurdistan," pp. 7-14.

[15]See Maria T. O'Shea, "Between the Map and the Reality: Some Fundamental Myths of Kurdish Nationalism," **Peuples Mediterraneens**, no. 68-69 (July-December 1994), pp. 77-94.

beauty and greatness of their country as well as the poverty and denial that are imposed on them. In Blau's words: "The new blossoming of Kurdish poets, writers, and intellectuals who belong to the Kurmanji group strikingly illustrates the relationship between cultural development and political freedom."[16] Another example is the sense of a common past represented in the form of storing up the collective memories and carrying them on to subsequent generations: the Kurds have a wealth of famous heroes and sacred dates and memorable places and unforgettable events that can fill historical catalogs in many volumes.[17] In such circumstances, Kurdish national feelings are almost impossible to be terminated from the minds and hearts of the Kurds.[18]

EDUCATION

The ban on the use of the Kurdish language in most parts of Kurdistan, and the shortage of both schools and teachers in Kurdish villages and towns has severely hindered the improvement of the Kurds' educational level. According to the available sources,[19] the illiteracy rate in Turkish Kurdistan was more than 72 percent in 1975 as opposed to 41 percent in areas populated by Turks. In Iranian Kurdistan, the illiteracy rate was 70 percent. Although in Iran, the illiteracy rate declined to 50 percent by 1986, the Kurds remain to be the second least literate of the major nationalities in the country (the Baluchis are first). Only in Iraq, Syria, and the former Soviet Union (where only 20-25% of all Kurds live) is the situation significantly better.

Urbanization seems to have a positive impact on education as could be suggested from the great increase in published works by Kurds living in the area.[20] However, given that more than half of the Kurds live in rural areas,

[16]Joyce Blau, "Kurdish Written Literature," in *Kurdish Culture and Identity*, edited by Philip Kreyenbroek and Christine Allsion (London: Zed Books, 1996), p. 27.

[17]Kawa and Newruz, Media Empire and the Republic of Mahabad are only a few examples.

[18]For further details, see *The Importance of Cultural Elements in the Struggle of the Kurdish People* (Amsterdam: Research Institute of Oppressed People, 1983); Philip Kreyenbroek and Christine Allsion, eds., *Kurdish Culture and Identity* (London: Zed Books Ltd., 1996); Kendal Nezan, "Kurdish Music and Dance," *World of Music* 21 (1979): 19-32; and O'Shea, "Between the Map and the Reality."

[19]Chaliand, *The Kurdish Tragedy* (London: Zed Books Ltd., 1994); A. R. Ghassemlou (Abdul Rahman), "Kurdistan in Iran," in *People Without a Country: The Kurds and Kurdistan*, edited by Gerard Chaliand (London: Zed Press, 1993), pp. 99-100; Izady, pp. 179-181; and Kendal (Kendal Nezan), "Kurdistan in Turkey," in *People Without a Country: The Kurds and Kurdistan*, edited by Gerard Chaliand (London: Zed Press, 1993) p. 40.

[20]For further details, see Amir Hassanpour, "The Creation of Kurdish Media Culture," in *Kurdish Culture and Identity*, edited by Philip Kreyenbroek and Christine Allison (London: Zed Books Ltd., 1996), pp. 48-84.

where education receives little local and government attention, the Kurds will continue to lag behind nationally as far as producing a highly literate stratum is concerned. Kurdish nationalists have for long argued that native tongue education is one of the indispensable means by which to protect their ethnic identity from assimilation efforts, but little planned efforts have been seriously considered by them. In other words, Kurdish nationalists need to give more and better attention to education. As Hassanpour has indicated in several of his works, there are various means or methods that can be used to achieve national rights; education is one of them (see bibliography).

ECONOMY

Kurdistan is known to be very rich in its natural resources. Not only oil and water, but also copper, chromium, iron, and sulfur are found with abundance in Kurdish soil. Agriculturally, Kurdistan is also affluent in its high-grade pasture lands as well as with its large and fertile mountain valleys (comprising 28 percent of Kurdistan's total surface area). Wheat, barley, and a great variety of cereals, vegetables, fruits and nuts are the common crops grown in Kurdistan. As for the cash crops, the most important are tobacco, cotton, olives, and sugar beets. Animal products are also of great importance in Kurdistan's economy with sheep being the most important.

Despite the huge economic production of Kurdistan, whether from its natural resources or from its agricultural goods, only a small portion of its benefits is geared towards the local population. Moreover, heavy modern industries in Kurdistan are almost non-existent. True that oil is produced with abundance from Kurdish areas (and is refined there), nevertheless, skilled laborers are almost entirely non-Kurds and indeed non-locals. Even in the mining sector, the Kurds constitute the main unskilled workers. Only light industries can be found in Kurdistan and these are mainly related to handicrafts, construction materials, sugar and textiles. Trade is also of growing importance in Kurdistan and represents a good source of income to many Kurds living near the trade routes. All this, along with the local governments' economic negligence of Kurdistan (e.g., limited investment) explains why Kurdish society is still mainly agrarian with most Kurds working on the land.[21] As a consequence, Kurdistan continues to suffer from a sharp increase in the emigration of its

---

[21]Chaliand, *The Kurdish Tragedy*, pp. 14-15; and Izady, pp. 221-234. Both Chaliand and Izady say that, contrary to what many peoples assume of the Kurds, only a very small number of Kurds (less than 3 percent) still practice a nomadic economy. It was the forced sedentarization policies, introduced in Turkey and Iran as of the 1920s that marked the beginning of the end of nomadism and its traditional modes of economic production. Since then, nomads became farmers, villagers, or even city dwellers.

productive population to urban centers where they are in effect "becoming urbanized but not industrialized."[22]

HISTORY

There is no doubt that the Kurds are one of the oldest nations in the Middle East. Distinct from their Arab and Turkish neighbors, many scholars agree that the Kurds are descendants of a mixture of peoples formed of indigenous inhabitants and subsequent Indo-European immigrants who settled the region for more than three thousand years. Their ancient history, which stretches from 3000 to 400 BC, was a period of high disturbances between Kurdistan and the neighboring powers. According to the records of those powers, a group of people residing in Kurdistan, known as the Gutis then, were able to establish a ruling dynasty in the region between 2250 and 2120 BC. For the next 1,500 years after the fall of the Gutis, however, Kurdistan was a scene for military invasions, looting, and destruction executed by their neighbors. Those actions which drove the entire region into a social and economic depression led to the transformation of Kurdistan (which was witnessing subsequent Aryan immigration waves) into an Indo-European-speaking society. Indigenous inhabitants along with other Aryan immigrants were able to establish their own empire—the Median Empire—which ruled vast areas of the Middle East between 612 and 549 BC. The establishment of the Median Empire and subsequent dynasties by the newly formed Kurdish people as well as by other peoples kept Kurdistan relatively independent of external rule until the Islamic conquest in the 7th century AD. After three centuries of Islamic rule, the Kurds started to reemerge powerfully again, particularly with the establishment of Kurdish dynasties that ruled large areas of the region. Among those dynasties were the Mamlanids or the Rawwadids (920-1071), the Buwayhid Daylamites (932-1062), the Shaddadids (951-1174), the Hasnawayhids (959-1015), the Marwanids (983-1085), and the Ayyubids (1169-15th century).

From the beginning of the 13th century, however, the Kurds started to experience a steady decline in various aspects of their lives. Several important causes were behind this decline but the most important were: (1) the destructive Mongol and Turkic invasions of Kurdistan; (2) the division of Kurdistan in 1514 among the Persian and the Ottoman empires; and (3) the economic isolation of Kurdistan which resulted from discovering new international trade routes that replaced the old routes that passed through Kurdistan. Sea transportation in particular, denied Kurdistan transit revenues as well as the influx of new technologies, information, and ideas.

Following the defeat of the Persians by the Ottomans at the battle of Chaldiran in 1514, the Kurds and Kurdistan became divided between two em-

---

[22]Chaliand, *The Kurdish Tragedy*, p. 41.

pires with the majority in the Ottoman part. Since then, vast portions of Kurdistan were systematically devastated and large numbers of Kurds deported to the
far corners of the Safavid and Ottoman empires. The magnitude of death and
destruction wrought in Kurdistan for nearly three hundred years resulted in
several Kurdish rebellions: the Baban revolt between 1806 and 1808, Prince
Mohammed of Soran's revolt between 1833 and 1837, the Badrkhan's revolt of
1847, the Yezdan Sher revolt of 1855, and the 1880 revolt of Sheikh 'Ubaydallah of Nehri. Although led by a religious leader, the revolt of 1880 was the
most important of all 19th century Kurdish rebellions for it included both the
Kurds of the Ottoman empire and those of Persia, and marked a beginning of
modern Kurdish nationalism.[23]

After the defeat of Sheikh 'Ubaydallah by the Ottomans in 1880, Sultan 'Abdulhamid II, hoping to secure the Ottoman domination of the eastern
provinces of the empire, decided to follow a different approach than his predecessors towards the Kurds. He made great efforts to integrate them into the
state system by allowing them to share in the advantages of the power. Successfully reflecting good intentions towards Kurdish feudals, and stimulating pan-
Islamic propaganda among them, 'Abdulhamid was able to create a special
Kurdish-dominated cavalry force known as the *Hamidiya* Cavalry which he
used to smash the Armenians, and later (under different name) to repress the
Kurds as well.[24]

Following the 'Young Turks' revolution in 1908 which overthrew the
rule of 'Abdulhamid and promised constitutional reform and representation, the
Kurds began to establish their own political organizations. However, the struggle between urban intellectuals and feudalists over leadership denied the Kurds
the positive outcomes of political organization and resulted in weakening of the
Kurdish movement. Consequently, the Kurds fell into the hands of the Turkish
rulers during World War I, and were used by them in fighting Turkish wars.[25]

As in the case with all other ethnic groups that were subjects to the
Ottoman Empire, the Ottoman's defeat in the First World War presented the
Kurds with an opportunity to set up their own national state. The Treaty of
Sevres (signed on August 10, 1920) anticipated an independent Kurdish state
to cover a small portion of the former Ottoman Kurdistan. Unconcerned with
the natives' call for independence, Britain and France divided former Ottoman

---

[23]The Kurdish rebellions of the 19th century are well analyzed in Kendal
(Kendal Nezan), "The Kurds Under the Ottoman Empire," in *A People Without A
Country: The Kurds and Kurdistan*, edited by Gerard Chaliand (London: Zed Press,
1993), pp. 11-37; McDowall, *A Modern History*, pp. 38-86; and Olson, pp. 1-25.

[24]Kendal (Kendal Nezan), "Ottoman Empire," pp. 24-26.

[25]McDowall, *A Nation Denied*, pp. 30-31; and Kendal (Kendal Nezan),
"Ottoman Empire," pp. 26-29. Two good surveys on this period of Kurdish history are
Kamal Madhar Ahmad, *Kurdistan During the First World War*, translated from the
Arabic by 'Ali Maher Ibrahim (London: Saqi Books, 1994); and McDowall, *A Modern
History*, pp. 87-112.

territories according to their needs, with Kurdistan apportioned to the new states of Turkey, Syria, and Iraq. This division was formalized in the Treaty of Lausanne that was signed on July 23, 1923 following the emergence of Ataturk. Since then, the Kurds, "victims of peace settlements,"[26] began to face a long series of protracted repressive measures by the subsequent governments of Turkey, Iran, Iraq, Syria, and the Soviet Union and its republics. Although these countries were at most times enemies, they all had one thing in common, that is, suppressing any attempt at Kurdish independence. The following is a brief summary of the history of the Kurds and Kurdistan in each of these countries. A brief discussion on the Kurds in Europe is also presented.

The Kurds in Turkey

Immediately after the signing of the Lausanne Treaty in 1923, Ataturk began a turkification process that included, among other things, the banning of all Kurdish schools, associations, publications, and other forms of cultural expression. The Kurds also discovered that the Muslim Patrimony they fought for alongside Ataturk, was nothing but a myth. After Ataturk achieved victory against the Greeks, Armenians and Russians, the Kurds were left out. Consequently, the Kurds revolted against Turkey in 1925, 1930 and 1937. These three revolts which were led by Sheikh Sa'id, the *Khoyboun* (Independence) Kurdish National League,[27] and Sayyid Reza of Dersim, respectively, were ruthlessly smashed.[28] Describing the 1925-1938 period of Kurdish history in Turkey, Nezan wrote:

> During these thirteen years of repression, struggle, revolt, and deportation... more than one and a half million Kurds were deported [or] massacred... The entire area beyond the Euphrates... was declared out of bounds to foreigners until 1965 and was kept under a permanent state of siege till 1950. The use of the Kurdish language was banned. The very words 'Kurd' and 'Kurdistan' were crossed out of the dictionaries and history books. The Kurds were never even referred to except as 'Mountain Turks.'[29]

Since then, all Kurdish attempts to resuscitate their cultural heritage or their identity in Kurdistan have been severely put down by the Turkish army.

Following the fall of Dersim in 1938, Turkey witnessed a wave of general discontent resulting mainly from the economic difficulties and famines

---

[26]Gidon Gottlieb, "Nations Without States," *Foreign Affairs* 73 (May/June 1994), p. 104.

[27]The *Khoyboun* was led by Ihsan Nouri Pasha and the Bedrkhan brothers.

[28]For details on these three revolts and their aftermaths, see Kendal, "Kurdistan in Turkey," pp. 51-58; and McDowall, *A Modern History*, pp. 184-213.

[29]Kendal, "Kurdistan in Turkey,", p. 58.

that took place during most of World War II years. Such discontent forced the Turkish government to liberalize its political system. This decision which took, among other things, the form of legalizing the formation of new political parties benefitted the Kurds. Though they were not allowed to establish their own parties, many Kurds who were in Istanbul and Ankara became politically involved. While attending universities in the major Turkish cities, many Kurds joined various Turkish political parties, especially the Democratic Party, with many Kurds eventually becoming members of the parliament or even state ministers. This period of liberalization in Turkey, however, was interrupted by a military rule between 1960 and 1961 in which a return to Kemalist orthodoxy took place aiming at "putting everything back in its right place," meaning, repressing the Kurds and other leftist forces.

But the Turkish army failed to suppress the invisible re-emergence of Kurdish nationalism. On the one hand, the Kurds in Turkey were delighted and influenced by the success of Barzani in the Iraqi part of Kurdistan and, on the other, they became "aware of both the cultural differences between eastern and western Turkey as well as of the highly unequal development of these two areas of the country."[30] The new constitution adopted by Turkey in 1961 (after the withdrawal of the military from office), moreover, created a new opportunity for the Kurds to establish themselves. Many educated Kurds, not allowed to form their own political parties, joined the newly founded Turkish Workers' Party (TWP) that, among other issues, took up the issue of underdevelopment of eastern and southeastern Turkey (i.e., Kurdistan).[31] Then in 1965, a group of pro-Barzani Kurds (mostly educated persons) decided to form their own political party that operated clandistinely under the name of the Kurdish Democratic Party of Turkey (KDPT).

Late in the 1960s and early 1970s, Kurdish political parties, more specifically, radical ones, grew in number. Feeling the rise of the Kurdish movement, along with the political disorder that was prevailing in the country, the Turkish army decided to step in power again on March 12, 1973 to restore order. This time it took three years before the army returned power to the civilians, but after making sure that no party would achieve a decisive victory in the government. The army was convinced that stability and powerful governments are the reasons behind the rise of the Kurds. Consequently, throughout most of the 1970s, the country went into a political deadlock and extremism with no party able to win a majority that would enable it to make vital decisions. At the same time, this period witnessed a turning point in the political demands of Kurdish organizations from economic development of Kurdistan and the recognition of elementary cultural rights of the Kurds to independence.

---

[30]Van Bruinessen, *Agha, Shaikh and State*, p. 32.

[31]In its Congress in October 1970, the TWP adopted a resolution which recognized the Kurdish people. It was the first time that an official body in Turkey take such a position. As a consequence of adopting this resolution, the party was banned.

According to van Bruinessen, two major reasons were behind this shift in the Kurdish movement. First, there was widespread dissatisfaction among the Kurds with the Turkish left, which seemed insufficiently responsive to the national dimension of the Kurdish struggle. Second, the weakness of the Turkish government allowed the Kurds considerable freedom thus making them able to organize themselves underground and make propaganda.[32] Edmund Ghareeb mentions a third reason, namely, the Islamic Revolution in Iran in 1979 that was associated with, or led to, the rise of the Kurdish national movement in Iran to the forefront.[33]

Towards the end of the 1970s, Kurdish organizations were able to control large areas of Kurdistan. However, the ideological differences and, in particular, personal rivalries between their leaders, caused many splits in, and conflicts among, them which counted more than ten by that time. The severe clashes between these organizations on the one hand, and their clashes with other Turkish groups, on the other, caused thousands of victims among both Kurds and Turks and exposed them to the eyes of the Turkish army. Consequently, the military took over power once again on September 12, 1980 in an attempt to "wipe out Kurdish nationalism."

Immediately after the coup, large scale military operations took place in Kurdistan to crush the Kurdish movement.[34] For the first time after more than 45 years, however, the Kurds confronted the Turkish army openly, particularly by the Kurdish Workers' Party (PKK), which proved to be the most violent of all Kurdish organizations. This war which is still going on was faced by severe Turkish military campaigns. Describing these campaigns, Laizer wrote:

> [The Turkish army campaign] is an all-out military on-slaught to end Kurdish resistance in the most brutal fashion (250,000 soldiers versus 15,000 guerrillas and Kurdish civilians). ... [Its aims are] murder, extra-judicial killings, and silencing of the Kurdish opposition—prominent writers, journalists, MP's, and even Kurdish businessmen shot, tortured, or imprisoned, and the opposition press forced into closure. The true face of the [campaigns] is in fact the military target of razing all rebellious Kurdish villages, mass deportations and massacres of the villagers themselves, and the arbitrary killing and detention of Kurdish civilians who refuse to become state-paid militia against the PKK. The killings are carried out by military and death squads with the civil governments' complicity.[35]

---

[32]Van Bruinessen, *Agha, Shaikh and State*, p. 33.

[33]Ghareeb, p. 9.

[34]A short but good account on these campaigns is Martin van Bruinessen, "The Kurds in Turkey," *MERIP Reports* 14 (February 1984), pp. 6-14.

[35]Sheri Laizer, "Gerard Chaliand's The Kurdish Factor," *Namah* 2 (Fall 1994).

Initially criticized because of its violent attacks on Kurdish collabora-
tors and their families, the extreme nature of PKK's activities against the
Turkish army nevertheless increased its popularity among Kurdish masses.
Such activities which were normally associated with Turkish military
repression of civilians, resulted in the evacuation and flight of millions of
Kurds westwards. Ironically, these displaced persons, now living in major
Turkish and European major cities, have made it impossible for Turkish public
opinion to ignore the Kurds any longer. The Kurdish population living outside
Kurdistan became more of a serious problem than those living inside it. A good
indication of this is the role the Kurds play in today's Turkish national
elections as well as their success in exposing their nation's plight not only to
the West but also to the Turks themselves.

The success of the PKK in mobilizing the Kurds in Turkey and
fostering Kurdish nationalism there and throughout the world received a
serious blow with the capture of the party's leader Abdullah Ocalan. What
made things even worse was the behavior of Ocalan afterwards. According to
Kutschera, rather than behaving heroically, Ocalan immediately abandoned the
idea of transforming his trial into a trial of the Turkish state, giving up on
pleaing the cause of the Kurds for whom he had fought for 20 years. Moreover,
Ocalan repudiated the cause for which thousands of Kurds had been sent to
prison or to their deaths; he repudiated the armed struggle and repudiated the
independence of Kurdistan.[36] The capture and trial of Ocalan, a major setback
in the Kurdish movement, put an end to his myth; however, it will not end the
Kurds' struggle for freedom and national rights. For the war to stop, both
Kurds and Turks have to negotiate with each other. Turkey, in addition, must
make some political concessions and show willingness to grant Kurds greater
freedom.

The Kurds in Iran

Although the Kurds in Iran have not been subjected to the level of bru-
tality as that of their counterparts in Turkey and Iraq, the Iranian government
has always been no less vehement in its opposition to any form of a separate
Kurdish entity. Iran's opposition stems from its fears of what such a prospect
may hold for other ethnic groups within its boundaries (such as Arabs, the Azeris, and the Baluchis) who may be encouraged by any Kurdish gains, and thus
demand a similar treatment.[37]

---

[36]Chris Kutschera, *Kurdistan Observer* (February 4, 2000).

[37]Perhaps the best authorities on the Kurds in Iran are William Eagleton, *The
Kurdish Republic of 1946* (London: Oxford University Press, 1963); A. R. Ghassemlou
(Abdul Rahman), pp. 95-121; and Archie Roosevelt, Jr., "The Kurdish Republic of
Mahabad," *The Middle East Journal* 1 (July 1947), pp. 247-269. Supplements to these
works can be found in McDowall, *A Modern History*, pp. 214-283, and Rouhollah K.

During the period between 1920 and 1930, Ismail Agha Simko, chief of the Shikak tribe, revolted several times against central authority. Though initially successful in capturing large areas of the Kurdish region, Simko failed in achieving Kurdish independence. After Simko's death, the Kurdish movement in Iran went into oblivion, or at least was not as active as in other parts of Kurdistan. A major turning point, however, was the founding of the Kurdistan Democratic Party in Iran (KDPI) in 1945, which was soon to proclaim the creation of the independent Democratic Republic of Kurdistan in Mahabad. The Mahabad Republic proved to be short-lived, however (January-December 1946). The KDPI was unable to attract local support to the small republic, especially from the tribes who were extremely reluctant to do away with the close relationship they had cultivated with the Tehran government in the years between Simko's death and World War II. As a result, immediately after the withdrawal of Soviet troops from Iran in December 1946, Tehran proceeded to crush the Mahabad Republic—something it did with relative ease considering the absence of a powerful protector of the Kurds. Thereafter, Kurdish nationalists went underground, only to be effectively suppressed by the SAVAK, the Shah's security service.

In 1978, Kurdish nationalists joined in the overthrow of the Shah thus creating a real opportunity to negotiate a new relationship with Tehran. Kurdish nationalists, mainly led by KDPI and Komala (The Kurdish Communist Party in Iran), were capable of mobilizing large masses both for the popular uprising that was to ensue, as well as for an autonomous Kurdish entity within Iran. However, the Islamic Revolutionary government was swift in rejecting any Kurdish request for autonomy because of the danger that autonomy for the Kurds could excite similar demands by other minorities, thus threatening to break-up the country. What followed was a gradual deterioration in relations between the Kurds and Tehran government, especially as the Shi'i character of the new regime became increasingly apparent. Tehran's efforts to re-impose central authority over Kurdish regions led to a protracted guerrilla warfare in which the Kurds were no match for the technologically and numerically superior government forces.

Although the Kurds were able to exploit Iraq's surprise attack on Iran to their advantage by capturing large areas of land in Iranian Kurdistan, the balance was soon tilted in Iran's favor. By 1983, not only Iran had regained territories captured by Iraq and Iranian Kurds but had virtually pushed KDPI out of most of the Kurdish regions. By the end of the Iran-Iraq war, Tehran government had successfully crushed the Kurdish resistance movement which by then had became extremely minimal.

Even the KDPI's attempts to seek a compromise with the government ended in failure too. Indeed, the two occasions on which the Islamic Republic

Ramazani, "The Autonomous Republic of Azerbaijan and the Kurdish People's Republic: Their Rise and Fall," in *The Anatomy of Communist Takeovers*, edited by Thomas T. Hammond (New Haven: Yale University Press, 1975), pp. 448-474.

had agreed to negotiate with the Kurdish movement were dedicated more by necessity rather than a sincere desire to resolve the Kurdish question. First, in October 1979, when it felt both weak and threatened; and, second, in July 1989, when Tehran's aim was the assassination of the KDPI's leader, Abdul Rahman Ghassemlou, the party's major thinker, strategist, diplomat and organizer.[38] The assassination of Ghassemlou in Vienna, as well as of his successor Sadiq Sharafkandi in Berlin in September 1992, left both the party and the Kurdish movement in Iran in disarray. Although subsequent Kurdish leaders in Iran continue to aspire for Kurdish autonomy, they are as far from achieving their aims as ever before.

The Kurds in Iraq

In World War I, Britain decided to create the state of Iraq. Initially, the plan was to unite the two provinces of Basra and Baghdad and making them fall within the jurisdiction of the British mandatory power under the provisions of the Sykes-Picot Agreement of 1916. However, the discovery of oil in the predominantly Kurdish province of Mosul made the British change plans. Britain then wanted Mosul to be part of the newly planned state of Iraq. Consequently, it occupied Mosul in November 1918 (still under Ottoman jurisdiction) despite the armistice of Mudros signed on October 31, 1918. Britain was aware that the population of Mosul was mainly Kurdish. Therefore, it planned to set up one or several semi-autonomous Kurdish provinces to be loosely attached to the emergent state of Iraq. The Kurds, however, were against being included in Iraq. Eventually, they came into direct confrontation with the British authorities.[39]

From 1919 to the mid-1940s, there was a long series of Kurdish rebellions against the British army and Iraqi regime for some form of real autonomy for Kurds in Iraq. All attempts by Sheikh Mahmud Barzinji and the Barzanis (Sheikh Ahmad and Mulla Mustafa), however, failed. Only with the overthrow of the monarchy on July 14, 1958 by General Qassim, did the Kurdish national movement in Iraq re-emerge powerfully. Qassim's coup raised Kurdish expectations for more equal participation in the state. He welcomed Mulla Mustafa back from exile and jointly dealt with many mutual enemies. Hoping to gain some civil and cultural rights to the Kurds, Barzani accepted to assist Qassim in his efforts to eliminate the government's opposition groups. However, Qas-

---

[38]Omar Sheikhmous, "The Kurdish Question: Conflict Resolution Strategies at the Regional level," in *Building Peace in the Middle East: Challanges for States and Civil Society*, edited by Elise Boulding (Boulder, Colo.: Lynne Rienner Publishers, 1994), p. 149.

[39]Ismet Cheriff Vanly, "Kurdistan in Iraq," in *People Without a Country: The Kurds and Kurdistan*, edited by Gerard Chaliand (London: Zed Press, 1993), p. 143.

sim's regime disappointed Kurdish hopes and, eventually, the Kurdish movement erupted again in 1961.

Qassim's efforts to bring Barzani to heel failed and the war between the latter and successive Iraqi governments continued until March 1970 when a peace agreement between the Kurds and the Ba'th regime was concluded which gave significant cultural, political and economic rights to the Kurds. However, although the March agreement was supposed to be implemented within a period of four years, it proved to be no more than a cease-fire agreement. Consequently, fighting resumed between the Kurdish forces and the Iraqi army in which the Kurds were overtly supported by the Iranians and covertly by the United States. In an attempt to defuse the escalating crisis, the Iraqi government resorted to a carrot and stick policy of which it offered Iran a revision of the agreement governing the demarcation of the disputed Shatt al-Arab waterway and in return both Iran and the U.S. withdrew their support of the Kurds. This agreement in effect signaled the death knell of the Kurdish revolt and the outcome was several hundreds of thousand Kurds either dead or refugees on the Iranian border. Less than two years later, both Jalal Talabani and Brazani's children continued the struggle on.[40]

An Iranian-Kurdish rapprochement was once again effected during the Iran-Iraq war, 1980-1988, through which the Kurds seized and controlled large portions of Iraqi Kurdistan. Displeased with the Kurds' military gains, the Iraqi regime could not have been more brutal, as demonstrated by the use of chemical weapons on the Kurdish town of Halabja in March 1988. Despite evidence of the use of chemical weapons, not a single country in the world condemned such brutal behavior by Iraq. Then, after Iran's acceptance of a cease-fire in August 1988, the Iraqi army directed its attention to squashing the Kurdish movement. In the process, thousands of Kurdish villages were razed to the ground, with the large majority of their inhabitants either executed or resettled in new towns or concentration camps in the south. The army also routinely used chemical weapons. According to various sources, up to 100,000 may have been killed in what was described as military operations tantamount to a full-fledged genocide campaign.[41]

As relations deteriorated to a new low between the Iraqi government and the Kurdish population, many Kurds concluded that their situation could only be improved with the removal of Saddam Hussein, under whose reign the

---

[40]See Alexis Heraclides, *The Self-Determination of Minorities in International Politics* (London: Frank Cass, 1991), pp. 129-146; McDowall, *A Modern History*, pp. 368-391; and Vanly, "Kurdistan in Iraq," pp. 153-190.

[41]Kenneth Anderson, *The Anfal Campaign in Iraqi Kurdistan* ... (New York: Human Rights Watch, 1993; George Black, *Genocide in Iraq: The Anfal Campaign Against the Kurds* (New York: Human Rights Watch, 1993); Joost Hiltermann, *Bureaucracy of Repression: The Iraqi Government in Its Own Words* (New York: Human Rights Watch, 1994); and Kanan Makiya, *Cruelty and Silence: War, Tyranny, Uprising, and the Arab World* (New York: W. W. Norton, 1993).

abuse of their human rights had become flagrant. By the start of military operations against Iraq in February 1991 a coalition formed by the Kurds, Shi'ites,
and other dissenters, declared the removal of Saddam Hussein as its goal. But
the outcome of the Kurdish and Shi'i rebellions were grossly miscalculated. As
in 1975, the U.S. once again withdrew its support of the Kurds. Only under
Allied protection did the Kurds escape much more losses than they did—
thousands of victims and over 2 million refugees. The subsequent establishment
of a Kurdish enclave in northern Iraq proved to be no more than a limited
guarantee of security, and failed to resolve the underlying problems.[42]

Indeed, some of the major obstacles to a permanent solution of the
Kurdish question in Iraq are related to deep internal rivalries between the various Kurdish factions. However, equally important are the reservations entertained by the international community concerning the repercussions of establishing a Kurdish state on regional powers including Iraq itself.

The Kurds in Syria[43]

During the French mandate, 1918-1945, the Kurds in Syria enjoyed
many cultural and political rights as perceived by the existence of Kurdish
political and social organizations, publications, use of the Kurdish language,
and recruitment into the army and administration. Following Syrian
independence, however, these rights began to gradually diminish.

The rise of hostile Arab nationalist movements (e.g., Ba'thism and
Nasserism) and the Union of Syria and Egypt into the United Arab Republic
(UAR) in 1958, marked the first round of oppressive conduct *vis-a-vis* the
Kurds. One of the pretexts for starting the oppressive campaigns was the establishment of the Kurdish Democratic Party in Syria (KDPS) in 1957. KDPS
called for the recognition of the Kurds as an ethnic group and for democracy in
Syria. It also unveiled the lack of economic development in Kurdish areas and
exposed the discriminatory practices against the Kurds in education and recruitment to the police, military academies, and other civil services. Immediately after the announcement of the Union between Syria and Egypt, Kurdish
leaders were arrested and Kurdish publications were outlawed.

Following Syria's secession from the UAR in 1961, political repression against the Kurds intensified and took on a legal dimension in its execution. This culminated in the promulgation of Decree 93 which called for a special census in the Kurdish area of Jezira and resulted in loss of Syrian citizenship by 120,000 Kurds. After the accession of the Ba'th to power in 1963, the
oppression of the Kurds went even farther. An arabization plan was effected
that took the form of creating an Arab Belt (*al-Hizam al-Arabi*). It covered

---

[42]See McDowall, *A Modern History*, pp. 343-367.
[43]For more details on the Kurds in Syria, see McDowall, *The Kurds of Syria*.

most of the Kurdish regions bordering both Iraq and Turkey. This plan aimed to expropriate the Kurds from their lands and push them to emigrate from the border regions to other places in and outside Syria. The evacuated regions and villages were populated by Arabs and were renamed to give them an Arab identity.[44]

Only with the coming of Hafiz Assad into power in 1972, the conditions of the Kurds began to improve although not significantly. Assad needed the Kurds for both external and internal reasons. First, he sought to please them, declaring the end of forced transfers from Jezira (1976). Then he used them to wipe out Arab opposition movements, particularly the Sunni radicals. Assad also used the Kurds to fight Arab wars for him; for example, several thousand Kurds served in the Syrian army and died during the Lebanese civil war.[45]

Unlike the leaders in the neighboring Turkey, Assad allowed the Kurds some cultural freedom. As of the 1980s, the Kurds were allowed to perform and sell tapes of their native songs and speak Kurdish in the streets. On the other hand, however, more than 200,000 Kurds continue to be denied citizenship. Teaching in Kurdish language is still prohibited. The Kurds may celebrate *Newruz* (New Year's Day), however, only in the countryside—away from public attention. Moreover, Kurds are still not allowed to form their own political parties. The success of the Kurds in electing fifteen Kurdish candidates to the Syrian Parliament in 1991 was a necessity rather than a sincere desire to lift the restrictions on the Kurds. The future of the Kurds in Syria is no less bleak than those of their compatriots elsewhere.

The Kurds in the Former Soviet Union

Today, there are about 500,000 Kurds living in Azerbaijan, Armenia, Georgia, Tajikstan, Turkmenia, Uzbekistan, Kazakhstan, Kirghizstan, and different republics or regions of Russia like Krasnodar and Siberia. Like the Kurds in Israel and Lebanon, the Soviet Kurds moved in there in waves with the first apparently taking place in the 1st century BC.[46] Later in the 10th century AD, some Kurdish tribes moved into the Caucasus to discover new fertile lands. Among these tribes were the Shaddadis who ruled a large part of the area between 951 and 1174 AD. In the 16th century, many Kurdish tribes moved into Central Asia as a result of their use by the Persian Shahs to guard

---

[44]McDowall, *The Kurds of Syria*; Middle East Watch, *Syria Unmasked*, pp. 96-98. See also Mustafa Nazdar, pseud., "The Kurds in Syria," in *A People Without a Country: The Kurds and Kurdistan*, edited by Gerard Chaliand (London: Zed Press, 1993), pp. 198-201; and Ismet Cheriff Vanly, "The Kurds in Syria and Lebanon," in *The Kurds: A Contemporary Overview*, edited by Philip G. Kreyenbroek and Stefan Sperl (London: Routledge, 1992), pp. 143-170.

[45]Chaliand, *The Kurdish Tragedy*, p. 87.

[46]"You Too Armenia," *Kurdish Life*, no. 9 (Winter 1994), p. 1.

Central Asia as a result of their use by the Persian Shahs to guard their eastern border, thus marking the third main wave. The fourth phase of Kurdish migration into the Caucasus took place the 19th century. The wars between Russia and Turkey (1804-1813, 1828-1829, 1853-1856, 1877-1878) and the Kurdish revolts throughout the century swelled the number of Yezidi Kurdish population with a flood of refugees seeking safety in the region. A final wave took place at the end of the 19th century and early 20th century when tens of thousands of Kurds moved from the Ottoman empire into Armenia and Georgia fleeing persecution.[47] Kurdish permanent settlement in the Soviet republics was not final, however.

Soon after the creation of the Soviet state, the two Kurdish-dominated districts of Jewanshir (with its capital Kelbajar) and eastern Zangazur (with its capital Lachin) both in Azerbaijan were joined and officially designated in 1920 as "Kurdistan." After three years, the political status of this Kurdish province was elevated to become the "Kurdish Autonomous Province," better known as "Red Kurdistan" with its capital Lachin. However, the period of Kurdish autonomy was very brief. In 1929, "Red Kurdistan" was no longer an entity and Kurds ceased to be reported in Azeri population censuses. Moreover, beginning in the 1930s, the Kurds, like many other Caucasian nationalities, began to face a series of repressive measures implemented by Stalin. Thousands of Kurds were deported from Armenia in 1937, and from Georgia in 1944 to Central Asia and Kazakhstan. The men were deported to secret places and the women and children were deported shortly afterwards to a different place.[48] Repressive measures against the Kurds did not stop until the late 1950s, but to be repeated in the 1990s, at the hands of the Armenians, Azeris, and Georgians. The war between Armenia and Azerbaijan since 1988 over Nagorno-Karabakh resulted in the complete destruction of the Kurdish areas of "Red Kurdistan" and the deportation of more than 150,000 Kurds from their lands let alone the Muslim Kurds deported from Armenia.[49] Today, there are no more indigenous Kurdish territories left in the former Soviet Union.

Socio-economically speaking, the Kurds of the former Soviet Union can be divided into two main groups: advantaged and disadvantaged. The former mostly located in Armenia and Georgia (mainly Yezidi Kurds) while the latter in Azerbaijan and other republics (mainly Muslim Kurds). Unlike the Kurds in Azerbaijan, who are facing continuous cultural repression and grim

---

[47]For further details on Kurdish immigration into the former Soviet Union, see Ismet Cheriff Vanly, "The Kurds in the Soviet Union," in *The Kurds: A Contemporary Overview,* edited by Philip G. Kreyenbroek and Stefan Sperl (London: Routledge, 1992), pp. 193-199.

[48]J. Otto Pohl, *Ethnic Cleansing in the USSR, 1937-1949* (Westport, CT: Greenwood Press, 1999), pp. 129-136.

[49]See Nadir Nadirov, "What Do the Soviet Kurds Want?" *Asia and Africa Today,* no. 1 (January-February 1991), pp. 74-76; Vanly, "The Kurds in the Soviet Union," pp. 211-218; and "You too Armenia?" *Kurdish Life,* pp. 1-5.

living conditions, under the Soviet auspices, the Kurds of Armenia and Georgia
were, until the early 1990s, enjoying a great degree of state assistance. For example, in Armenia, the Kurds were very well treated and given both encouragement and state funds to develop their culture and improve the socio-
economic conditions of their communities. Kurds there had their own network
of schools, an institute of Kurdish studies at the Academy of Sciences at Yerevan, and a modest national press which includes a bi-weekly Kurdish newspaper *Reiya Taze* (The New Course), published since 1930 in Yerevan with a
circulation of 2,500-3,500 copies. Kurds studying in Moscow and Leningrad's
universities were also a major source for the development of the socio-economic
conditions of the local Kurds. All this resulted in the Kurds' preservation of
their national identity and cultural heritage as well as in their social and economic prosperity. Had the situation of the Kurds in Azerbaijan and other republics been the same as it was in Armenia and Georgia, it would have been easier
to talk about a real use of the Soviet Kurds as agents or propagandists of Kurdish nationalism: Kurds in Armenia were very few and in Azerbaijan were (and
still are) repressed.[50] As things turned out, it was only a Soviet policy to foster
Kurdish culture in Armenia and Azerbaijan. Once the Soviet Union was disintegrated, Armenians and Azerbaijanis almost instantly fell upon the Kurds with
vengeance, stripping them of all those privileges. Most of the Kurds who were
living in the Caucasus republics fled to Russia or Western Europe.

The Kurds in Europe[51]

Kurds have been migrating to Western Europe for over a century;
however, this migration gained more intensity in the last four centuries. In the
1960s and 1970s Kurds from Turkey were migrating primarily for economic
reasons whereas those from Iraq and Syria were migrating particularly for political reasons. Kurds from Iraq and Syria were either fleeing persecution by
their respective governments or leaving for Europe at the request of Mulla
Mustafa Barzani for educational purposes and for disseminating news about the
Kurdish national movement. Prominent examples of these Kurds are Ismet
Cheriff Vanly and Noureddine Zaza.
       Most Kurds who migrated from Turkey knew no language other than
Turkish and were reluctant to be involved in politics. The 1980 coup in Turkey

---

[50]See T. F. Arsitova, "Kurds," in *Encyclopedia of World Cultures, vol. VI:
Russia and Eurasia/China*, edited by P. Friedrich and N. Diamond (Boston, Mass: G.K.
Hall & Co., 1994), pp. 224-227; and Kendal, "The Kurds in the Soviet Union," in *A
People Without a Country: The Kurds and Kurdistan*, edited by Gerard Chaliand
(London: Zed Press, 1993), pp. 205-209.
       [51]This section relies largely on the work of Martin van Bruinessen, "Shifting
National and Ethnic Identities: The Kurds in Turkey and the European Diaspora," *Jour-
nal of Muslim Minority Affairs (JMMA)* 18, no.1 (April 1998), pp. 39-52.

and its aftermath changed that. This coup led to a great influx of politicized, mostly young Kurds as asylum seekers. Their presence, and the news about the guerrilla war in Turkey that erupted in 1984, worked as a catalyst of the Kurds' ethnic self-awareness. With their growing self-awareness, many Kurds started to discover that they were not Turks but Kurds. As a result, while in the early 1980s estimates were made of approximately 600,000 Kurds in Europe, by the late 1990s estimates reached close to 2 million Kurds, the result of "rediscovery" rather than increased immigration.

The Kurdish diaspora in Europe has acquired central importance for the Kurdish movement in Turkey, the same way as the Kurdish diaspora in Lebanon had in the 1960s and early 1970s for the Kurdish national movement in Iraq and Syria and in the 1980s and early 1990s for the Kurdish movement in Turkey.[52] Large sums of money were and still are raised in Europe to financially support military and non-military activities in Turkey. As in Kurdistan and other parts of the world, Kurdish young men residing in Europe were and still are recruited either for fighting or as organizers, diplomats, and technicians of various sorts. In addition, the PKK and its support organizations continue to publish a wide range of journals and magazines in Kurdish, Turkish, and the major European languages through which it voices its struggle against Turkey. Perhaps even more important in the long run than the political mobilization in the Kurdish diaspora are the cultural activities by Kurdish intellectuals in Europe which will also have a long-term political impact. Not only Kurmanji became a widely used language in Kurds' writings, but also Kurdish journals and books gradually increased in number and Kurdish cultural institutions were founded almost everywhere in Europe, including Belgium, Denmark, Finland, France, Germany, Sweden, and United Kingdom. According to van Bruinessen: "The Kurdish institutes, Kurdish print media and Kurdish language courses that operate in western Europe, largely impervious to control by the Turkish state, have provided the Kurdish movement with instruments of nation building comparable to those traditionally employed by states." Moreover, Kurds in Europe were able to form their own associations, with little or no harassment from the state. In 1995, a powerful instrument was added to this arsenal, the satellite television station MED-TV, which broadcast to the Middle East and Europe, among other regions.

All of these developments in the Kurdish movement led Bruinessen to conclude: "However one defines what a nation is, by practically every definition the Kurds have over the past two decades become more of one, and have dissociated themselves somewhat from the Iraqi and Turkish 'state-nations'."

---

[52]See Meho, 1995.

The Kurds in Lebanon

There are thousands of studies on the Kurds living in Kurdistan and the countries dividing it. Even the relatively more recent Kurdish communities in Europe and the United States gained more research attention than the older Kurdish community in Lebanon. The reason for this negligence is two fold: First, despite their relatively long stay in Lebanon, the Kurds have failed to establish themselves powerfully, primarily because of the social and political status that was imposed on them by the Lebanese confessional politics. The Kurds in Lebanon never gained public or official attention except at times when Kurdish youngsters were needed to fight a certain battle for a certain party, or at times when Kurdish votes were needed by a local *za'im* (leader) to be successful in a certain election. Furthermore, almost never were the social and political problems of the Muslim, non-Arab Kurds of prime concern to any of the Lebanese successive governments or leaders. Second, at a time when no body was interested in studying the Kurdish community in Lebanon, the Kurds, on the other hand, have failed to produce the necessary cadre or intelligentsia that would be able to do so. Because virtually nothing is published on the Kurds in Lebanon, I will discuss the topic in some detail (see next chapter).

CONCLUSION

As made evident by the twentieth century Kurdish experience, Kurdish national rights has been hindered by three interrelated problem areas: problems of communication (linguistic and religious diversity); problems of common political action (political disunity); and most importantly, problems of external influence, repeated manipulation, and lack of a superpower's support in the midst of such repressive regimes as Turkey, Iran, Iraq, Syria, and Armenia and Azerbaijan.

It is true that all Kurds realize that they belong to a common entity and all have occasionally taken part in Kurdish nationalist movements, yet, there has never been a united Kurdish movement. Division by personal, tribal, regional, and sect has been the rule rather than the exception. The geopolitical situation moreover has made the Kurds vulnerable to manipulation by outside powers. Throughout their revolts, Kurdish leaders have always hoped to achieve national rights through foreign support. However, they seldom realized that they were fighting others' wars. The Kurds' limited alternatives and perhaps more importantly the foreign powers' carelessness about their fate, encourage outside powers to exploit the Kurds and leave them to death. The drawing of well-guarded state boundaries dividing Kurdistan has, since 1921, afflicted Kurdish society with such a degree of fragmentation that its impact is tearing apart the Kurds' unity as a nation.[53]

The future of the Kurds remains uncertain. Kurdish national identity has developed considerably in the last few years and will never disappear despite military pressure. Surrounded from all sides by enemies, however, Kurdish national rights will continue to be denied for a long time to come. This is particularly true given the carelessness of the United States, Russia, the European countries, and the United Nations about the violation of Kurdish human, civil, and national rights by the countries occupying Kurdistan and mistreating its people.

---

[53]*International Journal of Kurdish Studies* 11, nos. 1-2 (1997), p. 254.

The Kurds in Lebanon: An Overview

Lokman I. Meho

GENERAL BACKGROUND

The present Kurdish community in Lebanon is a product of several waves of immigrants.[1] The first major wave took place in the two decades following World War I, when thousands of Kurds fled the violence and poverty that struck Kurdistan in those years. Most of these Kurds came from the villages of Mardin/Tur 'Abdin. The second major wave took place in the period between World War II and the early 1960s. A large portion of these new immigrants arrived from Turkey, however, the vast majority came from Syria fleeing the socioeconomic, cultural, and political repression that began there in 1958 (see below). The relative improvement in the living conditions of the Kurds in Lebanon, and the proximity of the country to Kurdistan, played an important role in encouraging these new immigrants to choose Lebanon as their new home or temporary place of residence.

All Kurds in Lebanon are Sunni Muslims. However, they are divided into many tribal or communal groups with each linked to the village or region from which it came. These communal groups are named after their villages of

---

[1]Kurdish presence in Lebanon goes as far back as the twelfth century A.D. when the Ayyubids arrived in there. Over the next few centuries, several other Kurdish families (or tribes) were sent to Lebanon by various powers (e.g., the Ottomans) to maintain order in the regions; others moved in as a result of poverty and violence in Kurdistan. These Kurdish groups settled in and ruled many areas of Lebanon for long periods of time. Examples include the Sayfa *Emirs* (princes) in Tripoli, Mir'bi family in 'Akkar, the Junblat's and the 'Imads of Mount Lebanon, and the Hamiyya family in Baalbeck. Detached from their homeland for so many years, these Kurdish families became fully integrated into Lebanon's social and political structure and were completely arabized by the end of the 19th century.

origin such as al-Rajdiyeh, Ma'sarteh, al-Mkhashniyeh, al-Mnezil, Marjeh, Jibl-Graw, Kinderib, Marska, Zeni, Fafeh, and Matina. Linguistically, the Kurds in Lebanon are divided into two main groups: those who speak the North Kurmanji (also called Bahdinani) dialect and those who speak the Mardin dialect, a mix of Arabic, Kurdish, Syriac, and Turkish with the dominant tongues Arabic and Kurmanji. Kurmanji speakers have greater ease in understanding Mardinli speakers than vice versa.

Today, there are 20 different religious and ethnic groups who live in Lebanon.[2] Of these, the Kurds represent the second largest non-Arab group; only the Armenians outnumber them. However, there is no official census or an accurate number of the Kurds. There are two main reasons for this: first, because no official census has taken place in Lebanon since 1932 and, second, because Kurds are still denied their ethnic distinction from other Lebanese groups. Unlike the Armenians, who are ethnically and religiously recognized as a distinct group, Kurds in Lebanon are considered as Sunni Muslims with no special status accorded to their ethnicity. Estimates about the number of Kurds prior to 1985 varied between 60,000 and 90,000 persons.[3] Given that thousands of Kurdish families have fled the country during the civil war, it is believed that their population in Lebanon today ranges between 75,000 and 100,000.

Most of the the Kurds who had arrived in Lebanon settled in different low-income areas in Beirut such as 'Ayn al-Mrayseh, al-Basta, Burj al-Brajneh, Burj Hammoud, the down-town sector, Furn al-Shubbak, Raml al-Zarif, and Zqaq al-Blat. Others, especially those who came from Syria, settled in the impoverished area of al-Karantina-al-Maslakh. Outside Beirut, most Kurds stayed in, Sidon, Tripoli, and the Biqa' area near the Syrian borders. The Kurds' residential compounds primarily reflected their tribal organizations, each according to its lineage.

Like their kinsmen elsewhere, many Lebanese Kurds have experienced various forms of forced resettlement; in many cases, more than once. For example, in early 1976, most of the Kurds who survived the Christian Maronite massacres in al-Karantina-al-Maslakh moved to West Beirut, Khaldeh, al-Jnah, and other areas of the 'Misery Belt' where new low-income residential areas were being built.[4] By 1978, almost all Kurds from the down-town sector, Furn al-Shubbak, and Burj Hammoud were forced by the Maronites to move out to the

---

[2]These include Sunni Muslims, Twelver or Imami Shi'as, Druzes, Isma'ilis, 'Alawis, Christian Maronites, Greek Catholics, Roman Catholics, Greek Orthodox, Protestants, Jacobites, Assyrians or Nestorians, Chaldean Catholic, Copts, Armenian Orthodox or Gregorian, Armenian Catholics, Kurds, Circassians, Bahais, and Turkomens.

[3]Ahmad Muhammad Ahmad, in his *Akrad Lubnan wa Tanzimimihim al-Ijtima'i wa al-Siyasi* (Unpublished Master's Thesis, Lebanese University, 1984-1985); *al-Maruni* [an Arab weekly newspaper published in Beirut], no. 3, 1980; Fadl Shruru, *al-Ahzab wa al-Tanzimat wa al-Qiwa al-Siyasiya fi Lubnan 1930-1980* (Beirut: Dar al-Masira, 1983); and Sami Zubyan, *al-Haraka al-Wataniya al-Lubnaniya: Al-Madi wa al-Hadir wa al-Mustaqbal min Manzur Istratiji* (Beirut: Dar al-Masira, 1977).

[4]The Belt of Misery is the poorer residential areas surrounding the capital Beirut, particularly on the east and south sides of the city.

'Misery Belt' and to areas where Kurds already had large concentrations. Then in the 1980s, Lebanon lost approximately one-fourth of its Kurdish population when whole families began to emigrate to Europe as a consequence of: (1) the 1982 Israeli invasion; (2) harassment by Christian-dominated government forces in 1982-1983; and (3) internal conflicts with the Lebanese Shi'ites (see below).[5] In the 1990s, almost all the low-income residential areas that were illegally built during the war by the Kurds, Shi'ites, and Palestinians were destroyed by the government, thus forcing thousands of families to move elsewhere. Families living in houses that were evacuated by the Christians and later on occupied by Kurds and other Lebanese, Syrian, and Palestinian groups during the war, were also forced to move out. Only a few of these families were financially compensated.

THE CITIZENSHIP ISSUE

In a 1995 study that surveyed 308 people, it was found that the adverse socioeconomic and political conditions of the Kurds in Lebanon were largely a result of their lack of Lebanese citizenship. Their poverty, lack of property and occupational skills, high illiteracy rate, feeling of insecurity and alienation, and their ill-treatment by various Lebanese groups were all found significantly related to the Kurds' status as noncitizens.[6]

Ever since the establishment of Greater Lebanon by France in 1920, the numerical balance of different confessional and ethnic communities in the country has been a critical matter. At that time, Christians probably outnumbered Muslims, and that predominance increased with the influx of thousands of Armenian refugees who escaped Turkish genocide during World War I and its aftermath. In 1924, France theoretically gave Lebanese citizenship to all erstwhile Ottoman citizens living in Lebanon. Thus, these Armenian refugees further reinforced Christian hegemony in Lebanon. A 1932 census showed that Christians outnumbered Muslims by a ratio of 6:5. The knowledge that Muslims tended to have high birthrates prompted Christian Maronites to make every effort possible to prevent any new census taken and to deny citizenship to Muslim immigrants in order to maintain their political predominance in the country.

Until 1940 it remained possible to acquire Lebanese citizenship provided the applicant had resided in Lebanon continuously for at least five years, or had married a Lebanese wife and resided in the country for one year after their marriage (1925 Decree). However, many Kurds failed to recognize the

---

[5]Ibid, pp. 120-123

[6]Lokman I. Meho, *The Dilemma of Social and Political Integration of Ethnoclass Groups within Pluralistic Societies: The Case of the Kurds in Lebanon*, Unpublished Master's thesis (Beirut: American University of Beirut, 1995). Study participants were drawn from a list of members of the Lebanese Kurdish Philanthropic Association. Snowballing was employed to include as many non-Kurmanji speakers as possible. All respondents were from Beirut and its suburbs (31% female and 69% male; 30% citizens and 70% noncitizens).

value of acquiring citizenship. Travel, for example, which usually necessitates the holding of citizenship ID cards was—until 1946—possible without these cards; people could have done so then by a certificate issued by the French authorities. According to a Kurdish local, had that not been the case, more Kurds would have applied for citizenship, especially because many of them traveled back and forth to Syria and Turkey.

It was mainly the introduction of war-time rationing in 1941 that made Kurds recognize the value of citizenship. During World War II, the majority of the Kurds were deprived from food ration cards because they did not have Lebanese citizenship. Although this incident made many Kurds rush into applying for citizenship, the appreciation of it, however, began too late. Legislation in 1940 made Lebanese naturalization theoretically impossible, particularly for the Kurds, and later in the decade for the Palestinian Muslim refugees (Palestinian Christian refugees were granted citizenship).[7]

Realizing that they were purposely deprived of acquiring Lebanese citizenship, many Kurds resorted to other methods to obtain it. For example, on February 1, 1956, 17 Kurdish families agreed in a court in the Christian town of Junieh to change their religious status from Sunni Muslims to Maronite Christians in return for naturalization.[8] This decision was to cause considerable national contention that ended with the Kurds re-registering themselves as Sunni Muslims. They kept the citizenship. Later in the year, a group of Chaldean Christians were granted citizenship. This incident created another national crisis. In order to resolve the conflict, the Christian Maronites agreed to naturalize an equal number of Kurds.[9] After this incident, virtually no Kurd was granted citizenship despite the various appeals to settle the naturalization problem. Following is an example of such appeals.

In a statement to the members of the Lebanese Parliament on August 1, 1960, Sa'ib Salam, a Sunni Muslim leader, addressed the Parliament stating: "There are people born in this country like you, and they have legitimate rights as you and I do; however, they are deprived of exercising ordinary citizens' rights ... There are some of them who cannot legally marry, have children, or even die ... and if they get sick, they are deprived of hospitalization and medical care." Soon after Salam became Prime Minister, he issued a decree which called for applications to be filed for citizenship. Most Kurds applied. However, action on all applications was immediately frozen. An article in the Christian daily newspaper, *an-Nahar*, reported that the naturalization process was canceled because some of the [Christian] officials objected to it for fear of the long-term political consequences of such an action. The report added that these officials

---

[7]Despite the various obstacles created by the Christian Maronites, some Kurdish families were still able to get naturalized, usually through *wasta*, the influence they could bring to bear through money or contacts. For example, in 1947, when Sami al-Sulh was Prime Minister, a number of Kurdish families were granted Lebanese citizenship on the basis of the 1925 Decree in return for electoral votes.

[8]*an-Nahar* [Beirut], (March 9, 1956).

[9]*an-Nahar* [Beirut], (June 24, 1956).

were afraid that if naturalized, the high birth-rate among Muslim Kurds would soon undermine Lebanon's precarious sectarian balance.[10]

Between 1961 and 1962, the naturalization problem witnessed new twists when Kamal Junblat, Minister of Interior in Rashid Karami's government, sought a solution to the noncitizens dilemma which by then became recognized as part of Lebanon's general confessional problem. Junblat granted the Kurds 'non-specified citizenship' which allowed their children to acquire Lebanese citizenship by judicial decrees in accordance with the law. The Article on which the judicial decree was based stated that: "everyone born on Lebanese territory to parents of non-specified citizenship is considered a Lebanese." As a result, some Kurdish children were granted citizenship. But due to Christian opposition, the granting of non-specified citizenship was soon abandoned and was replaced with '*qaid al-dars*' ('Under Consideration') ID cards. Despite the fact that the issue of naturalizing the Kurds and other stateless minorities was raised in Parliament in more than a dozen of cabinets founded between 1970 and the early 1990s, all efforts ended in failure due to the objection of the Christian Maronites.[11] As a result, most Kurds were left for decades living a minority complex, burdened with an imposed alien status that hindered their integration into Lebanese society. By the mid-1990s, fewer than 20% of Lebanon's Kurds had citizenship and approximately 10% were without any form of identity or had been registered as Syrians or Palestinians. The remaining Kurds, over 70%, held Under Consideration ID cards.

The Under Consideration ID card was granted for a period of either one or three years after which it could be regularly renewed. The card was valid for all members of the immediate family. To obtain the card, fingerprints and official applications were required in addition to application fees. It is important to note here that most noncitizen Kurds suffered from the complicated transactions when renewing their ID cards. These transactions not only cost them application fees but also entailed costs resulting from brokerage. For a lower class family composed of six members, the 1994 application fees represented more than 15% of the household's annual income. Furthermore, Kurds residing in European countries and elsewhere had grave problems when officials at Lebanese embas-

---

[10]*an-Nahar* [Beirut], (September 14, 1961).

[11]Each cabinet would focus on the humanitarian aspect of the problem and the civil rights of the people who had been in the country for decades. For instance, after his cabinet was formed in November 1974, the Sunni Prime Minister Rashid al-Sulh insisted that the formal government statement include an article committed to resolving the issue of minority naturalization before the situation becomes too grave. A heated debate followed between al-Sulh, on the one hand, and the Christian Phalangist Party (al-Kata'ib) and the National Liberal Party (Hizb al-Wataniyyin al-Ahrar) on the other. In the midst of his argument against the proposition, George Saadeh, the Phalangist minister then, drew attention to the political ramifications of naturalizing the Kurds by stating: "We, the Phalangists, have worked hard in the past to give the Armenians Lebanese nationality and this was accomplished. But what was the result? They have become the electoral balance in the districts they live in. So if the Prime Minister wants his electoral fate to be determined by the Kurds, we are with him." Cited in *Rohilat*, no. 9 (November 1974), p. 2.

sies refused to renew their cards. Kurds then incurred financial loss as a result of having to travel to Beirut with their families in order to complete the transactions. This is not to mention those Kurds whose applications were turned down.

These burdens on the Kurds did not come to an end until June 21, 1994 when, despite strong opposition by many Christians, the government of Rafiq al-Hariri issued a citizenship decree, whereby those who had no citizenship were invited to file applications. Unfortunately, many Kurds could either not afford the cost of the application, were abroad and thus unable to travel and file for themselves, or simply did not believe in it. As a result, only 18,000 Kurds benefited from the decree. The processing took about two years. After 1996, there were attempts to issue another decree, particularly for those who missed the first opportunity. Over the last five years (1996-2000), the issuing of the second decree has been repeatedly postponed primarily because not enough Christian applicants were available. The issue is still pending.

THE SOCIOECONOMIC STATUS OF THE KURDS

In addition to legal obstacles that the Kurds have faced in Lebanon for over half a century, they also encountered social discrimination. To best describe this type of discrimination, it might suffice to give a picture of the social class that the vast majority of Kurds belong to, namely, the lower class.[12] A summary of related findings of my 1995 study is also presented.

In general, the lower class includes working people who possess neither office nor wealth, and little or no education. They include taxi drivers, vegetable peddlers, barbers, sharecroppers, unskilled day laborers, servants, office boys, craftsman or tradesman who worked as employees or apprentices. Many of them form a sub-proletariat who are employed in menial jobs in construction, road building and small industries, for the most part with no social or medical insurance, or trade-union rights.[13] Often working on temporary bases and easily dismissed, lower class people are low-paid and do not have the adequate property or savings which they could use as an insurance during times when work becomes slack. Additionally, many members of the lower class, especially those who had been denied citizenship, are severely vulnerable to discriminatory treatment by others and treated unjustly and perceived as aliens. Kurds, in particular, face greater adversity than most other members of the lower class (such as the Shi'is, Syrians, and Arab noncitizens). The very fact that Kurds are not Arabs denies many of them employment, humanitarian support, and equal treatment in government offices, even if the Kurdish person is Lebanese in citizenship.

---

[12]Lebanese society today, similar to how it was on the eve of the civil war, can be easily divided into five broad definable social classes: the national elite, the upper class, the middle class, the upper lower class, and the lower class.

[13]Theodor Hanf, *Coexistence in Wartime Lebanon: Decline of a State and Rise of a Nation*. Translated from German by John Richardson. London: The Centre for Lebanese Studies, in association with I.B. Tauris & Co Ltd., Publishers, 1993), p. 199.

Assuming that in Lebanon education both reinforces the position of many traditionally high status groups and provides others with an important channel for upward mobility,[14] the fact that lower class people are relatively overwhelmed by the pressure to provide their families with adequate resources for survival, they have neither the money nor the time to send their working-age children to schools. As a result, they become the least literate class in Lebanon and the easiest to be exploited and manipulated by others. According to Khuri, mobility from the lower to higher class not only requires wealth but also social and psychological mobility which means that the family has to transform itself from an extended family sub-culture—a characteristic of lower class communities—to new forms of family ties and duties often represented in nuclear types of families, and from social and economic dependence to social and economic independence.[15] Such a transformation process is still in its infancy as far as the Kurds are concerned.

In the study that I undertook in 1995, it was found that 85 percent of the Kurds live either within the poverty line or below it. Their educational attainment is also extremely deficient. Almost 60 percent of the Kurds are virtually illiterate while 97 percent of their parents are in the same category. Most Kurds have large families, exceeding six children in about 44 percent of the cases. Kurds also overwhelmingly lack property; most of them are either renters or occupants of houses that were evacuated by the Christians during the civil war (these houses are now given back to their original owners). The vast majority of the respondents maintained that the Lebanese people perceive the Kurds as aliens or inferior to them. More than three quarters of the respondents indicated that the Lebanese government mistreat the Kurds in comparison to other minorities, and almost 60 percent revealed that the political structure in Lebanon does not allow ambitious Kurds to acquire important positions in the government. Now that a larger proportion of Kurds have become citizens, it remains to be seen how far and quick they will be able to change their current socioeconomic status and integrate into Lebanese society.

THE POLITICAL STATUS OF THE KURDS

As mentioned earlier, most Kurds were until the mid-1990s noncitizens. As a result, they were forced to: (1) be part of a clientalist system that was generally working at their expense, and (2) to join forces against those who imposed on them their underprivileged status or threatened their very own existence. Having said this, it is important to understand how this clientalist system in Lebanon specifically affected (and still affects) the Kurdish community. It is

---

[14]Paul D. Starr, "Lebanon," in *Commoners, Climbers and Notables: A Sampler of Studies on Social Ranking in the Middle East*, edited by C. A. O. Van Nieuwenhuijze (Leiden: E. J. Brill, 1977.), p. 212.

[15]Ibid, p. 38.

also important to describe how the Kurds contested their adversaries and what the outcome of their struggle was.

The Kurds in the Lebanese Clientalist System

Throughout most of its history, Lebanon has essentially been characterized by the division of its population into competing families and religious confessions politically organized in what is known as patron-client relationships.[16] Such a relationship, involving an interchange of unequal goods and services between patrons (za'ims or leaders) and clients (followers), has a profound effect on the social and political culture of the Lebanese. In exchange for their support of a za'im, usually in the form of votes or more active forms of political participation, the followers expect to receive assistance or favors in securing employment, government benefits, and mediation with government officials or other prominent persons.[17]

Until the 1980s, three main categories of clients comprised the za'ims' resources of patronage: First, and most important, were the rich clients who usually belonged to large families and had adequate money to support the za'im. Second, were the poorer and politically less important voters, who made up the majority of the za'im support base. Such people generally had simple requests which could be dealt with by the assistants of the za'im. The third category of clients comprised two groups of people: those who voted in another constituency and the disenfranchised Kurds and Palestinian refugees who had not been naturalized, a problem that meant they had nothing to offer the za'im and, as a result, were largely excluded from clientalist networks.[18]

With the increase in the number of Kurds carrying the citizenship, candidates began to communicate with them for electoral support, yet, these interactions did not result in assistance offered to the Kurdish community. This was because the disunited Kurds have always supported more than one political figure or bloc. As a result, the Kurds denied themselves the concentrated power that could be efficiently used to exert pressure on local za'ims for benefits. There is little reason to suggest that this situation has changed today in comparison to the period between the mid-1940s and mid-1970s. The 1992 and 1996 parliamentary elections showed that the Kurds became better organized than

---

[16]According to Powell, three basic factors lie at the core of the patron-client relationship: first, the patron-client tie develops between two parties unequal in status, wealth and influence; so, in other words, it is a lopsided friendship. Second, the formation and maintenance of the relationship depends on reciprocity in the exchange of goods and services. Third, the development and maintenance of a patron-client relationship rests heavily on face-to-face contact between the two parties or, in other words, proximity. See John Duncan Powell, "Peasant Society and Clientalist Politics," in *Political Development and Social Change*, 2nd ed., edited by Jason L. Finkle and Richard W. Gable (New York: John Wiley & Sons, Inc., 1971), pp. 520-521.

[17]Starr, p. 208.

[18]Michael Johnson, *Class and Client in Beirut: The Sunni Muslim Community and the Lebanese state 1840-1985* (London: Ithaca Press, 1986), p. 94.

before but they are still far from acting as a cohesive group. The Kurds are still divided among themselves and continue to be manipulated for their electoral power with little or nothing in return. Even their several attempts at running for parliamentary elections ended in failure. The only Kurdish candidate in the 1992 elections received only 5,000 votes; that is, less by 10,000 votes that would have qualified the person for membership in the Parliament.[19] In the 1996 elections, results were no better, and Kurdish votes were more distributed than ever. The· electoral power of the Kurds is steadily growing; however, lacking resources and leadership, this power will continue to be exploited. The next Lebanese parliamentary elections are scheduled for August and September 2000.

The Kurds During the Civil War (1975-1991) and After

On the whole, the Kurds had little reason to take sides in Lebanon's civil war. That to some extent changed with the purging of Kurds in East Beirut and perhaps more importantly in al-Karantina/al-Maslakh area in January 1976 by the Christian Maronite Phalange forces. The inhabitants of this latter area, mainly Kurds and Palestinians, were either shot (if male) or raped and driven out (if female), and their hovels leveled. Only a few managed to escape. Describing the massacres of al-Karantina-al-Maslakh, Johnson wrote:

> The press accounts, films and photographs of the subsequent massacre were horrifying. The hovels were looted for whatever small items of value they contained, bodies of men and women were piled in the streets, and at least one terrified slum dweller shot his daughters rather than see them raped. At the end of it all, the shacks of al-Karantina were bulldozed, burying the dead to create a level empty space.[20]

Following this massacre, and because of other atrocities committed before and after it, some Kurds decided to take up arms against the Christian-dominated Lebanese Front (*al-Jabha al-Lubnaniya*). Kurds either took up arms as members of their own Kurdish political parties (see below) or joined the Lebanese Communist Party, the Sunni Movement of Independent Nasserites (*al-Murabitun*) and, later on, the Druze-dominated Progressive Socialist Party (*al-Hizb al-Taqaddumi al-Ishtiraki*). Many Kurds also joined Palestinian organizations, especially the Popular Front for the Liberation of Palestine (PFLP) and the Democratic Front for the Liberation of Palestine (DFLP). The Kurds sought common cause with these progressive and Palestinian parties particularly because they thought that upon victory these forces would deliver them from per-

---

[19]The first time a Kurd nominated himself or herself to the Lebanese parliamentary elections was in 1968, when Jamil Mihhu (see section on Political Parties) unsuccessfully participated as a candidate for the 2nd district in Beirut.

[20]Ibid, pp. 190-191.

manent political, economic, and social misfortunes imposed on them by the Maronites.

In the early years of the war, Kurdish participation in the war focused primarily on fighting the Christian militias in East Beirut. Thus, following Israel's invasion of Lebanon in 1982, Kurds residing in Khaldeh and the areas surrounding West Beirut became subject to expulsions and detention by both the Israeli forces and their Lebanese Christian allies. Most Kurds who managed to escape before Israeli arrival moved to the Beirut and the Biqa' area. Then following Israel's violation of its own undertaking not to enter West Beirut in mid-September 1982 and the establishment of a pro-Israeli/pro-US Phalange dominated regime under Amin Gemayel, Christian dominated government forces began to harass the "unwanted people" in Lebanon, mainly Kurds and Palestinians, rounding them up, and detaining or expelling those without proper papers. Consequently, tens of thousands of Kurds and others were forced to emigrate to Europe. Barely a year later, Druze, Shi'i, and Sunni militia forces, backed by Syria, ousted Israel's Maronite surrogates from predominantly Muslim areas.

In late 1983, Amal, the main Shi'i militia then, began to exert its power to achieve ascendancy in South and West Beirut on behalf of Syria. Although its main focus was the suppression of the Palestinian camps' population in a series of nightmare sieges, Amal also fought the Sunni militias and had them rapidly eliminated. Unhappy about the idea of Shi'i control of the Sunni-dominant West Beirut, both the Druzes and the Kurds joined forces to resist Amal's encroachments into vital areas of West Beirut.[21] This they did with astonishing success. Kurdish militiamen were strong enough in their areas of concentration that they kept the Shi'is at bay in every battle they participated in. Fighting lasted until 1987 when an agreement between Syria and the warring factions was reached to withdraw all militias from Beirut and handover public order and security to Syrian forces. At the request of the Syrian authorities, the Druze Progressive Socialist Party (PSP) retreated to its heartland in the Shuf mountains. However, the Shi'i forces remained in Beirut. They were still needed to maintain control over the areas around Palestinian camps. This left the Kurds vulnerable to Syrian surveillance and harassment as well as to Shi'i vengeance. Hundreds of Kurds, primarily those who were members in PSP, Palestinian organizations, and anti-Syrian Kurdish organizations, were either killed or jailed by the Syrians and Shi'is. Thousands others either fled the country to Europe, or moved out to the Biqa' region and the Druze mountains.

The consequences of the Kurds' involvement in the war not only cost them lives and resulted in their displacement, but it further exposed the extent of prejudice they face in Lebanon. For instance, at the time when the Sunnis were fighting the Christians in the mid-1970s, it was reported that the Kurds were asked to volunteer their services as auxiliaries to the Sunni Murabitun militia of Beirut. These services were willingly given. Yet, when it came to sharing out

---

[21]Hanf, p. 304 and Rosemary Sayigh, "The Beirut Experience 2: Disillusionment" *Middle East International*, no. 271 (March 21, 1986), p. 16. It is argued that Kurdish identification with the Druzes had to do with Junblat family's Kurdish origin.

relief supplies from Europe and the United Nations, the Kurds lost out. "Supplies were usually divided into four parts and handed over to the Maronites, the Druze, the Shi'is, and the Sunnis." As Christians, the Armenians received a share from the Maronites and the Kurds, as Sunnis, ought in the way to have had a similar share from their co-religionists. But then, "for the Murabitun, the Kurds are just Kurds."[22]

In summary, it appears that the Kurds were among those peoples who suffered the most during the civil war. They lived beyond Lebanese society and were beset by a crippling sense of indignation, injustice, and impotent bitterness against a system which had denied them legitimate human rights as citizens. Hoping to change their situation, they mistakenly entered the civil war which further divided and impoverished them. Until today, the Kurds in Lebanon still feel relatively friendless. They have found few in Lebanon willing to fight their corner, or represent their interests. Based on the findings of my 1995 study, the Kurds have suffered from each and every major sectarian group in the country. The Christian Maronites denied them citizenship on the basis that such action will tilt the sectarian balance of the country towards the Muslims. The Sunnis, influenced by several rival Arab ideologies (e.g., Nasserism, Ba'thism), did not like the Kurds, thus doing little effort to naturalize them. For the Shi'ites, the Kurds were nothing but Sunni combatants or Druzes' allies. For the Druzes, the Kurds were good fighters. The Druzes, as well as the Sunnis wanted and used the Kurds to fight their wars, but when the Kurds were no longer needed they were ignored and disregarded. As far as local leaders are concerned, the study found that, with a few exceptions, Kurds mistrust all Lebanese political elites, consider them as unhelpful, and accuse them of being opportunists.[23]

SOCIAL AND POLITICAL ORGANIZATION OF THE KURDS

Before the late 1950s, the Kurds in Lebanon had virtually not taken part in any significant social or political activity. Only after the events that took place in 1958 and after did the Kurds start to think about such activities. First, following the 1958 civil war in Lebanon, the country witnessed a tremendous rural-urban migration the extent of which was that during the 1960s alone nearly one-fifth of Lebanon's rural population migrated to urban areas, mostly to Beirut and its suburbs.[24] These newcomers in Beirut made life harder for the Kurds as they

---

[22]Interview with one of the Lebanese Kurdish refugees in Sweden, cited in Ismet Cheriff Vanly, "The Kurds in Syria and Lebanon." In *The Kurds: A Contemporary Overview*, edited by Philip G. Kreyenbroek and Stefan Sperl, 143-170. London: Routledge, 1992), p. 167.

[23]The main exceptions are Sami al-Sulh, Sunni Prime Minister in the 1950s and 1960s, Kamal Junblat, Druze chief and leader of the leftist Arab nationalist forces during the civil war (assasinated by Syria in 1977), Salim al-Hoss, Sunni Prime Minister in the 1970s, 1980s, and 1990s, and Rafiq al-Hariri, Sunni Prime Minister in the 1990s.

[24]Salim Nasr, "The Crisis of Lebanese Capitalism," *MERIP Reports*, no. 73 (December 1978), p. 10.

both sought the same kind of jobs and shared the same residential areas; however, unlike their new competitors, the Kurds did not hold any citizenship rights. Consequently, the Kurds suffered severe economic losses and therefore started voicing their concerns over the citizenship issue.

Also in 1958, the union between Syria and Egypt was announced, a political act that had significant negative consequences on the social, economic, and political conditions of the Kurds in Syria. The end result was ultimately felt in Lebanon. The union initiated the first oppressive measures against the Kurds in Syria. In due course, many thousands of Syrian Kurds—mostly politicized students, workers, refugees and asylum seekers—moved to Lebanon. Despite the temporary presence of most of these Kurds, they nevertheless were able to help in making the Kurds in Lebanon better aware of the importance of social and political activism. They even helped in establishing and participated in the activities of Lebanese Kurdish social and political organizations, particularly in the late 1960s and early 1970s.

Finally and perhaps the most important factor for initiating Lebanese Kurds' social and political awareness was the fall of the monarchy in Iraq in 1958 which ultimately led to the outbreak of the 1961-1975 Kurdish war. Mulla Mustafa Barzani needed a publicity platform for the war. He found that platform in the liberal city of Beirut where thousands of Kurds live. Having their national self-awareness boosted by the Kurdish war, many Lebanese Kurds began to sense their impoverished status and started to think about methods for changing that status. One method was through establishing social and political organizations. What follows is a survey of these organizations detailing the formation and evolution of each organization, including its interaction with other Kurdish and Lebanese groups.

Voluntary Associations

al-Jam'iya al-Khairiya al-Kurdiya al-Lunaniya (Lebanese Kurdish Philanthropic Association). This was the first legal Kurdish body to be established in Lebanon. It was founded on September 19, 1963 when Kamal Junblat was the Minister of Interior. Among its primary goals is consolidating friendship ties among Lebanese Kurdish youth and expanding the social and public services of, and fostering education and knowledge among, the Kurdish community.[25] Its major activities included the establishment of an infirmary in October 1967 and the distribution of humanitarian supplies. This association was and still is the only legal/official organization in which the Kurmanji speakers group of Kurds form the majority, a fact that reflects the division of Kurdish organizations according to linguistic and communal lines. Although not very effective, the activities of the association went beyond merely providing direct services to its members. It sought and still is seeking to change the social, economic, cultural, and legal conditions of Lebanon's Kurds. For example, it targeted the

---

[25] The Association's by-laws.

naturalization problem as its prime concern, just like all other Kurdish organizations had done. Known as the largest and most active Kurdish association in Lebanon, LKPA recently faced Syrian harassment after showing high capacity for social and political activism on the Kurdish and Lebanese levels. Its president, Khalid Uthman, was detained by Syrian authorities in 1995. He was released a few days after.

Jam'iyat al-Arz al-Riyadiya al-Thaqafiya (al-Arz Athletico-Cultural Association). This association was established on March 18, 1969 under the name of Jam'iyat al-Arz al-Riyadiya to enhance Kurdish athletic activities. Three years later, it widened its scope of activities to include cultural ones, hence the full name *Jam'iyat al-Arz al-Riyadiya al-Thaqafiya*. The founders of the association viewed that the primary need for an illiterate and unorganized group like the Kurds would be a cultural center like *Jam'iyat al-Arz*.[26] Members of this association are almost exclusively from the Mardinli speakers of Kurds. Among its prominent figures was Faysal Fakhru who founded the Rezgari party (see below). One of the distinguishing activities of the association was the establishment of a soccer team which often plays in the Lebanese Division II soccer league.

Ittihad al-Talaba al-Akrad fi Lubnan (Kurdish Student Union in Lebanon). This association was established on June 19, 1970 by a group of students who took advantage of Kamal Junblat's term of office as Minister of the Interior. The Union's goals were to work towards enhancing the intellectual and social status of Kurdish students in Lebanon, to offer educational services to those Kurds who are unable to attend universities in Lebanon, and to strengthen relations with Lebanese students and other student unions. The activities of the Union were very weak because the number of Kurdish students in Lebanon was marginal. Furthermore, the internal conflicts which arose among its committee members in 1974 over leadership and planning paralyzed its activities. Thus it failed to achieve its goals and collapsed at the outbreak of the civil war.

al-Jam'iya al-Kurdiya al-Thaqafiya al-Ijtima'iya (The Kurdish Socio-Cultural Association). This association was established on May 3, 1975 by *Munazzamat al-Parti al-Kurdi al-Yasari fi Lubnan* to encourage education and social interaction with other Kurdish cultural organizations and to improve the social and cultural status of the Kurds in Lebanon. However, its activities, which included a literacy program and the publication of a bulletin entitled *Reber* (The Guide) as well as a few other pamphlets on Kurdish literature, came to an end a few months after the Israeli invasion of Lebanon in June 1982. The association was known for its close ties with several Palestinian organizations, a fact that made many of its supervisors leave Lebanon before the Israelis arrived. It was known to have a large and unique collection of books on the Kurds in various languages. The library collection was haphazardly distributed among or sold to

---

[26]*Rasti* [Beirut], no. 10 (1973), p. 5. Cited in Ahmad, *Akrad Lubnan*, p. 109.

interested people. The internal conflicts among the remaining members of the Association marked its final dissolution in January 1983.

   Majlis al-A'yan al-Kurdi al-Lubnani al-A'la (The Lebanese Kurdish Supreme Council of Notables). This association was founded on December 17, 1994. Its primary goal was to give attention to Kurdish social, cultural, educational, and developmental activities in order to enhance the conditions of the Kurds in Lebanon and to unite all Kurdish groups, families, political parties, clubs, and associations found in Lebanon.[27] The individualistic style of its formation and leadership, however, denied it both the popular support and the co-operation of other existing Kurdish organizations. In fact, its name reflects the kind of members it recruits: Kurdish notables who are usually elderly people, have money but not education or the necessary mechanisms for improving the general status of the Kurdish community.

   In summary, it can be concluded that Kurdish voluntary associations remained largely ineffective in changing the socioeconomic status of the Kurds. Exacerbated by the breakout of the civil war in 1975, they were too weak to have demonstrated any real effect in changing the conditions of their own members, let alone the Kurds as a whole. For example, they were unable to build a single school, hospital, or even plan a social orientation program as they have declared in their agendas upon foundation. Moreover, the associations failed to provide the Kurdish society with fresh cadres of leaders who would have new perspectives on problems, thereby stimulating social change. The associations were very weak in exerting pressure on Lebanese authorities and they failed to integrate the Kurds into the Lebanese society. Such results made many Kurds entertain the idea of establishing familial leagues which began to emerge in the mid-1970s to group the members of the family within one body and serve their own interests. The formation of such leagues were seen as a reaction to their dissatisfaction or inadaptation with the Kurdish associations discussed above. Yet, the leagues whose aims and functions did not differ from those of the voluntary associations did no better than the associations themselves. Unfortunately, the outcome was the further incohesiveness of the Kurdish community.

Political Parties

   al-Hizb al-Dimuqrati al-Kurdi fi Lubnan - al-Parti (The Kurdish Democratic Party in Lebanon, better known as al-Parti). This was the first legal Kurdish party to be established in Lebanon (1970). Founded by Jamil Mihhu, a house painter, the party started to operate clandestinely in July 1960 under the name of *Munazzamat al-Shabiba al-Kurdiya* (the Organization of Democratic Youth in Lebanon). It was a group formed by a cluster of young Lebanese and

---

   [27]*Al-Wahj* [Beirut], no. 1 (1995), p. 13. The founder of the association, Wahhaj al-Shaykh Mussa, a member of a wealthy Kurdish family, ran for parliamentary elections in 1992 but lost.

Syrian Kurds with the assistance and encouragement of the Kurdish Democratic Party in Syria (KDPS).[28] Initially, the activities of the Organization were limited to communication with local Kurds and dissemination of 'statements' explaining the social, cultural, and political conditions of the Kurdish community and outlining methods to improve them, with particular emphasis on the citizenship problem. As of 1961 and upon the recommendation of the KDPS, activities developed to include assisting Kurdish representatives sent by Mulla Mustafa Barzani to publicize the Kurdish national movement in Iraq.

The group's political activities remained underground until 1970 when Mihhu, attending the Eighth Congress of the Democratic Party of Kurdistan (KDP) that was held in August 1970 in Iraq, was told by Barzani about the importance of organizing Kurdish political activities through a legal body which would serve both the Lebanese Kurds as well as the Kurdish national movement. Because Barzani knew that Mihhu was going to face some challenges from Salah Badreddine, an ex-leader of KDPS and a person disliked by Barzani but with a large number of followers in Lebanon, Barzani decided to give Mihhu a letter addressed to the Lebanese Kurds revealing that Mihhu had been chosen by him (i.e., Barzani) to lead the Kurds in Lebanon. The fact that the Lebanese Kurds viewed Barzani as the champion of the Kurdish cause meant that anything he says will be willingly accepted.

The selection of Mihhu as the representative of Barzani increased the former's popularity in Lebanon, a fact which enraged Badreddine who accused Mihhu of lying about the contents of the letter. However, soon after he came back from Iraq, Mihhu, a Lebanese citizen, succeeded in mobilizing many Kurds to rally behind his party and asked the Lebanese government to legalize its status. On September 24, 1970 this was done and the Kurdish Democratic Party in Lebanon, better known as al-Parti, was born. However, Badreddine did not surrender to this setback. He soon started a campaign against Mihhu accusing him of being oriented towards the Iraqis for financial reasons. Mihhu's popularity then began to deteriorate dramatically as he failed to prove the opposite. Later on, Mihhu was also accused of nepotism. Consequently, Barzani sent for Mihhu and put him under house arrest in Iraqi Kurdistan for three years between 1971 and 1974.

After his return to Lebanon, Mihhu consistently used his newspaper *Sawt al-Akrad/Denge Kurd* (The Voice of the Kurds) to declare his opposition to Barzani and his support of Baghdad's autonomy plans for the Kurds. This led to more internal divisions among the Kurdish community in Lebanon, factionalization of al-Parti, and weakening of Mihhu's position as the leader of the community. Locally, al-Parti operated within the framework of the Lebanese National Movement until 1976 when it withdrew on the pretext that al-Parti was no longer welcomed by the Lebanese Communist Party (LCP). LCP insisted on substituting al-Parti with *Munazzamat al-Parti al-Kurdi al-Yasari fi Lubnan*. Mihhu was arrested and jailed by the Syrian authorities in 1977. He was released

---

[28]The slogans of the group were "Citizenship is one of the rights of the Kurds" and "Unite ... then ask for your rights."

two years later. Al-Parti ceased activities after the death of Mihhu in 1982. It lost its legal status in 1991 at the request of Syrian authorities.

al-Parti - al-Qiyada al-Markaziya (al-Parti - Central Leadership). After discovering Mihhu's orientation towards the Iraqis, several members of al-Parti split off in 1971 and joined those friends whose membership applications to al-Parti were declined earlier by Mihhu, to form the Kurdish Democratic Party in Lebanon - Central Leadership. This group was characterized by its full cooperation with, and loyalty to, Mulla Mustafa, a fact that contributed to its popularity among many Lebanese and Syrian Kurds. This party issued a bulletin entitled *al-Parti* and applied several times to the Lebanese government for a license, but in vain. Its primary activities included making material contributions to the Kurdish national movement in Iraq as well as disseminating news of the movement in Lebanon and abroad. After the collapse of the Kurdish movement in March 1975, the activities of the party went into gradual decline and ended with the assassination of its General Secretary, Ghazi Farah, in June 1978. Attempts to revive its activities in the 1980s completely failed.

Rezgari (The Lebanese Kurdish Party): Three reasons were used by Faysal Fakhru to justify the founding of this party on April 3, 1975: the failure of al-Parti to appeal to non-Kurmanji speakers, Mihhu's support for the Iraqi regime's plans for Kurdish autonomy, and the leadership structure of al-Parti which seemed to have been transformed into a Mihhu family organization rather than representing the interests of the whole Kurdish community.

Soon after its formation, the Rezgari declared through its bulletin, *Xebat* (The Struggle), its support for the Lebanese government and its neutrality towards the various factions participating in the civil war. Accordingly, it participated in Jabhat al-Ahzab wa al-Qiwa al-Qawmiyya wa al-Wataniyya fi Lubnan, which was in favor neither of the policies adopted by the Muslim-dominated Lebanese National Movement nor those of the Christian-dominated Lebanese Front.

In a surprise move, on December 4, 1976, Mihhu and Fakhru put their differences and verbal attacks aside and announced the formation of *al-Jabha al-Wataniyya al-Kurdiyya al-'Arida* (The Broad Kurdish National Front) whose main goals were to unify Kurdish political action in Lebanon, guarantee the unity of the Kurdish community in Lebanon, improve their social and political status, and to uphold the rights of Lebanese Kurds in employment and citizenship. They also agreed to support the Lebanese National Movement and, at the same time, welcomed the intervention of the Arab Deterrence Forces led by Syria, an act seen by them as the best solution to end the war. The Front ceased exsitence in less than a year due to the imprisonment of Mihhu by the Syrians. Keeping a very low profile on the Lebanese scene after 1977, Rezgari continues to exist today.

Rezgari II (The Lebanese Kurdish Party): Following the creation of the Broad Kurdish National Front between al-Parti and Rezgari, a faction within the latter split off accusing General Secretary Fakhru of "reconciling with Mihhu and returning to Kurdish tribalism." Led by 'Abdi Ibrahim, this new faction also protested Mihhu's domination of the Front and accused Fakhru of following Mihhu's pattern in not appealing to various Kurdish groups. In addition, Fakhru was accused of favoring Baghdad's autonomy plans for Iraqi Kurdistan. In early 1977, Ibrahim announced that he would maintain and preserve the basic principles of the parent party and denounce the establishment of the Front. As a result, he declared the formation of a new party, the Lebanese Kurdish Party (or Rezgari II) which replaced Rezgari in Jabhat al-Ahzab wa al-Qiwa al-Qawmiyya wa al-Wataniyya fi Lubnan. Rezgari II continued to function until the Israeli invasion in June 1982. Thereafter, the party practically ceased to exist when its General Secretary left for Syria; his attempt to revive the party three years later eneded with failure. In fact, soon after Ibrahim left in June 1982, Jamil Hasan, a leading member in the party broke away in November of the same year to establish the *Lebanese Socialist Rezgari Party*. Hasan himself was thrown out of the new faction after re-allying himself with Fakhru and declaring the merger of both the Socialist Party and Rezgari in late 1984. Witnessing more break-ups, the Socialist party ceased existence in 1985.

Munazzamat al-Parti al-Kurdi al-Yasari fi Lubnan (The Leftist Kurdish Democratic Parti Organization in Lebanon). This Marxist-Leninist oriented party (the Parti Organization herefater) is an offshoot of the mother party--*al-Hizb al-Dimuqrati al-Kurdi al-Yasari* (LKDP). LKDP was founded on August 5, 1965 by Salah Badreddine after he split off from the Kurdish Democratic Party in Syria (KDPS). The beginnings of the Parti Organization in Lebanon go back to the early 1960s when several immigrant Syrian Kurds became members in, and cooperated with, *Munazzamat al-Shabiba al-Kurdiya*. This cooperation continued until 1969. In that year, relations between Badreddine's LKDP and Barzani deteriorated as the latter openly expressed support for the KDPS. As a consequence, Badreddine decided to move to Lebanon. There, he found great difficulties because most Lebanese Kurds were loyal to Barzani.

The Parti Organization began its activities formally in 1970.[29] During the first half of the 1970s, it was mainly concerned with recruiting Lebanese Kurds since most of its initial members were Syrians. This the Parti Organization achieved in various ways. For example, it openly criticized Jamil Mihhu for his orientation towards the Iraqis[30] and Syrians as well as his move away from the Lebanese National Movement, a fact that led several followers of al-Parti to join the Parti Organization. Mihhu blatantly accused the Communists (with whom the Parti Organization were on good terms) of instigating the dissension movement. As a consequence, al-Parti withdrew from the Lebanese National Movement to be replaced by the Parti Organization. Practically speaking, the Parti Organization, which changed its name into *al-Ittihad al-Sha'bi al-Kurdi fi*

---

[29]The word 'Leftist' was added by the end of 1975.
[30]Ironically, Salah Badr al-Din went into compromise with the Iraqis as of 1975.

Lubnan (The Kurdish Popular Union in Lebanon), ceased existence in Lebanon when its General Secretary Badreddine fled to Cyprus after the Israeli invasion. Before that, it witnessed a dissident movement in 1979 that ended with the formation of a breakaway faction named *Munazzamat al-Parti al-Kurdi al-Yasari fi Lubnan - al-Haraka al-Tashihiya* (The Lebanese Kurdish Leftist Parti Organization - the Corrective Movement) which ceased existence with the Israeli invasion as well.

 Munazzamat al-Taqadumiyyin al-Akrad fi Lubnan (The Organization of Kurdish Progressives in Lebanon). This party was one of the break-away factions from the Parti Organization that was led by Ahmad Jamhur and Mustafa Sufi. The dissenters accused Badreddine of treason because of his relations with the Iraqi regime in 1975. Then in June 1976, Jamhur and Sufi distributed a statement under the name of *al-Qiyada al-Shar'iya lil-Munazzama* (the Legal Leadership of the Parti Organization). By mid-1978, it changed its name into the Organization of Kurdish Progressives in Lebanon. Its activities included the formation of *Rabitat al-Taqaddum al-Fikriyya* (The Intellectual League of Progress), holding festivals and seminars and publishing several pamphlets. Nevertheless, it too was short-lived and collapsed with the Israeli invasion of Lebanon in June 1982.

 al-Hizb al-Dimuqrati al-Kurdi fi Lubnan - al-Parti/al-Qiyada al-Mu'aqqata (The Kurdish Democratic Party - al-Parti - Provisional Leadership). After the formation of The Broad Kurdish National Front in 1976 by al-Parti and Rezgari, Muhammad Mihhu, son of Jamil Mihhu, split off from his father's party and formed his own in May 1977. Muhammad began to confront his father openly through his bulletin *Sawt al-Shabiba al-Kurdiyya* (Voice of the Kurdish Youths) criticizing him for his advocacy of the Iraqi policy against Barzani as well as his move away from the Lebanese National Movement. However, both Muhammad and his father shared the same views concerning those Kurds who did not speak the Kurmanji dialect, a fact which did not fail to leave its negative effects on *al-Parti/al-Qiyada al-Mu'aqqata*. Muhammad was killed during a clash with the Shi'ite Amal Movement on April 16, 1982, and event that marked the final dissolution of the party.

 Kurdish organizations, whether voluntary associations or political parties, have failed to achieve their desired objectives because the Kurds took little part in their activities. Participation for the majority of Kurds seemed irrelevant to their primary concerns which centered around finding jobs and securing food and medical aid for their families. The ignorance by the Kurds about the significance/importance of well-organized political activity was another reason. Most importantly, the organizations, especially the political parties, did not emerge out of Lebanese Kurdish social and political consciousness; instead, they were either instigated by outside actors or were haphazardly established as a reaction to dissatisfaction with the existing parties. Moreover, the leaders or notables of the Lebanese Kurds not only dominated the power apparatuses of the organizations, but also exploited their resources for personal goals and inhibited many Kurds from membership. Besides, the leadership lacked both the education and political literacy which are prime requisites of any genuine organization. Parties were thus riddled with internal conflicts and were severely factionalized. This drove the little educated Kurdish individuals away from political action. In addition, at a time when most of the organizations were incapable of supporting themselves financially,[31] they still promised, as their programs indicated, to build schools and hospitals which were completely beyond their means. This behavior further alienated the organizations in the eyes of the Kurdish public.

Two other important reasons for the failure of Kurdish organizations to improve the social and economic status of the Kurds include: (1) At various times, national issues (i.e. events in Kurdistan) prevailed over local ones and interfered with the primary activities of the organizations, a fact that led to the emergence of conflicts between the different parties which caused them to neglect efforts to improve the general status of their community in Lebanon. (2) The Kurds' broad lack of Lebanese citizenship denied many people from effectively participating in the activities of the organizations. It should be noted here that establishing any organization in Lebanon requires that two-thirds of its officers be Lebanese citizens. Since very few Kurds held citizenship, the result was relying on any Kurdish persons who have held citizenship regardless of their qualifications for the offices to be run.

In short, the record of Kurdish political parties has been dismal. They were very weak to an extent that they were unable to institutionalize mass support. In fact, they not only lacked mass appeal but also did not develop the organizational and institutional framework for organizing mass support. The nature of their political literature and party rhetoric proved to be misleading and disguising more than was informing and revealing. Many of the parties even tried to reconcile their narrowly based membership with their lofty slogans to broaden their appeal. Moreover, the parties were too weak to have demonstrated any real adaptability, especially since they were always led by their founders whose absence (as a result of death or fleeing) marked their dissolution. Most of the parties, functioning with illegal status, collapsed soon after the establishment of an Israeli-backed Lebanese government in 1982. All that survives today from different Kurdish political parties is Rezgari which currently has very little support base. As for the voluntary associations, the Lebanese Kurdish Philanthropic Association and al-Arz Athletico-Cultural Association continue to operate.

CONCLUSION

Until the end of the civil war in the late 1991, the Kurds were still held in low esteem and were often objects of contempt, hatred, ridicule and violence.

---

[31]The income of Kurdish organizations, especially the voluntary associations, were mainly generated from membership fees. Contributions represented a marginal portion.

In terms of public policy, the Kurds, like all noncitizen groups in the country, were frequently singled out for special treatment. Their property rights were restricted, they did not enjoy the equal protection of the law, were deprived of the rights of suffrage, and were excluded from public office. The majority have had to seek employment without the security and benefits of contractual relations and were, as a result, subject to arbitrary dismissal.

The 1995 study revealed that citizenship status had a great impact on the socio-economic status (SES) of the Kurds in Lebanon. In all SES items, citizen Kurds had, by far, better SES scores than noncitizen Kurds. Moreover, noncitizen Kurds were barred from employment in the public sector or public firms. Doctors, engineers, and lawyers are rare among the Kurds because being one requires that she or he be a member of a syndicate or union before being able to practice the profession. For that to be realized, however, the person should be a Lebanese citizen. The lack of citizenship denied the Kurds the right to participate in the political life of Lebanon, to make demands and reciprocate with votes. It also made them subject to discriminatory treatment by the system. Such treatment led the Kurds to occupy a distinct social strata in Lebanon and become disproportionately concentrated, in terms of status, at the bottom of the political, social, and economic hierarchy of Lebanon. In short, the perplexities of Lebanon's social and political life and the negative repercussions it had on the Kurdish community made it virtually impossible for the Kurds to alter their social position or effect any change in their status. On the other hand, although aware of the discriminatory treatment they are facing, the Kurds never succeeded in producing a leader or a cadre that would ease their relations with the Lebanese state, its administrative system, and secure its services. In relation to this, it should be noted that the socioeconomic characteristics of the Kurds, whether measured by income, occupation, or education, no doubt account in part for the low status that is attributed to them by most of the Lebanese people.

The 1995 study revealed some seemingly paradoxical findings regarding the nature and degree of Kurds' attachment to Lebanon. Despite their strong sense of Kurdish identity (measured by their level of use of Kurdish as a daily language, their high interest in Kurdish music, their patterns of self-identification and associational behavior, their negative attitude toward other Lebanese groups, and their low desire to intermarry with members of other groups), about 85 percent of the Kurds hesitate to emigrate to anywhere including an independent Kurdistan. This finding reflects the Kurds' desperate hope to find a secure and dignified place within Lebanese society.[32]

In summary, the degree of discrimination against the Kurds was and still is relatively high. They continue to be reminded that they are different and at great personal costs. Yet, after several decades in Lebanon, the Kurds seem to

---

[32]The Kurds' strong sense of ethnicity is perhaps a result of, or is in effect defined and reinforced by, the Lebanese dominant groups who labeled them as a distinct category of people and practiced discriminatory treatment towards them. The kind of interactions with dominant groups made Kurds more self-consciously aware of defining differences: they were Kurds in an Arab society; they dressed and acted differently in social situations.

have acquired a dual life style and did not give up its efforts to identify itself as Kurdish as well as Lebanese. In other words, the Kurds in Lebanon accepted the society they live in as the home base, as the prime focus of allegiance, and as the place where personal ambitions are formed, achieved and enjoyed. All what the Kurds needed (and still need) is the formalization of their existence and their recognition as Lebanese by the Lebanese political system and by the Lebanese people as a whole. The naturalization of the Kurds, finally attained in 1996, will definitely lessen the degree of discrimination they had to face and will enhance their opportunities for upward mobility and integration into a pluralistic society like Lebanon.

PART II
BIBLIOGRAPHY

1

General Works

1 Attalah, H. (rev.). "Kurds." In *Worldmark Encyclopedia of Cultures and Daily Life*. Vol. 3, pp. 414-417. Detroit: Gale, 1998.

Outlines the history, geography, and demography of the Kurds and Kurdistan and then briefly discusses Kurdish language, folklore, religion, major holidays, rites of passage, interpersonal relations, living conditions, family life, clothing, food, education, cultural heritage, work, sports, entertainment and recreation, folk art, crafts, hobbies, and social problems.

2 Blau, Joyce. *Le Probleme Kurde: Essai Sociologique et Historique*. Brussels: Centre pour l'etude des problemes du monde musulman contemporain, 1963. 80 p.

In this book, Blau has drawn from scholarly works by such experts as Minorsky and Nikitine to give an excellent thumbnail sketch of the cultural and historical background of the Kurds. The major part of the book is devoted to Kurdish political history, divided into three main parts according to the countries in which the majority of Kurds now live: Turkey, Iran and Iraq. The book is largely an account of numerous Kurdish insurrections that erupted during the 19th and 20th centuries, but the earlier ones are cut mercifully short by Blau. The author comes to several conclusions: if the move for Kurdish autonomy is successful, the next logical step would be an independent state; the Kurds would prefer to be neutral in international politics, but if the West continues to be indifferent to their plight, they may be driven into the Soviet camp; and, if the Arabs do not show some sympathy for the Kurdish demands for autonomy, the Kurds may procure the situation into their own hands. (abridged, Lettie Wenner/*MEJ* 19, Winter 1965: 95)

3   Bois, Thomas. "Les Kurdes: Histoire, Sociologie, Litterature, Folklore."
            Al-Machriq 53 (1959): 101-147, 266-299.

A comprehensive annotated bibliography of works dealing with Kurdish
history, society, literature, and folklore. Also covered are Kurdish periodicals and previously published bibliographies.

4   Bois, Thomas. *The Kurds*. Translated from the French *Connaissance des
            Kurdes* (1965) by M. W. M. Welland. Beirut: Khayats, 1966. 159 p. Bib-
            liography: p. [155]-159. The French version was translated into Arabic by
            Muhammad Sharif 'Uthman (Najaf, Iraq: Matba'at al-Nu'man, 1973) un-
            der the title: *Lamhah 'an al-Akrad* and the English version was trans-
            lated into Arabic as well by Araz Zangi (Baghdad: Matba'at al-Jahiz,
            1975) under the title: *Ma'a al-Akrad*.

Father Thomas walks arm-in-arm not only with the Kurds but also with
their history and aspirations. A Dominican monk, Bois has studied Arabic
and Kurdish, has lived many years in the Middle East and has written extensively about the Kurds. Opening his book with a striking reference to
Kurdistan as "land without frontiers," Father Thomas proceeds with un-
failing skill and intellectual mobility to describe the socio-economic and
religio-cultural aspects of Kurdish life. Although there is frequent obei-
sance to the "fathers" of modern Kurdology, Minorsky, Nikitine, and
Rondot, there is a great deal of original observation and what may be
construed as empathy even with some of the Kurdish ancestral superstitions. Fact and myth, nevertheless, are differentiated and assessed; not
easy tasks with a mythogenic group like the Kurds. The reader gets a
corporate image of the people: their social system, family, villages,
homes, education, occupations, art, skills, folklore, weddings, feasts,
religious observances, magic rites, leisure hours, joys and sorrows—all
following a thematic sequence. Perhaps the best and the most edifying
chapter in the book deals with the language and the literature of the
Kurds. The author indicates familiarity with the cultural heritage of the
people and a hopeful awareness of their intellectual ferment. Also covered is the Kurds and their relations with the Christians.

5   Bois, Thomas. "The Kurds and their Country Kurdistan." In *Encyclo-
            pedia of Islam*. New ed. Vol. 5. Edited by C. E. Bosworth and others,
            439-447. Leiden: E. J. Brill, 1986.

Father Bois wrote this essay before his death in 1975. It is a summary of
essential information on the Kurds and Kurdistan. Topics discussed include: (A) The Territorial Extent of Kurdistan; (B) The Ethnic and Geographical Extent of Kurdistan; (C) Numerical Extent of the Kurds and;
(D) The Geography of Kurdistan: 1) Physical aspect; 2) The living landscape and habitat; 3) The human aspect.

6   Bruinessen, Martin van. "Kurdish Society, Ethnicity, Nationalism and Refugee Problems." In *The Kurds: A Contemporary Overview*. Edited by Philip G. Kreyenbroek and Stefan Sperl, pp. 33-67. London: Routledge, 1992.

This paper excellently surveys Kurdish society, ethnicity, nationalism and refugee problems. Those familiar with van Bruinessen's doctoral dissertation, *Agha, Shaikh and State* will find further insights. Analyzing the movement of large numbers of Kurds away from Kurdistan, as migrant workers, displaced persons (due to warfare), or political refugees, van Bruinessen argues that as a result a purely territorial nationalism, aiming at political independence, has become highly unrealistic.

7   Bruinessen, Martin van. *Agha, Shaikh, and State: The Social and Political Structures of Kurdistan*. London; Atlantic Highlands, NJ: Zed Books, 1992. 373 p.: ill. Includes bibliography (p. 344-361) and index.

This is a revised edition of the author's doctoral dissertation, which originally appeared in 1978. Since then it has become a classic of Kurdish studies, which has been translated into German, Kurdish (Sorani), Persian, and Turkish. This authoritative study of the Kurdish people, written by a distinguished social anthropologist, provides a varied insight into one of the largest primarily tribal communities in the world. The introductory chapter, which contains general information on Kurdistan, has been thoroughly updated since 1978 and includes sections on the Kurdish national movement from 1960 to 1985, on the effects of the Iran-Iraq war, and on recent trends in the policies of the Iranian, Iraqi, and Turkish governments towards the Kurds. The second chapter deals with tribes, examining questions of tribal structure and leadership, and the relations between tribal and non-tribal Kurds. The following chapter, 'Tribe and State,' stresses the importance of national politics on the fate of tribes. It is based on an impressive mass of historical data, and comes to the intriguing conclusion that Kurdish society has passed through what are generally recognized as crucial stages in social evolution: tribe, chiefdom and (proto-) state, but in descending order. Much of the material presented in the treatment of religious institutions in the fourth chapter, entitled 'Sheikhs: Mystics, Saints and Politicians,' is fascinating, and sometimes difficult to find elsewhere in Western literature. The fifth chapter, a well-documented history of the revolt of Sheikh Sa'id in Turkish Kurdistan in the mid-1920s, has been included because the movement involved all the major elements with which the study is concerned. It is followed by a brief concluding chapter, an appendix dealing with family trees of the major Kurdish families of *Sheikhs*, an explanatory list of Oriental terms, and a very good bibliography. The excellent quality of the work's eleven maps should be remarked upon. (abridged, Philip Kreyenbroek/*Ethnic and Racial Studies* 17, January 1994: 172)

8   Bruinessen, Martin van. *The Kurds in Movement: Migrations, Mobilisa-
tions, Communications and the Globalisation of the Kurdish Question*.
Tokyo: Islamic Area Studies Project, 1999. 20 p. [Islamic Area Studies
Working Paper Series; 14]

9   Busby, Annette. "Kurds." In *Encyclopedia of World Cultures, Volume
IX: Africa and the Middle East*. Edited by John Middleton and Amal
Rassam, pp. 174-177. Boston, MA: G.K. Hall and Co., 1996.

Topics discussed include: Orientation, History and Cultural Relations,
Settlements, Economy, Kinship, Marriage and Family, Sociopolitical Organization, and Religion and Expressive Culture of the Kurds.

10   Edmonds, Cecil John. *Kurds, Turks, and Arabs: Politics, Travel, and
Research in North-Eastern Iraq, 1919-1925*. London; New York: Oxford University Press, 1957. 457 p.: ill. Bibliography: p. [436]-437.

This book, covering the period from 1919 to 1925, is the first installment
of the author's diaries and notes based on his long experience in Iraq, first
as an officer under the British administration, and later, in the service of
the Iraqi government, as an advisor to the Ministries of Interior and Foreign Affairs. This book is more than a mere record of the author's experiences during 1919-1925. It combines a study of the geography of Iraqi
Kurdistan, based on the author's extensive travels and study, and an intimate knowledge of the history, customs and manners of the people and
their leading personalities. The author also records and assesses the services of his colleagues and predecessors as administrative officers of
north-east Iraq under both the British and Iraq administrations. As a detailed study of the geography and people of this part of Iraq, the book has
an added value to the scholar who needs an accurate and detailed study of
Iraqi Kurdistan. No less significant a feature of the book is the account of
British policy aimed at frustrating the separatist tendencies among the
Kurds, led by Sheikh Mahmud, in order to make possible the integration
of south Kurdistan, ceded by Turkey under the Treaty of Lausanne
(1923), with Iraq. Mr. Edmonds discusses not only the methods used to
prevent Sheikh Mahmud from realizing his ambition, but also his own
role in carrying out such a policy successfully to Iraq's advantage. The
author makes no apology for his opposition to Sheikh Mahmud, justified
only, it seems, by raison d'être; but Mr. Edmonds does not allow in his
account the interpretation that Sheikh Mahmud's "rebellion," viewed
from a different angle, was not a manifestation of a Kurdish nationalist
movement. The last part of the book is devoted to a detailed account of
the investigations of the League of Nations' Commission on the disputed
area between Iraq and Turkey. The Mosul Commission, on which Mr.
Edmonds served as a liaison officer, reported to the League three recommendation: the first was to keep the disputed area within Iraq, provided
the British Mandate was to extend another 25 years (after 1925); the sec-

ond, to give it back to Turkey; and the third to divide the area into two. The first was the preferable recommendation for economic, geographical and ethnic considerations, and the last was offered as a compromise solution. (abridged, Majid Khadduri/*MEJ* 12, Fall 1958: 469-470).

11   *Encyclopaedia of Islam*. New edition. Leiden: E. J. Brill, 1960, 1965, 1971, 1978, 1986, 1991, 1993, 1995, and 1997 for vols. I, II, III, IV, V, VI, VII, VIII, and IX, respectively.

In this widely known encyclopedia, several entries are written on (or are related) to the Kurds. These entries include: in volume (I): Agri; 'Anna-zids; Ardalan; Ayyubids; Baban; Badrkhani, Thurayya and Djaladat; Bahdinan; Baradust; Barzan; Bidlis; Bidlisi, Idriss; and Bidlisi, Sharaf Khan. (II): Colemerik; Dersim; Djaf; Djanbulat; Djawanrud; Fadlawayh; and Guran. (III): Hakkari; Hamawand; Hasnawayh; and Ibn 'Umar, Djazirat. (IV): Kadi Muhammad. (V): Kirkuk; Kitab Al-Djilwa; Kurds, Kurdistan; Lak; Madjnun Layla; and Mahabad. (VI): Maku; and Mar-wanids. (VII): Mustafa Barzani; Amir Nizam. (VIII): Oramar; Rawandiz; Rawwadids; Sakkiz. (IX): Sanandadj; Sarliyya; Sawdj-Bulak; Shabak; Shabankara; Shaddadids; Shahrazur; Shakak; Shamdinan; Sindjabi; Sisar; Somay; and Sulaymaniyya.

12   Gewranî, Ali Seydo [Gurani, 'Ali Saydu al-]. *Min 'Amman ila al-'Amadiyah aw Jawla fi Kurdistan al-Janubiyah*. [A description of a travel from Amman, Jordan to 'Amadiya, Iraqi Kurdistan] Cairo: Matba'at al-Sa'ada, 1939. 272 p.: illus., fold. col. map, ports.

13   Gewranî, Ali Seydo [Gurani, 'Ali Saydu al-]. "al-Lur wa-Luristan." [An overview of the Lur and their country Luristan] *Majallat al-Majma' al-'Ilmi al-Kurdi* 2, no. 2 (1974): 108-181.

14   Ghassemlou, Abdul-Rahman. *Kurdistan and the Kurds*. Prague: Publishing House of the Czechoslovak Academy of Science, 1965. 304 p.

This is a comprehensive analysis, from a Marxist Leninist point of view, written by the former General Secretary of the Kurdish Democratic Party of Kurdistan in Iran who was assassinated in 1989 in Vienna by Iranian government agents. The book is made up of three parts. The first provides a condensed geographical and historical outline of the Kurds and Kurdistan. The second investigates the economic life of the Kurds: land-tenure, living standards, industry, commerce and petroleum. The last part discusses the Kurdish question and the right of self-determination.

15   Great Britain. Colonial Office. *Report by His Majesty's Government in the United Kingdom of Great Britain and Northern Ireland to the Council of the League of Nations on the Administration of 'Iraq*. London: His Majesty's Stationery Office, 1922-1932.

16   Hakim, Halkawt (ed.). *Les Kurdes par-dela l'Exode*. Paris: L'Harmattan, 1992. Includes bibliographical references (p. 269-[272]).

An excellent collection of papers that discuss Kurdish history, economy and literature.

17   Iran. Markaz-i Amar-i Iran. *Salnamah-i Amari-i... Kishvar. Iran Statistical Yearbook*. Tehran: Markaz, 1972-. Annual.

English editions are published irregularly under title *Iran Statistical Yearbook* or *Statistical Yearbook of Iran*. Contains information on climate and geography, as well as statistics on population, including data on births, deaths, divorces, and marriages. Other tables present data on economic affairs, elections, and social and cultural topics.

18   Iraq. al-Jihaz al-Markazi lil-Ihsa'. *al-Majmu'ah al-Ihsa'iyah al-Sanawiyah. Annual Abstract of Statistics*. Baghdad: Central Statistical Organization, Publications & Public Relations, 1969-. Annual.

Continues *Statistical Abstract* (issued until 1966) and *Annual Statistical Abstract* (1967). A compendium containing statistical data on demographic, economic, social, and cultural affairs.

19   Izady, Mehrdad R. *The Kurds: A Concise Handbook*. Washington, D.C.: Crane Russak, 1992. p. 268.: maps. Includes bibliographical references.

The author offers a good reference work on the Kurds. According to the preface, Izady has written this book as a reference manual for the public, the press, teachers, students, scholars, and travelers. He brings together in an encyclopedic format, current information on the Kurds. The book includes ten chapters on the geography; land and environment; history; human geography; religion; language, literature and the press; society; political and contemporary issues; the economy; and culture and arts of the Kurds and Kurdistan. Coupled with a thorough introduction to many aspects of Kurdish society, the book is a good starting point for those beginning a study of the Kurds. The book also features 42 maps, several tables and diagrams, and each section and chapter is followed by a thorough bibliography of other sources.

20   Jalil, Jalili. *Nahdat al-Akrad al-Thaqafiyah wa-al-Qawmiyah fi Nihayat al-Qarn al-Tasi' 'Ashar wa-Bidayat al-Qarn al-'Ishrin*. [An overview of the Kurdish national and cultural development in the late 1800s and early 1900s] Translated from Russian by Bavi Naze. Beirut: Dar al-Katib, 1986. 228 p.

21 Kreyenbroek, Philip G.; Allison, Christine (eds.). *Kurdish Culture and Identity*. Atlantic Highlands, NJ: Zed Books, 1996. Includes bibliographical references (p. [174]-180) and index.

While Saddam Hussein's persecution of the Kurds and his military attacks on them have drawn world attention to the political plight of the Middle East's largest ethnic minority, much less is known of their culture. The present volume seeks to remedy this gap. Its contributors, who include both leading Western and Kurdish scholars, provide excellent overviews and some detailed examinations of various dimensions of Kurdish culture and its historical underpinnings. Making clear the differences that exist in a community that is spread across four countries in the region—Iraq, Iran, Turkey and Syria—and recognizing that Kurdish culture is in the process of change, successive chapters look at Kurdistan's written literature as well as its oral tradition, material culture including textiles and costume, and religion. The book contains chapters on Kurds' current position and their historical background, influence of the media, written literature, oral tradition, religion, Ahl-i Haqq, material culture, costume, rugs and weaving.

22 Mawsili, Mundhir. *'Arab wa-Akrad: Ru'yah 'Arabiyah lil-Qadiyah al-Kurdiyah: al-Akrad fi Watanihim al-Qawmi wa-fi al-Jiwar al-'Iraqi -al-Turki- al-Irani..wa-fi Suriyah wa-Lubnan*. 2nd ed. Beirut: Dar al-Ghusun, 1991. 621 p. Bibliography: p.[599]-607 and index.

Includes a general background on the Kurds and Kurdistan and a discussion on the Kurds' origins, anthropology, history, religion, language, literature, press, society (including character, social life and customs, costume, and women), tribes and tribal life, as well as the Kurds in Syria and Lebanon. Also discussed is agricultural and economic life and conditions of the Kurds and Kurdistan.

23 Minorsky, Vladimir. *al-Akrad: Mulahazat wa-Intiba'at*. Translated from Russian, and commented on, by Marouf Khaznadar. Baghdad: Matba'at al-Nujum, 1968. 99 p. Russian version was published in 1915.

Includes discussion on Kurdish social life and customs, religion, language, literature, and women, and a brief account on the Kurds in Russia.

24 Mokri, Mohammad. *Contribution Scientifique aux Etudes Iraniennes: Etudes d'Ethnographie, de Dialectologie, d'Histoire et de Religion (parues dans les annes 1956-1964)*. Paris: Klincksieck, 1970. 418 p.: illus., plates. Includes bibliographies.

Topics discussed include: social life and customs, sedentarization, marriage, the history and development of Kurdish studies in the former Soviet Union, folklore, magic rites, music, religion, Ahl-i Haqq, poetry, mythology, and legends.

25 Mokri, Mohammad. *Persico-Kurdica: Études d'Ethnomusicographie, de Dialectologie, d'Histoire et de Religion Parues dans les Annees 1964-1978: Mythes et Mots*. Louvain: Editions Peeters, 1995. 505 p.: ill. Includes bibliographical references.

26 Nikitine, Basile. *Les Kurdes: Etude Sociologique et Historique*. [The Kurds: Sociological and Historical Study] Paris: Editions d'Aujourd'-hui, 1975. viii, 351 p.: maps. (Reprint of the 1956 ed. published by Klincksieck, Paris). Bibliography: p. [311]-326.

The author served as Russian Consul (1915-18) in Urmia where he gained first-hand knowledge and experience in Kurdish affairs. He has since sustained a scientific interest in every phase of this comparatively little known and frequently misrepresented ethnic minority. The volume is devoted to the diverse aspects of the Kurdish problem that stems from the desire of the politically fragmented Kurds to preserve their national culture and character and to attain an independent state. Though the author realizes that no solutions are yet in sight for most of the questions posed by the complexity of the Kurdish situation, he sets himself the exacting task of critical analysis and summary of the scientific researches of leading Kurdologists on the sociology and history of the Kurds. One of the contributions of the present study is that it alerts the free world to the sustained and purposeful interest of Soviet Russia in the Kurdish problem. Not only the views of Western scholars, but also those of the Kurds themselves, past and present, are taken into consideration and presented critically yet objectively to the reader. The scope of the work is indicated by the themes of its twelve chapters: racial origins, geography, way of life, character and psychology, family life and the role of women, tribal organization both social and economic, history and distribution of the various tribes, national aspirations pre- and post-fifteenth century, steps in the modern nationalistic movement, religious life, and Kurdish literature. The sociology of the Kurd is treated at greater length than is his history, partly for lack of adequate historical materials and partly because of the author's predominantly sociological interest and method. The fifteen maps, placed to good advantage throughout the work, clarify the shifting geographical distribution of the tribes, indicate natural resources, political boundaries, areas of revolt, religious distribution, and the Kurdish nationalist's conception of a viable Kurdish state as presented to the San Francisco Conference of 1945. The twelve plates placed at the end of the volume convey a realistic idea of the land and its people. (abridged, Nabia Abbot/*Journal of Near Eastern Studies* 18, January-October 1959: 96-98)

27   Rawlinson, Henry C. "Kurdistan." In *The Encyclopaedia Britannica: A Dictionary of Arts, Sciences, and General Literature*, vol. 14, pp. 155-160. New York, C. Scribner's sons, 1878-89.

Includes a detailed discussion on the geography, history, demography, and antiquities of Kurdistan and its climate, productions, and flora and fauna. The character, language, and religion of the Kurds are also discussed. An important paper that provides a 19th century perspective of the Kurds.

28   Sweetnam, Denise L. *Kurdish Culture: A Cross-Cultural Guide*. Bonn: Verlag fur Kultur und Wissenschaft, 1994. 335 p.: ill. Includes bibliographical references (p. [301]-325) and index.

Chapters include Kurdish generosity, hospitality, honor, shame, loyalty, unity and community, patience, religious beliefs, religion, anthropology, cooking, and food with some recipes.

29   Syria. Mudiriyat al-Ihsa'. *al-Majmu'ah al-Ihsa'iyah. Statistical Abstract of Syria*. Damascus: Matba'at al-Hukumah, 1948-. Annual.

Arranged in topical chapters. Information in climate and area is followed by statistical tables—some containing long time series—offering data on demography and on economic, social, and cultural activities.

30   Turkey. Devlet Istatistik Enstitüsü. *Istatistik Yilligi. Annuaire Statistique. Statistical Yearbook of Turkey*. Ankara: Istanbul Cumhuriyet Matbaasi, 1928-. Annual.

Title varies; issuing body varies. Not published between 1954 and 1958; resumed in 1959. The first volume was published in French only. From 1929 to 1968, it was published in both French and Turkish. From 1968 on, it was published in English and Turkish. Provides a statistical summary of various geographical, social, and economic aspects of the country.

31   Turkey. Devlet Istatistik Enstitüsü. *Il ve Bölge Istatistikleri=Provincial and Regional Statistics*. Ankara: T.C. Basbakanlik Devlet Istatistik Enstitüsü, 1994-. Annual.

Provides similar information as item number 30, but with more details on individual provinces and regions.

2

Anthropology

32   Barth, Frederik. "Father's Brother's Daughter's Marriage in Kurdistan."
      Southwestern Journal of Anthropology 10 (Summer 1954): 164-71. Ap-
      pears also in *Peoples and Cultures of the Middle East: An Anthro-*
      pological Reader, edited and with an introduction by Louise E. Sweet,
      vol. 1, pp. 127-136 (New York: The Natural History Press, 1970); and in
      Journal of Anthropological Research 42 (Fall 1986): 389-396.

      Assumptions in past writings concerning marriage patterns among the
      Muslims of the Middle East suggest that close family endogamy and
      preferential father's daughter marriage are associated with a desire to
      maintain family property in the face of Koranic rules of inheritance.
      Among the Kurdish in the southern districts of Iraq this assumed associa-
      tion is not correct. Data gathered in the field by the author suggest that the
      Kurdish utilize father's brother's daughter marriage to reinforce the po-
      litical implications of the lineage by solidifying the first potential lines of
      fission and segmentation within the minimal lineage itself. Thus a
      nephew, upon becoming a son-in-law, pledges political allegiance to the
      father-in-law uncle. Evidence related to this new association of cousin
      marriage and political allegiance among the Kurdish is offered as (1) ex-
      pressed norms, (2) relatively lower bride-price for nephews, and (3) ac-
      tual statistical occurrence.

33   Dawod, Hocham. "Materiaux et hypotheses pour une etude de la societe
      traditionnelle kurde." [Materials and hypotheses for a study of the tradi-
      tional Kurdish society] *La Pensee*, no. 281 (1991): 85-94.

      The field study, among the Kurds in Turkey, helps to specify the knowl-
      edge of traditional Kurdish social groups and the features which charac-

terize them, concerning the environment of the space they occupy, their language, the seminomadism and the pastoral nomadism. (A)

34   Dziegiel, Leszek. "Traditional Food and Daily Meals in Iraqi Kurdistan Today." *Ethnologia Polona* 7 (1981): 99-113.

The author discusses traditional food and typical daily diet of the Northern Iraq Kurds basing on his own field studies conducted in 1977/1978. The subject of this study is the present state of nutrition of the rural populations and its changes. The author presents the basic components of Kurdish diets: wheat flat cake and cereals, rice, leguminous plants, vegetables, fruit, meat, animal and plant fats, milk and milk products, and imported foodstuffs. He draws attention to the scarcity of indigenous foods supplemented by imports, and also to the rise in wealth of the Kurdish peasants arising from the oil boom, which contributed to the liquidation of traditional want in Kurdistan. He describes, at some length, the customs of consuming meals, drawing analogies with the cultures of the Kurds' neighbors: the Turks, Arabs, Persians, Afghans and Armenians.

35   Dziegiel, Leszek. "Life Cycle within the Iraqi Kurd Family." *Ethnologia Polona* 8 (1982): 247-260.

36   Dziegiel, Leszek. "Hygiene and Attention to Personal Appearance among the Iraqi Kurds." *Archiv Orientalni* 50 (1982): 43-50.

As member of a Polish Agricultural Team of Experts, the author carried out field research in 78 villages and country towns of Iraqi Kurdistan in 1977, 1978, and 1980. This paper deals with contemporary Iraqi Kurdistan that since 1975 has been a scene of intensive development carried out by the Iraqi government for political reasons. The Iraqi oil boom has enabled the once poverty-stricken and rather isolated Kurdish villagers to participate in the economic and material advance of the country as a whole.

37   Dziegiel, Leszek. "Villages et petites villes kurdes dans l'Irak actuel: construction traditionnelle, formes et fonctions dans leur processus de changement culturel." [Kurdish villages and small towns in contemporary Iraq: traditional construction, forms and functions in the processes of cultural change] *Studia Kurdica*, no. 5 (1988): 127-156. Was published in Arabic in the same journal in 1992, pp. 47-60.

The author, an anthropologist, carried out fieldwork in 80 villages and small towns in the Dohuk, Arbil and Sulaymania areas of Iraqi Kurdistan during 1977-1980. This essay describes the rural lifestyle, forms of houses and farms, and the changes that had begun to affect the Kurds, economically and politically after the signature of the peace agreement between Mulla Mustafa Barzani and the Iraqi government in 1970.

38   Kandler-Palsson, A. "Zur Anthropologie nomadisierender und sebhafter Kurden und Armenier im Nahen Osten." [Contributions to the anthropology of nomadic and resident Kurds and Armenians in the Near East] *Homo* 35, no. 3-4 (1984): 193-198. [In German.]

39   Khasbak, Shakir. "Badw al-'Arab wa-Ru'at al-Akrad: Muqaranah bayna Mazahir wa-Muqawwimat Hayatihima." *Majallat al-Jam'iyah al-Jughrafiyah al-'Iraqiyah* 6 (June 1970): 99-116.

      Argues that although nomadism and tribalism represent the backbone for the economic and social lives of the Arab bedouins and Kurdish nomads, there are many differences between these two groups of people. The paper illustrates these differences.

40   Khasbak, Shakir. *al-Akrad: Dirasah Jughrafiyha Ithnughrafiyah.* [A geographical and ethnographic study of the Kurds] Baghdad: Matba'at Shafiq, 1972. 560 p.

41   Kren, Karin. "Kurdish Material Culture in Syria." In *Kurdish Culture and Identity.* Edited by Philip G. Kreyenbroek and Christine Allison, pp. 162-173. Atlantic Highlands, NJ: Zed Books, 1996.

      This chapter seeks to draw attention to the importance of the study of ethnographic specimens in the documentation of a culture. In the case of Kurdish culture such research is especially urgent, as the Kurdish people have now been under threat for many years. Before doing so, a definition of what material culture is is provided as well as an explanation of the methodological background of a study of this kind.

42   Leach, Edmund Ronald. *Social and Economic Organisation of the Rowanduz Kurds.* London: Percy Lund, Humphries & Co., Ltd., for the London School of Economics and Political Science, 1940. 74 p.: ill., maps. [Monographs on Social Anthropology, No. 3]

      This short monograph is based on material obtained during a five weeks' field survey in northeastern Iraq. The survey was intended to be preliminary to a longer and more intensive study of one Kurdish community there, but because of the political situation Mr. Leach was unable to continue his work as planned. Mr. Leach's object in making this study was to present "a society in functioning existence at the present time." He has on the whole been successful in achieving this object, although the unavoidable meagerness of the material permits him to sketch only the framework of the structure. As the title of the monograph indicates, Mr. Leach is concerned almost wholly with the social and economic organization of the Rowanduz Kurds. He does not, however, overlook technology as a vital part of the economy of the group, and supplements his chapter on this subject with a series of excellent photographs and sketches illustrating

equipment used by the Kurds. A part of the monograph is devoted to a
consideration of the present social and economic problems with which the
Rowanduz Kurds are confronted as the result of recent intensification of
western cultural influences upon Iraq. Mr. Leach avoids for the most part
any inquiries into historical contacts of the Kurds with their neighbors
which might have influenced the development of their present culture.
Yet even in this avowedly functional study he has perforce resorted to a
certain amount of reconstruction, and does occasionally hint at historical
borrowings. [E. Bacon/*American Anthropologist* 43, 1941: 288-290]

43 Mokri, Mohammad. "Le foyer kurdes." *L'Ethnographie* N.S. 55 (1961):
79-95.

44 Papoli-Yazdi, Mohammad-Husayn. "La motorisation des moyens de
transport et ses consequences chex les nomades kurdes du Khorassan,
Iran." [The motorization of transport and its effects among Kurdish nomads of Khorassan, Iran] *Revue Geographique de l'Est* 22 (1982): 99-
115.

The 2300 nomadic Kurdish families living in northern Khorassan use
mainly camels, as beasts of burden. Since 1972, they have begun to replace their camels by motorcars—they can fetch water from remote
places to new dry pastures and avoid trouble in keeping camel flocks out
of cultivated lands. Once most of the families in a pastoral unit have sold
their camels, others are obliged to do so to follow the group. Important
socio-economic change is bound to the ownership of vehicles. People
owning a vehicle get additional income from the remaining families in the
same camp. The nomads of northern Khorassan now understand that vehicles bring various drawbacks as well as advantages, and they try now to
keep some camels as 'stand-by vehicles.'

45 Papoli-Yazdi, Muhammad Husayn. *Le nomadisme dans le nord du
Khorassan, Iran*. [Nomadism in North Khurasan, Iran] Paris: Institut
francais de recherche en Iran, 1991. 434 p.: ill., maps. (Bibliotheque
iranienne; no. 34)

Abridgment of the author's doctoral dissertation (Universite de Paris IV-
Sorbonne, 1982) presented under the title: *Le nomadisme et le semi-
nomadisme dans le nord du Khorassan: etude de geographie humaine*. A
compilation of anthropological research conducted primarily from 1968
to 1977 on small groups of nomads among the Kurdish population of
Khurasan in northern Iran. The book opens with a historical survey, beginning with the first appearance of the Kurds in Khurasan. Following are
discussions of the geography of the region, land ownership, dwellings,
migratory patterns, transport, the economy, and sedentarization. Numerous tables, maps, and graphs, as well as photographs, are provided (*MEJ*
46, Winter 1992: 130).

46   Yalcin-Heckmann, Lale. *Kinship and Tribal Organization in the Prov-
           ince of Hakkari, Southeast Turkey*. Ph.D., London: London School of
           Economics, 1987.

Based on data collected through a total of 18 months of stay (1980-1982)
in a mountain village and in the sub-district's central town on the plain.
After a general socio-economic background to the province and village
level organization, the history of tribal organization is presented as elicited from written and oral sources. The discussion of tribal organization
today focuses on the criteria for identifying and belonging to tribes, inter-
tribal and state relations and the political role of tribal leaders. Kinship
and marriage strategies are subsequently examined as forms of local and
regional organizational principles. Finally, a complex case study is presented to draw the themes of overlapping or conflicting ethnic, kinship
and tribal loyalties together. The anthropological problem of the thesis is
centered on the overlapping kinship and tribal structures in the region. On
the one hand, tribal relations could be seen as historical relics of a tribal
confederational past; on the other hand, its own internal dynamics restruc-
ture the inter- and intra-tribal relations in response to wider political and
economic processes. Tribal confederational structures disappear, yet
lower tribal structures continue to exist. At the ideological level, tribal
membership is a political issue with a potential for claiming pasture usage
rights, yet at the practical level it is hardly distinguishable from complex
kinship organization. The thesis shows, first, the complexity of the kinship organization and tribal relations, and secondly the interplay between
different levels of kinship, tribal and ethnic structures as a response to or
to activate internal and external political processes. (A)

47   Yalcin-Heckmann, Lale. "On Kinship, Tribalism and Ethnicity in Eastern
           Turkey." In *Ethnic Groups in the Republic of Turkey*. Edited and com-
           piled by Peter Alford Andrews with the assistance of Rudiger Benning-
           haus, pp. 622-632. Wiesbaden: Ludwig Reichert Verlag, 1989. (Beihefte
           zum Tubinger Atlas des Vorderen Orients. Reihe B. Geist-
           eswissenschaften; Nr. 60)

The present Turkish state having inherited a micro-model of the population composition from the late Ottoman Empire, yet with radically different goals and proposed political structure has had to come to terms with
various social formations within its territory. Among these, especially in
relation to Eastern Turkey the questions of ethnicity, tribalism, and kinship to a degree, are more salient from a sociological point of view. Any
sociological research on Kurds in Turkey has to deal with the above social formations along with the level of economic and political development of the area and of Turkey. Here the author presents an outline of the
dominant principles of ethnic, tribal, and kinship organization in Eastern
Turkey with special reference to anthropological data collected in a limited area during 1980-1982 as well as the arguments and analyses pre-

sented in the sociological studies of Kurdish society by Besikci, Nikitine, and van Bruinessen.

48   Yalcin-Heckmann, Lale. *Tribe and Kinship among the Kurds*. Frankfurt am Main, Germany: Peter Lang, 1991. 328 p. ill. maps. bibliog. (European university studies. Series XIX, Anthropology-Ethnology. Section B, Ethnology, 0721-3549; vol. 27). Revision of the author's thesis (item 46).

Although Kurdish national aspirations and their political difficulties have become relatively well known, scientific studies of the Kurdish society are rare. Yalcin-Heckman completed this work as her doctoral dissertation in anthropology at the University of London. The basis for her writing is drawn from her fieldwork in the Hakkari region of northern Kurdistan, the remotest corner of the Republic of Turkey from Ankara, in the extreme southeast. The very rugged nature of this mountainous region has kept it remote from modern changes that have taken place in other parts of Turkey and Kurdistan at large. Therefore, this research is of additional value for studying what may be the most traditional section of Kurdistan's society. The study is primarily concerned with relationships between various aspects of Kurdish identity, tribal organization and kinship in the Hakkari region and its interaction with the Turkish state, its representatives (such as civil servants, military and police) and agents in the region. Using a gun-running incident as a springboard, the more complex story involving conflicting ideologies and interests and shifting kinship, tribal and political alliances are tackled on various levels with convincing strength. The issue of kinship and tribal structures in Hakkari vis-a-vis the state, and the State's perception of the overlapping phenomenon of tribal and ethnic identity, constitute the secondary theme of the work, and the more attractive part of it. An admirable perception of the minutest detail in her fieldwork leaves the reader fascinated with many of the characteristics of the Kurdish village that is the subject of her study. The lively development of individual characters in many sections of the work even borders on the theatrical. The description achieves near visual quality through the author's unceasing supply of details. Since it is the fieldwork that provides the preponderence of the data, relatively few other sources are cited or used in this work. Yalcin-Heckman draws most heavily on Martin van Bruinessen's doctoral dissertation for her textual sources, and like van Bruinessen she readily excludes the much larger Kurdish society that is neither rural nor traditionalist. Through the efforts of scholars such as Yalcin-Heckman and van Bruinessen much is now known about the fast-shrinking rural Kurdistan: family structure, kinship relationship, tribal, social and political alliances and structure. (*IJKS* 1993)

See also items: 7, 22, 28, 71, 73, 142, 166, 167, 170, 171, 172, 173, 358, 649, 650, 651, 652, 653, 654, 655, 656, 661, 685, 772, 815, 861, and the chapter on Archaeology

3

Archaeology

49 Bazin, Marcel. "L'habitat rural dans la vallee de l'Euphrate a l'est de Malatya (Turquie)." *Journal Asiatique* 277, no. 1-2 (1989): 19-46.

The Karakaya Dam on the Euphrates, as part of the Grand Anatolian Project (GAP—Project of South-East Anatolia), will destroy totally, or partially, 97 Kurdish villages located in West and East of Malatya, and some archaeological sites in Turkish Kurdistan. In ethno-archaeological perspective, Bazin addresses the architectural heritage of these villages and its archaeological sites before its destruction or disappearance under the waters of the dam. Bazin argues that the vernacular habitat of Turkish Kurdistan is composed of the cultural heritage of the Kurds. (Joyce Blau/*AI* 13: 323)

50 Braidwood, Linda. *Digging Beyond the Tigris: An American Woman Archeologist's Story of Life on a "Dig" in the Kurdish Hills of Iraq*. New York: H. Schuman, 1953. 297 p.: ill.

This is the story of an archaeological expedition organized by the Oriental Institute of the University of Chicago. This expedition worked in Iraq in 1949 and the book discusses its development from the original planning stage to the actual fieldwork in the Kurdish hills. It is not only a book on archaeology for it relates the events of the happy journey that the members of the expedition made through this region. It also includes notes on the customs and way of life of the local people (i.e., the Kurds) together with fifty photographs.

51 Braidwood, Linda, and others (eds.). *Prehistoric Archeology along the Zagros Flanks*. Chicago, Ill.: Oriental Institute, 1983. ix, 695 p.: ill.

The Iraq-Jarmo Prehistoric Project sponsored by the Oriental Institute saw three seasons of work between 1948 and 1955, published in preliminary fashion as *Prehistoric Investigations in Iraqi Kurdistan* (Chicago, 1960). Its goals were to investigate the transition from food-collecting to food-producing economies in Southwest Asia in an area reasoned to be a "nuclear habitat zone," a natural environment favoring the wild ancestors of the earliest domesticates. The 1983 volume presents final reports on the excavations and soundings in northeastern Iraq at Jarmo, Karim Shahir, Banahilk, M'lefaat, Ali Agha and al-Khan. The report consists of an "Introduction" and 22 sections devoted to individual categories of remains from the excavations and soundings. The papers are the work of a variety of authors, not all affiliated with the original project, and were completed at various times during the 1960s and 1970s. (abridged, Ann C. Gunter, *American Journal of Archaeology* 89, January 1985: 175-176)

52   Braidwood, Robert J. "The Agricultural Revolution." *Scientific American* 203 (September 1960): 130-152.

Until some 10,000 years ago all men lived by hunting, gathering and scavenging. Then the inhabitants of hills in the Middle East domesticated plants and animals, and founded in Kurdistan the first village in the region.

53   Braidwood, Robert J.; Braidwood, Linda. "The Earliest Village Communities of Southwest Asia." *Journal of World History* (1953): 278-310.

It is commonly understood that the earliest village communities of the Middle East were, in fact, the earliest such communities anywhere in the world. There is ever increasing documentary evidence, of a comparative nature, for this idea. Unfortunately, few radioactive carbon dates are yet available from the area. The worldwide Carbon 14 dates in hand do, however, directly support the idea of earliest beginnings in established village life in southwestern Asia (i.e., Kurdistan and the neighboring regions). In this article, the authors are concerned with a description of the available primary archeological documentation. Their attention is focused on the nuclear Middle East.

54   Braidwood, Robert J.; Howe, Bruce; with contributions by Hans Helback and others. *Prehistoric Investigations in Iraqi Kurdistan*. Chicago: University of Chicago Press, 1960. 184 p.: plates, maps. Bibliography. (Oriental Institute of the University of Chicago—Studies in Ancient Oriental Civilization, no. 31).

This is the story of the first three field campaigns carried out by an archaeological expedition working on the Iraq-Jarmo Project. The work of the expedition was mainly to investigate the great changes in mankind's way of life at the time of the first appearance of the settled village-farming society. This volume is a study of early society in the light of archaeological evidence and observations. The book has an extensive bibliography and is illustrated by a series of twenty plates.

55 Braidwood, Robert J., and others. "Beginnings of Village-Farming Communities in Southeastern Turkey." *Proceedings of the National Academy of Sciences* 68 (1971): 1236-1240.

Since the end of World War II, much evidence has accrued of the primary phase of village-farming community life in southwestern Asia, which began about 7000 B.C. The remains of (usually) several of the positively domesticated animals (dog, sheep, goat, pig) and plants (wheat, barley, legumes such as peas and lentils) assure us that these settlements were based on effective food production, although collected wild food, also remained a significant portion of the human diet. Evidence of a transitional phase (or phases) that must have immediately preceded the primary phase of effective food production has, however remained very elusive. Part of a breakthrough appears to have been made in the autumn 1970 field campaign at Cayono Tepesi in southeastern Turkey, where the expansion and deepening of earlier exposures has yielded evidence that may span a significant portion of the transition. (A)

56 Braidwood, Robert J., and others. "Beginnings of Village-Farming Communities in Southeastern Turkey—1972." *Proceedings of the National Academy of Sciences* 71 (1974): 568-572.

The mound known as Cayonu Tepesi in Turkish Kurdistan is one of the increasing number of early village sites which, since World War II, have been excavated archaeologically in greater southwestern Asia. The evidence recovered in the autumn 1972 campaign of the Joint Istanbul-Chicago Prehistoric Project is briefly described, with particular attention to Cayonu architectural remains, which are most remarkable, considering the site's date of about 7000 B.C. There was evidence of domesticated food plants from the beginning but animal domesticates were not present (save the dog) until later in the major prehistoric phase of occupation. (A)

57 Evans, Christopher. "On the Jube Line: Campsite Studies in Kurdistan." *Archaeological Review from Cambridge* 2 (Autumn 1983): 67-77.

This study was conducted as an attempt to examine the spatial organization of a transhumant community's seasonal campsites and tent dwellings. The work was undertaken as part of a general research program to study the contemporary population of Zardeh basin. The program of ethnographic research was approached as an extension of the overall archaeological project in the basin, in which the present Zardeh communities are the most recent or final phase in its settlement sequence.

58   Garrod, D. A. E. *The Paleolithic of Southern Kurdistan: Excavations in the Caves of Zarzi and Hazar Merd*. New York: Kraus Reprint, 1968. 43 p. Originally published in 1930 as issue no. 6 of the *Bulletin of the American School of Prehistoric Research*.

59   Kramer, Carol. "An Archaeological View of a Contemporary Kurdish Village: Domestic Architecture, Household Size, and Wealth." In *Ethnoarchaeology: Implications of Ethnology for Archaeology*. Edited by Carol Kramer, pp. 139-163. New York: Columbia University Press, 1979.

Utilizing data on residential architecture in a contemporary village (Hasanabad) in central Iranian Kurdistan, Kramer attempts to pinpoint some of the causal relationships between variation in architectural features, household size and composition, and economic rank. She suggests that while both economic variation and aspects of household size and composition might be inferred from the archaeologically retrievable architectural remains of this village, different classes of data may be required to reconstruct each of these aspects of village organization. The article bears on the analysis of excavated early village architecture in Southwest Asia as well as on the more general issue of architectural variability. In short, Kramer provides excellent illustrations and details in her attempt to correlate architectural factors of compounds, household size, wealth, and economic rank; she also suggests which architectural attributes might be indicators of household size and composition in archaeological situations.

60   Kramer, Carol. "Ethnographic Households and Archaeological Interpretations: A Case from Iranian Kurdistan." *American Behavioral Scientist* 25 (July/August 1982): 663-675.

This article shows how archaeological interpretation based strictly on the evidence of architectural remains may lead to inaccurate conclusions about social patterns in extinct societies. An ethnographic study of an Iranian Kurdish village is used to illustrate the possible variations of residential social relationships within buildings with similar architectural features.

61   Laessoe, Jorgen. *The Shemshara Tablets: A Preliminary Report*. Kobenhavn: I Kommission hos Ejnar Munksgaard, 1959. 106 p.: ill., fold. plan. Includes bibliographical footnotes.

This report is a preliminary inquiry into a collection of clay tablets, inscribed in the cuneiform character, which were uncovered by the Danish Dokan Expedition in the remains of a building in Tell Shemshara, an ancient mound situated on the right bank of the Lesser Zab, near Rania in Iraqi Kurdistan. The tablets, which were discovered in the summer of 1957, were provisionally registered in the field and the present writer took some field photographs of individual tablets in good state of preservation. 146 tablets were discovered, and the field numbers SH. 800-SH. 945 were assigned to them.

62   Matheson, Sylvia A. *Persia: An Archaeological Guide*. 2nd ed., rev. London: Faber and Faber Ltd., 1976. 358 p.: ill., maps.

Iran has been estimated to have some 250,000 archaeological and historic sites, and Matheson's book provides a guide to all the most significant of them, which range in period from the earliest known cave dwellers and primitive open settlements some 40,000 years ago, to the turbulent Saljuqs whose power was effectively brought to an end by the Mongol invasion in A.D. 1220. When the author was asked to prepare a new edition, she realized that in the short period since publication, tremendous changes had taken place in Iran. Hotel accommodation and air and land communications have been greatly expanded, entirely new roads often superseding old ones; there have been continuing developments in existing archaeological sites and many new sites discovered. For this second edition the book has been brought up to date as far as humanly possible when changes are taking place so rapidly and constantly. Several photographs, plans and line illustrations have been replaced by new ones.

63   Merpert, N. Y.; Munchaev, R. M.. "Early Agricultural Settlements in the Sinjar Plain, Northern Iraq." *Iraq* 35 (1973): 93-113.

In the spring of 1969, the Soviet archaeological expedition began extensive studies of early agricultural sites in northwestern Iraq. Up to that time, the investigation of archaeological cultures representing the early stages of development of food-producing economies in Mesopotamia had been confined to northeastern Iraq and western Iran, the mountains of Kurdistan and the Zagros with their foothills and valleys. But in northwestern Iraq, from Mosul to the Syrian frontier, there are areas whose natural resources offer an equally fruitful prospect for investigation of this process. One such area particularly favorable to agriculture from its earliest stages is the broad and fertile Kurdish Sinjar plain, the topic of discussion of this paper.

64   Sinclair, T. A. *Eastern Turkey: An Architectural and Archaeological Survey*. London: Pindar Press, 1990. 4 vols.: ill., maps. Includes bibliographies.

Over the course of a number of years Sinclair has been systematically traveling in Eastern Turkey collecting materials for this work which surveys, in a remarkably comprehensive way, the historical buildings and archaeological sites in the area. His aim, as he explains in the preface to volume 1 (1987), is to provide a survey of the "archaeological landscape" of that part of Turkey "whose monuments need justice done to them."

Coverage in time is from Neolithic to Ottoman times, and the work is arranged regionally; Volume I, besides including four introductory chapters, covers the Van region and Kars-Ararat; Volume II (1989) deals with six further regions, Tao-Klardjeti and the Georgian churches, Pontus, Erzerum and the Saltukid principate, Sivas and Tokat, the Upper Euphrates, and the Anti-Taurus. Volume III (1990) continues with the regions of the Upper and Lower Euphrates, and of the Tigris, while volume IV (1990) covers the region between Diyarbakir and Antakya.

65   Smith, Philip E. L.; Montensen, Peder. "Three New Early Neolithic Sites in Western Iran (Kurdistan)." *Current Anthropology* 21, no. 4 (1981): 511-512.

This article reports on the discovery of three new sites in Kurdistan, discovered on an archaeological survey in 1977. It gives a brief description of recent discoveries in central-western Iran that augment knowledge of the early food-producing period.

66   Solecki, Ralph S. "Prehistory in Shanidar Valley, Northern Iraq." *Science* 139 (1963): 179-193.

The archaeological investigations of two sites in Shanidar Valley have been made more significant through the use of interdisciplinary studies. The combined information provide concrete data regarding man and his environment in this region from the Middle Paleolithic age to the present. The significance of the Shanidar Valley investigations is that here, in this one locality, there is an almost continuous sequence of human history dating from the time of the Neanderthals. The information derived from these investigations contributes to biological, paleontological, climatological, and geological studies, as well as archaeological and anthropological ones—the major concerns of the project. The project is of further special interest because Shanidar lies within the area where domesticated plants and animals—the basis for the great Neolithic economic, social, and cultural revolution—appear to have been first developed. The Shanidar excavations provide data reflecting the effect on the people in this remote valley of the introduction of the new mode of living, which was dependent on the products of the fields and on tamed animals rather than exclusively on the hunt. (A)

67   Solecki, Ralph S. *Shanidar: The First Flower People*. New York: Knopf, 1971. xv, 290 p.: ill. maps, ports. Bibliography: p. [273]-280. A newer version was published in 1972 under the title: *Shanidar: The Humanity of Neanderthal Man* (London: Allen Lane, 1972).

This book, which is part the archaeologist's tale and part an account of how to get along in Kurdistan, is the first popular description of what was found in Shanidar in Iraqi Kurdistan. It provides a background for the archaeological excavations at Shanidar Cave where skeletons of Neanderthal men were unearthed. This discovery led to new and interesting details about these ancient people. Analysis of the soil surrounding some of the skeletal remains showed microscopic pollen from trees, grasses, and flowers as well as fragments from at least eight species of flowers. This and other evidence indicating that the bodies were buried with flowers gave the author a new perspective to the study of the Neanderthals. The belief is presented that these first "Flower People" were endowed with traces of human emotional qualities, that they cared for the aged, assisted the wounded, and thus came closer to present day man than scientists had previously expected. The author's evidence should remove objections to the inclusion of Neanderthal in our family tree. (A)

68   Solecki, Ralph S. "Contemporary Kurdish Winter-time Inhabitants of Shanidar Cave, Iraq." *World Archaeology* 10 (February 1979): 318-330.

A contemporary seasonal settlement of about 45 Kurds with their animals at Shanidar Cave, a major archaeological site, presents an interesting study. It has possibilities for inferences to the top cultural horizons in the recent archaeological deposits in the cave. The inhabitants occupy what appear to be unusually small, flimsily constructed huts ranged around the interior of the cave. The floor area of the houses per inhabitant is much smaller than that generally found to be true in ethnographic examples quoted in the literature. The reason for the exception here appears to be that the Shanidar inhabitants sacrificed their house sizes to provide shelter for their animals in the limited cave area. Moreover, but in secondary importance, because the cave formed a primary shelter, large houses were not needed.

69   Speiser, E. A. "Southern Kurdistan in the Annals of Ashurnasirpal and Today." *The Annual of the American School of Oriental Research* 8 (1926-1927): 1-41.

70   Watson, Patty Jo. "Architectural Differentiation in Some Near Eastern Communities, Prehistoric and Contemporary." In *Social Archeology: Beyond Subsistence and Dating*. Edited by C. Redman and others, pp. 131-157. New York: Academic Press, 1978.

Part I of this chapter concerns ethno-archeological research the author carried out in the village of Hasanabad (Iranian Kurdistan) in 1959-1960, and the discussion centers on spatial organization. In Part II, comparative attention is given to the wide variety of spatial organization present in some prehistoric Mesopotamian and Anatolian communities. The book in which this chapter occurs is a collection of case studies which constitutes a source book of the newest approaches, methods, and organizations in archaeology. The articles are written by 20 leading scholars representing diverse regions, subject matters, time periods, and theoretical positions.

Taken together, they demonstrate modern archaeology's increasing methodological rigor and sophistication, and its growing ability to interpret
complex societies and deal with such meaningful cultural problems as the
origin of states. They also discuss the movement to cultural resource
management and the changes it has helped bring about in the organization
of archeology.

71   Watson, Patty Jo. *Archaeological Ethnography in Western Iran*. Tuc-
son: University of Arizona Press, 1979. xv, 327 p.: ill. (Viking Fund publications in anthropology; no. 57). Bibliography: (p. 307-322). Includes
index.

A study conducted in three Kurdish villages in Iran (Hasanabad, Shir-
dasht, and Ain Ali). In presenting the results of this study the author intended to accomplish two purposes: (1) to make available as much data as
possible on details of technology and subsistence within the context of
village life in the region studied so these may serve as sources of hypotheses for archaeologists working with relevant material; (2) to make a
contribution to our knowledge of behavioral correlates for material culture, and in particular to the relationship between settlement pattern and
domestic architecture and equipment on the one hand, and population size
and economic and social organization on the other. Part I of this book is a
corpus of descriptive material presented essentially as limited-scope eth-
nographies of the three villages where data were gathered. Throughout
the first part, information is included that is not directly or strictly relevant to archaeological ethnography bearing on the time range that most
interests the author as an archaeologist. However, published ethnographic
data are still rather limited for Iran and the Kurds for that matter, and
hence it seems worthwhile to include whatever reliable information was
obtained. The corpus also contains specific references to archaeological
parallels for the objects and activities observed in the living villages, and
includes various other data relevant to the generalizations discussed in
Part II. Part I, then, consists of three bodies of ethnographic data, one for
each of the communities studied. Part II is a description and discussion of
some archaeologically-useful relationships and uniformitarian principles
that can be derived from the ethnographic data presented in Part I. The
bulk of the data contained in this account comes from a village of share-
cropping tenants in the Kermanshahan Ostan of western Iran. The author
worked in Hasanabad from November 29, 1959, to February 9, 1960,
from March 27, 1960, to May 9, 1960, and from May 28, 1960, to June
16, 1960. During this time the author stayed, not in the village, but in a
nearby residence complex, an orphanage managed by American missionaries.

See also items: 358, 881, and the chapter on Anthropology

4

Decorative, Fine, and Performing Arts

GENERAL

72   Fischer, Lothar. "Hasim Saydan: Ein Kurdischer Kunstler in Berlin."
[Hasim Saydan: a Kurdish artist in Berlin] *Graphische Kunst* 30, pt. 1
(1988): 21-24. [In German]

The author places the work of Saydan (b.1954), a painter, engraver and
musician, in the context of Kurdish cultural life, explaining the functions
of the various scenes, dances and figures such as traveling musicians, and
the artist's skill in capturing the vitality of a people surrounded by unrest.
These almost idyllic scenes are contrasted with the monumental paintings
showing the sufferings of the Kurdish people since 1980.

73   Kren, Karin. "La culture materielle des Kurdes syriens et turcs." [Material
Culture of Syrian and Turkish Kurds] *Peuples Mediterraneens*, no. 68-69
(July-December 1994): 95-108.

Information we get concerning Syrian Kurdistan is based on results from
field research carried out in 1988 and 1990 and concerns clothing and
jewelry, pottery, tannery, rug weaving, and other forms of habitation. Material culture is being modified: disappearance of certain elements, adoption of others. But, as in all the Kurdish territory, some very important
changes are apparently the causes of which are first of all economic and
the consequences social. The traditional technological methods of work
are in the process of disappearing. In Syrian Kurdistan, the subsistence
production is today marginalized, and one could foresee that in no more
than a generation, traditional technologies will have disappeared.

74   "The Living Fire." Festival of Kurdish Arts and Culture. *The Middle East*
          [London], no. 222 (April 1993): 46-47.

          Dubbed "The Living Fire," the festival offers a rare and comprehensive
          glimpse into the richness, vitality and strength of the Kurdistan identity.
          The festival features a month-long program of concerts, films, exhibitions
          and workshops at selected venues throughout London. It was launched to
          coincide with the Kurdish new year.

75   Wilkinson, Charles Kyrle. *Ivories from Ziwiye and Items of Ceramic
          and Gold*. Bern: Abegg-Stiftung, 1975. 80 p.

See also items: 1, 4, 19, 59, 518, 596, 706, 833

COSTUME

76   Andrews, Peter Alford. "Kurdish Clothing in [Kermanshah]." In *Ency-
          clopaedia Iranica*. Vol. 5, pp. 824-825. Costa Mesa, CA: Mazda Publish-
          ers, 1992.

          Describes Kurdish men's and women's clothing and discusses the distinct
          vocabulary used for naming the various kinds of costumes.

77   Andrews, Peter Alford; Andrews, M. "Turkic and Kurdish Clothing of
          Azerbaijan." In *Encyclopaedia Iranica*. Vol. 5, pp. 836-840. Costa Mesa,
          CA: Mazda Publishers, 1992.

          According to the author, in Azerbaijan as a whole, including both Persian
          and former Soviet territories, the traditional costume, now worn largely in
          a tribal context, retains the form of garments much as they were at the end
          of the 19th century; it is maintained primarily by women, and it is only
          among Kurdish, rather than Turkic, men that elements have survived the
          reforms of Reza Shah in everyday wear. Describes Azeri and Shahsevan
          and Qaradaghi Turkic dress as well as Kurdish costume, more specifically
          those of the Milan, the Zarza, the Kurds of Mahabad, the Harki, and the
          Kurds of Yerevan. Includes a detailed bibliography.

78   Criel, Jean-Marie; Jamil, Pervine. *Costume et Tapis kurdes*. [Kurdish
          Costumes and Rugs] Brussels: Institut Kurde de Bruxelles, 1995. 95 p.:
          maps, ills., col. photographs. Includes bibliographical references.

          The collection of costumes of the Kurds provided here is so authentic and
          clearly photographed as to make this rather small book a treasure to lov-
          ers of Kurdish costumes and fabrics. The work divides into three distinct
          sections: costumes, rugs and political/dynastic history. While the treat-

ment of rugs is interesting and adequate, the costumes presented and discussed constitute a treasure throve of information. In contrast to the wealth of female costumes, the book presents only two males from western Kurdistan, one from Adiyaman, the other from Diyarbekir. Even though the two specimens are extremely valuable in their own right, the authors are remiss in not including more examples from western Kurdistan, one of the richest regions of that land in men's costumes. (Anahid Akasheh/*IJKS* 10, no. 1-2, 1996: 157)

79   Dziegiel, Leszek. "Iraqi Kurdish Traditional Costume in its Process of Europeanization." *Acta Ethnografisca Academiae Scientiarum Hungaricae* [Hungary] 33, no. 1-4 (1984-1985): 93-112.

80   Mohseni, Shirin. "Kurdish Clothing in Persia." In *Encyclopaedia Iranica*. Vol. 5, pp. 822-824. Costa Mesa, CA: Mazda Publishers, 1992.

According to the author, Kurds can easily be recognized by their dress, which has quite distinctive features. Describes female dress, male dress, children's dress, and the variations in Kurdish clothing, reflecting differences in age, designed for special occasions, or adapted to the changing seasons. Includes a detailed bibliography.

81   O'Shea, Maria T. "Kurdish Costume: Regional Diversity and Divergence." In *Kurdish Culture and Identity*. Edited by Philip G. Kreyenbroek and Christine Allison, pp. 135-155. Atlantic Highlands, NJ: Zed Books, 1996.

This chapter draws attention to the emergence of a 'universal' Kurdish costume which is instantly recognizable, can be used occasionally at festivals and on special occasions, and conforms to moderns aesthetics and function. Some general observations are made also on the regional types, without detailed reference to changing fashions. These regional types are probably widely recognized by Kurds as markers of regional origins. Local variations would only be recognized by inhabitants of the region in question, and they are subject to an even more rapid decline than the basic regional variation. Finally, the changes in Kurdish fashion are illustrated by a discussion of the developments of Kurdish costume in and around the city of Sanandaj in Iran. (A)

See also items: 1, 21, 73, 114, 167, 357, 358, 676, 786, 829, 831, 833, 851

KILIMS, RUGS, TEXTILE FABRICS

82   Azadi, Siawosch. "Tribal Carpets." In *Encyclopaedia Iranica*. Vol. 4, pp. 893-896. Costa Mesa, CA: Mazda Publishers, 1990.

According to the author, the term "tribal carpets" includes both floor coverings and other objects woven by nomads and semi-nomads for their own needs. Describes Kurdish carpets and discusses the state of research on this topic. Includes a comprehensive list of relevant sources.

83   Biggs, Robert D. (ed.). *Discoveries from Kurdish Looms*. Evanston, Ill.: Mary and Leigh Block Gallery, Northwestern University, in conjunction with the Chicago Rug Society, 1983. 116 p.: ill (some col.). [Issued to accompany an exhibition on view at the Mary and Leigh Block Gallery, December 9, 1983 to February 19, 1984.]

This excellent catalog of an exhibition held at Northwestern University, from December 1983 through February 1984 is an important first step toward academic appreciation of the hitherto unsystematically studied field of Kurdish weaving. It features more than 80 illustrations, 12 of which are in color, of pile, flat-woven, and kilim rugs, mats, bag faces, salt bags, saddle and horse covers, and the like from Iran, Iraq, and Turkey, accompanied by descriptive commentaries. In addition, the volume includes six brief essays: John Perry's "The Kurds," Murray Eiland's "The Kurdish Rugs of Iran," Amedeo de Franchis's "Kurdish Rugs from Northeastern Iran," John Wertime's "The Principal Types and Woven Structures of Kurdish Weavings in Northeastern Iran," William Eagleton's "The Weavings of Iraqi Kurdistan," and Ralph Yohe's "The Kurds of Turkey and their Weavings."

84   Bolour, Y. "Knotted Persian Saddle-Covers." *Hali: The International Magazine of Antique Carpet and Textile Art* 3, pt. 4 (1981): 268-272. [Also in German] 45 illus.

Developed from early nomadic saddle-covers, used on wooden frames, more recent Persian saddle-covers appear to have been decorative, and in the 19th and 20th centuries their use has been reserved for special occasions such as religious, marital, tribal or family. The author surveys the variety of saddle-covers produced in Iran during the last 150 years, drawing on examples from the A. J. prior collection, now in the United States, and in the Fitzwilliam Museum, Cambridge, England. The tradition was strongest in Kurdistan and pieces in the 'Senneh' technique and colors are among the most numerous to have survived. The illustrations are annotated.

85   Eagleton, William. *An Introduction to Kurdish Rugs and Other Weavings*. New York: Interlink Books, 1988. 144 p. Includes bibliographies and index.

A beautifully illustrated description and classification of Kurdish weavings from Iran, Iraq, and Turkey. The author, a former U.S. ambassador in the region, has compiled this catalog from his extensive experiences there. Information on Kurdish history and a list of over 200 Kurdish tribes is also included. Concurring with rug authority Murray Eiland, Eagleton characterizes Kurdish weavings in this way: "If we were to designate a fifth major category of Oriental rugs, there would be a convincing argument to suggest that Kurdish weaves are an entity in themselves...and Kurds should rank among the most imaginative and prolific of weavers." Taking this judgment further, he adds, "Indeed, among the peoples producing tribal and village rugs in traditional ways, the Kurds perhaps rank first."

86   Eagleton, William. "Kurdish Rugs and Kilims: An Introduction." In *Kurdish Culture and Identity*. Edited by Philip G. Kreyenbroek and Christine Allison, pp. 156-161. Atlantic Highlands, NJ: Zed Books, 1996.

Although we do not have examples to prove it, we can assume that the Kurds have been producing flat weaves and pile rugs for many hundreds of years. The earliest rugs now in collections that are attributed to the Kurds are large garden carpets dating from the eighteenth century. These are of sophisticated design and were certainly produced at the time for a wealthy urban clientele. For the authentic tradition of Kurdish weaving, however, we must go much further back, to those women providing the essentials for nomadic and village life. Even today the most authentic Kurdish rugs and kilims are those made by individual women in tribal or village contexts for use either by the immediate family or in some cases for barter in the marketplace. This paper tries to uncover some of the common characteristics of Kurdish weaving, its design and color, and classification by region.

87   Eiland, Murray L. *Oriental Rugs: A New Comprehensive Guide*. 3rd ed. New York: New York Graphic Society, 1982. 294 p.: ill., maps. Includes index and bibliographies.

One of the more reliable introductory guides to Oriental carpets from Turkey, Iran, U.S.S.R., and Afghanistan as well as to technical aspects of weaving. It includes both black and white and color plates. The book is superior in its coverage of old and new rugs to any other general publication of recent years. The author does not always give full acknowledgment of his sources of information for maps of rug-weaving regions and for descriptions of specific types. A short bibliography follows each chapter.

88   Ellis, C. G. "Garden Carpets and their Relation to Safavid Gardens." *Hali: The International Magazine of Antique Carpet and Textile Art* 5, pt. 1 (1982): 10-17.

The gardens of Persia stood in such marked contrast to the dry land about them that they captivated the imaginations of Persian poets, miniature

painters and weavers. The author discusses the characteristics and variations of the safavid garden, in particular the plans of its watercourses, and
demonstrates the ways in which these have been reflected in individual
carpets. It describes those carpets which embody the 'chahar bagh' or
four-fold garden concept and shows how those garden carpets made in
Kurdistan around 1800, possibly for export, use a design which represents
a single garden of the four in the 'chahar bagh' theme. In later Kurdish
rugs, the 'chahar bagh' was telescoped to meet the requirement of smaller
dimensions and finally 'watered down' to leave a rug not readily recognizable as a garden carpet at all.

89   Ford, P. R. J. *The Oriental Carpet: A History and Guide to Traditional
Motifs, Patterns, and Symbols*. New York: Harry N. Abrams, Inc., Publishers, 1981. 352 p.: ill.

This book is both more and less than its subtitle implies. Ford's stated
intent is to provide a handbook for rug identification for the buyer of
modern Orientals. While his work is not really a history, although he discusses the historical development of many rug patterns, it is by far the
best practical guide to Orientals (primarily Persian, although Chinese, Indian, and others are included) that this reviewer has seen. The basic arrangement is by pattern or design; within this framework the author discusses at length examples of each design manufactured in different rug-
producing areas (including Kurdistan). (abridged, *Library Journal* 106,
November 15, 1981: 2230)

90   Gans-Ruedin, E. *Splendeur du Tapis Persan*. [The Splendor of the Persian Carpet] Photos by Leo Hilber. Fribourd, Switzerland: Office du
Livre, 1978.

This excellent work on the Persian carpet includes a section on Kurdish
rugs, discussed on pp. 241-275.

91   Gibson, M. "Discoveries from Kurdish Looms." *Arts of Asia* 14, no. 1
(1984): 129-139.

Describes Kurdish rugs and rugs industry. Carpet dealers in the Middle
East avoid describing rugs as Kurdish since the people of that region generally consider Kurdish pieces inferior to more formal floral rugs. This attitude has found its way into the international trade. Many collectors have
avoided them or possess only Sennehs and Bijars, which are Kurdish rugs
disguised under town names. The result has been that Kurdish weavings
have been one of the great bargains in Oriental carpets for those who appreciate their good composition, subtle combinations of colors and use of
traditional materials. Constituting as they do a large proportion of the traditional rug-making population of the Middle East, the Kurds today may
be producing a better range of weavings than any other single group, but

their rugs as a class have not been the subject of a major exhibition nor have they been studied in their entirety. Scholarly work on Kurdish production has concentrated mainly on Sennehs and Bijars. Only occasionally has there been any investigation by ethnographers or textile specialists on the rugs of the Kurds, who live as settled villagers or as nomads in several countries of the Middle East. Now, with the exhibition "Discoveries from Kurdish Looms" at the Mary and Leigh Block Gallery of Northwestern University, Evanston, Illinois (December 9th, 1983 to February 19th, 1984), Kurdish rugs are beginning to receive the attention that they deserve. (A)

92   Helfgott, Leonard Michael. *Ties that Bind: A Social History of the Iranian Carpet*. Smithsonian Institution Press, 1994.

This is a study of the development of the Iranian carpet industry from the fifteenth century to the present... (Helfgott) divides the period into three stages: the fifteenth to early eighteenth centuries, generally known as the Safavid period; the early eighteenth to mid-nineteenth centuries... and the period from 1875 to the present, when the Iranian carpet industry boomed... (The author) devotes one-third of his work to the impact of the mid-nineteenth- century boom in the Persian carpet trade on Western European elites and emerging middle-class tastes... The remaining two-thirds of the book focuses on nomadic, village, and town production of Iranian (Kurdish, Turkic, and Persian) carpets in the nineteenth and twentieth centuries. (A)

93   Housego, Jenny. *Tribal Rugs: An Introduction to the Weavings of the Tribes of Iran*. New York: Van Nostrand Reinhold Co., 1991 178 p.: ill. (some col.).

This book paints a fascinating picture, not only showing superb examples of tribal rugs, but also the woven and the life of the tribes themselves. The author's many years of study and close association with the tribes people responsible for these stunning rugs and fabrics enables her to speak with authority, not only about well-known groups such as the Qashqa'i of southwest Iran, the Baluch of the southeast, the widespread Kurds and the Turkoman, but also such important weaving groups as the Shahsavan of the north regions. In short, the author is able to describe the rich elements in the design as well as giving technical notes on the weaving so that the text and pictures together form an essential introduction for anyone who knows or cares about rugs.

94   Hull, Alastair; Luczyc-Wyhowska, Jose. *Kilim: The Complete Guide: History, Pattern, Technique, Identification*. Introduction by Nicholas Barnard. With 649 illustrations, 394 in color and 18 maps. Line drawings by Miranda MacSwiney. London: Thames and Hudson Ltd., 1993. 352 p.

Bold, distinctive patterns, brilliant colors, astonishingly diverse decoration, and affordability - these are some of the characteristics that explain
why the marvelous flat-woven textiles known have become so popular in
the West. In recent years, demand for them has reached unprecedented
levels, fueled by a new recognition of the special qualities of handmade
ethnic craft. There is now an urgent need for a comprehensive survey of
the field. This book answers this need, unraveling the complex questions
surrounding the origins and history of these unique flat-weaves and of the
peoples who make them. Hundreds of illustrations, many in color and
many specially taken, offer a remarkable blend of information and the
dazzling visual allure for which kilims are famous. A detailed account of
techniques--embracing materials, dyes and dyeing tools, kilim structures
and weaving--is followed by a systematic analysis of motifs and symbol-
ism. Here, the complex relationship between Islam and the animistic or
shamanistic traditions that preceded it is explored, but so too are the many
pitfalls that await any researcher who does not take into account the lore
of the bazaar or the marketplace. The core of the book is devoted to the
specific characteristics of region, tribe and kilim type. Four major sections present the fruits of much original research, fully informing the
reader about the kilims he is likely to encounter; those from the North African countries of Morocco, Algeria and Tunisia; the kilims of Anatolia;
the riches of Persia and the Caucasus; and—for some the most attractive
of all—the creations of the Afghani and Central Asian nomads. Chapters
on new kilims and the uses of kilims—as bags and trappings as well as
rugs—together with a reference guide to collecting, care and further
study, conclude what will swiftly become the standard work on a widely
appealing subject. Kurdish kilims in Turkey are discussed on pp. 112-
121; those in Iraq on pp. 122-128; and in Iran on pp. 183-195.

95   Ittig, A. "A Group of Inscribed Carpets from Persian Kurdistan." *Hali:*
        The International Magazine of Antique Carpet and Textile Art 4, pt. 2
        (1981): 124-127.

        The author argues that, contrary to common assumption, the fall of the
        Safavid dynasty did not necessarily coincide with a decline in the stan-
        dard of carpet weaving in Persian Kurdistan. As evidence she discusses
        four inscribed carpets produced in the late 19th century.

96   Klingner, James H. "Captivating Anomalies." *Hali: The International*
        Magazine of Antique Carpet and Textile Art 17, no. 3 (June-July 1995):
        76-81.

        Discusses the traditions of rug weaving in northeast Turkey. The author
        describes the fieldwork he did there and traces the origins of the variety
        of rugs known as 'Kagizman' that were produced in that area at the end
        of the 19th century and the beginning of the 20th. He examines the charac-
        teristics of older Turkish and Kurdish rugs that he found there, and states

that it is almost impossible to discover anything about Armenian textile traditions from the same period, due to the ethnographic changes that have occurred in the region.

97   Landreau, Anthony N. *Anatolian Rug Weaving: Mirror of Change* Ph.D., Temple University, 1996. 332.

Rug weaving in Anatolia mirrors changes in the social relations of production of Turkish peasants, particularly weaving women. During the past 150 years there has been a transition from use value and local exchange production to fully commoditized production driven by an accelerating external capitalist market. This transformation represents a metamorphosis from "oriental rug" to "occidental rug." It is a tangible and ideological change from a traditional rural craft to an alienated product. The Western rug market boom was fueled by a notion of authenticity spawned by collectors, dealers and museums. It, along with the general expansion of capitalism, drastically changed the lives of the producers. The author's theoretical perspective is that of political economy. Results are based on ethnological fieldwork completed during the years 1972-1982. The fieldwork included an intensive residence in a Yoruk village in Icel Province, and surveys in Kurdistan and among commercial weaving centers in Western and Central Anatolia. The author demonstrates, through analysis of material culture, that changes in technology mirror changes in production relations. These changes include the differential lowering of the status of rural women depending of various specific historical circumstances. (A)

98   Levi, A. "Tappeti curdi classici: la produzione in Persia e in Anatolia." *Ghereh* 1, no. 2 (1993): 33-39. [In Italian]

99   Levi, A. "Renewal and Inovation: Iconographic Influences on Kurdish Carpet Design." *Hali: The International Magazine of Antique Carpet and Textile Art* 15, no. 4 (1993): 85-93, 120.

100   MacDonald, Brian W. *Tribal Rugs: Treasures of the Black Tent*. Woodbridge, Suffolk: Antique Collectors' Club, 1997. 302 p.: ill. (some col.), col. maps. Includes bibliographical references (p. 298- 299) and index.

Includes a chapter on the Kurds.

101   Opie, James. *Tribal Rugs*. Portland, Oreg.: Tolstoy Press, 1992. 328 p.: col. ill.

This book is an important contribution to understanding the relationships of woven tribal art from Iran, Anatolia (Turkey), the Caucasus, Afghanistan, and other parts of Central Asia. The author's *Tribal Rugs of Southern Persia* was the beginning of his extensive studies, and now, after

much travel in Asia and experience in the commercial field, he presents
the best, yet-published view of Asian tribes, their woven art, and the life-
styles that provided the underpinnings for their creations. Part I covers
tribal culture and art history including an examination of ancient motifs,
design origins, and even urban influences on tribal rugs. Part 2 is the heart
of the book, providing a survey of each of the major tribal groups. Given
Opie's apparent special interest in Persian weavings the tribal products
from the Caucasus, Anatolia, and Central Asian areas receive less consideration. Some of his views concerning the origin of motifs have been regarded as controversial, but his support for them is very convincing. The
text is well written and is accompanied by dazzling illustrations. There
are interesting, extensive notes for each chapter and a good glossary. (L.
G. Kavaljian/*Choice* March 1993: 1134)

102   Petsopoulos, Yanni. "The Qajar Kilims of Sehna." *Hali: The Interna-
        tional Magazine of Antique Carpet and Textile Art* 8 (July-September
        1986): 42-47.

Examines the kilims, or flat-weave carpets, originating in the Sehna region of Persian Kurdistan during the time of the Qajar dynasty, which
ruled from the late from the late 18th to the early 20th century. Unlike the
kilims woven in other regions, which are characterized by their geometric
designs in bold colors, Sehna kilims are decorated with delicate and intri-
cate motifs, and are renowned for the fineness of weave.

103   Stanzer, Wilfried. *Kordi: Lives, Rugs and Flat Weaves of the Kurds in
        Khorasan*. Vienna: Adil Besim OHG, 1988. (Expanded ed., 1993). xxiv,
        223 p.: maps, color photographs, tables.

This book did not arrive a moment too soon. There is so little in English
on the arts and crafts of the Kurds in northern Khurasan, that production
of a book of this richness marks a watershed. The current dearth of
knowledge about the Khurasani Kurds is not limited to their arts and
crafts. Our general knowledge of this populous Kurdish enclave has been
virtually non-existent. This book richly documents the potential resiliency
of native arts and crafts in face of all natural and man-made obstacles. As
the subtitle of the book implies, the text does in fact deal with "lives,
rugs, and flat weaves" of the Kurds in Khurasan and more. By far the
largest portion of the book is dedicated to full-page, color reproduction of
important weaves supplemented on their facing page with a complete
technical description of the piece. Unfortunately, *Kordi* lacks a bibliography, leaving it to guesswork by the readers to figure out where and when
the cited sources were published (if published at all). No index is likewise
provided. The book contains the original German and English translation
of the text side by side in two columns. Most of the information on the
maps is also translated into English, but not all. The English translation is
however awkward, uneven, often ungrammatical, and occasionally amus-

ing. The book is absolutely indispensable to the admirers of Kurdish weaving, and very helpful to all those interested in the Kurds of Khurasan as a community. Photographs are very clear and of high quality. Maps are done beautifully, and put into very good use by a numbering system that helps locate place of the weave for each item discussed in the text. (Anahid Akasheh/*IJKS* 115-118).

104   Zipper, Kurt; Fritzsche, Claudia. *Oriental Rugs: Vol. 4: Turkish*. Woodbridge, Suffolk, England: Antique Collectors' Club Ltd., 1981. 264 p. [Originally published in German]

This volume, fourth in the highly successful Oriental Rugs series, serves as a detailed introduction to the fascinating range of carpets and rugs from Turkey. The history of the region and the art of carpet weaving and knotting are explained, and the various types and styles of rugs produced are traced through the traditions and differing techniques found throughout the Anatolian peninsula. Turkey lies in a geographical position of some importance, separating as it does the Eastern and Western cultures. Despite the proximity of the Persian influence, Turkish rug makers largely retained their own traditional motifs, and the language of their designs and ornaments is explained. The main text leads into a pictorial catalogue in which 210 full color plates illustrate rugs from the numerous towns and villages throughout Anatolia. Comprehensive and detailed captions describe some 225 examples, ranging from antique and very rare museum exhibits right through to good quality modern pieces which are readily available today. This comprehensive book provides definitive coverage of the rugs and carpets of Turkey. It is an essential volume for all lovers of fine carpets, and will appeal equally to the acknowledged expert and the fascinated but inexperienced beginner.

See also items: 21, 247

PERFORMING ARTS

105   Armes, Roy. "Guney, Yilmaz." In *International Dictionary of Films and Filmmakers - 2: Directors*. 3rd ed. Edited by Laurie Collier Hillstrom, pp. 407-410. Detroit: St. James Press, 1997.

Provides a biographical sketch of the Kurdish actor, author, director, and filmmaker, Yilmaz Guney. Lists all the films he made and/or directed and those he acted in. Also lists his publications.

106   Aufderheide, Pat. "Yol." In *Magill's Survey of Cinema: Foreign Language Films*. Vol. 7, pp. 3467-3470. Edited by Frank N. Magill. Englewood Cliffs, NJ: Salem Press, 1985.

Review and critique of the movie, *Yol*, also known as *The Road* and *The Way*, released in 1982 and played by the late Kurdish actor, director, novelist, and playwright, Yilmaz Guney. The movie won the Gold Palm at Cannes in 1982.

107   Coryell, S. "Yilmaz Guney: le cineaste revolte." *Cemoti* 19 (1995): 460-468.

108   Hasinov, A. A. *Yilmaz Guney: al-Hayat al-Khalidah*. [Biography of the Kurdish actor, director, novelist, and playwright Yilmaz Guney] Translated from Russian by Ahmad Ahmad. Revised and introduced by Muhammad Nuri Khurshid. Aleppo, Syria: Markaz al-Inma' al-Hadari lil-Dirasat wa-al-Tarjama wa-al-Nashr, 1993.

109   Jaffar, Shwan. "Trots formes du théâtre traditionnel kurde." *Bulletin de l'Association ties Anciens élèves de l'INALCO* B (1991): 83-98.

110   Jaffar, Shwan. "Le theatre kurde." [The Kurdish theater] In *Les Kurdes par-dela l'exode*. Edited by Halkawt Hakim, pp. 207-231. Paris: L'Harmattan, 1992.

111   Pennet, Jean-Marc. "Istilham al-Majal al-Tabi'i fi Sinima Yilmaz Guney: ('al-Amal' wa 'al-Qati')." *Studia Kurdica* (1992): 61-73.

Based on the author's Master's paper titled: *Temporalites dans l'ouevre cinematographique de Yilmaz Guney*, Universite de Paris VII, 1989 (125 pages).

112   Shani, Sabah Hurmuz. *al-Taqlidi wa-al-la-Taqlidi fi al-Masrah al-Kurdi: Majmu'at Maqallat Naqdiyah*. [A collection of critiques on Kurdish theater] Stockholm, Sweden: Sahari lil-Tiba'a wa-al-Nashr, 1993. 80 p.

113   Wakeman, John (ed.). "Guney, Yilmaz." In *World Film Directors: Volume II (1945-1985)*. pp. 405-409. New York: The H. W. Wilson Company, 1988.

Provides a detailed biography and description of the works of the most famous of all Kurdish directors, filmmakers and actors. Also provides a list of works Guney was involved with as a director and actor and lists journal, magazine, and newspaper articles published about him.

5

Description and Travel

DESCRIPTION AND TRAVEL (PRE-1900)

114 Bird, Isabella L. *Journeys in Persia and Kurdistan*. London: Virago, 1989. 2 vols.: ill. Vol. 1 has a new introduction by Pat Barr. Vol. 2 has a new introduction by Shusha Guppy. Originally published in London by John Murray, 1891.

In January 1890 Isabella Bird (1831-1904) began one of the toughest single journeys of her life. Already a veteran of expeditions to the Rocky Mountains, Japan and Malaysia, her challenge this time was a series of punishing journeys into Persia and Kurdistan. Escorted by Major Herbert Sawyer, she left Baghdad and tolled for six weeks in appalling winter conditions, across uncharted mountainous territory, to arrive 'nearly blind from fatigue' in Tehran. A month later she set out on another, hardly less exacting exploration of a remote part of Luristan. Exceptionally courageous and stoical, she yearned for the 'untrammeled freedom of the wilds' and relished every new experience– from wandering disguised in city bazaars to enduring squalid caravanserais, from meeting by chance the Shah of Persia to administering to the nomadic Bakhtiari Lurs. In Volume II, she sets off in the blazing heat of summer, longing for the chill winds, fog and rain of Britain, for several months traveling northwards, through deep valleys and lofty mountain passes, to Trebizond. At the mercy of warring tribes, plagued by robbery and fever, she maintains her keen interest and detailed descriptive power as she tells of the day-to-day customs, beliefs, dress and activities of the people, to whom she continues to minister as a healer, despite appalling difficulties. On her much-loved horse, Boy, she visits cities both spectacular and decayed, traverses fertile plains and scorched landscapes. She meets proud Kurdish

tribesmen and dedicated ladies of the Anglican mission. Despite the vaga-
ries and vicissitudes of her journey, when at last she reaches its end, she
reflects: "Such is the magic charm of Asia that I would willingly have
turned back at that moment to the snowy plateau...and the savage mountains..."

115   Bosworth, C. E. "The Intrepid Victorian Lady in Persia: Mrs. Isabella
          Bishop's Travels in Luristan and Kurdistan, 1890." *Iran* 27 (1989): 87-
          101.

116   Boyes, W. J. "Routes in Asia Minor, Armenia, Kurdistan, Georgia,
          Mesopotamia, and part of western Persia." In *Routes in Asia*. Calcutta:
          Office of the Superintendent of Government Printing, 1877-1878.

117   Bruinessen, Martin van; Boeschoten, H. E. (eds.). *Evliya Celebi in Di-
          yarbekir: The Relevant Section of the Seyahatname*. Leiden: E. J. Brill,
          1988. xvi, 270 p. [41] p. of plates (2 folded): ill.

In April and May 1655, the Turkish traveler Evliya Celebi spent a few
weeks in Diyarbekir, at that time still one of the major cities of the Ottoman Empire. He left us in the fourth volume of his *Book of Travels*, the
Seyahatname, a lively picture of this city which, especially if combined
with other contemporary sources, gives interesting insights in the social,
political, and cultural life, both of the city and of the province of the same
name, in a period that the Empire's heyday was over but the decline had
not yet really set in. One of the reasons that made the editors of this work
select Diyarbekir is that the eastern provinces of the Empire—especially
the Kurdish provinces of Diyarbekir, Van and Sulaymania—have so far
received relatively little serious attention from scholars as compared to
other parts of the Ottoman Empire, particularly the Balkans, Egypt, Palestine and the center of the Empire. Part I of the book discusses the Ottoman conquest of Diyarbekir and the administrative organization of the
province into the 16th and 17th centuries, the population of Diyarbekir, the
economic life in Diyarbekir in the 17th century, its religious life, the
physical aspects of the city, Evliya's style, his spelling and the editors'
transliteration, and the *Seyahatname* as a source for linguistic investigation. Part II of the book discusses Evliya's description of Diyarbekir.

118   Bruinessen, Martin van. "Evliya Çelebi and His Seyahatname." In *Evliya
          Celebi in Diyarbekir: The Relevant Section of the Seyahatname*. Edited
          by Martin van Bruinessen and H. E. Boeschoten, pp. 3-12. Leiden: E. J.
          Brill, 1988.

According to van Bruinessen, whatever is known about Evliya's life we
owe to his own remarks spread throughout the *Seyahatname*. He therefore
gives only a short summary of the most relevant facts.

119   Dankoff, Robert (ed.). *Evliya Celebi in Bitlis: The Relevant Section of the Seyahatname*. Leiden: E. J. Brill, 1990. 395 p.

Evliya Celebi (1611-1683?) is the most famous of Ottoman travelers. His ten-volume *Seyahatname* provides delightful reading. Despite his exaggerations and his love of a good story, he provides valuable information to historians, geographers, and other scholars. In this book, Dankoff offers a carefully edited transcription into modern Turkish letters, with facing pages of English translation, of sections of the work concerning an eastern Ottoman province. Bitlis, just west of Lake Van, was a provincial city of 5,000 houses and 1,200 shops, according to Evliya. Its governor was a Kurdish *khan*, of the Rozhiki tribe, subordinate, to the governor of the Van *eyalet* but in fact nearly independent. Evliya recounts three visits to Bitlis in 1655-1656, when he was in the suite of his uncle, Melek Ahmed Pasha, governor of Van. Uncle and retinue stayed in Bitlis ten days on the way out to Van and were royally entertained by the Kurdish governor, Abdal Khan. Then, after a falling out, Melek Pasha attacked Abdal Khan; a detailed account ensues of Melek's victorious siege, directed from his encampment before Bitlis. Finally, Evliya was sent to Bitlis to collect payments from the new *khan*, only to get caught there when Melek lost his governorship and Abdal Khan returned to Bitlis. Evliya made a hair-raising escape through winter snows. The action is colorful. It involves much cruelty, hundreds of heads struck off by both sides, deception, even the tricks of magicians. Evliya recreates dialogue. He provides his readers, further, with copious information on people, places, the city, buildings, weapons, foods, clothes and cloths, books, even attitudes. (abridged, Roderic H. Davison/*MEJ* 45, Autumn 1991: 692-693)

120   Ellis, Tristram James. *On a Raft, and through the Desert: The Narrative of an Artist's Journey through Northern Syria and Kurdistan, by the Tigris to Mosul and Baghdad, and of a Return Journey across the Desert by the Euphrates and Palmyra to Damascus, over the Anti-Lebanon to Baalbek and to Beyrout*. London, New York, Field & Tuer; Scribner & Welford, 1881. 2 v. illus., 30 pl. (incl. fronts., fold. map).

121   Floyer, Ernest Ayscoghe. *Unexplored Baluchistan: A Survey, with Observations Astronomical, Geographical, Botanical, etc., of a Route through Mekran, Bashkurd, Persia, Kurdistan, and Turkey*. 3rd ed. Pakistan: Nisa Traders, 1980. xvii, 507 p., [12 leaves of plates]: ill. Originally published in 1882 by Griffith and Farran (London).

122   Fowler, George. *Three Years in Persia with Travelling Adventures in Koordistan*. London: Henry Colburn, 1841. 2 v.: ill.

123   Galletti, Mirella. "The Italian Contribution to Kurdology (13th to 20th Century)." *The Journal of Kurdish Studies* 1 (1995): 97-112. This paper is a revised version of "Curdi e Kurdistan in opere italiane del XIII-XIX secolo," *Oriente Moderno*, 58, no. 11 (1978), pp. 563-596. The introduction is part of a lecture given at the 1st Kurdish Academy Congress, Vienna, August 2-4, 1991.

After Greek and Latin, Arabic and Kurdish classical sources, a European literature on the Kurds developed. The French, English and German writings are widely known, but the Italian sources, among the oldest, are also the least known, even though they are of extraordinary interest. The primary sources dating from the 13th to the 19th century demonstrate continuity in relations between Kurdistan and Italy and were written by travelers, diplomats, missionaries and merchants who crossed Kurdistan to get to Persia or Mesopotamia. With the exception of the works on the subject written by Domenico Lanza, Maurizio Garzoni, Giuseppe Campanile and Alessandro De Bianchi, Italian travelers left only short notes on the Kurds and Kurdistan because their acquaintance with the region was limited to the time necessary to cross it. Italian Catholic missionaries also carried on activities that led to a broadening of knowledge about Kurdistan and its peoples. Because of the presence of significant Christian communities (Armenians, Chaldeans, Jacobites, Nestorians, and others), some preaching friars frequently went to Mosul to win them back to the Catholic Church. As Mosul was an important trading center and a transit place between Aleppo and Baghdad, the town and its region were well known to travelers. In this paper, the author has divided Italian publications according to the centuries in which they were written in order to emphasize the evolution of the interests and activities of the Italian travelers in Kurdistan. Politics, trade and religion were the principal aims of their exploration. There were considerable differences between the simple reports of travelers such as Marco Polo and Ricoldo da Montecroce of the 13th century, who saw the Kurds as only one of the numerous peoples they met and who treated them mainly from a folkloristic perspective, and the literature on the Kurds written in the 18th and 19th centuries, which displayed precise cultural and scientific interests. (A)

124   Hakim, Halkawt. "Missionnaires et voyageurs, les débuts de la connaissance des Kurdes en Europe." *Bulletin de L'Association des Anciens Elèves de l'INALCO* (Avril 1990): 25-32.

125   Harris, Walter B. *From Batum to Baghdad via Tiflis, Tabriz, and Persian Kurdistan*. Edinburgh: W. Blackwood and Sons, 1896. xii, 335 p., [17] leaves of plates (1 folded): ill., maps.

126   Heude, William. *A Voyage up the Persian Gulf and a Journey Overland from India to England in 1817: Containing Notices of Arabia Felix, Arabia Deserta, Persia, Mesopotamia, The Garden of Eden, Babylon, Bagdad, Koordistan, Armenia, Asia Minor, &c. &c*. New ed. Reading: Garnet, 1993. x, 252 p., [6] p. of plates: ill. Originally published: London:

Longman, Hurst, Rees, Orme, and Brown, 1819. With new introd. Includes bibliographical references.

127   Jones, James Felix. *Memoirs of Baghdad, Kurdistan and Turkish Arabia*. Slough: Archive Editions, 1998. xxxiii, xxii, 500 p.: ill., maps (some col.). [Selections from the records of the Bombay Government; new ser., no. 43. Originally published in the series under title: *Memoirs*. Bombay: The Govt., 1857. Three folded maps in pocket. Includes bibliographical references (p. xxxii-xxxiii) and index.

128   Khaznadar, Marouf (tr.). *al-Rahalah al-Rus fi al-Sharq al-Awsat*. [Russian travelers in the Middle East] Beirut: s.n., 1981. 430 p.

129   Kinneir, Sir John Macdonald. *Journey through Asia Minor, Armenia, and Koordistan in the Years 1813 and 1814 with Remarks on the Marches of Alexander and Retreat of the Ten Thousand*. London: J. Murray, 1818. xii, 603 p., [1] leaf of plates: map.

130   Layard, Austen Henry. *Nineveh and its Remains: With an Account of a Visit to the Chaldean Christians of Kurdistan, and the Yezidis, or Devil-Worshippers; and an Inquiry into the Manners and Arts of the Ancient Assyrians*. New York: G. P. Putnam, 1849. 2 vols. illus., plates (part fold.), plans (part fold.), map. An abridged edition was published in 1970 by Routledge & Kegan Paul (London) with an introduction by H. W. F. Saggs.

Detailed reviews of the expedition appeared in many journals of the day, for example: *The Dublin Review* 28 (June 1850): 354-398; *Littell's Living Age* 20 (February 24, 1849): 358-367; *Littell's Living Age* 21 (April 7, 1849): 19-43; and *The North American Review* 69 (July 1849): 110-142.

131   Layard, Austen Henry. *Discoveries among the Ruins of Nineveh and Babylon with Travels in Armenia, Kurdistan, and the Desert: Being the Result of a Second Expedition Undertaken for the Trustees of the British Museum*. New York: G.P. Putnam, 1853. xxii, 686 p., [12] leaves of plates (some folded): ill., 2 maps. 2nd ed. New York: Cincinnati: A. S. Barnes; H. W. Derby, 1856. 549 p.: ill., pl., maps, plans. Abridgment of author's larger work.

Detailed reviews of the expedition appeared in many journals of the day, for example, *The Dublin Review* 35 (September 1853): 93-138.

132   Lynch, Harry Finnis Blosse. *Armenia: Travels and Studies*. Beirut: Khayats, 1965. 2 vols.: illus., maps. Bibliography: v.2, pp. 471-496. [Khayats oriental reprints; no. 15] Originally published in London by Longmans & Green, 1901. v.1. The Russian provinces.--v.2. The Turkish provinces.

This is a good composition, still valuable for its encyclopedic nature as
well as for being a standard work on the Armenians. The volumes contain
the author's observations following his journeys to the Armenia and Kurdistan in 1893-94 and 1898. The book provides not only a comprehensive
account of his travels and studies but also an impression of the life of the
people at that time. Volume II affords a view of Ottoman Kurdistan before it was apportioned to Turkey and other countries.

133   Marsh, Dwight W. *The Tennesseean in Persia and Koordistan: Being
       the Scenes and Incidents in the Life of Samuel Audley Rhea*. Philadel-
       phia: Presbyterian Publication Committee; New York, A. D. F. Randolph,
       1869. 381 p. incl. illus., 11 pl. 2 maps.

134   Millingen, Frederick. *Wild Life among the Koords*. London: Hurst and
       Blackett, 1870. xiii, 380 p. map.

135   O'Shea, Maria T. "The Image from the Outside: European Travellers and
       Kurdistan Before the Great War." *Geopolitics and International
       Boundaries* 2, no. 3 (Winter 1997): 70-89.

This article examines the origins of some of the sources of information
upon which the Great Powers relied when determining their policies regarding Kurdistan. The nineteenth and early twentieth centuries were an
unparalleled period in the European exploration and the study of Kurdistan, and the volume of work was to inform European agents during, and
perhaps more crucially, after the First World War. The article examines
some of the reasons for European interest in Kurdistan, the nature of research and intelligence gathering in the region, and the significance of the
personalities involved. The personalities of writers, as well as their purposes, affected both their own views and also the ways in which those
views influenced external policies towards the Kurds. The difficulties inherent in examining 'British' policy in the region are also explored, given
that British policy was both fluid and multi-faceted. (A)

136   Rich, Claudius James. *Narrative of a Residence in Koordistan, and on
       the Site of Ancient Nineveh: with Journal of a Voyage Down the Tigris
       to Bagdad and an Account of a Visit to Shirauz and Persepolis*. Amer-
       sham, England: Demand Reprints, 1984. 2 v.: ill., maps (some folded).
       Reprint. Originally published: London: Duncan, 1836.

Travel account by an Englishman who spent the years 1816-1821 in Iraq
and Kurdistan, collecting manuscripts and antiquities. A 15-pages long
review article that describes the book in detail and provides some additional historical context of Rich's experience in Kurdistan appeared in
The Edinburgh Review, volume 64 (October 1836).

137 Southgate, Horatio. *Narrative of a Tour through Armenia, Kurdistan, Persia and Mesopotamia, with an Introduction, and Occasional Observations upon the Condition of Mohammedanism and Christianity in those Countries*. New York: D. Appleton & Co., 1840. 2 v. in 1. front., illus., plates, fold. map.

138 Ussher, John. *A Journey from London to Persepolis: Including Wanderings in Daghestan, Georgia, Armenia, Kurdistan, Mesopotamia, and Persia*. London: Hurst and Blackett, 1865. xiii, 703 p., [17] leaves of plates: col. ill. Title on cover and half title: London to Persepolis.

DESCRIPTION AND TRAVEL (SINCE 1900)

139 Balsan, Francois. *The Sheep and the Chevrolet: A Journey through Kurdistan*. London: Elek, 1947. 176 p.: ill.

This is an account of a motor tour in Kurdistan by the author and his wife in 1939. The record, unfortunately, is irritating, and misses most of the important angles. Worst of all, there is no map. In fact, the route was by train to Malatya, through Caesarea and Sivas, by horse carriage to Elazig, and on by Chevrolet down the Murad Valley to Van, skirting the southern shores of the lake, then southeast 100 odd miles to the Iranian frontier near Khanasur. No dates, no mileage, no seasons, no altitudes. One suspects this was a light account of the trip for the children, put later into literary battle-dress with forty excellent photographs.

140 Bruni, Mary Ann Smothers. *Journey through Kurdistan*. Austin, TX: Texas Memorial Museum, 1995. 127 p.

In a remarkable journey through Kurdistan, Bruni captures in both words and photographs the sentiments and history of the Kurdish people. From 1991 to 1993, the author explored Kurdistan, interviewing countless Kurds of various faiths, including Christian, Jewish, Muslim and Yezidi. She describes in detail their rituals and practices. Numerous full-page color photographs feature scenes of Kurdish life and customs.

141 Coan, Frederick Gaylord. *Yesterdays in Persia and Kurdistan*. Foreword by Robert E. Speer. Claremont, CA: Saunders Studio Press, 1939.

142 Coon, Carleton. *Caravan: The Story of the Middle East*. New York: Holt, Rinehart and Winston, 1952. viii, 376 p.: ill., maps. Includes bibliographical references and index. An Arabic translation was published in 1959 by Dar al-Thaqafah (Beirut).

Professor Coon has set out in this volume to provide a background of geographical and cultural information, and hence of understanding, for

Americans interested in the Middle East. He covers practically all the peoples, past and present, of the countries from Morocco to Afghanistan, before that impact [of the West] had been felt. Although Professor Coon's extensive wanderings in the Middle East seem to have been concerned largely with archaeology and anthropometry, he has also carried out some first-hand ethnographic research. It is the attempt to survey a vast and complex civilization with an anthropologist's interests and anthropological concepts which is the striking and original feature of the book. Professor Coon tells us a great deal about customs and social institutions, and continually seeks to see these customs and institutions in a functional framework. It is the complex inter-dependence of the parts of the mosaic which fascinate him. (abridged, Paul Stirling/*International Affairs* 29, October 1953: 518-519)

143 Douglas, William O. *Strange Lands and Friendly People*. New York: Harper, 1951. xv, 336 p.

Justice Douglas presents an unusual combination of romantic sensibility and clear, practical intelligence. This has enabled him to provide his readers with both an exciting tale of travel and a penetrating analysis of some of the basic social problems of the Middle East. Most of the book is devoted to Iran and to the countries of the Fertile Crescent, and Kurdistan.

144 Glazerbrook, Philip. *Journey to Kars: A Modern Traveller in the Ottoman Lands*. Viking: Penguin Books Ltd., 1984. 246 p.

Philip Glazerbrook, born in 1937, is the author of four novels. Inspired by the ancient voyagers, he journeyed through the world. This voyage to the region of Kars, a Kurdish homeland, is the end of a long journey of more than 10,000 square kilometers of a talented writer who had read a lot, studied, and particularly wished for such adventure. He wanted to go through the roads traced by his famous predecessors whose narratives aroused the dreams of entire generations. Accompanying their ghosts, in the shade of their works, he traveled till this "fortress where Turks, Russians and Persians" disputed since old times. This book where the present and the past meet harmoniously is proper to read, yet, it bears little useful information about the actual life of the Kurds in that region. (Joyce Blau/*AI* 9: 635)

145 Hamilton, Archibald Milne. *Road through Kurdistan: The Narrative of an Engineer in Iraq*. With a foreword by Major-General Rowan-Robinson. New York: AMS Press, 1975. 331 p., [25] leaves of plates: ill. (Reprint of the 1937 ed. published by Faber and Faber, London). Two new editions appeared in 1945 and 1958 by Faber & Faber. Translated into French by Thomas Bois under the title: *Ma route a travers le Kurdistan Irakien: recit d'un ingenieur neo-zelandais en Irak* (Paris: Harmattan, 1994).

This is the story of an engineer who for close to five years supervised the building of a road from Arbil to Rowanduz through the mountains of Kurdistan to the Iranian border. It includes much on the local politics and social tensions of the area at the time. When the task was finally achieved the author "left secretly during the full swing of the day's work, saying no word of farewell to the vast army of workmen whom through stress and travail I had led for so long; even an engineer is human, and frankly I could not have faced them." The author explains a very human and understanding account of all people whom he came across in Kurdistan: rival chieftains, warring tribes, and the motley crowd of Kurds, Arabs, Assyrians, Armenians, and Turks employed on the road. Descriptions of the formidable ranges and canyons near Rowanduz are graphic and illustrated by excellent photographs.

146   Hay, William Robert. *A Soldier in Kurdistan: Rupert Hay's Two Years in Kurdistan*. Cambridge: Allborough, 1991. xxiii, 324 p. A reprint of the 1921 edition, *Two Years in Kurdistan: Experiences of a Political Officer, 1918-1920*, published by Sidgwick & Jackson (London). An Arabic translation was published in 1973 by Matba'at al-Jahiz (Baghdad).

This is a reprint with a new introduction of the personal account of Hay's experiences while administering the largely Kurdish region of Arbil for the Indian Political Service from 1918 to 1920.

147   Hubbard, Gilbert Ernest. *From the Gulf to Ararat: An Expedition through Mesopotamia and Kurdistan*. Edinburgh: W. Blackwood, [1916], 1917. xv, 273 p. front., plates, ports.

148   Ignatieff, Michael. *Blood and Belonging: Journeys into the New Nationalism*. New York: Farrar, Straus and Giroux, 1994. 263 p., [16] p. of plates: ill.

Modern nationalism is a language of the blood: a call to arms that can end in the horror of ethnic cleansing. But it is also a language of belonging: a call to come home. In this book, Ignatieff explores both sides of nationalism in a personal odyssey that begins in the nightmare of former Yugoslavia and ends with his return to his adopted homeland, Great Britain's disunited kingdom. When he visits the mountains of Kurdistan, he notes that the world's largest stateless people—the Kurds—are fighting the Turks, the Iraqis, and themselves to establish their own nation-state. This is a good work that shows the diversity, complexity, agonies and horrors of nationalism with greater depth and insight than most, if not all, academic treatises and does so in elegant, passionate and memorable prose.

149   Matbi'i, Hamid. *Rihlati ilá Shamal al-'Iraq*. Baghdad: Sharikat Matba'at al-Adab al- Baghdadiyah, 1986. 376 p.: ill., maps, ports.

150   Noel, Edward William Charles. *Diary of Major Noel on Special Duty in Kurdistan*. Baghdad: s.n., 1920. 76 p. illus.

151   Soane, Ely Bannister. *To Mesopotamia and Kurdistan in Disguise: Narrative of a Journey from Constantinople through Kurdistan to Baghdad, 1907-1909, with Historical and Ethnographical Notices of the Various Kurdish Tribes and of the Chaldaeans of Kurdistan and an Index*. 2ⁿᵈ ed. with a memoir of the author by Sir Arnold T. Wilson. Amsterdam: Armorica Book Co., 1979. xix, 421 p.: ill., map, ports. Reprint. Originally published: London: J. Murray, 1912 and in 1926.

This is an account of a journey across Mesopotamia and through Southern Kurdistan. Includes a detailed description of the places and people of the region with historical and ethnographical notices of the various Kurdish tribes, and of the Chaldeans of Kurdistan. An Arabic version appeared in 1970. It was translated, reviewed, introduced, and commented on by Fuad Jamil under the title *Rihla Mutanakkirah ila Bilad ma bayna al-Nahrayn wa-Kurdistan* (Baghdad: Matba'at al-Jumhuriyah, 1970). His detailed account on the Kurdish tribes has been translated into Arabic and commented on by Fu'ad Hama Khurshid under the title: *al-'Asha'ir al-Kurdiyah* (Baghdad: Matba'at al-Hawadith, 1979. 159 p.).

152   Sykes, Mark. *The Caliph's Last Heritage: A Short History of the Turkish Empire*. New York: Arno Press, 1973. xii, 638 p.: ill. (Reprint of the 1915 ed. published by Macmillan, London).

The first part of the book is a sketch of the origin and rise of Islam as a political power in south-west Asia, culminating in the Ottoman Empire. Colonel Sykes gives no authorities for his historical statements, which are illustrated by many acute reflections and striking characterizations. The second part of the book contains the diaries of the author's travels during the years 1906-1913. He published the diaries just as they were originally written. The first journey, by far the most extensive, was made in 1906. It led east from Aleppo over the Euphrates and across the Jazireh to Mosul, then north-west to Diyarbekir and Erzerum. Finally, Mosul was once again reached by way of Mush, Bitlis, and Van. Colonel Sykes describes this journey with a freshness, a vigor, and even a dogmatism. He revels in the natural beauties of the country, and his observation on the peoples he met are full of interest and acuteness. The close study he made of the Kurds is shown by the valuable appendix in which their tribes are classified and their characteristics and distribution classified.

153   Thesiger, Wilfred. *Among the Mountains: Travels through Asia*. London: HarperCollins, 1998. xv, 250 p.: ill. Includes index.

The author devotes the first 12 pages of the preface to describe his journey in Iraqi Kurdistan in 1950-1951.

154   Thornhill, Teresa. *Sweet Tea with Cardamom: Journey through Iraqi Kurdistan*. England: Pandora, 1996. 240 p.

Thornhill explores the Middle Eastern world through the eyes of its women. In each chapter, the reader meets a girl or woman who shares her experience of living under Hussein's regime in Iraqi Kurdistan. Cultural mores, such as the difference between honor and shame, are explained in tales like that of a 14-year-old girl whose mother had to kill her in order to save the family's honor after the girl brought shame upon them by being raped in a field by strangers. The passion and poignancy of these stories, brought to life through Thornhill's warm, descriptive prose, make this book hard to put down.

155   Wigram, William Ainger; Wigram, Edgar Thomas Ainger. *The Cradle of Mankind: Life in Eastern Kurdistan*. London: A. and C. Black, 1914. xii, 373 p. illus. 2nd ed., 1922 (430 p.).

This book is written by two brothers, one of whom had spent years as a member of the Archbishop's Mission to Assyrian Christians, the other who had made a tour of three months in the Iraq and Kurdistan. They give a fresh eye and excellent photographs, as well as the accurate information and insight of the resident of years. They describe their journey to Kurdistan from Aleppo, and again their journey from Mosul to Baghdad. Incidentally, they give a considerable amount of history, Roman, Sassani and modern Turkish, descriptions of Assyrian, Babylonian and Roman antiquities, and an insight into the peculiar ecclesiastical and ecclesiological conditions in that region. After finishing the book, the reader will be able to distinguish clearly between a Nestorian and a Jacobite Christian, and will know either apart from a Chaldean or any other form of Uniat. The reader will know about the Yezidis and the relations of various sects to their Mohammedan neighbors, and will be introduced to the intricacies of Turkish misrule, both ancient and modern, and the interaction of Persian, Turkish and Russian politics. The whole is brilliantly illustrated, not only by capital photographs, but also by a number of most excellent and racy stories. The book is neither a missionary book nor a book on Islam, except incidentally, but the authors hold strong views on the need for the regeneration of the Oriental Churches as a preliminary to the evangelization of the Moslem world. (Ruth Rouse/*The Moslem World* 4, 1914: 434)

See also items: 10, 11, 12, 13, 399, 876, 919, 925

PICTORIAL/PHOTOGRAPHIC WORKS

156   Brisley, Maya; Dewran, Hasan; Kashi, Ed. "The Struggle of the Kurds." *Left Curve*, no. 19 (1995): 31-39.

This work is a collection of photographs, texts and poems highlighting the plight of the Kurds and their struggle for an independent state. The article reproduces photographs, and a foreword, by American photographer Ed Kashi from the book *When the Borders Bleed: The Struggle of the Kurds* (New York: Pantheon Books, 1994). The photographs show Kurdish refugees in Turkey and Iran, Kurdish youths in Berlin, Kurdish dissidents, a Kurdish chieftain who has won power by coming to an accommodation with the Turkish government, and the Kurdish Workers Party. Kashi's foreword describes his involvement with Kurdish rights groups since 1990, and his work on the book. A chronology by Maya Brisley, reprinted from the same book, provides an ethnographic account and history of the Kurdish people from the 7th century to the present, focusing on Kurdish efforts in the 20th century to establish a separate nation and their suppression by Iraq, Iran and Turkey. Poems by Hasan Dewran (b. 1958), are taken from his unpublished volume *Fire Since Zarathustra*.

157   Harris, M. "Meiselas, Susan (selected photographs from the forthcoming book '*In the Shadow of History, Kurdistan: A Photographic History of the Kurds from the 1880s to the Present*')." *Aperture*, no. 133 (Fall 1993): 24-33.

In a series of interviews, documentary photographer Susan Meiselas discusses her book project *Kurdistan: In the Shadow of History*, a photographic history of the kurds from the 1880s to the present, in which she tries to represent a culture which, because of its chaotic history, may be virtually without a self-image. Reproductions of Xeroxes and photographs from Meiselas's source books for the Kurdish project accompany the text.

158   Kashi, Ed. "Ed Kashi." *Photo Metro* 13, no. 123 (November 1994): 15-18.

An American photographer who describes his interest in the plight of the Kurdish people and his subsequent visits to Kurdistan to document the suffering of the population and the Kurdish struggle for survival in the middle of wars and conflicts. Kashi describes his recent book *When the Borders Bleed: The Struggle of the Kurds* (London: Chatto and Windus, 1994), from which the accompanying photographs are taken, and laments the fact that the Kurds are now only of secondary importance as a news item.

159   Kashi, Ed.; Hitchens, Christopher. *When the Borders Bleed: The Struggle of the Kurds*. Photographs by Ed Kashi; introduction by Christopher Hitchens. New York: Pantheon Books, 1994. 140 p.: chiefly col. ill., map.

"The Kurds have no friends—no friends but the mountains." This powerful photo essay masterfully illustrates this Kurdish saying as it chronicles the Kurds' seemingly endless struggle for survival. Hitchens, columnist for the *Nation* and *Vanity Fair*, describes the history of the Kurds in a 30-page introductory essay, documenting their legacy as victims of geopolitics. The 100 photographs by photojournalist Kashi, who traveled to Kurdistan, Turkey, Iraq, Syria, Iran, and even Germany, powerfully reveal the plight of contemporary Kurds. This book is unquestionably an apologia for the Kurds meant to keep alive awareness of their struggle. Nevertheless, there is criticism of the Kurds' internal divisiveness; their situation is not entirely a result of actions beyond their control. The book succeeds as a cohesive work. The prose is clear and succinct, the photographs persuasive and directly related to the prose. (Ruth K. Baacke/*Library Journal* 120, February 1, 1995: 89-90)

160   Kisra'iyan, Nasr Allah; Arshi, Ziba; Zabihi, Khosro. *Kurdistan: Photos*. Ostersund, Sweden: Oriental Art Publications, 1990; London: Kegan Paul, 1991. 139 p.: chiefly col. ill., map. Includes bibliographical references (p. 138-139).

Kisra'iyan, an Iranian photographer, is known for many years. He has traveled more often across Iranian Kurdistan and reported his images on the country. This volume, with its more than 127 color photographs and knowledgeable text by Ziba Arshi and Khosro Zabihi, gives the reader an insight into the customs, history, and way of life of the Kurds. The photos were taken during the winter season in Kurdish regions that are hardly accessible and known.

161   Kohl, Engelbert. *Kurdistan: Schmelztiegel der Hochkulturen zwischen Anatolien und Mesopotamien.* Aufl. Graz [Austria]: Weishaupt Verlag, 1991. 227 p.: ills, maps. Includes bibliographical references (p. 225). [In German.]

162   Meiselas, Susan. *Kurdistan: In the Shadow of History* London: Random House, 1997. Includes glossary, bibliography, index, maps.

This volume presents photographs, taken by Meiselas and others, aiming to document the Kurds' struggle for survival and independence over the past 125 years. Chronologically arranged, each chapter begins with a historical overview by anthropologist, Martin van Bruinessen. The body of each of the six chapters consists of primary source information from oral histories, diaries, letters, newspapers, memoirs, British and American government documents, and telegrams, (juxtaposed with photographs).

163   Young, Gavin. *Iraq: Land of Two Rivers*. Photos by Nik Wheeler. London: Collins, 1980. 280 p.: col. ill., maps.

Iraq is a land of beauty and turmoil. Young and Wheeler give an impression of this unusual country of twin rivers, and provide some idea of the life of the people who live there (both Arabs and Kurds, Muslims and Christians, and others). This book is mainly concerned with the landscape and people of Iraq and it presents an absorbing study of the place accompanied by beautiful color photographs.

6

Economy and Development

164 Bazin, Marcel. "L'impact du barrage de Karakaya sur la vallee de l'Euphrate a l'Est de Malatya." *Revue Geographique de l'Est* 28, no. 1 (1988): 3-17.

The Euphrates valley between the dams of Keban and Karakaya is populated with Kurdish villages getting their irrigation water from the surrounding mountains and not from the river itself. The prosperity won thanks to the apricot cash crop is unequally distributed amongst landlords and tenants. Additional incomes are sought for in Malatya and mostly in Istanbul. (A)

165 Bumke, Peter J. "Gecitveren—zur Wirtschaftlichen Situation eines Ostanatolischen Dorfes." [Gecitveren: The economic situation of an east-Anatolian village] *Mardom Nameh* 2 (1976): 2-22. [In German]

Data were collected in the summer of 1974 during field work in a Kurdish village of East Turkey. The economic organization of Gecitveren's peasant households is described and classified according to production and demand for wheat. Strategies of bridging the gaps of demand employed by each household are traced. These strategies consist of a migration of labor resulting in wage transfers from industry into agriculture. On the other hand, connected with this migration are new possibilities of taking lease of additional land. This process is based on traditional institutions of kinship relations. (A)

166 Dziegiel, Leszek. "Uprawa ruslin w rolnictwie chlopskim kurdystanu rackiego." [Peasants agriculture in modern Iraqi Kurdistan] *Lud* 65 (1981): 121-143. [In Polish]

167   Dziegiel, Leszek. *Rural Community of Contemporary Iraqi Kurdistan Facing Modernization*. Krakow, Poland: Agricultural Academy of Krakow, 1981. 208 p.

Dziegel's study was carried out within the framework of a wider agro-economic field-survey by the Polish Institute of Tropical and Subtropical Agriculture and Forestry at Cracow, in the northern Iraqi provinces of Dohuk, Sulaymania, and Arbil. The surveys were carried out in autumn 1977, spring 1978, and summer 1979 and 1980. The aim of the research was to investigate socio-economic changes amongst the Kurdish population of these provinces after the collapse of the Barzani revolution. The discussion of this work is primarily descriptive. The part dealing with economic changes in the agricultural and pastoral relevant to the Kurdish population comprises only one fifth of the book. The remaining chapters deal principally with changes in the material culture of the Kurdish population, the domestic and private sphere of Kurdish households (i.e., clothing, hygiene and care over personal appearance), sex relationships and school education. (abridged, E. Orywal/*Sociologia Ruralis* 22, 1982: 202-203)

168   Emmanuelsson, A.C. "Chasing the Rainbow: Economic and Social Constrains Facing Kurdish National Aspirations in Iraq." *The International Journal of Kurdish Studies* 8, no. 1-2 (1995): 110-125.

The author shows how the Iraqi government exploits the natural resources in and agricultural products of Kurdistan with little benefit to the Kurdish people. The author also discusses the impact of forced migration and re-settlements on the economic conditions of the Kurds in Iraq. Particular emphasis is put on the impact of the 1991 Gulf war and its consequences.

169   Fleming, Glenn, Jr. "The Ecology and Economy of Kurdish Villages." *Kurdish Times* 4 (Summer-Fall 1991): 28-41. French version: "L'ecologie et l'economie des villages kurdes." In *Les Kurdes par-dela l'exode*. Edited by Halkawt Hakim, pp. 157-181. Paris: L'Harmattan, 1992.

170   Gotlieb, Yosef. *Geo-Ethnic Imperatives of Development: The Inter-Dynamics of Territory, Society and State in the Third World (Political Geography, Kurdistan)*. Ph.D., Clark University, 1991. 489 p.

This study addresses the problems of entrenched underdevelopment and persistent ethnic unrest in the Third World. The thesis suggests that these phenomena constitute a single problem. The relationship between these phenomena is adduced from an exploration of evolving theory, historical accounts, and cartographic and quantitative studies. An explanation of the problem is based on the social and spatial configuration of post-colonial states. These states are largely contiguous with the imperial entities that preceded them. The colonies were demarcated to further the economic and geostrategic interests of the metropolitan powers. Accordingly, the indigenization of colonial space in the form of the post-colonial state perpetuates territorial incongruities between historical geo-ethnic regions and formal borders. Such incoherence has socioeconomic, environmental and political implications that obstruct development: societies emerge which are characterized by weak economies, ethnic stratification, degraded environments and oppressive regimes. These conditions render societies incapable of sustained development. Kurdistan constitutes the case study; it is considered representative of those ethno-regions whose populations suffer doubly from the imperialist legacy of the post-colonial state: the Kurds not only endure the privations of a developing people, but they also suffer subjugation at the hands of the elites governing the post-colonial states into which Kurdistan has been apportioned. The historical and contemporary relationship of the Kurds to Kurdistan exemplifies both the integrity of ethnicity and territory and the disastrous consequences for development which obtain when this relationship is violated. Principles relating to the articulation of modes of production, ethno-science and the imperatives of reversing internal colonialism in post-colonial states are among the building blocks of an incipient geo-ethnic approach to development. The conclusion draw from this study is that the integral albeit dynamic relationship between society and territory is an essential precondition for development. The spatial realm of development activity should be defined by anthropological and ecological continuities. (A)

171 Gotlieb, Yosef. "Retrieving Life-Place from Colonized Space: Transcending the Encumbrances of the Post Colonial State." *Political Geography* 11 (September 1992): 461-474.

The thesis advanced in this paper is that the phenomena of impeded development and ethno-national unrest in the Third World are inextricable from one another. Their origins are identified in the spatial structure of post-colonial states, which produce societies that are anthropologically, economically, and ecologically fragmented. Such fragmentation derives from the drawing of colonial borders in a manner aimed at maximizing economic benefit and/or geostrategic advantage to the metropolitan powers. Boundaries drawn in this way did not serve interests of indigenous social formations since they frequently divided such groups and the ecosystems of which they are part. The post-colonial state today is essentially indigenized colonized space. These political perpetuate the fragmentary ethnic and ecological territories pieced together as part of the imperial enterprise; de-colonization simply entailed the transfer of control over these polities to indigenous elites. In this context, the territorial composition of the post-colonial state renders it resistant to sustainable development. The social fragmentation that is so dominant a feature of post-colonial societies seriously challenges the possibilities for nation building as well as for development. The fragmentation of the Kurdish Ethno-region as a result

of the establishment of the post-colonial states into which it is divided
serves as the illustrative case of this study.

172   Gotlieb, Yosef. *Development, Environment, and Global Dysfunction:
        Toward Sustainable Recovery*. Delray Beach, Fla.: St. Lucie Press, 1996.
        xi, 188 p.

        Argues that international, growth oriented development, is inevitably ac-
        companied by poverty, environmental degradation, and socio-political un-
        rest, and that global priorities must be reordered toward local devel-
        opment and sustainable communities. Includes case study of Kurdistan.

173   Gotlieb, Yosef. "Irreconcilable Planning: The Transformation of Life-
        place into Economic Space in Iraqi and Turkish Kurdistan." *Progress in
        Planning* 47, no. 4 (1997): 321-332.

        The thesis advanced in this paper is that the violence found in Kurdistan
        is the outcome of two divergent views of the region. On the one hand
        governments seek to rationalize and maximize the potential of Kurdish
        areas as a resource frontier rich in soils, water and minerals. The official
        view of Kurdistan is based on its uses as economic space in the service of
        the state as a whole. For the Kurds, however, Kurdistan is life- place and
        represents the integrity of the society- nature relations prevalent in the re-
        gion since time immemorial. Where the state centers see modernization
        and aggregate economic growth as the primary objective of their policies
        in all areas under their jurisdiction, the Kurds see economic exploitation
        and cultural imperialism.

174   Hussein, Fuad; Leezenberg, Michiel; Muller, Pieter. *The Reconstruction
        and Economic Development of Iraqi Kurdistan*. Proceedings of the in-
        ternational conference on the reconstruction and development of Iraqi
        Kurdistan, Zeist, The Netherlands, September 4-6, 1992. Amsterdam:
        Stichting Nederland- Koerdistan, 1993. 112 p.: ill. Includes bibliographi-
        cal references (p. 112).

175   Iran. Sazman-i Barnamah (Iran). Umuri Iqtisadi. *The Third Development
        Plan of Iran, 1341- 1346 [i.e., 1962-1967]*. Tehran: Plan Organization,
        Division of Economic Affairs, 1961. 10 vols.

        Title of each volume varies slightly. Some volumes have special titles
        only. (1) General introduction to the Third Development plan of Iran. (2)
        Outline. (3) Education plan frame. (4) Electricity. Third draft. (5) Health
        plan frame. (6) Industry and mining. (7) Manpower. (8) Statistics. (9)
        Transport and communications. (10) Urban and rural development plan
        (plan-frame).

176 Iran. Bank-i Markazi-i Jumhuri-i Islami-i Iran. Idarah-i Barrasiha-yi Iqtisadi. *Annual Review*. Tehran: The Bank, 19? Annual.

177 Iraq. al-Bank al-Markazi al-'Iraqi. *al-Taqrir al-Sanawi=The Annual Report of the Central Bank of Iraq*. Baghdad: The Central Bank of Iraq, 1950-. Annual.

178 Jafar, Majeed R. *Under-Underdevelopment: A Regional Case Study of the Kurdish Area in Turkey*. Helsinki: Social Policy Association in Finland, 1976. 153 p.: ill. (Studies of the Social Policy Association in Finland; no. 24). Bibliography: p. 148-152. Arabic version (Beirut: Matb'at Amiral, 1990), 342 p.

179 Jaff, Akram. *Economic Development in Kurdistan*. Tallahassee, FL: Badlisy Center for Kurdish Studies, 1993. 19 p.

180 Kazemi, Abbas Ali. *Economic Analysis of Modifying Cropping Patterns in Selected Regions in Iran*. Ph.D., University of Illinois at Urbana-Champaign, 1983. 253 p.

This dissertation examined the implications of modifying cropping patterns in four major regions in Iran (East and West Azerbaijan, Kurdistan, and Khuzestan). The objectives of this study were: (1) to investigate the overall economic situation, industry and agriculture in Iran; (2) to review regional differentiation in agriculture in these regions to show the factor combination that will improve productivity; (3) to compare the present cropping system with the proposed cropping pattern within the framework of the partial budgeting program; and (4) to evaluate the results of the analysis and suggest alternatives that may shift the operation to a more productive system in these major regions of Iran. The study shows that expansion of cultivated land on typical farms in regions under investigation lead to different results under each investigation. It is possible to encourage the farmers to change some of their current cropping pattern in cultivation and land utilization in order to increase productivity in the area. A sensitivity analysis was performed in this study in order to investigate the effect on the optimal solution provided by the budgeting program. The effect of variation in the parameters on the equilibrium was also observed. (A)

181 Kurdistan Committee of Canada. *The Economic and Human Dimensions of Ten Years of War in Kurdistan*. Ottawa: Kurdistan Committee of Canada, 1995. 45 p.: ill.

182 Lambton, Ann K. S. *The Persian Land Reform, 1962-1966*. Oxford: Clarendon Press, 1969. 386 p.

Professor Lambton's book provides a comprehensive account of land reform in Iran, and complements her *Landlord and Peasants in Persia* (London: Oxford University Press, 1953). It is based on data gleaned from Iranian legal and administrative documents, observation of a number of villages in Iran, and conversations with various officials of agencies charged with developing and implementing land reform programs. The author, professor of Persian at the University of London, treats the first stage of land reform, which began in 1962, and the second stage, which began in 1964, separately and devotes four chapters to irrigation and cooperatives. She concludes that the first stage changed the structure of land ownership and the second ended the crop-sharing agreement in most of the villages. Consequently, The social and political power of the landlord has been broken. The levy by them of dues and services from the peasant has been abolished. The peasants have thus been liberated from institutions now recognized as obsolete. Further, a major change in the attitude of the peasant has been brought about by convincing him for the first time that change is possible and by giving him a new spirit of confidence. Cooperative societies are considered by the author as the most important institutional arrangement of the land reform program by providing their members with practice in cooperation, fostering a spirit of self-help and independence, and encouraging a sense of responsibility. (abridged, G. H. Razi/*American Political Science Review* 69, March 1975: 324)

183   Leitner, Wilhelm. "Das Vanseegebiet (Ostanatolien) in wirtschafts- und sozial geographischer Sicht." [Economy and social geography of the Van lake region, eastern Anatolia] *Mitteilungen der Osterreichischen Geographischen Gesellschaft* 121, no. 2 (1979): 207-228. [In German]

This article was published just before the Turkish military coup of 1980. The Van lake region has been changed in its economic and social geographic structure. Labor reserves and natural resources help to diminish the existing disparities. The ethnic diversity of Kurdistan still exists though there is a new relation between Kurds and Turks brought about by the migration of Turks, and urbanization. The regional geographic description of the region stresses the opening up to the transverse line and the synoptic and hierarchic classification of central places. (A)

184   Nezam-Mafi, Mansoureh E. "Merchants and Government Tobacco and Trade: The Case of Kordestan, 1333 A.H./1919 A.D." *Iranian Studies* 20, no. 1 (1987): 1-15.

This article, based on Hajj Rahim's private papers, deals with the collection of the tobacco tax in Kordestan, which the government had farmed out to *Ettehadieh* in 1919-1920. Although the life of this tax farm was brief, this little-known transaction sheds considerable light on the then government's problems in administering tax collection, on the troubled relations between the merchant class and the government, on the changing attitudes toward the state, and on the factors that led, in the Pahlevi period, to the establishment of state monopolies over such items of trade as tobacco and opium.

185 Sajjadi, Mansour. "The State of the Economy in Kurdistan." In *Kurdistan: Political and Economic Potential*. Edited by Maria T. O'Shea, pp. 36-61. London: GIBRC, SOAS, 1992.

The objective is to present an introduction to the economic situation of different parts of Kurdistan and to show their levels of development. The Kurdish regions in the USSR are not covered in this paper and those of Syria are discussed very briefly. In different sections the emphasis is on the resources, agriculture and industry. Due to uneven development, the Kurdish regions of different countries constitute different kinds of underdeveloped areas within underdeveloped countries. To illustrate this, wherever possible, the differences in the levels of development between these regions and the other areas of their respective countries are discussed. The economic situation of the individual part differs in a number of specific aspects, related mainly to the economy of their host countries. Yet these differences do not affect the general outline of the state of economy of all Kurdistan as a single unit, which is the subject of the final section. (A)

186 Semo, Ereb (Shamilov, Arab). *Hawla al-Iqta'iyah 'Ind al-Akrad fi Shamal al-'Iraq*. [Discusses feudalism in Iraqi Kurdistan] Cairo: s.n., 1967. 442 p.

187 Semo, Ereb (Shamilov, Arab). *Hawla Mas'alat al-Iqta' bayna al-Kurd*. [Discusses feudalism among Kurds] Translated from Russian by Kamal Mazhar Ahmad. Baghdad: Matba'at al-Zaman, 1977 [1984]. 104 p.

188 Skogseid, H. "Nomadic Pastoralism and Land Use Patterns in Eastern Turkey: The Case of the Kurdish Beritan Tribe." *The Middle East— Unity and Diversity: Papers from the Second Nordic Conference on Middle Eastern Studies, Copenhagen 22-25 October 1992*. Edited by H. Palva and K. S. Vikor, pp. 216-232. Copenhagen: Nordic Institute of Asian Studies, 1993. [Nordic Proceedings in Asian Studies, 5.]

189 Syria. Wizarat al-Takhtit. *Annual Report on the Economic & Social Development Plan of Syria*. Damascus: Bureau des documentations syriennes & arabes, 1961. Annual.

190 Türkiye. Basbakanlik Devlet Istatistik Enstitüsü. *Türkiye ekonomisi, istatistik ve yorumlar=Turkish Economy, Statistics and Analysis*. Ankara: T.C. Basbakanlik Devlet Istatistik Enstitüsü, 1989. Monthly.

191   Türkiye Cumhuriyet Merkez Bankasi. *Annual Report*. Ankara: The Bank, 1962-. Annual.

192   Türkiye Ticaret Odalari, Sanayi Odalari ve Ticaret Borsalari Birligi. *Iktisadi Rapor=Economic Report*. Ankara: Turkish Union of Chambers of Commerce and Industry and of Commodity Exchanges, 1985-. Annual.

193   White, Paul J. "The Economic Marginalization of Turkey's Kurds: The Failed Promise of Modernization and Reform." *Journal of Muslim Minority Affairs (JMMA)* 18, no.1 (Apr 1998): 139-158

The author shows that within Turkey, which is itself a developing country, a marked disparity exists between its Kurdish region and western Turkey. The evolving economic condition of the region is presented as the backdrop of overall developments in Turkey.

194   Yalcin-Heckmann, Lale. "Sheep and Money: Pastoral Production at the Frontiers." In *Culture and Economy: Changes in Turkish Villages*. Edited by P. Stirling, pp. 17-26. Hemingford Grey: Eothen, 1993.

This chapter is part of a volume that emerged from a conference that took place in June 1990 at the School of Oriental and African Studies in London, organized by Paul Stirling. Yalcin-Heckmann's chapter on Kurdish sheep smugglers makes an important contribution to this under-studied and difficult to access phenomenon. Issues such as accumulation, borders and money come together in her synthetic analysis of the social and political economy of smuggling (dealt with in depth in her monograph *Tribe and Kinship among the Kurds*).

See also items: 4, 9, 14, 15, 16, 19, 26, 27, 39, 42, 44, 45, 46, 47, 48, 117, 229, 322, 335, 348, 351, 354, 359, 364, 658, 670, 672, 680, 681, 706, 771, 775, 801, 808, 829, 843, 860, 885, 910, 912, 919, 920, 923

7

Education

195   Alrubaiy, Abdul Amir. "The Failure of Political Integration in Iraq: The Education of the Kurdish Minority." *Intellect* 102 (April 1974): 440-444.

This essay describes and analyzes the way in which the different Iraqi regimes have provided, unsuccessfully, for the education of the Kurds. An effort was made to assess the extent of the integration of the Kurdish minority into the mainstream of the Iraqi society.

196   Chatoev, Khalid. "Pages d'amitie armeno-kurde (Histoire de l'instruction des Kurdes aux annees 1920)." *Acta Kurdica: The International Journal of Kurdish and Iranian Studies* 1 (1994): 37-42.

197   Fikrat, Hikmat T. *Education in Kurdistan: An Overview*. Tallahassee, FL: Badlisy Center for Kurdish Studies, 1993. 16 p. Includes bibliographical references (p. 15- 16).

198   Hassanpour, Amir. "The Pen and the Sword: Literacy, Education and the Revolution in Kurdistan." In *Knowledge, Culture and Power: International Perspectives on Literacy as Policy and Practice*. Edited by Peter Freebody and Anthony R. Welch, pp. 35-54. Pittsburgh, Pa: University of Pittsburgh Press, 1993.

The struggle of the Kurdish people to promote their national language and education while under the control of hostile Ottoman, Arab, and Persian empires is described. The intimate connection between state power and literacy in the process of gaining independence for a unified nation is also examined. The history of the domination and repression of the Kurds is traced from the seventh century onward to explain Kurdish literacy and forced foreign-language education. Controlled at most times by some part of the Arab, Ottoman, or Persian empires, the Kurds who lacked political independence found it difficult to develop a literate tradition in their native tongue. The rise of Kurdish political power was found to coincide with the literary use of Kurdish in the fifteenth and sixteenth centuries, but the endless wars with the Ottomans and the Persians are blamed for the language's repression, but also for a sort of Kurdish national awakening. The accomplishments are related to two Kurdish poets and nationalists, Ahmad Khani and Haji Qadir Koyi, who worked to develop a prestigious Kurdish literacy. But in order to develop a Kurdish literate tradition, it is concluded that the Kurds must have political independence and the means to educate their peoples because language use is closely related to social, economic, and political power. (J. Repath/*SA* 94-0531)

199   Hassanpour, Amir; Skutnabbkangas, T.; Chyet, M.. "The Non-Education of Kurds: A Kurdish Perspective." *International Review of Education* 42, no. 4 (1996): 367-379.

Educational provision in Kurdistan (embracing parts of Iran, Iraq, Syria and Turkey) violates most of the language-in-education requirements of international law. The same is true for Kurds in diaspora in most parts of the world. Linguistic and cultural genocide is attempted, with the tacit complicity of the West. The future of Kurdish education depends to a large extent on the political situation in the Middle East. Political solutions are needed before educational problems can be tackled. Within international law, a new interpretation by the UN Human Rights Committee of Article 27 in the International Convenant on Civil and Political Rights (UN 1986) might give grounds for hope for the future. However it argued that only a democratic Kurdistan could promote education that fosters nation building, self-determination, and autonomy.

200   Iran. Vizarat-i Amuzish va Parvarish. Department of Planning and Studies. *Educational Statistics in Iran*. Tehran: Bureau of Statistics, 1971-. Annual.

201   Iran. Vizarat-i Farhang va Amuzish-i 'Ali. *Statistics of Higher Education in Iran*. Tehran: Center for Educational Planning, 1983-. Annual.

202   Iraq. Mudiriyat al-Ihsa' al-'Amma. *Report on the Education in Iraq*. Baghdad: Printed at the Republic Government Press, 19?. Annual.

203   Iraq. Qism al-Ihsa' al-Thaqafi. *Nata'ij al-Ihsa' al- Thaqafi*. Baghdad: Wizarat al-Takhtit, Da'irat al- Ihsa' al-Markaziyah, Qism al-Ihsa' al-Thaqafi, 1961-. Annual.

204   Iraq. Shu'bat al-Ihsa' al-Tarbawi. *al-Ta'lim al-Jami'i fi al-'Iraq*. Bagh-
      dad: Wizarat al-Takhtit, al-Jihaz al-Markazi lil-Ihsa', Da'irat al-Ihsa' al-
      Ijtima'i, 19?. Annual.

205   Iraq. Wizarat al-Tarbiyah wa-al-Ta'lim. *Annual Report [on] Educational
      Statistics. al-Taqrir al-Sanawi, al-Ihsa' al-Tarbawi*. Baghdad: Ministry
      of Education, 1967-. Annual.

206   Karim, Ahmad Malla. *Adwa' wa-Dirasat Hawl Mashakil al-Ta'lim fi al-
      'Iraq*. [A review of the problems of education in Iraq] Kirkuk, Iraq:
      Matba'at al-Baladiyah, 1972. 134 p.

207   Marduk[h], Abd-allah. "The *Madrasa* in Sunni Kurdistan." In *Encyclo-
      paedia Iranica*. Vol. 8, pp. 187-189. Costa Mesa, CA: Mazda Publishers,
      1998.

      Describes the educational system of the madrasas in Iranian Kurdistan.
      The students at the madrasa were engaged solely in Arabic-language and
      theological studies. In Iranian Kurdistan education was formerly in the
      hands of a few learned families, like the Barzinjis, the Curis, the Hayda-
      ris, and the Mardukjis. The important educational centers were the Dar al-
      Ihsan mosque in Sanandaj; the mosque at Sulaymania; Mahabad; Torjan,
      a village near Bukan; and Aba Obayda, a village in Iraqi Kurdistan. In-
      cludes a bibliography.

208   Syria. Wizarat al-Tarbiyah wa-al-Ta'lim. *al-Tarbiyah fi al-Jumhuriyah
      al-'Arabiyah al-Suriyah lil-'Am al-Dirasi...* Damascus: al-Wizarah,
      1993-. Annual.

209   Syria. Wizarat al-Tarbiyah wa-al-Ta'lim. Mudiriyat al-Takhtit wa-al-
      Ihsa'. *Ihsa'at al-Ta'lim wa-al-Imtihanat lil-'Am al-Dirasi...* Damascus:
      al-Mudiriyah, 1988-. Annual.

210   Turkey. Milli egitim istatistikleri. *National Education Statistics. Formal
      Education. Örgün Egitim Istatistikleri*. Ankara: Basbakanlik, Devlet
      Istatistik Enstitüsü, 1987-. Annual.

See also items: 1, 4, 20, 167, 175, 322, 323, 337, 691, 838, 840, 848, 888

8

Health Conditions

211　Ahmad, Abdulbaghi. "Symptoms of Posttraumatic Stress Disorder among Displaced Kurdish Children in Iraq: Victims of a Man-Made Disaster after the Gulf War." *Nordic Journal of Psychiatry* 46, no. 5 (1992): 315-319.

Interviewed 20 Kurdish children (aged 6-26 years) from families who were displaced in temporary camps on the Turkish border after the Gulf war about their experience of stress symptoms, focusing on posttraumatic stress disorder (PTSD). The interviews were conducted two months after the disaster and again at a two-month follow-up when the subjects had returned with their families back to the home regions. All of the subjects showed some PTSD symptoms. At the index interview, however, only four of them fulfilled the criteria for PTSD. Children's risk of developing PTSD symptoms is discussed with regard to family construction, social support, and the parents' previous exposure to violence.

212　Ahmad, Abdulbaghi; Kirmanj, Mohammad. "The Socioemotional Development of Orphans in Orphanages and Traditional Foster Care in Iraqi Kurdistan." *Child Abuse and Neglect* 20, no. 12 (1996): 1161-1173.

In order to investigate orphans' situation and development in Iraqi Kurdistan, samples from the two available orphan care systems, the traditional foster care and the modern orphanages, are examined at an index test and at one-year follow-up regarding competency scores and behavioral problems at both test occasions, and posttraumatic stress reactions at a one-year follow-up. Achenbach Child Behavior Check List (CBCL) and two instruments regarding posttraumatic stress disorder (PTSD) were used. While competency scores showed an improvement in both samples at the follow-up test, the problem scores increased in the orphanage sample and decreased among the foster care subjects. Moreover, the orphanage sample reported higher frequency of posttraumatic stress disorder (PTSD) than the foster care children. The results are discussed with regard to the value of the Kurdish society's own traditions in taking care of orphans.

213   Ahmad, Abdulbaghi; Mohamed, H. T.; Ameen, N. M. "A 26-Month Follow-Up of Posttraumatic Stress Symptoms in Children after the Mass-Escape Tragedy in Iraqi Kurdistan." *Nordic Journal of Psychiatry* 52, no. 5 (1998): 357-366.

In the aftermath of the Gulf War, an Iraqi military attack caused a mass-escape tragedy in Kurdistan. Two months later, a sample of displaced children on the Iraqi-Turkish border reported a high frequency of posttraumatic stress symptoms. Twenty percent of the examined children met DSM-III-R criteria for posttraumatic stress disorder (PTSD). After a decrease in symptoms at the four-month follow-up, the 14-month follow-up showed a significant increase in PTSD-related symptoms, which persisted even at the 26-month follow-up. The results are discussed in relation to the specificity of PTSD symptoms, their course over time, and the socio-cultural aspects in measuring posttraumatic stress symptoms.

214   Babille, M.; Colombani, P. De; Guerra, R.; Zagaria, N.; Zanetti, C. "Post-Emergency Epidemiological Surveillance in Iraq-Kurdish Refugee Camps in Iran." *Disasters* 18 (March 1994): 58-75.

Describes a computerized epidemiological surveillance system developed in 1991 to monitor health trends among 25,000 displaced Kurds in Now-sood and Saryas refugee camps in the Kermanshah region. Weekly population movements, attack rates, point-prevalence estimates, and case fatality ratios were calculated. The overall crude mortality rate (CMR) in the camps under study was still nine times higher than the reported CMR for Iraq. Health problems with very low rates included measles, meningitis, and tetanus. However, morbidity for the most common conditions (acute respiratory infections, diarrhea, skin infections, eye diseases, and typhoid fever) increased at the end of intervention. It is concluded that such epidemiological surveillance systems should be implemented during mass migrations in developing countries as well as post-emergency settings. (*SA* 94D-9032)

215   Bailly, L. "Les sequelles d'un traumatisme a l'echelle d'une population: l'exemple du Kurdistan Irakien." [Population wide sequelae of trauma: The example of Iraqi Kurdistan]. *JEUR* 9, no. 4 (1996): 161-164.

Political oppression creates intentional and planned catastrophes, surrounded by silence and secret. In such situations the intervention of a foreign psychiatrist is rather complicated and demands efforts of clarification on what the mission aims to achieve and how. Neglecting that aspect can lead to negative results. Iraqi Kurdistan has been exposed to severe political oppression: arbitrary imprisonment, torture, and chemical weapons have killed more than 500,000 of the 4 millions Kurds during the last decade. The Anfal operation was settled by Saddam Hussein government 'to get rid' of the Kurds. PTSD, depressions, psychosomatic diseases are so common that the need is one of a global public health program. (A)

216   Bat-Haee, Mohammad Ali. "Knowledge and Attitudes of Kurdish Men in Iran with Respect to Vasectomy and Other Means of Male Fertility Control." *The Journal of Family Welfare: Personal, Marital and Sociological* 33, no. 4 (June 1977): 3-22.

Voluntary male sterilization has not been an unusual method of contraception during the 1970's. Many reports in recent years have addressed themselves to the cultural as well as psychological effects of vasectomy upon vasectomized men. Upon reviewing more than 120 articles, Wortman and Piotrow stated that "... family men throughout the world have discovered that this simple, onetime procedure can spare their mates the inconvenience of daily pills or IUDs, not to mention the more complicated female sterilization." An examination of the available studies has resulted in the development of a list of eight generalizations pertinent to the advantages of vasectomy over other methods of birth control. The socio-cultural conditions of many Asian and Middle Eastern countries fit the conditions specified in these generalizations very well. It follows that under such socio-cultural circumstances, vasectomy should be considered "acceptable" and "preferable" by Iranians, particularly by such ethnic groups as the Kurds of Western Iran, whose score on the social characteristics is rather high. The purposes of this study, then, are (a) to test the Wortman and Piotrow generalization with a sample of Kurdish men in Western Iran in reference to vasectomy, (b) to report on the knowledge and attitudes of the sample not only towards vasectomy but also towards other means of male fertility control (the condom and coitus interruptus), and (c) to examine the effect of different levels of education upon the reproductive behavior of the sample. (A)

217   Gol-Anbar, Jalil. *A Descriptive Survey of Psychotherapy in Kurdistan and Western Cultures*. Ph.D., United States International University, 1983. 187 p.

The Problem: This is a study about psychotherapy practiced by native people living in the mountainous regions of Western Iran. It is concerned primarily with a single province where there is a high concentration of folk healers. This study explores the history of the Kurdish healer and the therapeutic techniques they employ. It also traces the origin of their psychotherapy, which is deeply rooted in Islam. The intent of the study was to present Kurdish psychotherapy within a coherent scientific framework.

This was achieved by including a general discussion and comparison of psychotherapy in Western cultures and Kurdistan. Questions regarding the meaning of psychotherapy, the function of the psychotherapist, the theories and techniques they utilize, are therefore answered from both perspectives. Method: The research method was descriptive survey. More specifically, the study was conducted by interview and direct observation of the healers at work over a period of six years, it was past oriented, as the researcher sought to trace the origin of Kurdish psychotherapy to material written by Muslim scholars dated as early as A. D. 620. Results: Psychotherapy used in Kurdistan is effective and rooted in scientific evidence and religious philosophy. The healers of Kurdistan have a well-designed place in their communities, promoting the physical and mental health of the members. In addition, it was found that both similarities and differences exist between psychotherapy practiced in Kurdistan and Western cultures. (A)

218   Iraq. Directorate of Vital Statistics. *Annual Bulletin of Health and Vital Statistics*. Baghdad: Directorate of Vital Statistics, 19?-. Annual.

219   Kneller, R. W.; Ingolfsdottir, K.; Revel, J.P.. "The Mortality Experience of Kurdish Refugees Remaining in Turkey." *Disasters* 16, no. 3 (1992): 249-254.

A survey of one of the camps still holding refugees from Iraq who crossed into Turkey in the spring of 1991 showed that the majority of the population was under 15 years of age and that increased mortality occurred during the first 20 days after the refugees left their homes in Iraq. Infants, young children, and the elderly suffered the highest mortality, with infant mortality rates (IMRs) over the first month of the crisis approximately 18-29 times the IMR in Iraq in the late 1980s. Still unexplained is a greater than two-fold excess mortality among males compared with females. Other demographic and health findings are also reported.

220   Kocak, R.; Alparslan, Z. N.; Agridag, G.; Baslamisli, F.; Aksungur, P. D.; Koltas, S. "The Frequency of Anaemia, Iron Deficiency, Hemoglobin S and Beta Thalassemia in the South of Turkey." *European Journal of Epidemiology* 11, no. 2 (1995): 181-184.

A survey on the prevalence of anemia, iron deficiency, and hemoglobinopathies (Hb S and beta thalassemia) was carried out in an ethnically mixed and carefully registered population of 45,000 living in an area in the Southern Turkey. A total of 1,223 subjects (representing the population with respect to sex and age group) were surveyed. The rate of anemia was found to be 16.9% overall with a highest prevalence of 18.3% in the children (0-2 ages) and 16.3% in the 14+ age group. The prevalence of iron deficiency using low transferring saturation as criteria was found to be 17.2% overall, being 48.0% in the infant group, 19.6% in the children, and 14.7% in the 14+ age group. The rate of Hb S using the sickling test was found to be 3.9% in the entire population without separating for ethnic groups. It was more prevalent (9.6%) in the Arabic speaking and not found at all in the Kurdish speaking people. The rate of beta thalassemia with a high HbS, was 3.4% overall and highest (7.1%) in the Kurdish speaking people.

221   Porter, J. D. H.; van Loock, F. L. "Evaluation of Two Kurdish Refugee Camps in Iran, May 1991: The Value of Cluster Sampling in Producing Priorities and Policy." *Disasters* 17, no. 4 (1993): 341-347.

Following the end of the Gulf War in March 1991, Kurdish refugees from Iraq crossed the border into Western Iran. To plan public health interventions and to assist in priority setting for scarce resources, a rapid epidemiological assessment of two camps, Hafez and Kaliche, was conducted in May 1991. A 30-cluster sampling method was used to determine the demographics of the camp population, the morbidity and mortality from certain diseases, and the nutritional status of the children less than five years of age. The survey identified that morbidity was less severe than in the Kurdish camps on the Turkish border and provided information for camp authorities to plan appropriate relief interventions.

222   Sharp, Trueman W.; Yip, Ray; Malone, John D. "US Military Forces and Emergency International Humanitarian Assistance: Observations and Recommendations from Three Recent Missions. (Kurdistan, Bangladesh, and Somalia)." *The Journal of the American Medical Association* 272, no. 5 (August 3, 1994): 386-391.

The purpose of this article is to examine recent military relief operations in Kurdistan, Bangladesh, and Somalia; describe advantages and limitations of using US armed forces for emergency international humanitarian assistance; and propose recommendations for increasing the effectiveness of military forces in future operations. The focus is on the provision of appropriate and effective medical and public health services.

223   Syria. Wizarat al-Sihah wa-al-Is'af al-'Amm. *al-Taqrir al-Sihi al-'Amm*. Dimashq: Wizarat al-Sihah wa-al-Is'af al- 'Amm. 1946-.

224   Turkey. Ministry of Health, General Directorate of Mother and Child Health and Family Planning. *Turkish Demographic and Health Survey, 1993*. Ankara, Turkey: Hacettepe University's Institute of Population Studies, for Turkish Ministry of Health, General Directorate of Mother and Child Health and Family Planning, 1994. xviii, 247 p.: ill., map. Includes bibliographical references (p. 119).

The TDHS is a nationwide survey of women of reproductive age designed to provided, among other things, information on fertility, family planning, child survival, and health of children. This survey is the most recent in a series of demographic surveys carried out in Turkey by Hacettepe University's Institute of Population Studies (HIPS).

225   Turkey. Saglik ve Sosyal Yardim Bakanligi. Tanitma ve Istatistik Birimi. *Türkiye saglik istatistik yilligi=Health Statistics Yearbook of Turkey*. Ankara: Saglik ve Sosyal Yardim Bakanligi, Tanitma ve Istatistik Birimi, 19?-. Annual.

226   United States. House. Select Committee on Hunger. International Task Force. *Humanitarian Dilemma in Iraq: Hearing, August 1, 1991*. Washington, DC: GPO, 1992. iii, 141 p.: tables. [102d Cong., 1st sess.; Serial no. 102-11; SD cat. no. Y 4.H 89:102-11]

Discusses concerns over the health and nutrition situation in Iraq exacerbated by the international trade sanctions. Also discussed are options for humanitarian action.

227   United States. House. Select Committee on Hunger. International Task Force. *Humanitarian Crisis in Iraq: Challenge for U.S. Policy: Hearing, November 13, 1991*. Washington, DC: GPO, 1991. iii, 96 p.: tables, charts, map. [102d Cong., 1st sess.; Serial no. 102-18; SD cat. no. Y 4.H 89:102-18]

Discusses the problem of health, nutrition, and welfare of the civilian population following the Persian Gulf war. US, UN, and international relief efforts are discussed too. The impact of medicine shortages, lack of drinking water, food, and other shortages on infants and children is also discussed.

228   'Uthman, Muhammad Amin. "al-Adwiyah al-Sha'biyah 'Ind al-Akrad." [Alternative or popular medicine among the Kurds] *al-Turath al-Sha'bi* 2 (September 1970): 28-35.

229   Weissman, Juliana. *The Syrian Arab Republic*. Washington: U. S. Department of Health, Education, and Welfare, Public Health Service, Office of International Health, Division of Program Analysis, 1977. xviii, 145 p.: maps. [Syncrisis: the dynamics of health; 23]

Part of an analytic series on the interactions of health and socioeconomic development. Prepared for, and funded by, the Agency for International Development. Discusses health conditions in the country, infant mortality and its causes, fertility, national health policy, and health education system, and health services.

230 Wittwer-Backofen, U. "Growth Study in Children of a Kurdish Village Population." *Homo* 47, no. 1-3 (1996): 147-162.

The paper presents growth data from Kurdish children from the age of three up to fifteen years. The children belong to a village population in southeast Turkey of which the demographic structure, as well as body measurements of the adults, was investigated. Hereditary effects measured as parent-offspring correlations in stature were high for above ten years. Growth in height and weight are demonstrated and estimated in comparison with international data. It is shown that growth development in the studied population differs from children of other Turkish studies and takes an intermediate position between those and Arabic samples.

231 Woodcock, Jeremy. "Healing Rituals with Families in Exile." *Journal of Family Therapy* 17, no. 4 (November 1995): 397-409.

Describes the use of healing rituals in therapy with families who have been subjected to torture and atrocity and forced into political exile. Therapeutic dilemmas when working with families affected by torture and atrocity are discussed. The culture of refugee families is a resource that can be used to enable them to integrate experiences of atrocity and adapt to life in exile. Case histories of Kurdish and Iranian families are presented to illustrate therapeutic strategies of passing time, use of a genogram, and enacting seasonal festivals and death rites.

232 Yip, R.; Sharp, T. W. "Acute Malnutrition and High Childhood Mortality Related to Diarrhea: Lessons from the 1991 Kurdish Refugee Crisis." *Journal of the American Medical Association* 270, no. 5 (1993): 587-594.

The objective of this study is to determine the extent, major causes, and contributory factors of high rates of morbidity and mortality among children at mountain camps along the Turkey-Iraq border during the 1991 Kurdish refugee crisis. Research design included a cross-sectional rapid nutrition survey among children and a retrospective mortality survey covering a two-month period from the onset of the crisis. Population studied was households of Kurdish refugees at a resettlement camp near Zakho. Main outcome measures included: prevalence of wasting (low weight-for-height) and mean weight-for-height status, prevalence of diarrhea, and crude and age-specific mortality rates. Results showed that weight-for-height measurements indicated that children under two years of age had suffered significant recent malnutrition. The elevated prevalence of wasting and the reduced mean weight-for-height status in this group indicated generalized weight loss. This weight loss was likely the result of the high rates of diarrhea, which still affected 50% of the younger children at the time of survey. The crude mortality rate for all ages was 8.9 per 1000 per month (expected rate, 0.6 per 1000); two thirds of the deaths occurred among children aged five years or younger, and half among infants younger than one year. An estimated 12% of all infants died during the first two months of the crisis. Most deaths were due to diarrhea, dehydration, and resulting malnutrition. It was concluded that the high rates of malnutrition and mortality related to diarrhea in infants and younger children of Kurdish refugees took place rapidly despite prompt relief efforts and a previously healthy population. This experience underscores the need for early and aggressive public health management of sanitation, water sources, and diarrhea control programs to augment the traditional focus on food and medical relief during the emergency phase of a refugee crisis.

See also items: 850, 904

9

Jewish Kurds

GENERAL

233 Ben-Yacob, Abraham; Gerson-Kiwi, Edith. "Kurdistan." *Encyclopedia Judaica* 10: 1295-1301. New York: Macmillan, 1972.

Presents the Jews of Kurdistan. Topics discussed include: Population, History, Economic Conditions, Instability of Living Conditions, The Organization of the Communities and their Spiritual Foundation, Kurdish Language, Aliyyot to Palestine, and Musical Tradition.

234 Ben-Yaakov [Ben-Yacob], Abraham. "Kurdish Jews in Israel." In *Encyclopedia of Zionism and Israel*. Edited by Raphael Patai, pp. 691-693. New York: Herzl Press, 1971.

235 Blady, Ken. *Jewish Communities in Exotic Places*. Northvale, NJ: Jason Aronson, 2000. xxvii, 422 p.: ill., map. Includes bibliographical references (p. 391-402) and index.

Presents the histories, economies, and religious life of 17 Jewish communities in the Middles East, Asia, and Africa. After describing the community's arrival in its host country, Blady focuses on the relationship between Jewish life and the country's culture. In particular, he considers which rituals were maintained and which customs adopted, showing that some communities had to balance their own culture with the need to adapt. Part III of the book is devoted to the mountain Jews of Kurdistan.

236 Cohen, Hayyim J. [Haim J.] *The Jews of the Middle East 1860-1972*. New York: John Wiley, 1973. 213 p.

Examines the social conditions, way of life, and experiences of Oriental Jews. Begins with historical background and then looks more closely at the Jewish communities in Iran, Iraq, Turkey, Syria, the Yemen and Egypt, examining education, demographic features, political activities, social change and economic development.

237   Franchetti, G. "A Kurdish Prime Minister of Israel?" [Yitzhak Mordechai] *Ponte* 55, no. 4 (April 1999): 31-36. [In Italian]

238   Gerson-Kiwi, Edith. "Kurdistan." *Encyclopedia Judaica*. CD-ROM edition. Shaker Heights, OH: Keter Publishing House Ltd., 1997.

Edith, an associate professor of ethnomusicology at Tel Aviv University, discusses the geographical distribution of the Kurdish Jews, their numbers, history, economic conditions, and instability of living conditions in Kurdistan. Edith also discusses the organization of the communities and their spiritual foundation. Their language and music tradition is also discussed.

239   Lipman, J. G. "Kurdistan." In *The Jewish Encyclopedia*, vol. 7, pp. 585-586. New York: Ktav Publishing House, Inc., 1964.

Describes the history of Jews in Kurdistan and their relationships with the various groups residing in Kurdistan, including the Muslim Kurds, Turks, Arabs, and the Christians. It also describes the Jewish Kurds' customs and lists their geographic distribution in Kurdistan and provides some statistical figures in that respect.

240   Mann, Jacob. "Documents Concerning the Jews in Mosul and Kurdistan." In *Texts and Studies in Jewish History and Literature*, vol. 1, pp. 477-549. Cincinnati: Hebrew Union College Press, 1931-1935. Reprinted in 1972 by Ktav Publishing House (New York).

241   Rejwan, Nissim. *The Jews of Iraq: 3000 Years of History and Culture*. Boulder, CO: Westview Press, 1985. ix, 274 p.

Covering nearly 3000 years of history, this fascinating and compelling work chronicles the Mesopotamian Jewish community from its beginnings during the Assyrian captivity to the Arab conquest (731 BC-641 AD), through its encounter with Islam (641-1850), and up to the last 100 years (1850-1951), a period of political upheaval and radical change which culminated in the massive exodus to Israel in 1950 and 1951. The book is comprehensive yet concise, and represents one of the first English language works to address the history of Iraqi Jewry in its entirety, with the broader framework of Jewish, Iraqi and regional history.

242 Sabar, Yona. "Jews of Kurdistan." In *Encyclopedia of World Cultures, Volume IX: Africa and the Middle East*. Edited by John Middleton and Amal Rassam, pp. 144-147. Boston, MA: G.K. Hall and Co., 1995.

Topics discussed include: Orientation (identification, location, demography, and linguistic affiliation); History and Cultural Relations; Economy; Kinship, Marriage, and Family; and Religion and Expressive Culture (religious beliefs and practices, medicine, handicrafts and oral arts).

ART AND MUSIC

243 Epstein, Shiftan. "Textiles of Union: On Festive Roundels Made and Used by the Jews of Irani Kurdistan." *Jewish Folklore and Ethnology Review*, no. 2 (1987): 1-5.

244 Gerson-Kiwi, Edith. "The Music of Kurdistan Jews: A Synopsis of their Musical Styles." In *Contributions to a Historical Study of Jewish Music*. Edited by Eric Werner, pp. 266-279. New York: Ktav Publishing House, Inc., 1976.

245 Schwartz-Be'eri, Ora. "Jewish Weaving in Kurdistan." *Journal of Jewish Art* 3/4 (1977): 74-89. Reprinted in *Kurdish Times*, vol. 4 (Summer-Fall 1991, pp. 86-96).

In 1975, the Department of Jewish Ethnography of the Israel Museum, with the aid of a grant from the Memorial Foundation for Jewish Culture, New York, and the Israel Ministry of Education and Culture initiated a survey of the material culture of Jewish immigrants from the Kurdish areas of Iraq, Iran, Turkey, and Syria. The survey was planned as an attempt to fill in the gaps in our knowledge of the occupations and objects characteristic of this Jewish group in its daily life.

246 Schwartz-Be'eri, Ora. "Kurdish Jewish Silvercraft." *Israel Museum Journal* 7 (Spring 1988): 75-86.

This article describes the work of silversmiths among the Jewish community of Kurdistan who immigrated into Israel and were still active in the 1930s. These Jews made jewelry as well as Jewish ritual objects. The author classifies their work according to the style and content of the decoration, and the type and quality of the material: ornamented objects in high quality silver, with elaborate and variegated surface ornamentation, often including a Hebrew inscription; smooth and flat inscribed objects: plain work on high quality silver, generally simply styled with clean lines and smooth areas bearing engraved inscriptions; folk art decoration: popular work on sheet alloy or copper with traditional folk motifs, chains, pendants and coins, usually without inscriptions.

247   Schwartz-Be'eri, Ora. "Clothing of the Kurdish Jews." In *Encyclopaedia Iranica*. Vol. 5, pp. 825-826. Costa Mesa, CA: Mazda Publishers, 1992.

The description provided by the author of the clothing worn since the beginning of the 20th century by the Jews of Persian and Iraqi Kurdistan is based on field observations and interviews among the immigrant community in Israel and on a visit to northeastern Iran in 1974-1979. Describes fabrics and men and women dress.

248   Schwartz-Be'eri, Ora. "Kurdish Jewish Silversmiths and their Craft." *The International Journal of Kurdish Studies* 6, nos. 1-2 (Fall 1993): 12-24.

In the course of field research on the material culture of Jews who emigrated from Kurdistan to Israel, the author undertook a study of Kurdish Jewish silverwork. The research of the author was based on interviews with makers and owners of silver pieces, their families, and *hakhamim* (sages) who served as teachers, cantors, circumcisers, ritual slaughters, etc. Silver pieces from homes, synagogues, and museums were examined both in Israel and Iranian Kurdistan, as was Kurdish jewelry in the Museum of Ethnography, Berlin.

HEALTH AND CHILD CARE

249   Abramovitch, Iva Bader; Abramovitch, Henry H. "Enuresis in Cross-Cultural Perspective: A Comparison of Training for Elimination Control in Three Israeli Ethnic Groups." *Journal of Social Psychology* 129 (February 1989): 47-56.

Investigating enuresis in the context of different styles of training for bladder control—among Israeli Jews of Moroccan, Kurdish, or Eastern European descent—semi-structured interviews were conducted in ethnically homogeneous agricultural villages with 46 mothers of 248 children aged 3-18. In contrast to previous British and U.S. studies, no sex differences were found, but there were higher rates of primary enuresis. Lower rates of secondary (regressive) enuresis were correlated among siblings in the Kurdish group only and with disorderly sleeping arrangements in the Moroccan group. The Moroccan and Kurdish groups had higher rates of enuresis than the Ashkenazi (East European) group. The higher rates appear to be related to differences in the age of onset of training and a lack of age-appropriate changes in the parent-child interaction, which lead to chronic enuresis and the inability to seek effective assistance. These results are discussed in terms of a proposed typology for training: an early symbiotic style, a strict toddler style, and a communicative partnership. (*SA* 90: V2689)

250   Edholm, Otto Gustaf. *Biological Studies of Yemenite and Kurdish Jews in Israel.* Published as volume 266, no. 876 (October 18, 1973) of the *Philosophical Transactions of the Royal Society of London (B. Biological Sciences)*, pp. 83-224.

Two communities of Jews living in Israel were selected for study. They consisted of Jews from Kurdistan and from the Yemen. They lived in five villages in the Negev area of Israel where the climate is hot in the summer months and cool to warm in the winter months. Studies were carried out in the summer (June, July) and in the winter (January, February). The studies were confined to the age group 20 to 30, and 75% of the population in this age group were examined. The investigations comprised: (a) clinical examination, (b) anthropometric measurements, (c) genetic study of blood markers, (d) habitual activity, (e) energy expenditure, (f) food intake, (g) climatic exposure, (h) measurement of physical work capacity, and (i) reaction to a standardized heat test. The environmental conditions of the subjects were similar for the two groups and the majority were engaged in farming. (A)

251   Frankel, Daniel G.; Roer-Bornstein, Dorit. "Traditional and Modern Contributions to Changing Infant-rearing Ideologies of Two Ethnic Communities." *Monographs of the Society for Research in Child Development* 47, no. 4 (1982): 1-51.

The modernization of infant-rearing ideologies was investigated by interviewing grandmother and granddaughter generations of two ethnic communities—Yemenite and Kurdish Jews—about pregnancy and delivery, postpartum care of the mother and newborn, and infant care and development expectations. The sample was limited to 60 biologically unrelated women who lived in ethnically homogeneous semi-communal farming villages. Results show that both traditional and modern influences affected the contemporary infant-rearing ideologies of the two communities. Traditional differences in the emphasis on the mother-infant relationship, cognitive development, motor development and physical/biological effects on development and health, as well as relative differences in developmental expectations, all were reflected in the ideologies of the granddaughter generation. Modern contributions were indicated by a rejection of much traditional ritual and the demise of spiritual/magical explanation. Modernization was also associated with an attribution of greater competence to the young infant and an increased recognition of the psychological characteristics of infant development and the psychological demands of infant care taking. Yemenites were more accepting of psychological explanations, while Kurds were more accepting of the medical/biological/physical explanations of infant behavior and development. (A)

LANGUAGE AND COMMUNICATION

252   Chyet, Michael L. "Neo-Aramaic and Kurdish: An Interdisciplinary Consideration of their Influence on Each Other." *Israel Oriental Studies* 15 (1995): 219-252.

It is tempting to assume that when whole linguistic categories are transferred from one language to another, the speakers of the languages in question have been in extremely close contact over a number of generations. It is ironic, however, that for two peoples to be in contact, it is not necessary for them to be fond of each other. As a matter of fact, from among the languages I have studied, it is generally the peoples who are on worst terms whose languages have borrowed the most from each other. How such phenomena came to be shared is the topic of this paper, giving special attention to the relationship between Kurdish and Neo-Aramaic. Rather than merely assume that such a "love-hate relationship" obtains with regard to the speakers of Kurdish and the neighboring Neo-Aramaic languages, I have amassed evidence in an attempt to shed light on this question. Although many of these findings are not surprising in view of the historical facts, until such research is carried out for a given *Sprachbund,* many assertions must remain hypothetical. My purpose in this exploratory article is to bring us closer to rendering as fact much that has hitherto been limited to the realm of the educated guess. (A)

253   Cohen, David. "Neo-Aramaic." *Encyclopaedia Judaica*. CD-ROM edition. Shaker Heights, OH: Keter Publishing House Ltd., 1997.

254   Garbell, Irene. "The Impact of Kurdish and Turkish on the Jewish Neo-Aramaic Dialect of Persian Azerbaijan and the Adjoining Regions." *Journal of the American Oriental Society* 85 (1965): 159-177.

This paper is the outcome of a study of the Jewish Neo-Aramaic dialect spoken in Persian Azerbaijan and the adjoining vilayets of Van and Hakkari, which was undertaken with the aid of the Mary E. Woolley Fellowship awarded to the author by the International Federation of University Women for the year 1956-1957.

255   Hoberman, Robert D. *The Syntax and Semantics of Verb Morphology in Modern Aramaic: A Jewish Dialect of Iraqi Kurdistan*. New Haven, CT: American Oriental Society, 1989. xii, 226 p. Bibliography: p. [199]-212. [American Oriental Society; 69]

The book is based on fieldwork, but it does not present the recorded corpus as a whole. Rather, it undertakes to analyze only the verbal system, This limitation in breadth is amply compensated for by the depth of the investigation. In the introduction (ch. 1, pp. 1-40), the author takes the reader on a guided tour through the labyrinth of modern linguistic theo-

ries, selectively accepting or rejecting statements with regard to their usefulness for the subsequent analytical effort. Then he gives a rapid overview of Neo-Aramaic verb morphology. The following chapters, "The Inflectional Categories of the Verb" (ch. 2), "Subjects, Objects, and Verb
Morphology" (ch. 3), "The Semantics of Tense, Aspect, and Mood" (ch.
4), contain a deep analysis of forms, meanings, and functions of the verb
from all possible angles, resulting in the most complete description of the
Neo-Aramaic verb ever undertaken. The four chapters of the book are followed by four appendices, "Phonology," "The Order of Major Sentence
Constituents," "Sample Texts," and "Paradigms." They are succeeded in
turn by a rich bibliography of references and an index of verbal roots.
(Georg Krotkoff/*Journal of the American Oriental Society* 111, 1, 1991:
138-139)

256   Hoberman, Robert D. "Formal Properties of the Conjugations in Modern
      Aramaic." *Yearbook of Morphology* (1991): 49-64.

Several inflectional classes are found in most Semitic languages. These
classes are characterized by differences in the canonical syllable shape of
their stems and the vowel melodies assigned to them. The system of verb
inflectional classes (binyanim) in Modern Aramaic is simpler than in
most Semitic languages, providing a convenient subject for study. The
system of conjugation in the Aramaic dialect of the Jews of 'Amadiya in
Iraqi Kurdistan is examined. It argued that each of the only two binyanim
is abstract and may trigger various other morphological operations. However, assignment of verbs to one binyanim or the other results not from
arbitrary marking in the lexicon but from the operation of a phonological
factor, i.e., whether the verb is mono or disyllabic. The possibility that
binyanim in other Semitic languages is also abstract is discussed. (*SA* 93:
3766)

257   Khan, G. "The Neo-Aramaic Dialect Spoken by Jews from the Region of
      Arbel (Iraqi Kurdistan)." *Bulletin of the School of Oriental and African
      Studies* (University of London) 62, no. 2 (1999): 213-225.

Topics discussed include: (1) The Jewish Neo-Aramaic dialects of Kurdistan; (2) The dialect of "Arbel" region; and (3) The relation between "Arbel" dialect group and other groups (Urmia and Zakho regions).

258   Krotkoff, Georg. *A Neo-Aramaic Dialect of Kurdistan: Text, Grammer,
      and Vocabulary*. New Haven, Conn.: American Oriental Society, 1982.
      172 p. (American Oriental series; v. 64) Includes bibliographical refer-
      ences (p. [171]-172) and index.

The author of this exemplary monograph on the dialect of Aradhin
(northwest of 'Amadiya) collected the materials for this study in 1959
from an informant from Aradhin then living in Baghdad. For many years

Krotkoff delayed publishing the present full descriptive account. Krotkoff has compressed an astonishing amount of information into a grammar of only 58 pages, and with admirable clarity, by keeping exposition to a minimum and citing numerous illustrative examples. Each example cited in the grammar is marked with the paragraph number of its source in the texts (the texts are provided with a facing English translation), enabling the reader to evaluate any issue of interpretation on the basis of the complete context. The texts are followed by a list of proper names and nicknames, a full glossary, and a helpful list of roots.

259   Sabar, Yona. "Nursery Rhymes and Baby Words in the Jewish Neo-Aramaic Dialect of Zakho (Iraq)." *American Oriental Society Journal* 94 (July 1974): 329-336.

The purpose of this paper is to make available further linguistic data of the Jewish Neo-Aramaic dialect from Zakho (Iraq). The sixteen nursery rhymes and the baby words were collected by the author among his immediate relatives who now live in Jerusalem. The linguistic material is analyzed grammatically and etymologically in an appended glossary.

260   Sabar, Yona. "First Names, Nicknames and Family Names among the Jews of Kurdistan." *The Jewish Quarterly Review* 65 (1974-1975): 43-51.

This paper was originally delivered at the annual meeting of the American Oriental Society, Washington, March 20, 1973. It is based primarily on oral communication with Kurdish Jews in Israel and his personal acquaintance with the Jews of Zakho, Iraq, the author's hometown and the largest center of Kurdish Jews until their emigration to Israel.

261   Sabar, Yona. "The Impact of Israeli Hebrew on the Neo-Aramaic Dialect of the Kurdish Jews of Zakho: A Case of Language Shift." *Hebrew Union College Annual* 46 (1975): 489-508.

This article is based on two papers, one delivered at the Second North American Conference on Semitic Linguistics, March 25, 1974, and the other at the Western Regional Conference of the National association of Professors of Hebrew, March 27, 1974, both at Santa Barbara, California. The article is a linguistic study of phonology, morphology and syntax, and vocabulary of the newer immigrants (1950-1952) from an important Jewish center in Iraqi Kurdistan now living in Israel. For a number of socio-linguistic reasons, Israeli Hebrew is gradually superseding the Neo-Aramaic dialect. The author argues that Jewish Neo-Aramaic being deprived of its source and natural habitat is coming to an end.

262   Sabar, Yona. "The Arabic Elements in the Jewish Neo-Aramaic Texts of Nerwa and Amadiya, Iraqi Kurdistan." *Journal of the American Oriental Society* 104, no. 1 (1984): 201-211.

The Neo-Aramaic manuscripts from which these Arabic elements were gleaned were mostly copied in the second half of the 17th century. The texts, however, indicate an earlier tradition of literary style, whose traces are well observed in the religious literature of the Kurdish Jews to nthe present day. The multilingual vicinity of the towns of Nerwa and 'Amadiya, with its cross-section of various ancient and new cultures, Hebrew-Aramaic, Kurdish, Persian, Turkish, and, particularly, Arabic, had made a strong impact on this literary style. Sections covered include: orthography, phonology (consonants and vowels), morphology (nouns, qualifiers and verbs), and lexicology. (A)

263   Sabar, Yona. "General European Loan Words in the Jewish New-Aramaic Dialect of Zakho, Iraqi Kurdistan." In *Studies in Neo-Aramaic*. Edited by Wolfhart Heinrichs, pp. 53-66. Atlanta, GA: Scholars Press, 1990.

Neo-Aramaic, like other old and new Semitic languages, has incorporated a certain number of loanwords from European languages. These loanwords are mostly from the semantic areas of modern technology, general western culture and medicine. Most of these words were probably incorporated in the spoken Neo-Aramaic dialect of the Jews of Zakho during the 1940's, just prior to their emigration en masse to Israel during 1950-51. They have been gleaned from the author's *Dictionary of Jewish Neo-Aramaic* and from his personal knowledge of the dialect. Sections covered include: orthography, phonology (consonants and vowels), morphology (nouns, qualifiers and verbs), and lexicology. Sections covered include: general notes, phonological observations, morphological observations, lexical observations, and list of the loanwords.

264   Sabar, Yona. "The Christian Neo-Aramaic Dialects of Zakho and Dihok: Two Text Samples." *Journal of the American Oriental Society* 115 (January-March 1995): 33-51.

Two texts illustrating the Christian Neo-Aramaic dialects of Zakho and Dohuk spoken in Iraqi Kurdistan are compared with each other and with adjacent Christian and Jewish dialects. The Zakho example is made up of a monologue and responses to a journalist's questions by a Chaldean Catholic priest. The Dohuk example comprises both casual conversation and responses to specific questions by an educated and wealthy Chaldean layman. It is noted that the latter employs a plain colloquial style that differs from the priests eloquent, rhetorical style. The interviews are printed in both phonetic transcription and English translations. Selected semantic and grammatical features of the layman's and priest's texts are analyzed.

LITERATURE AND FOLKLORE

265   Blau, Joyce. "Les Juifs au Kurdistan." [The Jews of Kurdistan] In *Melanges Linguistiques offerts a Maxime Rodinson*. Edited by Ch. Robin, pp. 123-132. Paris: Geuthner, 1985. (Suppl. aux Comptes Rendus du Groupe Linquistique d'Etudes ch. Amito-semitiques, 12).

Blau has gathered Jerusalem folkloric texts from Jews who came from Iraqi and Iranian Kurdistan. The collected texts are part of the Kurdish rich folkloric background. The folkloric corpus is preceded by a brief introduction of the history of the numerous Jewish communities (146) that lived in harmony with the agro-pastoral Muslim, Christian and Yezidi populations of Kurdistan. (*AI* 9: 875)

266   Gerstein, Mordicai. *The Shadow of a Flying Bird: A Legend of the Kurdistani Jews*. New York: Hyperion Books for Children, 1994. Retold and illustrated by Mordicai Gerstein. Includes ills.

Dedicated to the memory of Gerstein's father, who died in 1991, this strikingly illustrated picture book may be more of a catharsis for its author than a comfort to its target audience. Using a story found in the literature of the Kurdistani Jews, Gerstein presents a moving and evocative account of Moses and his last days on earth. Moses was one hundred and twenty years old when God showed him the Promised Land from the top of Mount Nebo and told him that he would never enter the land because he had come to the end of his days. When Moses pleads for more days, he is told that even a thousand years would seem like one day, that "A man or woman's life is like the shadow of a flying bird." Closing heaven's doors and windows to the prayers of Moses, God declares, "Everything born has a time to die. I cannot change that." Moses pleads with the hills and mountains and with the sun, moon, and the stars to intercede on his behalf; they answer that, in time, they too must come to an end. Thus Moses accepts his fate, but God's angels, Gabriel, Michael, and Zagzagle, are all unwilling to take Moses's soul. Only Sammael, the angel of death, wrapped "in a cape of hate, envy, and rage," is willing to go, but he is defeated by Moses's piety. Finally, the celestial presence of God descends and, with a kiss, takes Moses's soul. When God grieves over the death of his faithful servant, the angels comfort him by saying, "In death as in life, Moses is yours," and Moses's soul responds, "Always and forever!" Gerstein's oil paintings convey the magnitude of the heavenly debate with majestic, star-strewn images of the deity in contrast to the small, sculptural figure of Moses wrapped in white robes and standing on a mountain top. This biblical legend leaves a powerful image of death as the inevitable partner of life. (Hanna B. Zeiger/ *The Horn Book Magazine* 71, no. 2, March-April 1995: 205-206)

267   Noy, Dov. "Is There a Jewish Folk Religion?" In *Studies in Jewish Folk-lore: Proceedings of a Regional Conference of the Association for Jewish Studies Held at the Spertus College of Judaica, Chicago May 1-3, 1977*. Edited by Frank Talmadge, pp. 273-286. Cambridge, MA: Association for Jewish Studies, 1980.

Jewish folk religion is described here as the beliefs, rites and customs considered by the 'folk' as a part of their religion but not found in and even opposed to the official normative codes. The author analyzes in detail a story from a Kurdish informant in Jerusalem, which expresses some central characteristics of Jewish folk-religion. It is emphasized as a conclusion that "the element of tension which exists between folk and official levels of religion…is absent in Jewish folk religion, as the observers and performers see their views and practices as part of the official religion."

268   Rand, Barukh; Rush, Barbara. *Jews of Kurdistan*. Toledo: Toledo Board of Jewish Education, 1978. 67 p.

Presents ten folktales told by the Jews who once lived in Kurdistan.

269   Sabar, Yona. "Lel-Huza: Story and History in a Cycle of Lamentations for the Ninth of Av in the Jewish Neo-Aramaic Dialect of Zakho, Iraqi Kurdistan." *Journal of Semitic Studies* 21 (1976): 138-162.

This article is a publication and analysis of an important Kurdistani folk-epic, 'Lel Huza.' Lel Huza or 'the demon of Judea' is a cycle of three narratives sung by Kurdistani women on the night of 9th of Av. The author describes the performance and its elements, the structure of the cycle, its sources and language. The second part of the article consists of the publication of the original Neo-Aramaic text (in Latin transcription). This publication is a good example of a text which very few informants still remembered (in the 1960s) and which without its recording by a scholar would have disappeared.

270   Sabar, Yona. "A Survey of the Oral and Written Literature of the Kurdish Jews." In *Pesat Wayehi Besallah. A Neo-Aramaic Midrash on Beshallah (Exodus)* by Yona Sabar, 161-178. Wiesbaden: s.n., 1976.

This is a condensed survey of some types of Jewish folk-literature in Kurdistan. The author emphasizes the relationships between oral and written literature and the linguistic character of the literature. The genres discussed here (folktales and legends) are not classified according to the theory of genres in folklore.

271   Sabar, Yona. "Multilingual Proverbs in the Neo-Aramaic Speech of the Jews of Zakho, Iraqi Kurdistan." *International Journal of Middle East Studies* 9 (1978): 215-235.

The author has collected 153 Aramaic proverbs from Zakho, presented in their cultural-linguistic context. The proverbs were collected from Jews who immigrated to Israel. The author emphasizes the relationships between the different ethnic groups in Iraqi Kurdistan as reflected in the Jewish proverbs. This material is also very useful for the study of the linguistic integration of different ethnic groups in Israel.

272   Sabar, Yona. "Kurdistani Realia and Attitudes in the Midrashic-Aggadic Literature of the Kurdish Jews." In *Studies in Jewish Folklore: Proceedings of a Regional Conference of the Association for Jewish Studies Held at the Spertus College of Judaica, Chicago May 1-3, 1977*. Edited by Frank Talmadge, pp. 287-296. Cambridge, MA: Cambridge University Press, 1980.

The author classifies the literature of the Kurdish Jews into four categories: Midrashic-Agadic literature in Hebrew, Midrashic-Agadic literature in Neo-Aramaic dialects, epic versions of Agadic literature and narratives and lamentations performed orally by and for women. In the second part of his article, the author demonstrates how the life, folk-beliefs and attitudes of the Kurdish Jews are reflected in the above-mentioned types of folk literature.

273   Sabar, Yona (tr.). *The Folk Literature of the Kurdistani Jews: An Anthology*. Translated from Hebrew and Neo-Aramaic Sources, with introduction and notes by Yona Sabar. New Haven, Conn.: Yale University Press, 1982. 250 p. [Yale Judaica Series, 23.]

The Aramaic-speaking Kurdish Jews are members of an ancient Jewish community that, until its emigration to Israel, was one of the most isolated in the world. Throughout their long and turbulent history, these Jews maintained in oral form a wealth of Jewish literary traditions embellished with local folklore. This volume is the first translation and anthology of their richly imaginative literature. Sabar, himself a Kurdish Jew, offers representative selections from the types of Kurdistani literature: epic recreations of biblical stories, Midrashic legends, folktales about local rabbis, moralistic anecdotes, folk songs, nursery rhymes, sayings, and proverbs. Sabar's introduction and notes are a storehouse of information on the history and spiritual life of the Kurdish Jews and on their relationship to the land of Israel. Because almost all the Kurdish Jews now live in Israel and speak Hebrew, there is very little new literary activity in their Neo-Aramaic dialects. This delightful anthology captures the essence of Kurdish Jewish literature, presenting it for public enjoyment and preserving it for the future.

274   Sabar, Yona. "Studies of the Folklore, Ethnography and Literature of Kurdistani Jews: An Annotated Bibliography." *Jewish Folklore and Ethnology Review* 11, no. 1-2 (1989): 35-38.

275   Shai, Donna. "A Kurdish Jewish Variant of the Ballad of ('The Bridge over Arta')" *Association for Jewish Studies Review* 1 (1976): 303-310.

The ballad 'The Bridge of Arta,' about the girl who was buried alive as a sacrifice for a bridge, was previously considered to exist only in the folk literature of the Balkan Peninsula. The author publishes a Kurdish Jewish version of the ballad in Neo-Aramaic and English translation, and states that the Kurdish version appears to bear great resemblance to the Biblical theme of Jephtah's daughter and international themes and elements from the Muslim Kurdish environment.

276   Shai, Donna. "A Kurdish-Jewish Animal Tale in Its Sociocultural Context." In *Studies in Jewish Folklore: Proceedings of a Regional Conference of the Association for Jewish Studies Held at the Spertus College of Judaica, Chicago May 1-3, 1977*. Edited by Frank Talmadge, pp. 297-306. Cambridge, MA: Association for Jewish Studies, 1980.

The basic hypothesis of the article is that the "boundaries of humanness are defined through the animal metaphor." The author discusses here the tale about the fox that knows a hundred tricks but is caught by the hunters while the cat, which knows only one trick, climbs the tree and is saved. The author suggests that the "powerless minority... Kurdish Jews may identify with the trickster fox who lives by his wits" (in this Kurdish version the fox outlives the lion).

277   Shai, Donna. "Changes in the Oral Tradition among the Jews of Kurdistan." *Contemporary Jewry* 5 (Spring-Summer 1980): 2-10.

Prior to their migration to Israel in the 1950s, the Kurdish Jews of Iraq had developed an important tradition in oral literature, characterized by linguistic diversity, the use of both Jewish and Islamic literary and historical sources and other influences. According to a commonly accepted scholarly perspective, the modernizing elements in the movement to Israel presumably would weaken this tradition. This presumed weakening was tested among immigrants to Israel from Zakho, Kurdistan, by field research on folk songs and tales conducted in Israel between 1971 and 1974. Rather than the Kurdistan oral tradition being harmed by the immigration experience, analysis of recording indicates that Kurdish Jews have demonstrated a creative use of Israeli or Zionist themes in their folk tradition, and have been encouraged to continue their traditional expressive forms. (*SA* 83M: 9252)

SOCIAL LIFE AND CUSTOMS

278   Brauer, Erich. *The Jews of Kurdistan*. Completed and edited by Raphael Patai. Detroit: Wayne State University Press, 1993. 429 p.

Following World War II, members of the sizable Jewish community in
Iraqi Kurdistan left their homeland and resettled in Palestine where they
were quickly assimilated with the dominant Israeli-Jewish culture. Anthropologist Erich Brauer interviewed a large number of these Kurdish
Jews and wrote *The Jews of Kurdistan* prior to his death in 1942. Raphael
Patai completed the manuscript left by Brauer, translated it into Hebrew,
and had it published in 1947. This new English-language volume, completed and edited by Patai, makes a unique ethnological monograph available to the wider scholarly community, and, at the same time, serves as a
monument to a scholar whose work has to this day remained largely unknown outside the narrow circle of Hebrew-reading anthropologists. *The
Jews of Kurdistan* is a unique historical document in that it presents a picture of Kurdish Jewish life and culture prior to World War II. It is the
only ethnological study of the Kurdish Jews ever written and provides a
comprehensive look at their material culture, life cycles, religious practices, occupations, and relations with the Muslims. In 1950-51, with the
mass immigration of Kurdish Jews to Israel, their world as it had been before the war suddenly ceased to exist. This book reflects the life and culture of a Jewish community that has disappeared from the country it had
inhabited from antiquity. In his preface, Raphael Patai offers data he considers important for supplementing Brauer's book, and comments on the
book's values and limitations fifty years after Brauer wrote it. Patai has
included additional information elicited from Kurdish Jews in Jerusalem,
verified quotations, corrected some passages that were inaccurately translated from Hebrew authors, completed the bibliography, and added occasional references to parallel traits found in other Oriental Jewish communities.

279   Cohen, Claudine. *Grandir au quartier kurde: rapports de generations et
        modeles culturels d'un groupe d'adolescents israeliens d'origine kurde*.
        [Growth of a Kurdish neighborhood: a report of a generation and cultural
        models of a group of Israeli adolescents of Kurdish origin] Paris: Institut
        d'ethnologie Musee de l'homme, 1975. 184 p.: ill. (Memoires de l'Institut
        d'ethnologie. 12.)

280   Epstein, Shiftan. "The Jews of Kurdistan." *Ariel* [Jerusalem], no. 51
        (1982): 65-78.

This article is based on a survey of the material culture of Kurdish Jewry
held by the Department of Jewish Ethnography at the Israel Museum, Jerusalem between 1974 and 1981. Ora Schwartz-Be'eri conducted the survey and interviewed more than 300 people in some 35 Kurdish-Jewish
settlements in Israel. In 1977 she visited Iranian Kurdistan where she was
able to observe, document and photograph Jewish life intact. As a result
of the survey an exhibition, "The Jews of Kurdistan," was mounted at the
Museum in September 1981.

281   Feitelson, Dina. "Aspects of the Social Life of Kurdish Jews." *The Jewish Journal of Sociology* 1, no. 2 (1959): 201-216. Reprinted in *Jewish Societies in the Middle East: Community, Culture and Authority*. Edited by Shlomo Deshen and Walter P. Zenner (Washington, DC: University Press of America, 1982), pp. 251-272.

The mass exodus of Kurdish Jews to Israel in 1951 ended the stream of emigrants from the Kurdish mountains of Iraq which has been taking place for the past 40 years by transferring the whole group to Israel. From fieldwork undertaken in 1953-1954 an attempt is made to reconstruct the old social patterns of this group, since "at that time the impact of new surroundings and institutions had as yet left intact many of the usage practiced in Iraq." The following aspects of Kurdish life are treated: (1) The Community—physical surroundings, occupation, and Jews and their neighbors; (2) Culture-language and religion; (3) The Household—the dwelling, extended family, cohesion of the extended family, the men, and womanhood and its tasks; and (4) The Life Cycle of the Individual— marriage, the baby, the toddler, boy becomes man, and girl grows into woman.

282   Fischel, Walter J. "The Jews of Kurdistan: A Hundred Years Ago." *Jewish Social Studies* 6 (1945): 195-226.

The author of this article was a member of the faculty of the Hebrew University at Jerusalem. He gives an interesting account of the visit of Rabbi David D'Beth Hillel to the Jewish communities in Kurdistan (1824-28), and in addition to copious notes, he provides the reader with a map of the region. The article should be of special interest to people studying missionaries in Iran and Iraq.

283   Fischel, Walter J. "The Jews of Kurdistan: A First Hand Report on a Near Eastern Mountain Community." *Commentary* 8 (December 1949): 554-559.

284   Magnarella, Paul J. "A Note on Aspects of Social Life among the Jewish Kurds of Sanandaj, Iran." *The Jewish Journal of Sociology* 11 (June 1969): 51-58.

Data were collected in 1967-68 on the Jewish Kurds of Sanandaj, Iran, through one female, 28-years old native from this city. A few other sources are also used. The number of the Jewish Kurds of Iran was estimated then at 3,000-4,000. Many of them immigrated to Israel in the 1950s, while Jewish Kurds from Iraq sought refuge in Iran. Iranian Jewish Kurds speak both Kurdish and Persian in public, and "Jewish Kurdish" in their homes. At that time, there were two private Jewish schools in Sanandaj, one for boys (grades 1-9), the other for girls (grades 1-6). About 70% of the working Jewish Kurds of Sanandaj were employed in private familiar business, e.g., retail shops, cloth merchants, or MD's in private practice. Most of the remaining 30% work for the government. On the average, their standard of living was better than that of the Muslim Kurds. The ideal household was extended-patrilocal, but in practice, this was modified by a number of factors. The actual household composition was kept in flux due to education, business transfer, government assignment and military service of individuals in the family. The Jewish Kurds were concentrated in a special quarter of the city for residential and business purposes, though some of their shops were interspersed with those of Muslims in the larger bazaars. Polygamy was allowed, but rarely practiced. A male Jewish Kurd may marry any female in his own generation except his sister, niece, or daughter-in-law. Marriage with the matrilateral or patrilateral parallel cousin was preferred. A few marriages with Muslims have taken place. Some components of the marriage contract are described.

285   Magnarella, Paul J. "Jewish Kurds of Iran." *Jewish Digest* 15 (April 1970): 17-20.

286   Miller, E. "The Jewish Village that Moved to Israel." *Jewish Digest* 25 (April 1980): 33-37.

287   Shai, Donna. "Wedding Customs among Kurdish Jews in Zakho (Kurdistan) and in Jerusalem (Israel)." *Studies in Marriage Customs, Folklore Research Center Studies* 4 (1974): 253-266.

This article is divided into three parts. In the first two parts, the author describes the wedding customs that were prevalent in the Jewish community in Kurdistan prior to their immigration and contemporary wedding ceremonies in Jerusalem. The third part is an analysis of the changes that these customs underwent during the acculturation process. The changes are divided into five categories: deletions, additions, substitutions, rearrangements and transformations.

288   Shai, Donna. "Public Cursing and Social Control in a Traditional Jewish Community." *Western Folklore* 37 (January 1978): 39-46.

After some introductory remarks and definitions, the author discusses attitudes toward cursing in traditional Jewish literature. The author then describes cursing in public among Kurdish Jews in Israel, with particular reference to concepts of honor and shame, self-image, and local norms. Finally, the author discusses how traditional Jewish attitude towards cursing may affect the social behavior of persons in a situation of interpersonal conflict.

289   Shai, Donna. "Family Conflict and Cooperation in Folksongs of Kurdish Jews." In *Jewish Societies in the Middle East: Community, Culture and*

Authority. Edited by Shlomo Deshen and Walter P. Zenner, pp. 273-284. Washington, DC: University Press of America, 1982.

The author amplifies knowledge of Kurdish Jews by making use of their folksongs as texts for understanding their social world. Like many anthropologists, Shai assumes that words recited at important rites of passage like weddings and funerals reflect underlying tensions which exist in the society. She is particularly concerned with the role of women among the Jews of Kurdistan. Contrary to certain stereotypes, she finds that women could exercise considerable authority in certain spheres of activity, such as mate selection, and, like Feitelson, Shai's work shows the heterogeneous nature of the Kurdish region. (A)

290   Shapiro, O. "Nissam: A Hill Village Settled by Kurds." In *Rural Settlements of New Immigrants in Israel*. Edited by O. Shapiro, pp. 103-124. Rehovot, Israel: Settlement Study Center, 1971.

291   Soen, Dan; Ezrachi, Ruth. "Kurdish Immigrants: Culture Contact and Social Adjustment in Israel." *Sociologus* 40, no. 2 (1990): 97-120.

Discusses general problems of immigration and absorption of the different Jewish groups then discusses the general background of the Jewish community of Sanandaj, the capital of Iranian Kurdistan. The author then discusses the community's immigration to Israel, the hardships along the way, and absorption and adjustment.

WOMEN

292   Sered, Susan Starr. "The Liberation of Widowhood." *Journal of Cross-Cultural Gerontology* 2 (April 1987): 139-150.

An important aspect of the religious world of a group of elderly, pious, Kurdish Jewish women in Jerusalem, Israel, is examined, based on fieldwork. While previous scholars have stressed the connection between menopause (with the resultant loss in fertility, but also menstrual pollution) and the increased religious involvement of old women, it is argued that the broadening of the religious lives that these women experience in old age is connected above all to widowhood. The women studied see old age (and more specifically widowhood) as a time for deepening and expanding their religious lives. Now that they are no longer busy with the demands of husbands and small children, they can devote increased time and energy to religious pursuits. Specifically, the focus of their religious world shifts from the domestic to the public sphere. The synagogue, senior citizen's day center, cemeteries, and holy tombs are the most important public, sacred spaces frequented. (*SA* 88T3147)

293   Sered, Susan Starr. "The Synagogue as a Sacred Space for the Elderly
Oriental Women of Jerusalem." In *Daughters of the King: Women and
the Synagogue: A Survey of History, Halakhah, and Contemporary Realities*. Edited by Susan Grossman and Rivka Haut, pp. 205-216. Philadelphia: Jewish Publication Society, 1992.

While the notion of setting aside certain space as "sacred" or "holy" may
be universal, there is considerable variation in the location, the content,
and the nature of the activities carried out in such spaces. Furthermore,
even within one particular cultural context, different categories of people
may have access to or make different uses of the various spaces that are
identified as sacred. This chapter focuses on the use of one particular type
of sacred space (that is, the synagogue), by one particular Jewish population (elderly oriental Kurdish women living in Jerusalem).

294   Sered, Susan Starr. *Women as Ritual Experts: The Religious Lives of
Elderly Jewish Women in Jerusalem*. New York, NY: Oxford University
Press, 1992. 174 p. Includes bibliographical references (p. 161-169) and
index

A number of studies have noted the effects of modernization upon the
lives of women. As the traditional extended family disintegrates and
wage-labor replaces reciprocity, women often lose the power that derived
from their traditional social and economic expertise and from their kin-
and village-based support networks. In this chapter the author asks how
modernization affects women's religious lives. This question has received
little attention in studies of religious change, which have looked almost
exclusively at men's experiences. At the time of the author's fieldwork,
the female-oriented religious traditions of the Day Center women were
deeply threatened both by modern secular culture and by the masculine,
Ashkenazi religious establishment in Israel. Despite the rather vulnerable
status of women's religion, the Day Center women felt that modern Israel
provided them with new and meaningful opportunities for religious expression. Their interest in novel religious activities, however, was tem-
pered by their awareness of the decline of other of their rituals. Most of
the discussion concerns Kurdish Jews because the majority of the women
at the Day Center are Kurdish. (A)

295   Sered, Susan Starr. "The Religious World of Jewish Women in Kurdi-
stan." In *Jews among Muslims: Communities in the Precolonial Middle
East*. Edited by Shlomo Deshen and Walter P. Zenner, pp. 197-214. New
York: New York University Press, 1996.

Despite a promising early beginning, with the work of Erich Brauer in the
1930s, followed by Dina Feitelson in the 1950s, Donna Shai and Yona
Sabar in the 1970s, the study of Kurdish Jewry has not developed much
over the years. Those scholars attempted to reconstruct conditions in

Kurdistan on the base of fieldwork among immigrants in Israel, and they contended with the difficulties of doing "ethnography at a distance." But they lacked an advantage that other scholars had, who worked in a similar way in the field of North African Jewry. The latter benefited from a tradition of major anthropological scholarship, the work of Westermarck, Gellner, Geertz and numerous other leading anthropologists. That led to a rich corpus of theory, and hence the interest in the work of both Judaists and Islamists of North Africa. Work in the Kurdish field had little theoretical focus. The importance of the work of Susan Sered, Associate Professor of Anthropology at Bar-Ilan University, is that it breaks away from the old model of work in the Kurdish field, and operates with a theoretical model. It is part of the wave of feminist anthropology, which evinces afresh sensitivity to the activities of women and explores their particularities. This probing leads the present study, devoted to religiosity, to the discovery of a shade of piety that, Sered argues, constitutes a female specialty. The women were concerned in particular with practices that would be auspicious for the home and its members. They were little concerned with matters beyond the circle of intimacy. Sered brings evidence that Kurdish Jewish women even conceptualized the great Jewish national themes in terms of personally relevant matters. The author suggests that these traits constitute a 'nurturing characteristic' of Kurdish Jewish women's religiosity. The theoretical thrust of the paper leads the author at the end to raise questions in the general field of religion. (A)

10
Journalism, Mass Communication, and Freedom of the Press

296 Davidson, L. "Images for a Resistance: The Birth of Kurdish Television." *Vertigo*, no. 2 (1993): 8-11.

297 Davidson, L. "Rising from the Ruins: Local TV Helps Define a New Kurdish Identity." *The Independent* 16 (April 1993): 24-28.

298 Duran, Ragip. "Freedom of Expression and the Press: Turkish National Press Coverage of Kurdish Issues." In *A Democratic Future for the Kurds of Turkey*, pp. 67-74. Proceedings of the International Conference on North West Kurdistan (Southeast Turkey)... 1994. Brussels; London: Medico International, Frankfurt and Kurdistan Human Rights Project, 1995.

299 Edmonds, Cecil John. "A Kurdish Newspaper: 'Rozh-i-Kurdistan'." *Journal of the Royal Central Asian Society* 12 (1925): 83-90.

Discusses the reasons for the emergence of Kurdish written language and by what means. Gives the example of the Kurdish newspaper 'Rozh-i-Kurdistan'.

300 Hassanpour, Amir. *A Stateless Nation's Quest for Sovereignty in the Sky*. Paper presented at the Freie Universitat Berlin, November 7, 1995.

This paper begins with a brief account of the Kurds, their distribution in the Middle East and Europe, and their status as a non-state nation. The next section is about MED-TV's history, its organization, and programming. Section three provides information on Ankara's repression of the television program in Turkey and Europe. The concluding part deals with the political implications of Turkey's practice for Europe and the evolving international communication system. (A)

301   Hassanpour, Amir. "The Creation of Kurdish Media Culture." In *Kurdish Culture and Identity*. Edited by Philip G. Kreyenbroek and Christine Allison, pp. 48-84. Atlantic Highlands, NJ: Zed Books, 1996.

Kurdish society is often viewed, by both the specialist and the general public, as tribal or pastoral-nomadic. The culture and language of this society are accordingly perceived as oral and unwritten, or 'local' varieties of the dominant cultures and languages of the Middle East—Arabic, Persian and Turkish. Although these constructions of Kurdish culture are rooted in identifiable ideological and political terrains, ranging from racism to romanticizing, it must be conceded that knowledge of the topic is restricted by a dearth of information and research. This chapter examines one understudied process of cultural change in Kurdish society—the rise and spread of a media culture since the end of the nineteenth century.

302   Hassanpour, Amir. "Satellite Footprints as National Borders: Med-TV and the Extraterritoriality of State Sovereignty." *Journal of Muslim Minority Affairs* 18, no. 1 (1998): 53-72.

The launching of the first Kurdish satellite television channel opened a new site of conflict between the Kurds and the Middle Eastern states that rule over Kurdistan. Failing to achieve self-rule in Turkey, Iran, Iraq and Syria after decades of armed resistance, the Kurds feel that they have achieved sovereignty in the sky.

303   Hassanpour, Amir. "The MED-TV Story: Kurdish Satellite TV Station Defies All Odds." *InterRadio* 10, no. 2 (December 1998): 8-9.

MED-TV has become a national television station for the Kurds—the largest nation in the world today without a recognized homeland. The author analyzes how, despite Turkey's sever repression of the Kurdish right to communicate, this virtual community television station is an example of the openings created by new information and communications technologies.

304   Human Rights Watch. *Turkey: Violations of Free Expression in Turkey*. New York: Human Rights Watch, 1999. 122 p.

This report examines the state of free expression in Turkey. It focuses largely on the print and broadcast media, and to a lesser extent on freedom of speech in politics. The report deals with the period from 1995 to 1999; when necessary, however, earlier periods are also explored. This study uses representative cases of newspapers, authors or writers, and political groups to highlight violations of the internationally-protected right to free expression.

305   International Association for Human Rights in Kurdistan. *The Kurds and Kurdistan: Thinking is a Crime: Report on Freedom of Expression in Turkey*. Bonn: International Association For Human Rights in Kurdistan, 1996. 52 p. Includes bibliographical references.

This report presents the Turkish laws regarding freedom of expression in the country and then goes on to describe the suppression of both Kurdish and Turkish newspapers and journalists, censorship and banning of Kurdish books, prosecution of authors and publishing houses, prohibition of freedom of speech and Kurdish music.

306   Gundem, Ozgur; Ulke, Yeni. *How Journalists Are Murdered in Kurdistan*. Cologne, Germany: Representation of Ozgur Gundem Newspaper in Europe, 1993. 151 p. Includes ills, portraits, plates, facsimiles.

307   Petley, J. "Dishing the Dirt - Satellite Television in Kurdish Language: Med-TV." *Index on Censorship* 28, no. 4 (July-August 1999): 27-30.

Med-TV is a Kurdish-language satellite television station funded by investors from Kurdish communities in Europe. In April, the Independent Television Commission (ITC) revoked Med's license; the station had breached the ITC's clauses on impartiality and incitement to violence.

308   Rasul, 'Izz al-Din Mustafa. *Hawla al-Sahafa al-Kurdiyah*. Baghdad: Dar al-Jahiz, 1973. 39 p.

Discusses the contributions and the problems of Kurdish journalism in relation to the national liberation movement.

309   Woker, M. "Press Freedom under Attack in Turkey." *Swiss Review of World Affairs* 12 (December 1994): 21-22.

Daily press reports of clashes in eastern and southeastern Turkey between Turkish troops and partisans of the Kurdish workers party (PKK) are an old and familiar story. Most domestic publications take sides, supporting either the Turkish government or the armed Kurdish opposition. Independent reporting on the quasi civil war is almost unobtainable, as both parties try to manipulate journalists for their own purposes. Ankara denies international groups access to the conflict zone, and massive human rights violations go almost unnoticed by the international community.

310   Zimmerman, Ann. "Culture after Saddam: Video Artists Restore a Country's Identity in Iraqi Kurdistan." *High Performance* 17 (Spring 1994): 32-35.

Television and video as an outlet for political opposition in Iraqi Kurdistan are discussed. The author mentions that the Iraqi Kurdish opposition operates three television channels in the Kurdish language; these, however, are monitored by Saddam Hussein's intelligence. Each television station supports local artists, public commentary, and special interest representatives that were formerly censured by the Ba'th regime. Previously censored videotapes of government atrocities are also discussed.

See also items: 3, 8, 19, 20, 21, 159, 175, 298, 304, 305, 306, 309, 374, 430, 432, 525, 526, 530, 691, 693

11

Kurdish Diaspora

EUROPE

311   Ammann, Birgit. "Ethnische Identitat am Beispiel kurdischer Migration in Europa." In *Ethnizitat, Nationalismus, Religion und Politik in Kurdistan*. Edited by Carsten Borck, Eva Savelsberg, and Siamend Hajo, pp. 217-238. Mèunster: Lit, 1997. [In German]

312   Blau, Joyce. "Le Roman en Kurmanji dans la Diaspora Kurde Europeenne." In *Enjeux de l'immigration turque en Europe: les Turcs en France et en Europe: actes du colloque international de Strasbourg, 25-26 février 1991*. Edited by Alain Jund, Paul Dumont, and Stéphane de Tapia, pp. 123-128. Paris: CIEMI: L'Harmattan, 1995.

313   Boeschoten, Hendrik; Dorleijn, Margreet; Leezenberg, Michiel. "Turkish, Kurdish and other Languages from Turkey." In *Community Languages in the Netherlands*. Edited by Extra Guus and Ludo Th. Verhoeven, pp. 109-142. Amsterdam, Netherlands: Swets and Zeitlinger, 1993.

The use and acquisition of Turkish, Kurdish, and Christian language varieties spoken in the Netherlands are examined. Turkish is one of three languages with an officially acknowledged status in the Netherlands and has a well-defined place in the educational system. Turk, Kurd, and Christian minority communities are sketched, language choice patterns are addressed, and the status of varieties is compared. The relative dominant status of Turkish is supported by Dutch governmental policies.

314   Bozarslan, Hamit. "L'immigration kurde." [Kurdish immigration] *Migrants Formation*, no. 101 (1995): 115-129.

315   Bruinessen, Martin van. "Shifting National and Ethnic Identities: The
          Kurds in Turkey and the European Diaspora." *Journal of Muslim Minor-
          ity Affairs (JMMA)* 18, no.1 (April 1998): 39-52.

          In this paper, van Bruinessen examines the shifting national ethnic identi-
          ties of the Kurds living in Turkey, Iran and Iraq. He argues that the Turk-
          ish "national building" strategies that worked in the 1920s and 1930s
          seem to have the reverse effect today. Also discusses the impact of Kurds
          in Europe on the Kurdish national movement in Turkey.

316   Elmas, Hasan Basri. "Exode rural et migration des Turcs et des Kurdes
          vers l'Europe." *Hommes et Migrations*, no. 1212 (1998): 5-13.

317   Nezan, Kendal. "Les Kurdes, un Peuple en Detresse." *Hommes et Migra-
          tions* (November 1988): 29-35.

318   Ostergaard-Nielsen, Eva. "Trans-state Loyalties and Politics of Turks and
          Kurds in Western Europe." *SAIS Review* 20, no. 1 (Winter-Spring 2000):
          23-38.

          The author's analysis of Kurdish and Turkish communities in Germany
          and the Netherlands illustrates how diaspora activities affect politics in
          the homeland and the host country. In so doing, they break down the dis-
          tinction between domestic and foreign politics.

CANADA

319   Gardner, Sheena; Polyzoi, Eleoussa; Rampaul, Yvette. "Individual Vari-
          ables, Literacy History, and ESL Progress Among Kurdish and Bosnian
          Immigrants." *TESL Canada Journal* 14, no. 1 (Winter 1996): 1-20.

          An examination of the relationship between individual variables and Eng-
          lish as a second language progress among Kurdish (n=9) and Bosnian
          (n=7) adult immigrants, who arrived in Canada with virtually no English.
          Significant correlations are found in test data between oral and written
          progress, and literacy level, years of schooling, and ethnicity. Contin-
          gency, text quality, and text quantity are also examined. Given the limita-
          tions of this study, it is hypothesized that in 18-21 months high literates
          will progress from low beginner to advanced, semi-literates from pre-
          beginner to low intermediate, and pre-literates from pre-beginner to low
          beginner. Implications for course programming are outlined.

320   Higgitt, Nancy C.; Horne, Lena. "Resettlement Experiences: Refugees
          from Kurdistan and Vietnam." *Canadian Home Economics Journal* 49,
          no. 1 (1999): 24-31.

Compares how the two ethnic groups attempt to interact with Canadian society, and discusses the difficulties they face in the assimilation process. Based on focus group interviews conducted with Kurdish and Vietnamese refugees resettled in Manitoba, Canada, 1994.

321   Peralta, Judith B. *The Kurds in Canada: A Question of Ethnic Identity*. Master's Thesis. Carleton University, 1997. 101 p.

Kurdish ethnic identity in Canada has been shaped by a complex process. Some of the factors included in this process are the history of Kurds in Kurdistan, subsequent immigration experiences in Canada, and Kurdish politics and demographics, which all play a significant role. Factors which mitigated against the development of a Kurdish nation-state influence attempts by Kurdish refugees in Canada to create and maintain a shared sense of Kurdish identity. Identity among many Kurds is politicized. There exist external factors which are central issues for Kurds in their countries of origin. These external factors in turn have become important aspects of the Kurdish communities' discourse on what it means to be a Kurdish Canadian. The object of this thesis is to examine the construction of Kurdish ethnic identity in an immigrant context. The main purpose of this thesis is to provide an ethnic perspective through Kurdish narratives. However, since ethnic identity is the result of both in-group definitions as well as definitions imposed by outsiders, according to the author, she examines how Kurdish identity is also a response to categorization by, and power conflicts with outsiders. This reflects a dialogue between divisions which were externally imposed in their countries of origin, and those which are produced by internal divisions in Kurdish Canadian communities. (A)

322   Smith, C. "Kurds." In *Encyclopedia of Canada's Peoples*. Edited by Paul Robert Magocsi, pp. 890-893. Toronto: University of Toronto Press, 1999.

Discusses the origins of the Kurds in Canada and their migration, arrival and settlement. It also discusses their economic life, community life, family, culture, education, and religion. Their relations with other groups are also discussed.

DENMARK

323   Moldenhawer, Bolette. "The Ethnic Minority Group of Turkish and Kurdish Origin: Schooling Strategies and Structural Integration." In *Multiculturalism in the Nordic Societies: Proceedings of the 9th Nordic Seminar for Researchers on Migration and Ethnic Relations: Final Report*. Edited by Jan Hjarnø, pp. 274-286. Copenhagen: Nordic Council of Minis-

ters, 1994. [Nordic Seminar for Researchers on Migration and Ethnic Relations (9th: 1993: Esbjerg, Denmark).]

The population of Western Europe's multi-cultural composition has intensified attention on ethnic minority groups' structural adjustment. Their position and ability to cope successfully in school and within the educational system seems to play a decisive role in connection to this. With present research on school and education, culture and ethnicity, and immigrants and minority conditions, as the point of departure, the intention of this paper is to analyze the multi-cultural school as a cultural meeting point between the minority pupils' school yield and the school's capacity to incorporate multi-culturalism. Empirically the study is a qualitative research on Turkish and Kurdish pupils' schooling strategies and practice in the bi-cultural classes adopted by "Enghojskolen." The backdrop to the research is an assumption that school undertakes to—more or less explicitly—force ethnic minority pupils to meet the school's 'socializational' and 'qualificational' criteria. Ethnic minorities on the other hand need to consider how their daily lives and ethnic culture(s) i.e., the importance of ethnically define boundaries between private/public, man/woman, adult/child, individual/family, dependence/independence etc., are determined by schools' pressures *vis-a-vis* conforming demands. Using Bourdieu's habitus, field and practice concepts as a point of departure, minority pupils' behavior and why they behave as they do, is analyzed: How can their prospective profit from school be explained? What do their gains from school express? Would one pose the same questions to Danish pupils? Are there grounds to assume that minority pupils educational gains are different to Danish pupils? Even though ethnic minority pupils do not wish to become Danish (furthermore, it is doubtful whether they could if they wanted to) the question is, whether they could, via the school's demands on them to adapt, be forced to create other (and new) ways of behaving than those they via their upbringing have incorporated. How does a minority pupil with a habitus in transition and an incorporated cultural competence, meet school as a structuring system, become orientated and behave within this system? In the paper, the author draws special attention to the Turkish and Kurdish group's situation at school and within the educational system. Questions like, how they cope and why they cope in a certain way, are dealt with. (A)

ENGLAND AND FINLAND

324   Wahlbeck, Östen. "The Kurdish Diaspora and Refugee Associations in Finland and England." In *Exclusion and Inclusion of Refugees in Contemporary Europe*. Edited by Philip Muus, pp. 171-186. Utrecht: European Research Centre on Migration and Ethnic Relations, 1997. [Comparative studies in migration and ethnic relations; 3]

325   Wahlbeck, Östen. *Transnationalism and Diasporas: The Kurdish Example*. Transnational Communities Working Paper Series. Oxford: University of Oxford, Institute of Social and Cultural Anthropology. Paper presented at the International Sociological Association, XIV World Congress of Sociology, July 26-August 1, 1998, Montreal, Canada. Research Committee 31, Sociology of Migration.

This working paper is also available at: http://www.transcomm.ox.ac.uk. Wahlbeck argues that the notions of transnationalism and diaspora can provide sociology with some conceptual tools needed to study migrants in an increasingly global world. An ethnographic study of Kurdish refugee communities is drawn on to discuss the concept of diaspora, taking into account the refugees' specific transnational experiences and social relationships. The sociology of migration has much to gain from the contemporary diaspora discourse. It is argued that the traditional way of looking at ethnic relations, in terms of a relation between strictly localized minorities and majorities, is inadequate to describe refugees' experiences. The concept of diaspora, however, understood as a transnational social organization relating to both the country of origin and the country of exile, can enhance understanding of the social reality in which refugees live.

326   Wahlbeck, Oesten [Östen]. "Community Work and Exile Politics: Kurdish Refugee Associations in London." *Journal of Refugee Studies* 11 (Summer 1998): 215-230.

Ethnic associations play an important role for refugees in their new country of settlement; however, refugee communities are often politically divided and find it hard to create viable ethnic organizations. Here, this dilemma is highlighted via an ethnographic field study of Kurdish refugees in London, England. The British case is of special interest, since the refugee resettlement policy is characterized by a tendency to emphasize the role of the local community. Whether the politicization of the Kurdish associations in London has been a help or a hindrance for the creation of refugee assistance organizations is discussed. It is argued that, although there is no cohesive Kurdish community, the refugees have been able to establish well-functioning organizations of a more limited nature. In this process the political activism of the Kurdish refugees has been a resource rather than an obstacle. (A)

327   Wahlbeck, Östen. *Kurdish Diasporas: A Comparative Study of Kurdish Refugee Communities*. New York: St. Martin's Press in association with Centre for Research in Ethnic Relations, University of Warwick, Macmillan Press, 1999. x, 219 p. Includes bibliographical references (p. 202-214) and index.

In recent years both scholars and the general public have become familiar with the Kurdish struggle in Turkey and Iraq (and to a lesser extent, Iran) for identity, autonomy, or statehood; that struggle spans several decades. Two indispensable and complementary accounts of this struggle are Chahand's *A People without a Country* (1993) and Martin van Bruinessen's *Agha, Shaikh and State: The Social and Political Structures of Kurdistan* (1992). Wahlbeck (Abo Akademi University, Finland) has now addressed the remaining gap in this scholarship, the neglect of the new diasporic communities that Kurdish emigrants and refugees from Turkish and Iraqi violence are shaping in Europe. This study provides an illuminating and comparative account of the Kurdish diasporic communities in Britain and Finland and goes beyond sociological observations. It investigates the practices of inclusion and exclusion in the host society and challenges prevailing concepts concerning those processes. It considers the ways and degrees in which kinship and communal ties survive violence and misery, to a greater degree than has hitherto been supposed. It elucidates the emergence of transnational institutions and makes the theoretical case for replacing--in certain cases--inadequate concepts of ethnicity with diaspora-oriented approaches. (*Choice*, November 1999)

FRANCE

328   Petek-Salom, G. "Les ressortissants turcs en France et l'evolution de leur projet migratoire." *Hommes & Migrations*, no. 1212 (1998): 14-23.

GERMANY AND AUSTRIA

329   Blaschke, Jochen. "Die Diaspora der Kurden in der Bundesrepublik Deutschland." [The diaspora of Kurds in the Federal Republic of Germany]. *Osterreichische Zeitschrift fur Soziologie* 16, no. 3 (1991): 85-93. [In German.]

Although there are more than half a million Kurds in Europe, research on this new diaspora is extremely scanty. This article is one of the contributions to a special issue of the journal on "migration and diaspora." According to the author, there are in Germany between 300,000 to 500,000 Kurdish immigrants mostly from Turkey. It is argued that the German government has excluded the Kurds from multicultural programs in order to appease the Turkish government. This policy has marginalized the Kurds to the extent that the young generation of German Kurds are more preoccupied with the Kurdish nationalist struggle in Turkey than with their own rights in Germany. According to the author, the official policy of marginalization amounts to institutionalized racism. (A)

330   Bozarslan, Hamit. "La Presse et les Immigres en Allemagne: 1995-1996." *Migrations Societe*, no. 48 (1996): 105-115.

331   Heine, P. "Yezidi am Niederrhein: Eine Kurdische Minderheit im Span-
      nungsfeld von Tradition und Moderne." [Yezidi on the lower-Rhine: A
      Kurdish in the crossfire of tradition and modernism] *Archiv Fur Sozial-
      geschichte* 32, (1992): 271-282. [In German.]

332   Leggewie, Claus. "How Turks Became Kurds, Not Germans." *Dissent* 43
      (Summer 1996): 79-83.

      Turkish-Kurdish differences in Germany led many Turkish immigrants in
      Germany to discover their Kurdishness. Both the Turkish and German
      governments deny their Kurds many rights in one way or another, thus
      igniting the sense of Kurdish nationalism among them. In other words,
      Turks in Germany have become Kurds because the Turkish state denies
      them cultural recognition and the German state denies them political rec-
      ognition.

333   Leggewie, Claus. "Turks, Kurds and Germans: The History of a Migra-
      tion: From Social Stratification to Cultural Differentiation, 1961-1990."
      Mouvement Social, no. 188 (July-September 1999): 103-. [In German]

      At around two million, people of Turkish descent and origin make up the
      largest ethnic minority in today's Federal Republic of Germany. The
      largest proportion of Turks living in Germany has already been residing
      there legally for two or more decades, often already in the second or third
      generation. The overwhelming majority of younger Turks was born in
      Germany, but owing to Germany's anachronistic citizenship law, they do
      not possess German nationality, even if a growing number has dual citi-
      zenship. Still, there is not only an ethnic line of conflict and cleavage be-
      tween Germans and Turks, but also a divide within the community of
      Turkish citizens living inside Germany (and in other European societies).
      Since the end of the Seventies, above all, many Turks have discovered
      and played up their Kurdish origins. The article asks why a big part of
      former Turkish guest workers became Kurds, not Germans, and why at all
      self-identification with a transnational ethnic community abroad over-
      whelmed political inclusion as German citizens at home. (A)

334   Viehbock, Eveline. *Die Kurdische und Tuerkische Linke in der Heimat
      und Migration: Kurdische und Tuerkische Widerstandsorganisationen
      in der Tuerkei und im Deutschsprachigen Raum Unter Besonderer
      Beruecksichtigung von Tirol im Zeitraum von 1960-1990*. [The Kurdish
      and Turkish left in their native country and migration: Kurdish and Turk-
      ish resistance organizations in Turkey and in the German-speaking parts
      of Europe with special consideration of Tyrol from 1960 to 1990] Doc-
      toral dissertation. Universitaet Innsbruck (Austria), 1990. 830 p. [In Ger-
      man]

This doctoral thesis is a description of the history of the Kurdish and Turkish left, their illegal political organizations from 1960 to 1990 and, in case of the Kurdish left, their resistance movement in general but especially in Turkey. With labor migration to Western Europe in the 1960s and 1970s, political culture migrated too. Workers from Turkey founded their own clubs and mosque-organizations, mainly in the Federal Republic of Germany. The aim of this doctoral thesis is to reveal the origin of these new migration-clubs and to compare the political activities at home, in Turkey and Turkish Kurdistan, with the situation in the new 'home'. (In Turkey their first aim is the liberation of their country, in Europe, it is the improvement of labor conditions.) This comparison was done by research on publications, newspapers and leaflets of the Kurdish and Turkish left and by interviews with their representatives in Tyrol. In Tyrol, the Turkish right organization-mosques were also included in the research. The result is diagnosis of very scattered Kurdish, Turkish left and right communities at home and in migration, where personal conflicts are conflated with political-ideological motives. (A)

GREECE

335 Black, Richard. "Political Refugees or Economic Migrants? Kurdish and Assyrian Refugees in Greece." *Migration* [Berlin], no. 25 (1994): 79-109.

This paper considers the basis for distinction between "political refugees" and "economic migrants," using as an example recent flows from the Middle East to the Eastern Mediterranean. First, the causes and context of mass exodus in the region both before and after the Gulf War are analyzed. Patterns of migration are traced and the strategies and aspirations of migrants are outlined. Two groups of migrants currently staying in Greece—Kurds and Assyrians (both from Iraq)—are considered in detail. It is suggested that for both groups, political and religious persecution strongly determined decisions to leave their home region, a fact which would qualify all for refugee status under the 1951 Geneva Convention. However, subsequent social, economic, political and cultural factors within each group and in host countries, have interacted in a variety of ways to generate specific channels of movement and modes of incorporation into host societies and economies. Whilst recognition of these factors is important in the provision of assistance to these "refugees," they also act to reduce the willingness of governments to recognize specific groups as refugees. It is argued that this fundamental contradiction between the growing complexity of most refugee movements, and the simplicity and transparency necessary in refugee policy leaves many refugees unprotected. (A)

ITALY

336   Belaid, Abdeslam; Arush, Starlin; Chaifouroosh, Kamal; Maher, Vanessa.
"Islam in emigrazione: continuita e cambiamento dell'identita religiosa."
[Islam in Immigration: Continuity and Change of Religious Identity] *Religioni e Societa* 6, no. 12 (July-December 1991): 43-59. [In Italian]

Explores various examples of change in the religious and cultural lives of
Muslims, particularly migrants. The diversity of the social and political
importance of Islam in the native countries of immigrants to Turin, Italy,
from Iran, Kurdistan, Morocco, Somalia and Senegal is examined. In
Iran, the politico-religious revolution alienated many Iranians who supported the separation of powers. The Muslim Kurds are marginalized in
the national political systems of Iraq and Iran for nonreligious reasons.
The Senegalese and Somalian immigrants have radicalized and internationalized their meaning of Islam. Due to Muslim immigrants' contact
with Western culture, certain elements of modern life have changed their
Muslim identity. Some true Muslims have certain restrictions on their
lives that are not observed by others who still consider themselves Muslim; e.g., many urban Moroccan women are allowed to receive religious
instruction, while their rural counterparts are not. (A)

SWEDEN

337   Runfors, Ann; Sjogren, Annick. "Language, Dominance and Resistance:
An Ethnological Perspective on Teaching and Learning Swedish in an
Immigrant Environment in Sweden." *Migration* [Berlin], no. 23-24
(1994): 293-314.

While immigration appears to have favored the national level of education in Sweden, local investigations point to the opposite in immigrant
areas. Concern is spreading among educational authorities as regards
young generations, born and raised in Sweden, who are said to speak
worse Swedish than their own parents who came from Turkey or Lebanon
in their early years. An investigation was launched to study the relationship between language and environment, and this paper addresses some
of the questions raised by an ethnological pilot study on the subject which
centered on an immigrant suburb outside Stockholm, Botkyrka. Language
is here studied as a phenomenon which involves learning not only words
but also a way of conceiving the world. To understand the process of
teaching and learning languages it is therefore essential to take into account the various elements of daily life. The schools of the area see the
proportion of children with parents of foreign origin increase every year.
It is now between 40 and 95 percent. In the schools where the concern
about the poor quality of Swedish is greatest, two groups of language
dominate. One is Turkish and Kurdish, the other one is Assyrian/Syrian

also called Suryoyo. Ethnic groups from the Middle East have a functional multilingualism with a markedly pragmatic attitude to languages.
To speak Swedish is then only one among other possibilities of communication. This attitude is foreign to the Swedish one, based on a long tradition of literacy in one's own language. The ideas and goals of Swedish
teaching in junior school show that the teachers have three main goals in
their teaching: scholastic achievement a good life for the children, and,
ultimately, a better Sweden. These aspirations reflect the values and ideals of the educated Swedish middle class but when transposed to the
world of the Turkish/Kurdish or Assyrian/Syrian groups in Botkyrka, the
same aspirations of success at school and later in life can be interpreted
very differently-which leads to other linguistic expectations. The question
of how and on whose terms the ethnic and social diversity is organized
must be further investigated to understand the processes of teaching and
learning the necessary languages in a multicultural community. (A)

SWITZERLAND

338   Frischerz, Bruno. "Zweitspracherwerb durch Kommunikation. Eine
       diskursanalytische Untersuchung zum Zweitspracherwerb turkischer und
       kurdischer Asylbewerber in der Deutschschweiz." [Second-language ac-
       quisition through communication: A discourse-analytic investigation of
       second-language acquisition among Turkish and Kurdish asylum seekers
       in German-speaking Switzerland] *Bulletin Suisse de Linguistique Ap-
       pliquee* 65 (April 1997): 47-65. [In German.]

       Surveyed are language contacts and acquisition of Turkish and Kurdish
       asylum seekers (n=21) in the German-speaking part of Switzerland. A
       summary of results is provided: Language acquisition for the asylum-
       seeker is extremely taxing and contact with native Swiss is infrequent and
       at times unpleasant. It is held that successful language acquisition re-
       quires that the learner be active in the communicative process, particu-
       larly with the local population. Self-initiated self-repair, questions, re-
       quests, and communication checks are all shown through discourse analy-
       sis to be strategies of the successful language learner. Self-repair is seen
       to have a 70% success rate for corrections. It is also shown that depend-
       ence on the native-language-speaking discourse partner is universal for
       beginning learners. It is concluded that successful acquisition is a result
       more of active interaction than passive input. (A)

339   Hauptli, Walter. "Beitrag zu einer Sozialwissenschaftlichen Beschreibung
       von Asylbewerbern in der Schweiz: Zwei Fallstudien aus dem Kanton
       Zurich." [Contribution to a sociological description of asylum seekers in
       Switzerland: Two case studies in the Canton of Zurich] *Schweizerische
       Zeitschrift fur Soziologie/Revue Suisse de sociologie* 15, no. 1 (August
       1989): 95-113. [In German]

An attempt is made to describe the group of persons seeking political asylum in Switzerland, based on analysis of two sets of data: (1) written questionnaires (in Turkish and Kurdish) concerning professional careers prior to migration administered in 1988 to 120 male and 22 female asylum seekers of Turkish nationality at the Social Services Office in the town of Winterthur; and (2) the files of 518 applicants (312 families of 28 different nationalities) at the Refugee Reception Center in Zurich. The findings highlight collective characteristics that illustrate the problematic nature of the social status of the asylum seekers, and their downgrading into the lower classes. (A)

UNITED STATES

340   Kahn, Margaret. "Kurds." In *Harvard Encyclopedia of American Ethnic Groups*. Edited by Stephan Thernstrom, pp. 606-608. Cambridge, MA: Belknap Press, 1980.

Provides a historical background and a brief overview of the Kurdish community in the United States.

341   Kelley, Ron. "Kurds." In *Irangeles: Iranians in Los Angeles*. Edited by Ron Kelley and others, pp. 150-157. Berkeley: University of California Press, 1993.

Provides a historical background and a brief overview of the Iranian Kurdish community who fled to the United States after the overthrow of the Shah.

342   O'Connor, Karen. *A Kurdish Family*. Minneapolis, MN.: Lerner Publications Co., 1996. 56 p.

Describes the experiences of one Kurdish family that was driven from its home in Iraqi Kurdistan and moved to a new life in California and how they adjust to that while still preserving traditions from their homeland. The book sweepingly and uncritically contrasts good (Kurds) and evil (Iraqis and Turks) in the old world and continues in this vein in the new ("I like the United States. No one can do anything to you here"). California appears to be paradise after their savage treatment at "home." Still, O'Connor manages to put human faces onto a political issue which is, admittedly, rather abstract for American youth. A pronunciation guide and suggestions for further reading are appended. (Bulletin of the Center)

343   Robson, Barbara. *Iraqi Kurds: Their History and Culture*. Washington, DC.: Center for Applied Linguistics, 1996. 46 p. [CAL Refugee Fact Sheet Series No.13.]

Just after the Persian Gulf War in 1991, Iraqi Kurds again rebelled against the Saddam Hussein government of Iraq. The persecution they experienced led to the establishment of Operation Provide Comfort and the protective no-fly zone. Thousands of Kurds fled their homeland to Turkey and were eventually resettled in the United States. This fact sheet provides background information about the Iraqi Kurds and discusses the ways their culture and history might affect their resettlement in the United States. The Kurds are overwhelmingly Muslim, and many aspects of their daily life are determined by Muslim customs and requirements. Concrete suggestions are offered to help Kurdish refugees adapt to life in the United States. Because of the relative formality of their own society, those who are interested in helping Kurds with acculturation would do well to take a rather formal approach and to work to encourage a positive attitude toward the national government, something Kurds by history and culture may not find congenial.

12

Kurds in Syria, Lebanon, and Former Soviet Union

SYRIA AND LEBANON

344   Ahmad, Ahmad Muhammad. *Akrad Lubnan wa-Tanzimuhum al-Ijtima'i wa-al-Siyasi*. Hayy Madi, al-Dahiyah al-Janubiyah [Beirut]: Maktabat al-Faqih, 1995. 256 p. Originally presented as the author's thesis (master's)—American University of Beirut. Includes bibliographical references (p. 247-255).

345   Darwish, 'Abd al-Hamid. *Lamhah Tarikhiyah 'an Akrad al-Jazira (Rad 'ala Dr. Suhayl al-Zakkar)*. [A historical overview of the Kurds in the Jazira province in Syrian Kurdistan: A reply to a report by Dr. Suhayl Zakkar] Qamishli, Syria: 'Abd al-Hamid Darwish, 1996. 78 p.

346   Epstein, Eliahu. "Al Jezireh." *Journal of the Royal Central Asian Society* 27, no. 1 (January 1940): 68-82.

A descriptive survey of the Jazire region, lying between the rivers Tigris and Euphrates, in northeast Syria, describing in detail the topography, water resources, climate and soils of the area. It was found that the population included large Kurdish, Yezidi and Assyrian minorities as well as nomadic 'Anaze and Shammar tribes. Although sparsely populated in the 1930s, the author argues that it was potentially a very productive agricultural region.

347   Feili, Omran Yahya. "The Status of the Kurds in Syria." In *The Syrian Arab Republic: A Handbook*. Edited by Anne Sinai and Allen Pollack, 63-65. New York: American Academic Association for Peace in the Middle East, 1976.

348   Ma'oz, Moshe. "Muslim Ethnic Communities in Nineteenth Century
       Syria and Palestine: Trends of Conflict and Integration." *Asian and Afri-
       can Studies* [Haifa] 19 (1985): 283-307.

       Discusses the relations of the non-Arab Sunni Muslim ethnic and cultural
       communities with either the Muslim Arab majority, or the minority reli-
       gious communities. Ma'oz argues that very few attention has been paid to
       the role of the non-Arab Sunni Muslim ethnic and cultural minorities in
       the public and social life of the Fertile Crescent during the modern period.
       In this article, a preliminary attempt is made to examine the trends of con-
       flict and integration as they affected Kurds, Turkomans, North Africans
       and Circassians. Special attention is given to the political, economic and
       cultural factors that strengthened the tendencies of these minorities to
       come into conflict or integrate with other local communities in nine-
       teenth-century Syria and Palestine.

349   McDowall, David. *The Kurds of Syria*. London: Kurdish Human Rights
       Project, 1998.

       Provides an account of Kurdish-Arab relations in Syria during the twenti-
       eth century; describes the current situation of the approximately 1.5 mil-
       lion Kurds of Syria; describes Syria's discriminatory practices; explains
       how these violate international law and in some cases its own domestic
       law; recommends the steps necessary for Syria to conform with interna-
       tional law and norms. Includes an overview of the Kurds in Lebanon.

350   Middle East Watch. *Syria Unmasked: The Suppression of Human
       Rights by the Asad Regime*. New Haven: Yale University Press, 1991.
       215 p.

       This book looks at human rights in Syria during two decades of rule by
       President Hafez Asad. It also considers the human rights practices of
       Asad's predecessors, particularly the governments that emerged from the
       military coup d'état of March 8, 1963, under the banner of the Arab Ba'th
       Socialist party.

351   Mulla, 'Izz al-Din 'Ali. *Hayy al-Akrad fi Madinat Dimashq bayna
       'Amay 1250-1979 M: Dirasah Tarikhiyah, Ijtima'iyah, Iqtisadiyah*. Bei-
       rut: Dar Asu lil-Tiba'ah wa-al-Nashr wa-al-Tawzi', 1998. 282 p.

       Discusses the historical background of a large Kurdish neighborhood in
       Damascus, its demographic structure, houses, mosques, street network,
       water resources, people, sheikhs, writers, leaders, families, women. Also
       discusses the neighborhood people's involvement in social and political
       activities, and education. Social life and customs and a variety of cultural
       aspects of the people are also discussed.

352   Perouse, Jean-Francois. "Les Kurdes de Syrie et d'Irak: denegation, de-
       placements et eclatement." [The Kurds in Syria and Iraq: denial, transfers
       and explosion] *Espace, Populations, Societes*, no. 1 (1997): 73-84.

       According to the author, Kurdish populations in Iraq and Syria are less
       known and suffer from mistreatments from the central governments: their
       proper identity and their fundamental rights are denied. More, they are
       obliged to move from Kurdistan (sometimes far outside these two coun-
       tries) and become more and more urbanized and internationalized.

353   Sherry, Virginia N. *Syria: The Silenced Kurds*. New York: Human
       Rights Watch, 1996. 63 p.

       Examines the situation of stateless Syrian-born Kurds and charges that
       they have been arbitrarily denied the right to nationality in violation of in-
       ternational law.

354   Thoumin, Richard. "Deux quartiers de Damas. Le quartier Chretien de
       Bab Musalla et le quartier Kurde." [Two quarters of Damascus: the Chris-
       tian quarter of Bab Musalla and the Kurdish quarter] *Bulletin d'Etudes
       Orientales* 1 (1931): 99-136.

       Describes the physical characteristics, population size, economic and so-
       cial conditions in the Christian (Bab Musalla) and Kurdish (El-Akrad)
       quarters of Damascus in the late 1920s.

355   Vanly, Ismet Chériff. "The Kurds in Syria and Lebanon." In *The Kurds:
       A Contemporary Overview*. Edited by Philip G. Kreyenbroek and Stefan
       Sperl, pp. 143-170. London: Routledge, 1992.

       Vanly, a prominent and long-established Kurdologist, refutes the Syrian
       official denial of the nativeness of the Kurds on its territories, and argues
       for the historic presence of the Kurds in Syria which he declares is be-
       yond question. He notes, for example, the antiquity of local names such
       as the Kurd-Dagh, the Mountain of the Kurds (northwest of Aleppo). The
       name of the medieval Crusader fortress of Kirak [Crac] des Chevaliers,
       "Fortress of the Knights" (northwest of Damascus) which has been al-
       ways known to the Syrian Arabs as Husn al-Akrad, "Fortress of the
       Kurds," Vanly argues, further speaks to this fact. As for the much smaller
       Kurdish community in Lebanon, Vanly declares that it is essentially com-
       posed of immigrants who left the areas of Mardin and Bohtan in Turkish
       Kurdistan after the failure of the Kurdish uprisings in the early part of the
       century and headed to Beirut in the 1920's and 1930's. On the treatment
       and utility of the Kurds in those states, Vanly notes that although Syrian
       President Asad's regime has conceded absolutely nothing to the Kurds as
       a cultural and national minority, it has used them to help buoy up its mi-
       nority Alawite rule and has given the Turkish-based PKK what may justi-

fiably be called a strategic alliance. In Lebanon, meanwhile, there is no nationalist anti-Kurdish feeling as there is in Syria, Turkey and Iraq, Vanly observes. (abridged, Michael Gunter/*IJKS* 8, nos. 1-2, 1995: 137)

356   Vanly, Ismet Chériff (pseud. Mustafa Nazdar). "The Kurds in Syria." In *A People without a Country: The Kurds and Kurdistan*. Edited by Gerard Chaliand; translated from French by Michael Pallis; foreword by David McDowall, pp. 194-201. London: Zed Books Ltd., 1993.

Provides a historical background of the Kurds in Syria and discusses the "Legal" and "Ideological" basis for Syrian oppression, as well as the burden of this oppression on the Kurds.

See also items: 21, 22, 29, 41, 73, 159, 185, 189, 208, 209, 223, 229, 690, 702, 807, 808, 809, 813,879, 893, 895, 904, 908, 931

FORMER SOVIET UNION

357   Aristova, T. F. "The Kurds of Transcaucasia." *Central Asian Review* 7, no. 2 (1959): 163-174.

This article is a slightly abridged translation of an article which appeared in *Sovietskaya Etnografiya*, no. 6, 1958. A comment by C. J. Edmonds is appended at the end of the article. Discusses the distribution, historical background, tribes and clans, language, religion, farming, carpet making and other manufactures, living conditions, clothes, domestic utensils, songs and dances and literature of the Kurds in Armenia, Azerbaijan, and Georgia.

358   Aristova, T. F. "The Reflection of Ethnic Processes in the Traditional Domestic Culture of the Kurds of Azerbaijan and Turkmenia." *Soviet Anthropology and Archaeology* 20, no. 1 (1981): 3-24.

Discusses the distribution, historical background, dwellings, clothes, domestic utensils, food, living conditions, family life and marriage, and naming of children of the Kurds in Azerbaijan and Turkmenia.

359   Aristova, T. F. "Kurds." Translated by David Testen. In *Encyclopedia of World Cultures, Volume VI: Russia and Eurasia/China*. Edited by Paul Friedrich and Norma Diamond, 224-227. Boston, Mass.: G.K. Hall & Co., 1994.

This article presents the Kurds of the Commonwealth of Independent States (or the former Soviet Union). It deals with their orientation (identification, location and demography), history and cultural relations, language and literacy, settlements, economy, religion and culture.

360   Aristova, T. F.; Vasil'yeva, G. P. "Kurds of the Turkmen SSR." *Central Asian Review*, no. 4 (1965): 302-309.
Field work amongst the Kurdish population of the Turkmen Soviet Social Republics was carried out by T. F. Aristova and G. P. Vasil'yeva in 1963. Their results were embodied in an article published in *Sovetskaya Etnografiya*, No. 5 of 1964. The authors illustrated their text with numerous photographs, plans and sketches, and also documented it with copious notes. In the more or less complete rendering of the letterpress given in this article, sub-headings have been introduced and several implied sentences on which the argument hinged have been made explicit. Readers will find the material as thus presented to be easily comprehensible without the visual aids or the forest of footnotes. In Soviet official thinking the Kurds settled in the Union have never been attached to, or in any way associated with, the concept of a territorial Kurdistan. Little enough indeed has come specifically about them from Soviet pens. (A)

361   Flint, Julie. *The Kurds of Azerbaijan and Armenia*. London: Kurdish Human Rights Project, 1998.

A report on the human rights situation of the Kurds of Azerbaijan and Armenia.

362   Marlay, Ross. "Kurds." In *An Ethnohistorical Dictionary of the Russian and Soviet Empires*. Edited by James S. Olson, pp. 408-412. Westport, CT: Greenwood Press, 1994.

Provides a historical background and brief overview of the Kurdish community in the former Soviet Union.

363   Nadirov, Nadir. "What Do the Soviet Kurds Want?" *Asia and Africa Today*, no. 1 (January-February 1991): 74-76.

364   Nezan, Kendal. "Kurdistan in the Soviet Union." In *A People Without a Country: The Kurds and Kurdistan*. Edited by Gerard Chaliand; translated from French by Michael Pallis; foreword by David McDowall, pp. 202-210. London: Zed Books Ltd., 1993.

Includes a discussion on the geography, demography, history, and economic and social situation of the Kurds and Kurdistan in the former Soviet Union prior to 1980. Also included is a discussion on the Soviet Kurds' cultural life.

365   Pohl, J. Otto. *Ethnic Cleansing in the USSR, 1937-1949*. Westport, CT: Greenwood Press, 1999. [Contributions to the study of world history, 0885-9159; no. 65]

Includes a chapter on the Meshkhetian Turks, Kurds, and Khemshils, pp. 129-136.

366   Vanly, Ismet Chériff. "The Kurds in the Soviet Union." In *The Kurds: A Contemporary Overview*. Edited by Philip G. Kreyenbroek and Stefan Sperl, pp. 193-218. London: Routledge, 1992.

In this article, Vanly examines the little-known history of "Red" Kurdistan as an autonomous region with Lachin as its capital and Gussi Gajev as its first leader from 1923 until in 1929 the Baku government reduced Kurdistan from an *uyzed* to an *okrug*, the lowest territorial unit for the Soviet non-Russian nationalities. Regarding the current population, Vanly writes that the total number of Kurds living within the former U.S.S.R. is unknown. Soviet Kurds themselves give estimates that range from approximately 300,000 to a precise figure of 1,120,000. Although the Armenian response to the massacres of 1895-96 was to massacre the Kurds in Armenia and northern Kurdistan during the Russian incursions of 1914-15, Vanly adds that Armenia is the only Soviet republic which preserved and protected Kurdish cultural infrastructures after the persecutions under Stalin. The effects the current Armenian-Azeri conflict over Karabagh will have upon the former Soviet Kurds who live there and in the vicinity remain to be seen. (abridged, Michael Gunter/*IJKS* 8, nos. 1-2, 1995: 138)

367   Wurdi, Muhammad Tawfiq. *al-Akrad fi al-Itihad al-Suvyatti*. [A brief overview of the Kurds in the former Soviet Union] Baghdad: Matba'at al-Liwa', 1959. 23 p.

See also items: 23, 29, 77, 196, 486, 801, 920

13

Language Studies/Works

GENERAL STUDIES/WORKS

368   Blau, Joyce. "Le Kurde." In *Compendium Linguarum Iranicarum*. Edited by Rudiger Schmitt, pp. 327-335. Wiesbaden: Dr. Ludwig Reichert Verlag, 1989.

369   Blau, Joyce. "La Reforme de la Langue Kurde." In *Language Reform: History and Future*. vol. IV. Edited by Istvan Fodor and Claude Hagege. With an introduction by Joshua A Fishman, pp. 63-85. Hamburg: Helmut Buske Verlag, 1989.

370   Blau, Joyce. "al-Lughah wa-al-Adab al-Kurdiyahyn." *Studia Kurdica* (1985): 39-44.

371   Bois, Thomas. "De la langue a l'ame du peuple kurde." *Bibliotheca Orientalis* 20 (1963): 5-9.

372   Bois, Thomas. "Comment ecrire le kurde." *Al-Machriq* 59 (1965): 369-378.

373   Bois, Thomas. "Les dominicains a l'avant-garde de la Kurdologie au XVIIIe siecle." [The Dominicans are pioneers of Kurdology in the 18th century] *Archivum fratrum praedicatorum* 35 (1965): 265-292.

374   Edmonds, Cecil John. "A Bibliography of Southern Kurdish, 1920-1936." *Journal of the Royal Central Asian Society* 24 (1937): 487-497; 32 (1945): 185-191.

The first article is a bibliography of Kurdish periodicals and books published in Iraq up to the end of 1936, with a short introduction on the distribution of Kurdish dialects. The second article is an update.

375   Fuad, Kamal. "On the Origins, Development and State of the Kurdish Language." In *Yearbook of the Kurdish Academy 1990*, pp. 11-21. Ratingen, Germany: The Kurdish Academy, 1990.

376   Halacoglu, Yusuf. "The Evaluation of the Words Turk-Etrak, Kurd-Ekrad as they Appear in the Ottoman Documents." *Belleten* 60, no. 227 (April 1996): 147-154.

377   Jaba, Alexandre Auguste (ed. and tr.). *Recueil de notices et de récits kourdes servant à la connaissance de la langue, de la littérature et des tribus du Kourdistan: textes kourdes, réunis, publiés, traduits et annotés*. Amsterdam: APA - Philo Press, 1979. x, 111, 128 p. Text in French and Kurdish. Includes bibliographical references. Reprint. Originally published in 1860 by Eggers, St.-Pétersbourg.

378   Justi, Ferdinand. "Note sur les mots etrangers en kurde." *Revue de Linguistique et de Philologie Comparee* 6 (1873): 89-99.

379   Kurdoev, Q. *Tarikh Dirasat al-Lughah al-Kurdiyah wa-Lahajatiha*. [A historical overview of Kurdish language studies] Translated from Russian by 'Abd al-Majid Shaykhu. Damascus: s.n., 1991.

380   Lerch, P. *Forschungen über die Kurden und die iranischen Nordchaldäer*. St. Petersburg, Eggers, 1857-1858. 3 pts. in 1 vol. [In German]

Part one provides a general introduction on the Kurdish language and reviews previously published materials on the topic. Part two discusses his method of learning the Kurdish language—staying in a prison where 20 Kurds were jailed. He learned from them several dialects such as the northern Kurmanji and Zaza. He also learned about the social life, traditions, and customs of the Kurds. In this part, Lerch discusses the inadequacy of Arabic alphabet for use in the Kurdish language. He also discusses the uniqueness of the language and divides it into five dialects: Kurmanji, Luri, Kalhuri, Gurani, and Zaza. He places particular emphasis on northern Kurmanji and Zaza. Part three is composed of two dictionaries: an 84-page Kurdish-Russian (in north Kurmanji dialect) and a 24-page Russian-Kurdish dictionary (in Zaza dialect).

381   MacKenzie, David N. "The Origins of Kurdish." *Transactions of the Philological Society* (1961): 68-86.

After considering Kurdish as a "normal Iranian language," the author tries to define Kurdish by establishing the features which distinguishes it from other Iranian dialects.

382   MacKenzie, David N. "Kurdish Language." In *Encyclopedia of Islam*. New ed. Vol. 5, pp. 479-480. Leiden: E. J. Brill, 1986.

383   MacKenzie, David N. "The Kurdish of Mulla Sa'id Samdinani." *The Journal of Kurdish Studies* 1 (1995): 1-27.

Describes the life of a man who worked for Nikitine, the Imperial Russian Counsel at the time, and taught him the Kurdish language. The author also discusses some of Samdinan's writings and the phonology and morphology of the Kurdish dialect he was using. The bloodstained "Tale of Suto and Tato" is reproduced with transcription and revised translation from its original script, published by Nikitine with the help of Major E. B. Soane. According to MacKenzie, the story reveals several aspects of Mulla Sa'id himself—his cynicism, his vanity, but above all his powers as eloquent raconteur.

384   Ma'ruf, 'Abd al-Rahman. *Ma Kutiba 'an al-Lughah al-Kurdiyah*. Translated from Kurdish by Muhammad Amin Ghaffar al-Hawramani. Baghdad: Manshurat Akadimiyat al-'Ulum, 1978. 62 p.

A detailed thematic bibliography on Kurdish language.

385   McCarus, Ernest R. "Kurdish Language Studies." *The Middle East Journal* 14 (Summer 1960): 325-335; 15 (1961): 123-125.

An annotated bibliography of Kurdish language studies that were often written by missionaries, comparative Indo-Europeanists, and diplomats. The author briefly comments on or reviews books and articles written in a number of languages, including English, French, German, and Kurdish, among others. Includes an extensive list of Kurdish language studies.

386   McCarus, Ernest N. "Kurdish." In *International Encyclopedia of Linguistics*. Editor in chief William Bright. vol. 2, pp. 289-294. New York: Oxford University Press, 1992.

After a brief introduction on the Kurdish language, McCarus discusses the phonology of the language and it writing system, noun morphology, verb morphology, and syntax. All descriptions are based on the Sulaymania (Sorani) dialect.

387   Minorsky, Vladimir F. "The Kurdish Language." *Encyclopedia of Islam* 2 (1927): 1151-1155.

388   Sa'id, Zubayr Bilal. *Ta'rikh al-Lughah al-Kurdiyah*. [A historical overview of the Kurdish language] Baghdad: Matba'at al-Hawadith, 1977.

389   Sallo, Ibrahim Khidhir. "A Linguistic Analysis of Kurdish-Arabic Code-Switching." *Adab al-Rafidayn* 17 (1988): 139-54.

The author analyzes the choice of language among bilingual Kurdish and Arabic speakers from a linguistic viewpoint.

390   Tsabolov, Ruslan. "Notes on the Influence of Arabic on Kurdish." *Acta Kurdica: The International Journal of Kurdish and Iranian Studies* 1 (1994): 121-124.

The interrelations of Kurdish and Arabic have left a number of traces in Kurdish; some of them are quite evident, others may not be noticeable. In fact, the most obvious result of such contacts with Arabic, as in a majority of cases—right up to the Indonesian and African languages in the South and the European languages In the North—is the lexical borrowings from Arabic. The influence of the Arabic phonetic system on Kurdish is also visible, albeit faint. The occurrence of many "alien" phonetic peculiarities in Kurdish derive from this same influence. (A)

391   Vanly, Ismet Chériff. "Regards sur les origines des Kurdes et leur langue." [A glance on the origins of the Kurds and their language] *Studia Kurdica*, no. 5 (1988): 39-58.

The author describes the Indo-European origins of the Kurds and the Kurdish language, their Japheto-Caucasian roots, the Armenian-Kurdish relations in the Van Basin, and then proposes some linguistic observations.

See also items: 1, 4, 19, 21, 23, 24, 25, 27, 517, 696, 734

DIALECT STUDIES/WORKS

392   Asatrian, Garnik S. "Dimili." In *Encyclopaedia Iranica*. Vol. 7, pp. 405-411. Costa Mesa, CA: Mazda Publishers, 1996.

Provides a short overview of the Dimili (or Zaza), the indigenous name of the Kurds living mainly in Turkish Kurdistan, in the Dersim region and to a lesser extent in Bingol, Mus, Bitlis, Diyarbekir, Siverek, and Sivas. Describes their religion, language (phonology and morphology--nouns and pronouns, verbs, linguistic position of Dimili, survey of typical phonetic developments, morphological isoglosses, and lexical isogloses), and literature. Includes a comprehensive list of related sources.

393   Benedictsen, Age Meyer; Christensen, Arthur. *Les dialectes d'Awroman et de Pawä. Revus et publiés avec des notes et une esquisse de grammaire*. København, Andr. Fred. Høst & Søn, 1921. 128 p.

394   Blau, Joyce. *Le Kurde de 'Amadiya et de Djabal Sindjar: Analyse Linguistique, Textes Folkloriques, Glossaires*. [The Kurds of 'Amadiya and Djabal Sindjar: Linguistic analysis, folkloric texts, glossaries] Paris: Klincksieck, 1975. 252 p. Bibliography: p. 12-19. (Travaux de l'Institut d'Etudes Iraniennes de l'Universite de la Sorbonne Nouvelle; 8).

This work by Blau is a much more serious piece of scholarship than her *Dictionnaire kurde-francais-anglais*. It consists of a linguistic analysis, folkloristic texts with French translation, and accompanying glossaries of Kurmanji material she collected in 'Amadiya and the Yezidi region of Jabal Sinjar, Iraqi Kurdistan in 1967 and 1968 (*Kurdish Kurmandji Modern Texts Introduction: Selection and Glossary*). The two glossaries—one each for 'Amadiya and Jabal Sinjar—include the gender of nouns and the present stem of verbs, but fail to indicate transitivity. These are the glossaries for the accompanying oral texts, and are therefore reflective of the living spoken language of two particular localities, rather than the artificially devised journalese of her earlier work. These traits, together with the annotated bibliography at the beginning of the book, make this an important contribution to the study of the Kurds and their language. (Michael Chyet)

395   Blau, Joyce. "Gurani et Zaza." In *Compendium Linguarum Iranicarum*. Edited by Rudiger Schmitt, pp. 336-340. Wiesbaden: Dr. Ludwig Reichert Verlag, 1989.

396   Blau, Joyce. "Le Kurde lori." In *Etudes irano-aryennes offertes a Gilbert Lazard*. Edited by C.-H. de Fouchecour and Ph. Gignoux, pp. 37-58. Paris: Association pour l'Avancement des Etudes Iranniennes, diff. Peeters, 1989. (Studia Iranica, Cahier 7).

397   Blau, Joyce. "Le cagani: lori ou kurde?" [Cagani: Luri or Kurdish?] *Studia Iranica* 22, no. 1 (1993): 93-119.

The Luri-Feili Kurdish is classed among the Southern Kurdish dialects spoken essentially in West Iran. The author presents a description of one of the Luri-Feili dialects spoken by the Luris who have moved into Iraq at the turn of the 20th century. Natives of Poshtekuh region, these Luris are Shi'ites who emigrated to Iraq to become closer to the Shi'ite sacred places of Karbala and Najaf. Of course, there are others who came for economical reasons.

398   Bordie, John G. "Kurdish Dialects in Eastern Turkey." In *Linguistics and Literary Studies in Honor of Archibald A. Hill, Vol. II: Descriptive*

Linguistics. Edited by M. A. Jazayery and others, pp. 205-212. The Hague: Mouton Publishers, 1978.

399   Bruinessen, Martin van. "Les Kurdes et leur langue au XVIIeme siecle: Notes d'Evliya Celebi sur les dialectes kurdes." [The Kurds and their language in the 17th century: Evliya Celebi's notes on Kurdish dialects] *Studia Kurdica*, no. 5 (1988): 13-34.

In April and May 1655, the famous Turkish traveler, Evliya Celebi, spent a few weeks in Kurdistan. On this occasion, he made many linguistic remarks from which van Bruinessen reproduces Sorani and other dialects' vocabularies as well as the grammatical observations of Evliya Celebi. This is an important article for those who want to do research on the Kurdish language.

400   Edmonds, Cecil John. "Prepositions and Personal Affixes in Southern Kurdish." *Bulletin of the School of Oriental and African Studies* 17 (1955): 490-502.

This article is a brief description of the personal affixes (clitics) of Sulaymania Kurdish. It includes a brief list and description of the prepositions and postpositions of Sulaymania Kurdish, a description of the ways in which clitics are used in the dialect, and discusses the past-tense transitive construction of the Sulaymania, which Edmonds identifies as a passive construction.

401   Ellow, Agha Petros. *Assyrian, Kurdish & Yizidis: Indexed Grammar and Vocabulary, with a few Grammatical Notes*. Baghdad: Printed at Government Press, 1920. 87, iv p.

The Kurdish and Yizidis of this book is that spoken by all Yizidis and the Kurds between the Black Sea, Lake Urmia and Mosul, and is mostly a combination of Persian, Arabic and Turkish. It is entirely different to the Kurdish spoken in other parts of Kurdistan. (A)

402   Hadank, Karl. *Mundarten der Gûrân, besonders das Kändûläî, Auramânî und Badschälânî*. Berlin: Verlag der Preussischen Akademie der Wissenschaften: in Kommission bei W. de Gruyter, 1930. xix, 479: maps. [Kurdisch-persische Forschungen: Ergebnisse einer von 1901 bis 1903 und 1906 bis 1907 in Persien und der asiatischen Türkei ausgeführten Forschungsreise von Oskar Mann: Abt. III (Nordwestiranisch); Bd. 2 Kurdisch-persische Forschungen, Abt. III (Nordwestiranisch); Bd. 2.] Bibliography: p. [xviii]-xix.

403   Hadank, Karl. *Mundarten der Zâzâ, hauptsächlich aus Siwerek und Kor*. Berlin: Verlag der Preussischen Akademie der Wissenschaften: in Kommission bei W. de Gruyter, 1932. xiii, 398 p. [Kurdisch-persische

Forschungen: Ergebnisse einer von 1901 bis 1903 und 1906 bis 1907 in Persien und der asiatischen Türkei ausgeführten Forschungsreise von Oskar Mann: Abt. III (Nordwestiranisch); Bd. 4 Kurdisch-persische Forschungen, Abt. III (Nordwestiranisch); Bd. 4.] Bibliography:. [xi]-xii.

404   Hasanpoor, Jafar. *A Study of European, Persian, and Arabic Loans in Standard Sorani*. Uppsala: Uppsala University, 1999. 176 p. Originally presented as the author's thesis (Ph. D.)—Uppsala University, 1999. Includes bibliographical references (p. 163-176). [Reports on Asian and African studies. 1]

This dissertation examines processes of lexical borrowing in the Sorani standard of the Kurdish language, spoken in Iraq, Iran, and the Kurdish diaspora. Borrowing, a form of language contact, occurs on all levels of language structure. In the pre-standard literary Kurdish (Kirmanci and Sorani) which emerged in the pre-modern period, borrowing from Arabic and Persian was a means of developing a distinct literary and linguistic tradition. By contrast, in standard Sorani and Kirmanci, borrowing from the state languages, Arabic, Persian, and Turkish, is treated as a form of domination, a threat to the language, character, culture, and national distinctness of the Kurdish nation. The response to borrowing is purification through coinage, internal borrowing, and other means of extending the lexical resources of the language. As a subordinate language, Sorani is subjected to varying degrees of linguistic repression, and this has not allowed it to develop freely. Since Sorani speakers have been educated only in Persian (Iran), or predominantly in Arabic, European loans in Sorani are generally indirect borrowings from Persian and Arabic (Iraq). These loans constitute a major source for lexical modernization. The study provides wordlists of European loanwords used by Hêmin and other codifiers of Sorani. Most European loanwords are well established, used in magazines, books, and the spoken language although they are neither standardized in their spelling nor registered in Kurdish dictionaries. Some loan blends, loan shifts, creations, and pure Kurdish words introduced into Sorani are also established. However, under conditions of intensive language contact, borrowing and purification continue to be the main trends of standardization. (A)

405   Ivanow, W. "Notes on Khorasani Kurdish." *Journal and Proceedings of the Asiatic Society of Bengal (New Series)*, 23 (1927): 167-236.

According to Ivanow, the materials for the study of the dialect that is spoken by the Kurdish tribes inhabiting Northern Khurasan consisted, at that time, only of a number of words that were collected by A. Houtum-Schindler, and which were published by him in his "Beitrage zum kurdischen Wortschatze," *Z.D.M.G.*, vol. 38 (1884), pp. 43-116. In 1918-1920, during Ivanow's residence in that part of Persia, he collected about 400 specimens of Kurdish poetry and tales which give a more definite idea of the language which the Kurds of Khurasan speak. As the subject is one of considerable interest to students of Kurdish language, a brief outline of the main features of this dialect is here given, to which is added a vocabulary, and a number of typical specimens of popular poetry and prose. Historical information concerning Kurdish migrations to Khurasan were briefly summarized by Houtum-Schindler in his referred to and a short note on their present distribution in the province was given in a paper by Ivanow, "Notes on the ethnology of Khorasan," which was published in the *Geographical Journal*, Vol. LXVII, 1926, pp, 143-158. For the convenience of the reader the most essential points are here repeated.

406   Khurshid, Fu'ad Hama. "al-Tawzi' al-Jughrafi li-Lahajat al-Lughah al-Kurdiyah." [The geographical distribution of Kurdish language dialects] *Majallat al-Majma' al-'Ilmi al-Kurdi* 3, no. 2 (1975): 612-634.

407   Khurshid, Fu'ad Hama. *al-Lughah al-Kurdiyah: al-Tawzi' al-Jughrafi li-Lahajatiha*. [The Kurdish language and the geographical distribution of its dialects] Baghdad: Matba'at al-Wisam, 1983. 52 p.: ill., map. Includes bibliographical references (p. 48-52).

408   Lazard, G. "Le dialecte laki d'Aleshtar (kurde meridional)." *Studia Iranica* 21 (1992): 215-245.

409   LeCoq, Albert von. *Kurdische Texte*. [Kurmangí- Erzählungen und -Lieder aufgezeichnet von Yacib oclu Yüsib aus Belpunar nebst einer Zaza-Erzählung des 'Omar ibn 'Ali aus Cermuq.] Berlin: Gedruckt in der Reichsdruckerei, 1903. 2 vols. Teil 1. Die Texte in der Urschrift -- T. 2. Die Texte in Transkription.

410   MacKenzie, David N. "Bajalani." *Bulletin of the School of Oriental and African Studies* 18 (1956): 418-435.

The main purpose of this article is to publish some linguistic notes, collected in a matter of some five hours. Scanty and incomplete as they are they will serve to augment Mann's even barer notes on Bajalani from Xorsabad. After Hadank's exhaustive treatment of Mann's material further annotation is almost superfluous. This is an opportunity, however, to draw attention to one shortcoming in Mann's otherwise accurate notation, viz. the fact that nowhere in his texts, Kurdish or otherwise, is a distinction made between tapped *r* and rolled *r*, beyond occasional writings of *rr* for the latter. (A)

411   MacKenzie, David N. *Kurdish Dialect Studies, I and II*. London: Oxford University Press, 1961-1962. maps, diagrs. Includes bibliography. (London Oriental Series, vols. 9-10)

A study based on the author's Ph.D. thesis submitted to the University of London in 1957. Dr. MacKenzie had an opportunity of studying a dozen dialects in Iraq, the majority of which had not been recorded before. He has made excellent use of the extensive material he managed to collect (he spent ten months in Iraqi Kurdistan, 1954-55, gathering material for his study), and has published an important contribution to our knowledge of Kurdish. The book examines the various Kurdish dialects spoken in Sulaymania and Akre. It describes the Phonology (pp. 1-49), Morphology, Syntax and Word Formation of the language (pp. 50-219) and the geographical distribution of its different dialects (pp. 220-225). The Appendix (pp. 226-240) is a list of verbs from the various dialects. Volume II presents the texts which served as the basis for the analyses in Volume I. Many of the texts were recorded on tape and transcribed with the help of the speakers. The speakers were all male adults, for the most part long-time residents in their native linguistic communities, and for the most part semi-literate or unlettered. The texts are mostly folk tales, with a few autobiographical or descriptive accounts of everyday life; there are two instances of conversational give and take, so that the majority of the texts are narratives. The author details his difficulties in finding informants speaking "pure" varieties of their own dialect; indeed, for Arbil he used an informant who was not a native of that city at all, but came from an outlying village. (Ernest McCarus/*Journal of the American Oriental Society* 84, 3, 1964: 305-310)

412   MacKenzie, David N. "Some Gorani Lyric Verse." *Bulletin of the School of Oriental and African Studies* 28 (1965): 255-283.

413   Makas, Hugo. *Kurdische Texte im Kurmanjî-Dialekte aus der Gegend von Märdîn: Gesammelt, Übersetzt, Erklärt und miteiner Einleitung, Anmerkungen und einem Glossar versehen*. Nebst *Kurdische Studien: eine Probe des Dialektes von Diarbekir; ein Gedicht aus Gawar; Jezidengebete: Texte nerausgegeben mit Kommentar und Ünbersetzt*. 2 vols. in 1. Amsterdam: APA; Philo Press, 1979. Reprint (1st work). Originally published: St. Petersburg, 1897-1926. Reprint (2nd work). Originally published: Heidelberg: C. Winter, 1900. Texts in Kurdish (Roman); translations, notes and introductions in German.

414   Mann, Oskar. *Die Mundart der Mukri-Kurden*. Berlin: G. Reimer, 1906-1909. 2 vols. [Kurdisch-Persische Forschungen; Kurdische Dialekte, Bd. 3, T. 1-2 Abt. 4] [In German]

These two volumes are part of Mann's *Kurdisch-persische Forschungen*. They are based on two and a half years of stay among Kurdish Mukri tribes. Volume I is 407 pages long and is composed of 106 pages discussing Kurdish grammar, including phonology, morphology, and syntax. The remaining 301 pages are reserved for Kurdish folklore, including popular stories, fables, and legends such as *Mem u Zin* and *Zambil Frush*. These texts are written in Arabic and Latin alphabets with German translations. Volume II is 529 pages long with 51 pages discussion of the various Kurdish dialects spoken by Kurds in Iran and the remaining pages being compilations of works related to Kurdish folklore. These two volumes are considered among the best written books on Kurdish language and folklore, particularly on Kurdish Mukri dialect.

415   Mann, Oskar; Hadank, Karl. *Kurdisch-persische Forschungen. Ergebnisse einer von 1901 bis 1903 und 1906 bis 1907 in Persien und der asiatischen Türkei ausgeführten Forschungsreise*. Berlin: W. de Gruyter, 1932. 7 vols.

416   McCarus, Ernest N. "David N. MacKenzie Kurdish Dialect Studies, Vols. I and II, 1961-1962." *Journal of the American Oriental Society* 84, no. 3 (1964): 305-310. [Review article.]

417   Morgan, Jacques de. *Mission Scientifique en Perse. Tome V. Etudes Linguistiques*. Dialectes Kurdes. Langues et Dialectes du Nord de la Perse. Paris: E. Leroux, 1904. 194 p.

Includes a comparison between the phonology and morphology of 13 different Kurdish dialects.

418   Müller, Friedrich. "Kurmangi-Dialekt der Kurdensprache." *Sitzungsberichte der K. Akademie der Wissenschaften, Philolophisch Historische Klasse* [Wien] 46 (1864): 450-480. [In German]

A study on the grammar of the Kurmanji dialect. The author emphasizes the independence of the Kurdish language from that of the modern Persian and claims that there are many words in Kurdish that cannot be found in Persian.

419   Müller, Friedrich. "Zaza-Dialekt der Kurdensprache." *Sitzungsberichte der K. Akademie der Wissenschaftlen* 48 (1864): 227-245. [In German]

A study on the grammar of the Zaza dialect.

420   Nawabi, Mahyar. "Notes on the Interpretation of the Terms Soran and Sorani." *Acta Kurdica: The International Journal of Kurdish and Iranian Studies* 1 (1994): 79-80.

At the end of the 18th century Soran was the name of a small principality roughly corresponded with Arbil. The language of the population of this region is called Sorani-Kurdish, although in Iranological literature it implies often the whole system of Southern Kurdish dialects as opposed to Kurmanji symbolizing the Northern group of Kurdish idioms. These terms as far as the author knows, have not as yet a reliable explanation.

421   Nikitine, Basile. "Notes sur le Kurde." In *Oriental Studies in Honour of Cursetji Erachji Pavry*. London: Oxford University Press, 1933.

422   Soane, Ely Bannister. "A Southern Kurdish Folksong in Kermanshahi Dialect." *Journal of the Royal Asiatic Society* (1909): 35-51.

At the time, Soane was considering Kurdish language as "nothing more than a Persian dialect." Later, however, he described it as the least dialect influenced by foreign languages and that the "Kurdish tongues (for there are many dialects) present an almost fundamentally pure Persian dialect, though much spoiled by corruption in pronunciation." Soane then presents a poem that he uses to compare between modern Kurdish and Persian.

423   Soane, Ely Bannister. "Notes on a Kurdish Dialect, the Shadi Branch of Kurmanji." *Journal of the Royal Asiatic Society* (1909): 895-922.

Discusses the substantive, pronouns, and the adjective, and provides some specimens of prose.

424   Soane, Ely Bannister. "Notes on a Kurdish Dialect, Sulaimania (Southern Turkish Kurdistan)." *Journal of the Royal Asiatic Society* (October 1912): 891-940.

The author starts this article by saying that the short sketch of the Sulaymani dialect of Kurdish here presented is part of the result of a study during residence of several months in and about that town. The dialect is closely allied to, and its grammatical forms identical with, that of the Mukri, a widespread tongue probably meriting the title of the main Kurdish language. The author then argues that the Sulaymani dialect is the purest of all Kurdish dialects; that is, it is very little influenced by Turkish, Persian, or Arabic. He also says that it is very for Kurds speaking the Sulaymani dialect to understand Kurds living in today's Turkish Kurdistan, but they will be at pain understanding Kurds living further south. Offers some notes on the corruptions due to mispronunciation in Sulaymani. Topics discussed include: The Substantive; The Verb; The Conditional; Pronouns; Adverbs, propositions, etc.; and Poetry. Also included is an 11-pages list of verbs.

425   Soane, Ely Bannister. *Report on the Sulaimania of Kurdistan*. Calcutta: Superintendent government printing press, 1918. 161 p.

426   Soane, Ely Bannister. "Short Anthology of Guran Poetry." *Journal of the Royal Asiatic Society* (1921): 57-81.

427   Vahman, Fereidun. "Kurdish and Bakhtiari." *Acta Kurdica: The International Journal of Kurdish and Iranian Studies* 1 (1994): 109-110.

428   Vahman, Fereidun; Asatrian, Garnik S. "Gleanings from Zaza Vocabulary." In *Iranica Varia: Papers in Honor of Professor Ehsan Yarshater*. Leiden: E. J. Brill, 1990. (Acta Iranica 30-Textes et Memoires 16). pp. 267-275.

Because the main part of the region inhabited by the Zazas, as well as almost the whole part of Turkish Kurdistan, is not easily accessible to investigators, the authors collected in the autumn of 1988, from Zaza speaking refugees living in Denmark, some dialect materials of which a short sketch on the vocabulary of the dialect is presented.

See also items: 25, 374, 379, 387, 466, 467, 475, 477, 691

DICTIONARIES AND WORD STUDIES

429   Amindarov, Aziz. *Kurdish-English, English-Kurdish Dictionary*. New York: Hippocrene Books, 1994. 400 p.

This dictionary provides a comprehensive reference to the Kurmanji dialect. A guide to the pronunciation and parts of speech accompanies each entry. The author's method of transliteration, customized for the Kurdish and English phonetic systems, simplifies usage.

430   Blau, Joyce. *Kurdish-French-English Dictionary=Dictionnaire kurde-francais-anglais*. Brussels: Centre pour l'etude des problemes du monde musulman contemporain, 1965. xvii, 263 p. (Correspondance d'Orient, no. 9). Bibliography: p. xiii-xvi.

This was an early attempt by Joyce Blau of the Sorbonne to compile a dictionary of literary Kurmanji. The words which appear in it are largely taken from the Kurdish journals of the 1930's and 1940's, which endeavored to create a vocabulary to deal with modern issues. The English definitions are often mistranslations of the French definitions, themselves of questionable reliability, since many of the words never became part of the living language. Although the gender of nouns is included, according to Professor MacKenzie the gender is often incorrect, or at least in conflict which what is attested elsewhere. The present stem of verbs is regularly given, but the issue of transitivity is not addressed. Neither the aspirated/unaspirated dichotomy nor the guttural sounds are recognized. This work is basically an early mistake, which even Blau herself will concede. Fortunately, her *Le Kurde de 'Amadiya et de Djabal Sindjar*, makes up for it. (Michael Chyet)

431   Blau, Joyce. *Kurdish Kurmandji Modern Texts Introduction: Selection and Glossary*. Wiesbaden, Harrassowitz, 1968. 58 p.

Makes use of five texts that were taken from the works of five "modern" Kurdish authors. These texts are: "The lion (killed) with a stick" (Osman Sebri); "The Peasant's life" (Cegerxwin); "Tree of Miracles" (Ereb Samilov); "The Mourning of the Kurds" (Ehmed Mirazi); and At the Doctor" (Musa Anter).

432 Gewranî, Ali Seydo al- [Gurani, 'Ali Saydu]. *Ferhenga Kurdî Nûjen: Kurdî-Erebî = al-Qâmûs al-Kurdî al-Hadith: Kurdî-'Arabî*. [The modern Kurdish dictionary: Kurdish-Arabic] Amman: Sharikat al-Sharq al-Awsat lil-Tiba'a, 1985. 672 p. Includes bibliographical references.

This Kurmanji-Arabic dictionary is riddled with misprints. Neither the gender of nouns, nor the transitivity or present stem of verbs is indicated. Nevertheless, this dictionary by a Jordanian Kurd includes almost the entire vocabulary used in the important Kurdish journals *Hawar* and *Ronahî* and the newspaper *Roja Nû*, all of which appeared in the1930's and 1940's. Consequently, a good deal of journalistic vocabulary is included. With regard to phonetics, some attempt is made to use the gutturals , although not consistently. Moreover, neither emphatics nor aspirated consonants are indicated. (Michael Chyet)

433 Gharib, Kamal Jalal. *al-Qamus al-'Ilmi al-Musawwar: 'Arabi, Inklizi, Kurdi = Scientific Dictionary, Pictorial: Arabic, English, Kurdish. Yashmulu Majmu'a min al-Kalimat wa-al-Mustalahat al-'Ilmiyah fi Mawadi' al-Hayawan wa-al-Nabat wa-al-Adawat wa-al-Fizya' wa-al-Kimya' wa-al-Falak. Volume I*. [A pictroial science dictionary: Arabic-English-Kurdish] Tartib wa-istinsakh Faysal Mustafa Haji. Baghdad: Matba'at al-Ajyal, 19?. 102 p.: ill.

434 Gharib, Kamal Jalal. *al-Qamus al-'Ilmi: 'Arabi, Inklizi, Kurdi. Volume II*. [A science dictionary: Arabic-English-Kurdish] Baghdad: al-Majma' al-'Ilmi al-Kurdi, 1979. 403 p.

435 Hakim, Halkawt; Gautier, Gerard. *Dictionnaire Francais-Kurde*. Paris: Klincksieck, 1993. 247 p.

436 Houtum-Schindler, A. "Beitrage zum kurdischen Wortschatze." *Zeitschrift der Deutschen Morgenländischen Gesellschaft* 38 (1884): 43-116.

437 Houtum-Schindler, A. "Weitere Beitrage zum kurdischen Wortschatze." *Zeitschrift der Deutschen Morgenländischen Gesellschaft* 42 (1888): 73-79.

438 Jaba, Alexandre Auguste; Justi, Ferdinand. *Dictionnaire kurde-francais*. Osnabruck: Biblio-Verlag, 1975. 463 p. (Reprint of the 1879 ed. pub-

lished by Commissionaire de l'Academie imperiale des sciences, Saint Petersburg).

This is the first important early Kurdish-foreign language dictionary. The approximately 15,000 entries are in Arabic script with a rather unsystematic Latin transcription. Although this work predates the modern orthographies and is of little use for phonological purposes, the definitions are remarkably thorough and reliable, which is all the more praiseworthy considering the limited resources available at the time. Earlier vocabularies, such as those of Garzoni, Rhea, Lerch, and Prym and Socin, are subsumed into this work. The major drawbacks of the work are, in addition to the transcription system already mentioned, that the gender of nouns, as well as the present stem and transitivity of verbs, are not regularly given. (Michael Chyet)

439 Justi, Ferdinand. "Les noms d'animaux en kurde." *Revue de Linguistique, et de Philologie Comparee* 11 (1878): 1-32.

440 Khalidi, Diya' al-Din Pacha al- [Yusuf Diya' al-Din al-Khalidi al-Maqdisi]. *al-Hadiyah al-Hamidiyah fi al-Lughah al- Kurdiyah=Dictionnaire kurde-arabe*. 2nd rev. ed. Translated and edited by Mohammad Mokri. Beyrouth: Librarie du Liban, 1987. 240, 56 p. [Textes et études religieux, linguistiques et ethnographiques; no. 4.]

First published in 1892, this is a Kurdish-Arabic dictionary based on the dialect of Bitlis, Turkish Kurdistan. Diya' al-Din Pasha, a Palestinian Arab, was a high-ranking Ottoman official, and composed the dictionary while he was *kaymakam* (governor) of Motkî in the *vilayet* of Bitlis. It is in Arabic script, and although it predates the modern orthography, it employs a system that corresponds exactly to the later orthographies. Although neither the gender of nouns nor the transitivity of verbs is indicated, the present stem of verbs is regularly included. The meanings given are generally quite reliable. It was reissued in Turkey in 1978, with Turkish translations rather than the original Arabic, by M. Emin Bozarslan. Includes itroductions in French and English. (Michael Chyet)

441 Ma'ruf, 'Abd al-Rahman. "Mujaz Tarikh Wad' al-Qawamis al-Kurdiyah." [A historical overview of Kurdish dictionaries] *al-Majma' al-'Ilmi al-Kurdi* 3, no. 2 (1975): 705-728.

442 McCarus, Ernest N. *A Kurdish-English Dictionary: Dialect of Sulaimania, Iraq*. Ann Arbor: The University of Michigan Press, 1967. x, 194 p. (University of Michigan Publications in Kurdish; 5)

Produced under a contract with the U.S. Office of Education. The work has been underway for some six years and the collaboration of Professor McCarus with Mr. Abdulla of the Higher Institute of Languages at the

University of Baghdad. This dictionary contains all the words occurring in the *Kurdish Basic Course* and the three *Kurdish Readers*, some 3,500 entries. Each word is given in the Kurdish alphabet and in transcription. Every work of more than one syllable has the stress marked. The scope of this dictionary is considerably less than the recent Kurdish dictionary by Wahby and Edmonds, but it should serve adequately for additional reading. The McCarus volume has an advantage over that of Wahby and Edmonds in that a more accurate phonemicization is used. However, one who is familiar with the McCarus volume will have no difficulty in using Wahby and Edmonds. (abridged, E. R. Oney/*Journal of the American Oriental Society* 90, 1970: 295-296)

443 Mokri, Mohammad. *The Name of Birds in Kurdish=Namhai Parindga'n dar lehjahai kurdi*. Karachi, Pakistan: Saad Publications (Translation Division), 1978. 180 leaves: ill. [At head of title: From Iranology Society, Publications, no. 5, 1947, 155 p. "TT 77-53127." "Prepared for the Smithsonian Institute and the National Science Foundation, Washington, D.C." Translated from Kurdish.] Includes bibliographical references.

444 Mukriani, Giv. *al-Murshid: Qamus Madrasi fi-al-Lughahtayn al-'Arabiyah wa-al-Kurdiyah* [The guide: a scholastic dictionary in Arabic and Kurdish.] Irbil, Iraq: Kurdistan Press, 1950. xvi, 400 p.

445 Nizam al-Din, Fadil. *al-Najma al-Lami'ah: Qamus Kurdi-'Arabi*. Baghdad: al-Jamhuriyah al-'Iraqiyah, Wizarat al-I'lam, Dar al-Thaqafah wa-al-Nashr al- Kurdiyah, 1977. 774 p.

446 Omar, Feryad Fazil. *Kurdisch-Deutsches Wörterbuch (Kurmanci)/Ferhenga Kurdi-Elmani*. xiv, 721 p. Berlin: Kurdische Studien Berlin im VWB-Verlag für Wissenschaft und Bildung, 1992. [In German]

This is the only Kurmanji dictionary to provide main entries in both Arabic and Latin script, thereby making it accessible to Kurds in Iraq and Iran as well as to those in Turkey. The author says in the preface that the present work is intended for the use of Germans learning Kurdish and Kurds learning German. Mention is also made of meeting the needs of scholars. The needs of average users of a dictionary are obviously met when most of the words for which they need an equivalent can be found there. Considering the present state of Kurdish lexicography it would be unfair to criticize individual authors too heavily for failing to include words which might have been useful--we should be grateful for those that are there. Still, it seems legitimate to mention that the author's method of collecting Bahdinani material from some written sources only tends to make the dictionary less than adequate where this dialect is concerned; the same may be true for Armenian Kurdish. A quick comparison with the reviewer's very basic private notes on spoken Bahdinani showed that a large percentage of common words are not to be found in the present work. Similarly, the dictionary has seldom proved helpful to the reviewer in his work on Yezidi religious texts in Bahdinani. Still, those who mainly wish to know the German equivalent of common Kurmanji words will certainly find this dictionary helpful, and in spite of the few points mentioned above Kurdologists will also welcome this useful and generally reliable addition to the still limited number of Kurmanji dictionaries. (Philip G. Kreyenbroek/*BSOAS* 60, pt. 1, 1997: 143-144)

447 Rizgar, Baran. *Kurdish-English English-Kurdish Dictionary*. [Kurmanji] London: M. F. Onen, 1993. 400 p.

A dictionary of Kurdish in the Latin alphabet which includes words from all Kurdish dialects, but is based on Kurmanji which is spoken by most of the Kurds residing in Turkey, Syria and former Soviet Union and by many of those who are residing in Iraqi and Iranian Kurdistan. The work includes a survey of Kurdish grammar, and also a table of correspondences for Arabic and Cyrillic scripts.

448 Rodiger, E.; Pott, A. F. "Kurdische Studien." *Zeitschrift fur die Kundefdes Morgenlandes* 3 (1840): 1-63; 4 (1841): 1-42 and 259-280; 5 (1843): 57-83; and 7 (1850): 91-167. [In German]

449 Wahby, Taufiq; Edmonds, Cecil John. *A Kurdish-English Dictionary*. London: ABC Publishing, 1996. x, 179 p.: table. A reprint of the 1966 ed. (Oxford: Clarendon Press).

This is the first Kurdish dictionary to be published in a Western European language since 1879. The language is "the standard language of belles-lettres, journalism, official and private correspondence, and formal speech as it has developed on the basis of the Southern-Kurmanji dialect of Sulaymania in Iraq, since 1918, when Kurdish was established as the official language of the administration and of primary education in the *liwa* of that name and in parts of the *liwas* of Arbil and Kirkuk." It is also the language used in Kurdish publications and broadcasts sponsored by the Persian government. The dictionary is in Roman script. The spelling used is a transliteration of a modified Arabic alphabet devised by Taufiq Wahby, which is to be adopted by the Iraqi ministry of education for use in schools. It avoids invented letters and has a minimum of diacritical marks. The arrangement of the material is clear. Much useful grammatical information is to be found in the body of the dictionary. Two short appendices, one on the conjugation of the verb and the other on the construction of sentences having a transitive verb in the past tense, supplement the grammatical information in the body of the dictionary. Another appendix gives a piece of continuous Kurdish prose with an English translation. For Persian scholars as well as Kurdish there is much of interest in the book, not least the changes in meaning that some words undergo. The authors have put students of Kurdish and Persian in their debt by the publication of this dictionary and they are to be congratulated on an admirable piece of work, the meticulous care with which it has been produced, and the exactness and accuracy of their renderings of the Kurdish words and phrases into English. (abridged, Ann K. S. Lambton/*Asian Affairs* 54, February 1967: 84-85)

450 Zilan, Reso. *Ferhenga Swedi-Kurdi (Kurmanci)=Svensk-Kurdiskt lexicon (Nordkurdiska)*. Stockholm: SIL, Statens Institut for Laromedel, 1989. 311 p.: col. ill.

See also items: 394, 399, 405, 424, 451, 474, 691

GRAMMAR

451 Akrawy, F. R. *Standard Kurdish Grammar*. Great Britain: F. R. Akrawy, 1982. 200 p.

According to the author, *Standard Kurdish Grammar* is standardized from different dialects, for the first time, to be the literary Kurdish language. Contents of the book include: Introduction—Kurds, their country 'Kurdistan', distribution of their population, etc.; Foreign influence on the Kurdish language; The present status of the language, classification and distribution of its dialects; Features of and criteria for the *Standard Kurdish language*; Standard Kurdish alphabet, its phonemes, pronunciation and writing; and Grammar which covers all parts of speech in depth and detail with many examples and vocabularies. Composition, speech, punctuation and Index are also included. According to Akrawy, the book is a new and scientific way to write, learn and teach Kurdish.

452 Asatrian, Garnik S.; Livshits, Vladimir. "Origine du systeme consonantique de la langue kurde." *Acta Kurdica: The International Journal of Kurdish and Iranian Studies* 1 (1994): 81-108.

453 Bedir-Khan, Celadet Ali. *Grammaire kurde*. [Kurdish grammar] Damascus: s.n., 1937.

454 Bedir-Khan, Celadat Ali; Lescot, Roger. *Grammaire kurde (dialecte kurmandji)*. [Kurdish grammar (Kurmanji dialect)] Paris: Librarie d'Amerique et d'Orient, 1970. 372 p.

A grammar of the Kurdish Kurmanji dialect which is generally the language of communication and literature among most Kurds. Bedir Khan was a progressive Kurdish linguist who advocated the romanization of the Kurdish alphabet.

455   Bedir-Khan, Kamuran Ali. *Langue Kurde: eléments de grammaire extraits des cours donnés à l'Ecole nationale des langues orientales vivantes*. 3rd ed. Paris: s.n., 1968. 106 p.

456   Beidar, Paul. *Grammaire kurde*. Paris: Librairie orientaliste P. Geuthner, 1926. 77 p.

457   Bynon, Theodora. "The Ergative Construction in Kurdish." *Bulletin of the School of Oriental and African Studies* 42, pt. 2 (1979): 211-224.

This paper attempts to trace the way in which the ergative construction has disappeared from a certain area of western Iranian. It bases its arguments upon the assumption that the geographical continuum of the Kurdish dialects, whose grammars exhibit the whole range of possibilities from fully ergative systems in the north to fully accusative systems in the south, reflects the successive stages of a diachronic process. This being granted, it should be possible by ordering the synchronic patterns of representative dialects from the northern, the central and the southern regions, to arrive at a picture of the historical sequence of events that have led to loss of ergativity in the southern dialects and to isolate the mechanisms involved in their resultant restructuring. The author focuses particularly on the Kurdish of Sulaymania.

458   Bynon, Theodora. "From Passive to Active in Kurdish via the Ergative Construction." In *Papers from the 4th International Conference on Historical Linguistics*. Edited by Elizabeth Closs Traugott, Rebeca Labrum and Susan Shepherd, pp. 151-163. Amsterdam: John Benjamins B.V., 1980.

Examines the rise and fall of the ergative construction in western Iranian by tracing the development of the Old Iranian perfect passive, via the ergative construction of western Middle Iranian and northern Kurdish, to a nominative-accusative type active in certain southern Kurdish dialects. An attempt is made to show that, although the syntactic change involved may be summarized simply enough as the transfer of surface subject status from the goal to the agent, its implementation cannot be described in terms of constituent structure alone. Only if the descriptive framework is widened to include thematic structure can the developments be accounted for. It is true that the ergative construction resembles a passive regarding both concord and case marking. Deriving the ergative construction from an underlying transitive sentence in a nominative-accusative language by means of obligatory passivization, however, disregards its thematic structure. The topic of an ergative construction is the agent and not, as in the case of a passive, the goal. It is therefore necessary to postulate, in addition to obligatory passivization, obligatory agent topicalization. Evidence from the Kurdish dialects points to two distinct topicalization processes: a simple change in word order leaving case marking intact and repetition of the syntactic features of the morphologically unmarked agent by insertion of its pronominal copy into the body of the sentence. It can be shown that these topicalization processes had the effect of converting an originally marked structure (the passive) into an unmarked one (the ergative construction), a change motivated by the total loss in the past tenses of the old unmarked active. The final step, substitution of a nominative-accusative type concord for an ergative one, is confined to the extreme south (Sulaymania) and can readily be accounted for in purely syntactic terms as directly resulting from loss of the verbal endings marking ergative concord and the ensuing conflation of agent and surface subject.

459   Dorleijn, Margreet. *The Decay of Ergativity in Kurmanci: Language Internal or Contact Induced?* Tilburg [Netherlands]: Tilburg University Press, 1996. 183 p. Includes bibliographical references (p. [175]-179). [Studies in multilingualism, 3] [In Dutch.]

This study wants to give an impression of the influence of Turkish on the Kurmanji dialect of Kurdish. More in particular, it intends to offer a treatment of split ergativity in Kurmanji. The aim is to show, on the basis of emerging patterns of variation, how varieties of Kurmanji are on the road to becoming nominative/accusative altogether. One of the main findings is that, besides internal tendencies, contact with Turkish may be a determining factor in this process. (A)

460   Dorleijn, Margreet. "Loss of Ergativity in the Kurmanci Dialect of Kurdish Spoken in Turkey." *Dutch Studies* 2, no. 2 (1996): 193-204.

461   Fossum, Ludvig Olsen. *A Practical Kurdish Grammar with English Phonetic Pronunciation, Exercises for Translation into Kurdish, Short Stories Illustrating Kurdish Composition and Syntax, and Vocabulary.* Minneapolis: Inter-Synodical Evangelical Lutheran Orient- Mission Society, 1919. 279 p.

462   Friend, Robyn C. "Enveloping Ambiopositions in Sulaymania Kurdish." In *Select Papers from SALA-7: South Asian Languages Analysis Roundtable Conference*, held in Ann Arbor, Michigan, May 17-19, 1985. Edited by Elena Bashir, Madhav M. Deshpande, and Peter Edwin Hook, pp. 132-140. Bloomington, Ind.: Indiana University Linguistics Club, 1987.

This paper describes some of the issues surrounding the use of prepositions and postpositions in Sulaymania Kurdish, a north-western Iranian language spoken in Sulaymania, Iraq. Sulaymania Kurdish employs both prepositions and postpositions. These can be used together, with a preposition before the object noun-phrase (NP) and a postposition after the object NP. These types of constructions are called "ambipositions." Sulaymania Kurdish has many different prepositions, but only two commonly occurring postpositions: /(d)a/ and /awa/. Two issues concerning the use of ambiposition constructions in Sulaymania Kurdish are the following: (1) What is the difference in usage between postpositions?; and (2) What is the difference between a prepositional phrase with a postposition and a prepositional phrase without a postposition? Examination of these issues seems to indicate that the differences are lexical, i.e., each NP or preposition-NP combination determines whether or not a postposition is used, and in the case where a postposition is used, which one it will be. (A)

463   Garzoni, Maurizio. *Grammatica e Vocabolario della Lingua Kurda.* Rome: Sacra Congregazione di Propaganda Fide, 1787. 288 p. [In Italian]

This is one of the first books to be published on Kurdish grammar and vocabulary. The author lived among the Kurds of 'Amadiya for 18 years and used their dialect to collect data for this book. It is composed of two parts: a 64-page discussion of Kurdish grammar and a 208-page Italian-Kurdish vocabulary (approximately 5,000 words). Garzoni's book marks the beginning of Western European interest in studying the Kurdish language.

464   Haig, Geoffrey. "On the Interaction of Morphological and Syntactic Ergativity: Lessons from Kurdish." *Lingua: International Review of General Linguistics* 105, no. 3-4 (August 1998): 149-173.

A detailed analysis of ergativity in Kurdish demonstrates that ergativity is indeed a relatively superficial phenomenon without further consequences for other levels of grammatical organization. Hence the usefulness of alignment as a typological parameter is questionable. Kurdish data are presented on morphological alignment, several syntactic processes, & voice phenomena. Finally, evidence from the loss of ergativity in Kurdish (Dorleijn, M., 1996) is discussed to provide further support for the analysis.

465   Jardine, Robert Frier. *Bahdinan Kurmanji: A Grammar of the Kurmanji of the Kurds of Mosul Division and Surrounding Districts of Kurdistan.* Baghdad: Printed at the Government press, 1922 1 p. l., vii, 114 p.

466   Justi, Ferdinand. *Kurdische Grammatik.* Walluf: Sändig Reprint, 1976. xxxiv, 256 p. Reprint of the 1880 edition published by Eggers, St. Petersburg. [In German]

Most of the works on Kurdish during the nineteenth century, whether grammars or vocabularies, were comparative in nature, seeking to relate Kurdish to other Indo-European languages. The most famous of these is Justi's, which uses all existing literature then to compare Kurdish dialects with each other or with other Indo-Iranian languages. Phonology (pp. 1-

101), morphology (pp. 102-122), and syntax (pp. 146-256) are treated in some detail.

467 Kalbassi, Iran. "Essai de comparaison du systeme verbal des dialectes kurdes de Mehabad, Sanandadj et Kermanchah." *Acta Kurdica: The International Journal of Kurdish and Iranian Studies* 1 (1994): 125-137.

468 Lecoq, Pierre. "La grammaire historique du kurde." *The Journal of Kurdish Studies* 2 (1996-1997): 31-36.

469 MacKenzie, David N. "Gender in Kurdish." *Bulletin of the School of Oriental and African Studies* 16 (1954): 528-541.

In this article, MacKenzie argues that it is not yet generally accepted in European works that a distinction of grammatical gender exists in Kurdish. In the Northern group of Kurdish dialects the *Izafe* appears in a number of forms. Members of the princely family of Bedir Khan have made an analysis of these forms into a clear system, with two declensions according to grammatical gender. A comparison of all the available texts in the light of their analysis serves to confirm the general validity of the paradigms and therefore of a distinction of grammatical gender, disguised to a varying extent by the generalization of certain forms. The history of a number of words of known gender suggests that the distinction is inherited. A hitherto unexplained phenomenon is the appearance in the Central Kurdish Mukri dialect of two forms of the nominal oblique case ending, -e and -i. The similarity of these forms to the corresponding Northern dialect forms is obvious. A comparison of related words in the two groups of dialects shows that in the Mukri dialect also the difference of the forms marks a distinction of grammatical gender. (A)

470 Matras, Yaron. "Ergativity in Kurmanji (Kurdish): Notes on its Use and Distribution." *Orientalia Suecana* [Sweden], no. 41-42 (1992-1993): 139-154.

This paper aims at presenting some data on the formal use of the ergative construction in the Kurmanji variety of Kurdish. Data on spontaneous speech was collected from a number of native speakers of Kurmanji, most of whom are Kurdish Jews originating from northern Iraq ('Amadiya and Akre) and now living in Israel. In addition, data from the literary language used by Kurds from the Turkish and Syrian parts of Kurdistan and now living and publishing in Western Europe is also considered. The author argues that the ergative construction in Kurmanji is obligatory and is therefore synchronically speaking not subject to optional processes of focusing or topicalization.

471 Matras, Yaron. "Clause Combining, Ergativity, and Coreferent Deletion in Kurmanji." *Studies in Language* 21, no. 3 (1997): 613-653.

A distinction is commonly made between morphological or surface ergativity, and syntactic or deep ergativity, based on what Dixon has termed
the "pivot" behavior (S/A vs. S/O) of a language. Since marked constructions enable an S/A pivot to function even in some deep ergative languages, deep or syntactic ergativity might be interpreted as gradational,
depending on the degree to which ergative morphology interferes with the
grammar of clause integration and referent coherence. For spoken Kurmanji, a northwest Iranian language with surface ergativity, tentative restrictions on zero-anaphora in conjoined clauses are identified which relate to ergative agreement patterns. These are compared to the distribution
of zero-anaphora in other complex constructions involving clause combining. Surface ergativity is found to be one of a variety of factors which
may promote relocation of the subject referent in a language in which
non-finite structures play a peripheral role, and multi-clause constructions
are under pressure to replicate the structure of single proposition clauses.
(A)

472   McCarus, Ernest Nasseph. *A Kurdish Grammar: Descriptive Analysis of
the Kurdish of Sulaimaniya, Iraq*. New York: American Council of
Learned Societies, 1958. xi, 138 p.: map, tables. (American Council of
Learned Societies. Program in Oriental Languages. Publications. Series
B: Aids, no. 10) Bibliography: p. 119-124.

Originally a doctoral dissertation (University of Michigan, 1957), this
work is a synchronic description of the phonology, morphology, and syntax of Sulaymania Kurdish. The corpus of data was obtained by the author in the field as a member of a University of Michigan expedition to
Iraq and Iran in 1951. Texts were recorded in phonetic notation from several literate adult male natives of Sulaymania, and covered a period of
four months. In Chapter 1 there is a description of data collection. The
status of previous studies on Kurdish is described, with brief annotation
of certain works. In Chapter 2, nine vowels and thirty-one consonants are
described. The distribution of vowels and consonants and syllable structure are also presented. Also described in this chapter are morphophonemic process involving vowels and consonants. Morphology is presented
in Chapter 3, "Form classes and their inflections," and Chapter 4, "Word
Formation." Form classes are formally defined by their inflections; they
are nouns, adjectives, pronouns, verbs, and particles. Chapter 5, "Syntax,"
treats the structure of utterances larger than a word: nominal and verbal
phrases, both minimal, expanse, and clauses. Includes an Appendix that
contains two illustrative texts in phonemic transcription with interlinear
as well as free translations. McCarus's grammar should help to make basic information on the language more widely available. The morphology
seems to be adequately outlined without recourse to difficult technicali-
ties, but at the expense of an occasional lack of rigor. As is all too often
the case, the syntax is only briefly described, and the structure is not always made clear. It contains two short texts in Kurdish script and tran-

scription with literal and free translations. Past work on the language has not been neglected, and there are brief critical comments on several of the older grammars.

473 Melikian, Gourgen. "Some Judeo-Persian-Kurdish Lexical Parallels." *Acta Kurdica: The International Journal of Kurdish and Iranian Studies* 1 (1994): 147-148.

474 Rhea, Samuel A. "Brief Grammar and Vocabulary of the Kurdish Language of the Hakari District." *Journal of the American Oriental Society* 10, no. 1 (1872-1880): 118-154.

Discusses the phonology and morphology of the Kurdish language, including orthography, nouns, pronouns, adjectives, numerals, verbs, first, second and third conjugation, prepositions, conjunctions, and adverbs. Includes a 20-pages long vocabulary.

475 Soane, Ely Bannister. *Grammar of the Kurmanji or Kurdish Language*. London: Luzac and Company. 1913. xiii, 289 p.

The introductory notice gives a short account of the chief Kurdish poets, together with remarks on the main dialects of the Kurdish tongue, which the author derives from that of the ancient Medes, as distinct from that of the Persians. In the first part of the book, the grammar of the language is simply and clearly taught, in the second part the "Idiomatic Uses" of verbs, nouns, pronouns, conjunctions, prepositions, etc., are explained. Particular value must be attached to the comparatively large selection of specimens of prose and poetry, with notes, and to the English-Kurdish vocabulary, the third part of the book.

476 Soane, Ely Bannister. *Elementary Kurmanji Grammar*. Baghdad: Printed at the government press, 1919. 197 p.

An abridgement of *Grammar of the Kurmanji or Kurdish Language*. It discusses the language morphology and includes a 70-pages long English-Kurdish vocabulary.

477 Socin, Albert. "Die Sprache de Kurden." *Grundriss der iranischen Philologie* 1 (1898): 249-286. [In German]

A standard general work. The author discusses the distribution of Kurdish dialects, Kurdish literature, Kurdish phonology and morphology in relation to other Iranian as well as non-Iranian languages.

478 Todd, Terry Lynn. *A Grammar of Dimili (Also Known as ZAZA)*. Ph.D., The University of Michigan, 1985, 295 p.

Dimili is an Iranian language, part of the Indo-Iranian subgroup of Indo-European. It is spoken in central eastern Turkey. Our knowledge of the structure of the language and had been based exclusively on field work done before 1910 partly due to official policy restrictions in the area where Dimili is spoken. The present research was done in West Germany where a number of Dimili speakers live as guest workers and/or refugees. A sizable corpus resulting from two years of monolingual elicitation is the source of data for this dissertation. The analysis consists of three chapters presented in a format which is a accessible to linguists of varied theoretical backgrounds and is cross referenced to the only substantial grammar of Dimili previously published (Mann-Hadank, 1932). Chapter one systematically describes the phonology including syllable structure and stress. Chapter two presents word structure and inflection. Chapter three illustrates phrases, clause and sentence syntax. Three appendices provide illustrative verb data, texts with English translations and a Dimili-English glossary of more than 1200 entries. (A)

See also items: 399, 410, 411, 414, 415, 418, 419, 424, 506, 508, 509, 511, 513, 515, 691

LATINIZATION AND STANDARDIZATION

479   Edmonds, Cecil John. "Suggestions for the Use of Latin Characters in the Writing of Kurdish." *Journal of the Royal Asiatic Society* (January 1931): 27-46.

Edmonds begins his article with saying that the Kurdish language resembles the Persian in that it belongs to the Western Iranian group, but is distinguished from it by striking differences of sound, form, vocabulary, and syntax. He then adds that with a few exceptions, Kurdish was not ordinarily written before 1919. Kurdish was introduced as the written official language in parts of Iraqi Kurdistan only after the establishment of a semi-autonomous Kurdish province in Sulaymania, Arbil, and Kirkuk in the late 1910s. As the title of the article implies, the author offers some suggestions for the use of Latin character for the writing of Kurdish rather than the Arabic or Persian character.

480   Edmonds, Cecil John. "Some Developments in the Use of Latin Characters for the Writing of Kurdish." *Journal of the Royal Asiatic Society* (July 1933): 629-642.

An update of the author's "Suggestions for the Use of Latin Characters in the Writing of Kurdish." The changes suggested are based on Tawfiq Wahby's works and comments.

481   Izady, Mehrdad. "A Kurdish Lingua Franca?" *Kurdish Times* 2, no. 2 (1988): 13-24.

One of the problems that concern Kurdish intelligentsia is the unification of the Kurdish language. In this article, Izady proposes the formation of a synthetic language from a "northern Kurmanji" and a "meridional Kurmanji" (i.e., the central Kurdish). This language will be easily understood without difficulty by all Kurds, confirms Izady. (Joyce Blau/*AI* 12: 135)

482   Matras, Yaron; Reershemius, Gertrud. "Standardization Beyond the State: The Case of Yiddish, Kurdish and Romani." In *Standardization of National Languages: Symposium on Language Standardization, 2-3 February 1991*. Edited by Utta von Gleich and Ekkehard Wolff, pp. 103-123. Symposium on Language Standardization (1991: Hamburg, Germany). Hamburg, Germany: Unesco Institute for Education, 1991.

A standardized "national language" is still considered to be an important identity card of a sovereign national community. It reflects and transmits what people regard as their "national heritage" or "national culture". But what is the role of modern standardization other than to cater as a medium for state institutions, and how can a "national language" emerge without being able to rely upon the authority of government organs? The authors deal with this question, comparing three ethnic minority languages: Yiddish—a language of Medieval German origin spoken by Eastern-European Jews; Kurdish; and Romani-a language of Northwest Indian origin spoken by an estimated number of 10-15 million Roma (Gypsies) in Europe and in the Americas. The authors look at the way standardization becomes a function of the speakers' own initiative after generations of intensive contact with several different administration and state languages used when dealing with the population and institutions of various host countries or occupying forces, respectively. The authors also consider some essential differences between several background factors: For example, Yiddish and Romani have never been centered in one geographic area, except at the very beginning of their existence. They are therefore typically "diaspora languages." Kurdish, on the other hand, is one of the most important languages of the Middle East, and despite various attempts on the part of the occupiers to assimilate and displace the indigenous population of Kurdistan, it is still the majority language of the region. Its dialects are dispersed along a language-geographical continuum, merging ultimately with related languages such as Lur and Farsi. It is due to political circumstances during the last century that standardizers of one of the main Kurdish varieties, Kurmanji, have been reluctant to achieve their goals within their country and that the center of literary activity has been shifted into exile communities in Western Europe. (A)

483   Minorsky, Vladimir F. "Remarks on the Romanized Kurdish Alphabet." *Journal of the Royal Asiatic Society* (July 1933): 643-650.

Suggests that attention must be paid to what Edmonds had offered; that is, the use of the Latin alphabet in the writing of Kurdish. Describes the inconvenience of Arabic alphabet for the writing of Kurdish and suggests that the Latin alphabet for the writing of Kurdish be utilized in its most simple from with a few additions of conventional signs as possible. Summarizes the principles underlying Edmond's scheme and offers his own detailed observations on, and suggestions in regard to, the systems proposed by Edmonds in his 1931 and 1933 articles.

484   Resho, Hemresh. "On the History and Development of Writing the Kurdish Language in the Latin Alphabet." In *Yearbook of the Kurdish Academy 1990* (pp. 78-84). Ratingen, Germany: The Kurdish Academy, 1990.

485   Rondot, Pierre. "L'Alphabet kurde en characteres latins d'Armenie sovietique." *Revue des Etudes Islamiques* 3 (1933): 412-417.

486   Rondot, Pierre. "L'Adoption des characteres latins et le mouvement culturel chez les Kurdes de l'U.R.S.S." *Revue des Etudes Islamiques* (1935): 87-96.

487   Rondot, Pierre. "Trois essais de latinisation de l'alphabet kurde: Iraq, Syrie, U.R.S.S." *Bulletin d'Etudes Orientales* [Damacsus] 5 (1935): 1-31.

488   Rondot, Pierre. "Le probleme de l'unification de la langue kurde." *Revue des Etudes Islamiques* 3 (1936): 297-307.

See also items: 515, 404, 451, 524, 541, 691, 695, 696

PHILOLOGY, PHONOLOGY, AND MORPHOLOGY

489   Ahmad, Abdul-Majeed Rashid. *The Phonemic System of Modern Standard Kurdish*. Ph.D., The University of Michigan, 1986. 169 p.

Modern Standard Kurdish (MSK) is a written form of Kurdish adopted by the Iraqi Kurds to establish a standard written Kurdish substituting for the various Kurdish dialects spoken in Iraqi Kurdistan. MSK is based on the Sulaymania dialect, a sub-dialect of Southern Kurmanji (Sorani). Written documents published in Iraq after 1970 are the main source for this study. The documents include books and articles listed in the bibliography. They are written by speakers of various Kurdish dialects. The author used himself as the only principle reader, i.e., he was not able to find other readers of MSK in the United States; therefore, this initial study should be followed by additional studies. This study is based on the reading aloud of newly published documents and dozens of spectrograms. The author's native Kurdish dialect is the Babani dialect of the Kirkuk Altun Kopri area. Since MSK is based on the Sulaymania dialect, the sound system of MSK corresponds partially but not entirely to the dialect of Sulaymania. Differences between MSK and both Sulaymania and Babani dialects are presented. The environments for allophonic variations such as vowel length in different environments, and phonological changes such as substitution, deletion, and insertion are described. The ranges of vowel length are given based on spectrograms. Chapter One is a historical sketch of the written form of Kurdish in Iraqi Kurdistan. Pre-MSK is introduced from early period of written Kurdish, when there was no Standard Kurdish, until 1958, when the Republic of Iraq was established, and the standardization period evolved following its establishment around 1970. The evolution of Arabic script as adopted for Kurdish is discussed. Chapter Two introduces Kurdish vowels and gives rules for phonological change. In Chapter Three consonants are presented. Allophonic features such as voicing, and de-voicing, of consonants are described and rules for phonological processes such as deletion, substitution, and insertion are given. Chapter Four demonstrates the predictability of stress in terms of morphology. Chapter Five describes syllable structure in MSK and Chapter Six gives general conclusions. (A).

490   Bois, Thomas. "Etudes recentes de philologie kurde." *Bibliotheca Orientalis* 19 (1962): 10-17.

491   Chodzko, A. "Etudes philologiques sur la lange kurde." *Journal Asiatique* 9 (1857): 297-356.

The author, a specialist in Iranian studies at the time, took advantage of meeting with a Kurdish native from Sulaymania and learned the language from him. With the assistance of this native Kurd, Chodzko collected a wealth of primary material which was used to publish this paper. The article contains 12 pages of discussion on nouns, pronouns, and adjectives, 20 pages on verbs, and the last 20 pages on prepositions and a few verses of Nali's poems.

492   Darmesteter, James. *Études iraniennes: relatives à l'histoire des langues et des croyances de la Perse ancienne et moderne*. Amsterdam: Philo Press, 1971. 2 vols. in 1 (336, 380 p.). "Traductions indigènes du Khorda Avesta": vol. 2, p. [255]-343. Reprint of 1883 Paris ed.

493   Ferhadi, Ahmed. *Some Morphological and Morphophonemic Features of Arbili Kurdish*. Ph.D., The University of Michigan, 1990. 153 p.

This work represents the first major attempt to investigate Arbili (Hawleri) Kurdish which is spoken in Arbil Province. Never has this dialect of the *Sorani* group been studied in earnest before because it has been eclipsed by another *Sorani* dialect; viz. Sulaymania Kurdish (SLK), on which Standard Kurdish has been based. Studies of Arbili Kurdish (AK) are urgently needed since the speakers of AK have recently been moved out of their locale under duress to areas where either no Kurdish whatsoever is used or other forms of Kurdish are spoken. The perpetuation of the prevalent circumstances places the very survival of the dialect in dire jeopardy. This work is the first major contribution to recording AK. Furthermore, it provides first-hand data, which have been meticulously selected and checked for accuracy. These data can also be used for other meta-linguistic analyses and research purposes. In an endeavor to familiarize the Western linguists and /or scholars with the terminology and nomenclature of Kurdish dialects which their Kurdish counterparts prefer to nowadays, this study has provided the equivalency of what is familiar in the literature of both. The focus has been on presenting the phonology, morphology and morphophonemic of AK as it is actually spoken in everyday life without endeavoring to either deliberately approximate it to Standard Kurdish or purge it of loan words from neighboring languages-two common pitfalls that bedevil many Kurdish linguists nowadays. Emphasis has been placed on the complex system of *clitics* and their functions in AK. These *clitics* combine in a specific order according to their function. They are typologically rare in the sense that they may encliticize onto any element which appears immediately before the verb in AK, whose sentences are verb-final. AK has much more in common with some similar *Sorani* dialects spoken in Koye, Rawunduz and *Khoshnawati* areas than SLK does. Hence this study of AK can account for many of their linguist phenomena better than studies of the latter can. Areas of divergence from Standard Kurdish have been particularly elaborated upon. (A).

494 Friend, Robyn C. *Some Syntactic and Morphological Features of Suleimaniye Kurdish*. Ph.D., University of California, Los Angeles, 1985, 236 p.

This dissertation examines some syntactic and morphological features of the verbal system of the Sulaymaniya dialect of Southern Kurdish. This examination is based on the author's analyses of data in the form of sentences from Sulaymania Kurdish, which were gathered both from a native speaker and from written texts. The particular features under investigation in this dissertation are: the past transitive construction, person/number *clitics*, adpositions (particularly enveloping adpositions), compound verbs, and preverbal verbs. In the course of the author's analysis, she found evidence that the Sulaymania dialect of southern Kurdish employs a linguistically significant combination of two different systems of marking (i.e., distinguishing) subjects and objects in sentences. In the general linguistics literature, these two systems are termed ergative/absolutive and nominative/accusative. The author then undertook to determine the extent of ergativity in this grammar. This was accomplished by developing a set of test-criteria which could measure the degree to which the specified features (and the combination marking system), reflected the presence of an ergative/absolutive marking system, or on the other hand represented a nominative/accusative construction. The results of these tests demonstrated that there is obvious evidence of ergativity in Kurdish morphology in the past transitive tense, although there is no evidence of ergativity in the syntax. In addition to the examination of ergativity in Sulaymania Kurdish, this dissertation brings together the works of three other scholars in Kurdish linguistics: McCarus, MacKenzie, and Wahby, and presents their theories in a coherent way. (A)

495   Jastrow, Otto. "Zur Phonologie des Kurdischen in der Turkei." *Studien zur Indologie and Iranistik* 3, no. 8 (1977): 84-106. [In German]

496   Kahn, Margaret. *Borrowing and Variation in a Phonological Descriptive of Kurdish*. Ph. D., The University of Michigan, 1976. 164 p.

This work discusses the phonology of Northern Kurmanji as it is spoken around Rezaiyeh in Iranian Azerbaijan. The discussion is based on data collected in the field and includes a treatment of borrowing and variation as well as a traditional phonemic analysis. One feature, pharyngealization, is traced successively through phonetic, phonemic, and generative analyses and, finally, is considered in the context of loan assimilation and possible change in progress. The data are examined in relation to Kurmanji's complex multi-lingual social setting. Over time, Kurmanji has been in contact with Arabic, Turkish, Persian, Aramaic, and Armenian. Past and present political changes have caused the first three of these languages to carry prestige in relation to Kurmanji, a nonstandard language. For a long time Arabic was most prestigious, while in the present Persian appears to be a dominant influence. In order to provide a basis for later analysis of change and borrowing, the segmental phonemes, stress rules, and phonotactics of Kurmanji are discussed in detail. The assimilation of loan words, mainly from Arabic and Turkish, is considered according to the relative strength of prohibition against various types of incoming sequences. Kurmanji is shown to have had a high degree of tolerance for foreign segments in the past. This is reflected by two series of consonants, voiceless unaspirated and pharyngealized, which appear to have been borrowed. Finally, social information on the linguistic sources used in this analysis is compared to types of variation across speakers. A correlation is found between degree of education and/or bilinguality and the production of 'Persianized' variants. If the social change continues in the present direction and the sample taken here is representative of the population, then these variants indicate the direction of change in progress. The dissertation takes highly variable data from a linguistic crossroads and organizes it into a coherent phonological description. Although the main phonological description was seen as primary to a relatively unstudied language, evidence from borrowing and variation proved to be integral to that description. (A)

497   Mahamedi, Hamid. "Notes on Some Phonological Developments in Kurdish." *The International Journal of Kurdish Studies* 8, no. 1-2 (1995): 79-93.

Despite its large number of dialects and a rather large body of borrowed words from other Iranic/Iranian and non-Iranic/non-Iranian languages, Kurdish as a unit preserves its separate character and features. Kurdish, along with Persian, is thus the most important (and popularly spoken) West Iranian language. In this article, some of the phonological characteristics of Kurdish and its development are examined in comparison to those of other ancient and modern Iranian languages. The South Kurmanji dialect of Kurdish, better known as Sorani, is here used almost exclusively for the Kurdish paradigms. The article also shows that Parthian (Pahlawani) and Kurdish being both Northwest Iranian languages, reveal the most similarity in their phonological development.

498   McCarus, Ernest N. "Kurdish Phonology." In *Phonologies of Asia and Africa*. Vol. 2. pp. 691-706. Edited by Alan S. Kaye, Winnona Lake, Ind.: Eisenbrauns, 1997.

499   Soane, Ely Bannister. "Notes on the Phonology of Southern Kurmanji." *Journal of the Royal Asiatic Society* (1922): 191-226.

Soane cites Justi, Darmesteter, and Socin, and agrees with all of them that Kurdish is a language of its own. The author hopes that his notes may throw some new light upon the subject, and serve as a preliminary step to further investigation of a widely spoken language which has hitherto suffered neglect because of researchers' ignorance of it. Topics discussed include vowels, consonants, and losses of original letters and treatment of some consonant groups.

See also items: 375, 378, 380, 381, 383, 386, 387, 388, 391, 392, 398, 404, 411, 414, 417, 438, 464, 466, 471, 472, 474, 475, 476, 477, 478, 691, 696

STUDY AND TEACHING

500   'Abd al-Rahman, Rizgar 'Ali. *al-Wajiz fi Ta'lim al-Lughah al-Kurdiyah*. [A handbook for teaching the Kurdish language] Baghdad: Matba'at As'ad, 1987. 312 p.

501   Abdulla, Jamal Jalal; McCarus, Ernest Nasseph (eds.). *Kurdish Readers* (three volumes): *I. Newspaper Kurdish*. vii, 180 p.; *II. Kurdish Essays*. vii, 147 p.; *III. Kurdish Short Stories*. ix, 115 p. Ann Arbor: University of Michigan Press, 1967.

Assuming a mastery of the contents of the *Basic Course in Kurdish* (by the same authors), this reader presents a variety of 28 lessons selected from two Iraqi newspapers *Zhin* and *Khebat*. Each lesson begins with a selection written in Kurdish (modified Arabic-Persian) script, followed by phonemic transcription (in the first 15 lessons), a glossary, exercises on sentence structure and vocabulary, and a Kurdish proverb. The material contained in the three *Readers* gives a cross section of Kurdish writing, newspaper style, short stories and essays. The Newspaper Reader has phonemic transcriptions for the first fifteen selections. Each lesson is also followed by a vocabulary list and extensive exercises based on the lesson, a most useful feature which allows the student to continue a controlled development of his grammatical knowledge. On the Kurdish essays (12) and short stories (6), all selections are provided with vocabularies and notes. Although full phonemic transcriptions are no longer included, each word in the vocabulary list is transcribed. Original spellings are retained, giving the student experience with the different orthographic conventions which may be found. The six stories in this collection are written in the Kurdish dialect of Sulaymania, the language of official publications and textbooks in Iraqi Kurdistan. The various themes included are representative of Kurdish culture and tradition. Each selection (written in Kurdish script) is followed by vocabulary and explanatory notes in order of occurrence in the text. The introduction includes a brief history of Kurdish literary culture and a short bibliography. The vocabulary used in this reader and the preceding readers, *Newspaper Kurdish* and *Kurdish Short Stories*, is included in the *Kurdish-English Dictionary* by the same authors. (abridged, E. R. Oney/*Journal of the American Oriental Society* 90, 1970: 295-296)

502 Abdulla, Jamal Jalal; McCarus, Ernest Nasseph. *Kurdish Basic Course: Dialect of Sulaimania, Iraq*. Ann Arbor: University of Michigan Press, 1967. 482 p.

Produced under a contract with the U.S. Office of Education. The Sulaymania dialect is used in these volumes, the form which was adopted for purposes of administration and elementary education in Iraqi Kurdistan after the First World War. The *Basic Course* is divided into three sections. Section I contains a description of the Kurdish sound system with eight pronunciation drills concentrating on phonemic contrasts. The system of transcription is consistent and not overly complex. Section II consists of 13 dialogues for memorization, followed by additional vocabulary, grammatical notes and exercises. The latter are mostly substitution drills based on the dialogues. Most of the lessons have more than 20 such exercises. There is also provision for additional guided conversation. The Kurdish writing system is introduced in section III. The thirteen dialogues are repeated in the Kurdish script and three additional lessons, the last one a story about Mulla Nasr al-Din, from a transition from the conversational style to a more literary style. (abridged, E. R. Oney/*Journal of the American Oriental Society* 90, 1970: 295-296)

503 'Arif, 'Uthman. *Kayfa Nata'allam al-Lughah al-Kurdiyah*. [A handbook for learning Kurdish language without an instructor] Sulaymania, Iraq: s.n., 1971. 78 p.

504 Barzinji, M. *Ta'allam al-Lughah al-Kurdiyah Bidun Mu'allim*. [A handbook for learning Kurdish language without an instructor] Beirut: al-Jam'iyah al-Thaqafiyah al-Ijtima'iyah al-Kurdiyah, 1979.

505 Bedir-Khan, Kamuran Ali. *Le Kurde sans peine: cours pratiques de la langue Kurdes*. [Kurdish without pain: practical courses in Kurdish Language] Paris: Institut kurde de Paris, 1990. 206 p.

506 Blau, Joyce. *Manuel de kurde (dialecte sorani): grammaire, textes de lecture, vocabulaire kurde-francais et francais-kurde*. [Handbook of the Kurdish Language (Sorani Dialect): Grammar, Reading Texts, Kurdish-French and French-Kurdish Vocabulary] Paris: Klincksieck, 1980. 287 p.

This book opens with a full 63-item annotated bibliography of Sorani dictionaries and grammars, native and foreign, of which only one item (J. J. Abdulla and E. N. McCarus, Kurdish Basic Course: Dialect of Sulaymania, Iraq, Ann Arbor, 1967) predates it as a graduated primer in a European language. After a section on the alphabet (including, pronunciation and reading exercises), the grammar is divided into 31 sections. Unlike the American work, with its acres of "drills," Blau's is concentrated in a traditional way, each section having a short vocabulary and sentences, later passages, in French and Kurdish for translation. Longer reading exercises and fuller vocabularies, French-Kurdish and Kurdish-French, complete the work. The transcription is used wisely, practically identical with that of the excellent Kurdish-English Dictionary of Taufiq Wahby and C. J. Edmonds. But the Kurdish, i.e., augmented Arabic, script is also used throughout, in an admirably clear type. It also contains many appendices and a French-Kurdish and Kurdish-French glossary of more than 2,000 words. (D. N. MacKenzie/*BSOAS* 44, 1, 1981: 173-174)

507 Blau, Joyce; Hakim, Halkawt. *Perles d'un Collier, textes Kurdes (Sorani)*. [Pearls of Necklace, Kurdish Texts (Sorani)] Paris: Institut National des Langues et Civilisations Orientales, 1981. 85 p.

Twenty-seven texts chosen from a series of popular tales published by 'Ala' al-Din Sajjadi (*Ristey Mirwari*, Baghdad, 1957-1980). Each text is accompanied by lexical, grammatical and sociological notes, with a glossary at the end of the book summing up all the encountered words. It is an indispensable complementary work to *Manuel de Kurde (dialecte sorani)*. This work puts into the disposition of the Francophones the necessary instrument for studying one of the most important forms of Kurdish languages at present. (Dominique Ferrandini/*AI* 5: 665)

508 Kurd, Rashid. *Qawaʻid al-Lughah al-Kurdiyah*. [Kurdish grammar] Translated from Kurdish by Muhammad Jazzaʻ. Beirut: s.n., 1991.

509 Mukriyani, Kurdistan. *Qawaʻid al-Lughah al-Kurdiyah*. [Kurdish grammar] Baghdad: Wizarat al-Thaqafah wa-al-Tawjih, al-Qism al-Kurdi li-Mudiriyat al-Thaqafa, 1989. 208 p.

510 Minorsky, Vladimir F. "Livres scolaires en kurde." *Revue des Etudes Islamiques* 4 (1930): 157-160.

511 Pikkert, P. *A Basic Course in Modern Kurmanji*. Genk, Belgium: Alev Books, 1991. 59 p.

512 Rizgar, Baran. *Learn Kurdish: A Multi-Level Course in Kurmanji*. London: Rizgar, 1996. 299 p.

513 Sajjadi, ʻAlaʼ al-Din al-. *Dastur wa-Farhang-i Ziman-i Kurdy- ʻAraby-Farsy: Dalil Yabhathu ʻAn Qawaʻid wa-Muʻjam al-Lughaht al-Kurdiyah wa-al-ʻArabiyah wa-al-Farsiyah*. Baghdad: Matbaʻat al-Maʻarif, 1961. 240 p.

514 Wafi, ʻAbd al-Rahim. *Kayfa Tataʻallam al-Lughah al-Kurdiyah bi-Dun Muʻallim*. [How to learn Kurdish without an instructor] Baghdad: Matbaʻat Asʻad, 1959. 176 p.

515 Wahby, Tawfiq. *Qawaʻid al-Lughah al-Kurdiyah*. [Kurdish grammar] 2 vols. Beirut: Matbaʻat al-Bayan, 1956.

In August 1929 Lieut.-Colonel (now Senator) Taufiq Wahbi published the first half of his *Dastur-i Zman-i Kurdi*, a now Kurdish grammar in Kurdish for Kurds, in which for the first time a Kurdish scholar born and bred in Kurdistan sought to apply the methods of European scholarship to the analysis of his own language. The second half of the *Dastur* was unfortunately never published; but the author, by his other publications and for a time as Minister of Education in Iraq, has continued to exercise a profound influence on the development of the dialect of Sulaymania as a literary language adapted to the needs of administration, legal proceedings, and modern journalism. A knowledge of the language of local government, if not compulsory in the technical branches of the civil service, is a very desirable accomplishment for any official or officer assigned to the Kurdish areas of Iraq, as well as for unofficial merchants and travelers. The present work, based on the original *Dastur* but now recast in Arabic, is likely to be welcomed in that country as a contribution both to mutual understanding between the races and to the efficiency of the administration. So far only the first two chapters, in separate parts, have been received; it is much to be hoped that this laudable project will not go the way of so many others of its kind, and that publication of the remaining parts will not be unduly delayed. Chapter I is described as an independent essay on spelling, a favorite subject of discussion in the contemporary Kurdish press, but one in which practice cannot always march with theory owing to typographical difficulties. Chapter 2 deals with the parts of speech and the parts of the sentence in the manner of a school primer; its principal value for European students will lie in the liberal allowance of exercises and folk stories, all with Arabic translations, with which it, like Chapter 1, is provided. The printing is good and clear. A list of errata accompanies each fascicule, but a few misprints, mostly omissions of diacritical marks, have been overlooked. [C. J. Edmonds/*BSOAS* 19: 593-594]

14
Literature, Folklore, and Oral Traditions

GENERAL STUDIES/WORKS

516 Ahmed, Abdullah Mohammed. *Essai sur l'histoire de la litterature kurde au Kurdistan meridional (1820-1920)*. [Essay on the history of Kurdish literature in southern Kurdistan (1820-1920)] Ph.D., Universite de Paris III-Sorbonne Nouvelle, 1988.

This study is divided into three parts: 1) 1820-1860, a period during which central Kurdish is revealed to be a literary language: the pioneers; 2) 1860-1908, the expansion of this literary language, the great names in literature; 3) 1908-1920, the development of the press and modernization of central Kurdish. (Joyce Blau/*AI* 12: 863)

517 Allison, Christine. "Old and New Oral Traditions in Badinan." In *Kurdish Culture and Identity*. Edited by Philip G. Kreyenbroek and Christine Allison, pp. 29-47. Atlantic Highlands, NJ: Zed Books, 1996.

Discusses Kurdish oral traditions in the Kurmanji dialect, with particular reference to Bahdinan, the northern province of Iraqi Kurdistan. Many of the observations made in this chapter may also apply to other parts of Kurdistan, but the establishment of Kurdish authority in the Bahdinan region made it possible to study traditions there within their social context. The chapter outlines the status of the Kurdish language, before moving on to a discussion of some key features of oral, as opposed to written literature. A brief description of the political situation and the effect on Kurdish society of recent social changes, especially collectivization, is given also. Two oral genres are highlighted: one using old material and the other using modern material in traditional form, namely oral history as

performed by Yezidis and laments as sung by Muslim women of the Barzani tribe. Each of the two groups and their social situation are described
before examples of their songs are considered.

518   Allison, Christine. *Views of History and Society in Yezidi Oral Tradition*. Ph.D., London School of Oriental and African Studies, 1996.

The Yezidis are a Kurdish-speaking religious minority living mainly in
Northern Iraq. In the past their religion forbade literacy. Thus their accounts of their history and their descriptions of their society have been
preserved orally. This thesis considers how the Yezidis use oral literature,
or verbal art, to represent themselves and their past. It is based largely on
fieldwork carried out in Northern Iraq. The theoretical perspective of this
work combines elements of both literary and social studies by considering
both text and social context. The genre of a tradition has major implications for its content; three genres considered in detail are lyrical song,
prose narrative and extemporized lament. Yezidi discourse about the past
stresses their distinctive identity and their endurance against adversity and
persecution. This is reflected in the oral traditions, especially in the lyrical
song, which is performed at festivals and is extremely popular; prose narratives of events predating the immediate past, on the other hand, are in
decline. Most love songs and stories feature historical figures; the performance of lyrical love songs, many of which depict conflict between
the wishes of the individual and the rules of a society where marriage is
arranged, provides an outlet for the audience's own emotions. Laments
are performed by women. Using traditional imagery, they are a vehicle
for the expression of a variety of emotions by the performer. Their performance is a social duty and is likely to remain so. The texts included in
this work comprise variants of two historical themes, Ferîq Pasa and
Dawûdê Dawûd; variants of a theme of love, Derwêsê Evdî, and examples of women's lament, both semi-professional and personal. Some of
these were transcribed from material collected during fieldwork; all were
translated for this thesis. An appendix lists performers and informants.
(A)

519   Allison, Christine. "Oral History in Kurdistan: The Case of the Badinani
Yezidis." *The Journal of Kurdish Studies* 2 (1996-1997): 37-56.

Like other histories, Kurdish history is a construct of the past. However,
Kurdish history differs from the history of most other peoples in being
unsupported either by coherent propagation systems such as state education and media, or by international affirmation. Kurds must fashion their
own history, to meet their own needs, in opposition to many of the ideologies prevalent in the Middle East, some of which have sought to deny
the very existence of "Kurdish" history, and even of the Kurds themselves. Staking a claim to the past, by having one's own account of history, is a perfectly ordinary need of most communities; for the Kurds it

has become a key element of self-determination. Thus to make sense of Kurdish history, we must not only isolate the truth of past events, but also study the accounts the Kurds give, and attempt to determine why particular accounts have become dominant; for a satisfactory understanding, it is not enough to know what happened, but we must also discover what people believe to have happened, and try to determine why they believe this. The study of Kurdish history becomes an exercise in discourse analysis. The term "discourse" is used here in the sense of all kinds of active verbal communication, in other words the sum of what the Kurds say about events in the past. The Kurdish historical discourse receives much of its inspiration from the publications of Kurds in the diaspora, and some material published locally, but most of what is exchanged remains oral, partly because of the political climate in Iran, Iraq, Turkey and Syria, and also because many literate Kurds, educated in the official State language, are not sufficiently literate in Kurdish. In contemporary nation-states, the dominant discourse is usually expressed by written media and broadcast. Most histories are still written about those who rule. Oral history tends to chronicle the experience of those who have no input into "official" histories, and represents a perspective which is not that of the ruling group; thus by its very nature it is subversive to some extent. (A)

520   Badr-Khan, Rushin. *Safahat min al-Adab al-Kurdi*. [An overview of Kurdish literature] Beirut: Matba'at Samia, 1954. 71 p.

521   Blau, Joyce. *Memoires du Kurdistan: Recueil de la tradition litteraire orale et ecrite*. [Memories of Kurdistan: A Collection of the Oral and Written Literary Tradition] Paris: Editions Findakly, 1984. 220 p.

This work is the first real anthology of Kurdish literature compiled outside the Middle East, and the first to be published in a European language. With a preface by Maxime Rodinson, it contains translations into French of popular tales, poems, songs, proverbs, stories, etc., collected from Iraq, Iran, Turkey, Syria, Lebanon and the Soviet Union. The translations are by several Kurds and Kurdologists writing in French, those unsigned being presumably by the compiler herself. Unlike the rare works on the topic, it has the merit of not being limited to the traditional oral literature; it includes as well a large part of the written Kurdish literature—the second half of the book—where a selection of Kurdish literature from the 18th and 19th centuries and a larger collection of literary works from the modern period are presented. This is a work that is indispensable for any person interested in Kurdish literature. (Dominique Ferrandini/*AI* 8: 621)

522   Blau, Joyce. "Kurdes (Folklore et Litterarture)." In *Dictionnaire Universel des Litteratures*. Vol. 2, pp. 1952-1955. Edited by Beatrice Didier. Paris: Presses Universitaires de France, 1994.

523   Blau, Joyce. "La litterature kurde." (Kurdish Literature) *Peuples Mediter-*
raneens, no. 68-69 (July-December 1994): 77-94.

During their long turbulent history, the Kurds have tirelessly fought for
the preservation of their cultural identity. In modern time, first in the
midst of large pluralistic ethnic empires, then in nation-states among
which their country—Kurdistan—found itself split after the first world
war, the difficult struggle of the Kurds to gain recognition of their national rights is closely linked to the flourishment of their language and literature. The emergence of poets, writers, Kurdish intellectuals in Iraq and
in the U.S.S.R. first, then in Iran and today in Turkey, illustrates in a
striking way the parallels between national development and cultural development.

524   Blau, Joyce. "Kurdish Written Literature." In *Kurdish Culture and Iden-*
tity. Edited by Philip G. Kreyenbroek and Christine Allison, pp. 20-28.
Atlantic Highlands, NJ: Zed Books, 1996.

Blau tackles the troubled topic of Kurdish written literature. She explains
that a central problem for the history and development of Kurdish language literature has been that the language itself never took on one unified form. Instead, it has settled down as a number of regionally-defined
dialects and sub-dialects, not all of which have evolved a written form.
Unable to form a viable nation-state of their own, the Kurds have been
unable to develop a proliferating written culture until the last two or three
decades. Blau plots the difficult course charted by Kurdish intellectuals,
in their attempts to emerge freely and openly into the light of day as cultural exponents. A Kurdish intellectual elite has always existed, Blau reports, expressing itself in Persian, Arabic or Turkish, more often than
they did in Kurdish. In the sixteenth century, however, master poets such
as Melay Jeziri and Ahmede Khani emerged, who penned their epics in
Kurdish dialects. The progress of Kurdish literature this century is epito-
mized by the extreme difficulties faced by Kurds wishing to mass produce their writings. None of the ruling authorities in all host countries
containing segments of Kurdistan have ever looked dispassionately upon
Kurdish cultural endeavors this century. Blau shows the considerable difficulties faced by Kurdish intellectuals and their publishers, indicating
however that Kurdish literature--especially poetry--has flourished when-
ever circumstances permitted this. She notes the promising explosion of
Kurdish publishing from the onset of the 1980s up till the present day, especially in the Kurdish diaspora in Europe, which has also erupted in size
during the same period. The development of a lively range of cultural, social and political publications in Kurdish dialects in the diaspora has itself
been a factor in helping to force more openings for Kurdish publishing in
the Kurds' host countries. Blau does a good job in summarizing the con-
voluted history of the fight for a Kurdish written culture in such an
unavoidably brief but readable essay (Paul White).

525   Bois, Thomas. *L'Ame des Kurdes a la lumiere de leur folklore*. [The soul of the Kurds in the light of their folklore] Beirut: Les Cahiers de l'est, 1946. 57 p. Includes bibliographical references. [Originally published in *Les Cahiers de l'Est* (Beirut), nos. 5 and 6, 1946]

526   Bois, Thomas. "Coup d'oeil sur la litterature kurde." *Al-Machriq* (1955): 201-239.

       Contains a comprehensive survey of Kurdish literature and periodicals throughout the Middle East, which include translations of characteristic literary selections and remarkably detailed bibliographical data of both Kurdish language and literature.

527   Bois, Thomas. "Kurdish Folklore and Literature." In *Encyclopedia of Islam*. New ed. Vol. 5, 480-486. Leiden: E. J. Brill, 1986.

       Subheadings include: (A) Popular and Folk Literature; (B) Written or Learned Literature: 1) Origins and the classical period, and 2) The modern age; and (C) The Kurdish Press.

528   Haydari, Jamshid al-. "Tarikh Tatawur al-Nathr al-Fanni al-Kurdi fi al-'Iraq." *Studia Kurdica* 1 (1984): 82-93.

       A short summary of a doctoral dissertation submitted at Leningrad University in 1980. The original study starts with a lengthy historical overview of the development of Kurdish prose in general, then focuses on the period between 1925 and 1960 in Iraqi Kurdistan. Part I discusses the formation of Kurdish prose in Iraq (1925-1939). Parts II deals with the 1940s period. Part III discusses the development of Kurdish prose in the 1950s and 1960s.

529   Hilmi, Rafiq. *al-Shi'r wa-al-Adab al-Kurdi*. [An overview of Kurdish poetry and literature] Baghdad: s.n., 1955.

530   Hitchens, Keith. "Kurdish Literature." In *Encyclopedia of World Literature in the 20th Century*. Vol. 2. 3rd ed., completely rev. and enl. Edited by Steven R. Serafin and others, pp. 683-684. Farmington Hills, MI: St. James Press, 1999.

       Provides a brief but excellent overview on the history and development of Kurdish literature, including newspapers and books, poetry, and prose. A number of poets along with some of their works and impact on Kurdish literature are discussed in brief.

531   Khaznadar, Marouf. *Makhtutat Farida wa-Matbu'at Nadira=Unique Manuscripts and Rare Publications*. Baghdad: Matba'at al- Ma'arif,

1978. 86 p. [Dirasat Kurdiyah; 1]. Added t.p. and summary in English: Unique manuscripts and rare publications.

This study contains two parts, the first is a study of a number of manuscripts archived in the Institute of Oriental Studies of the Soviet Science Academy of Leningrad, these were written by A. Jaba, M. Hartmann, V. Minorsky, and others about Kurdish language, literature, and culture. The second part of the study contains a translation (into Arabic) or A. Chodzko's work on the Kurdish dialect of Sulaymania pertaining Kurdish literature. The secondd part also include a study that deals with what Jaba wrote in the 1850s on Kurdish classical poets. This collection is of special importance because much of it is based on materials recorded from conversations with educated Kurds.

532   Khaznadar, Marouf. *Mujaz Tarikh al-Adab al-Kurdi al-Mu'asir*. [A historical overview of modern Kurdish literature] Translated from Russian by 'Abd al-Majid Shaykhu. [Syria]: Hushang Qaradaghi, 1993. 199 p.

533   Khaznadar, Marouf. "Kurdish Prose (1945-1961)." *The Journal of Kurdish Studies* 2 (1996-1997): 65-70.

Discusses the development of Kurdish prose and its different forms, including, short fiction, short stories, novels, and allegories. A short biography of prose writers Muhammad Mustafa Kurdi, Ibrahim Ahmad, Shakir Fattah, Marouf Barzinji, and Muharram Muhammad Amin is presented. Also presented is a discussion of their works and their impact on Kurdish literature.

534   Lancaster, Pat. "Weapons in the War for Freedom." *The Middle East*, no. 164 (June 1988): 39-40.

There are more ways than one of winning a war and, after spending time living with freedom fighters, the *peshmergas*, the famous Kurdish nationalist poet, Sherko Bekas, still believes the pen and the poem can be as mighty as the sword. Here, he talks to Pat Lancaster.

535   Lescot, Roger. "Litterature kurde." [Kurdish Literature] In *Histoire des Litteratures. I. Litteratures Anciennes, Orientales et Orales*. Edited by Raymond Queneau, pp. 795-805. Paris: Gallimard, 1977.

Kurdish literature is a popular literature. Very few are those who know the existence of Kurdish written literature and fewer are those who appreciate its importance. Many written texts have disappeared during the decades- and centuries-old conflicts erupted in Kurdistan, and others are still unpublished. This is a brief survey on Kurdish literature.

536 Margueritte, Lucie Paul. *Dirasat fi al-Adab al-Kurdi al-Mu'asir*. [An overview of studies in modern Kurdish literature] Translated by Rafiq Hilmi. Baghdad: s.n., 1939. 66 p.

537 Muhsin, Fa'iz. *Dirasat fi al-Adab al-Kurdi*. [An annotated bibliography of Kurdish literature] Baghdad: Dar al-Adab, 1973. 45 p.

538 Prym, Eugen; Socin, August (comps.). *Kurdische Sammlungen*. St.-Pétersbourg: Commissionaires de l'Académie impériale des sciences, Eggers et cie et J. Glasounof, 1887-1890. 2 vols.

539 Rasul, 'Izz al-Din Mustafa. *al-Waqi'iyah fi al-Adab al-Kurdi*. Saida, Lebanon: Manshurat al-Maktaba al-'Asriyah, 1966. 235 p. Includes bibliographical references.

Originated from a larger version of the author's doctoral dissertation submitted to the Oriental Institute in Azerbaijan, former Soviet Union. Provides a comprehensive historical overview of Kurdish literature and its various literary forms, including but not limited to Kurdish short story; prose; oral histories; epic literature; types of epics; proverbs, maxims, and popular sayings; songs; and allegories. Focusses discussion on realism in Kurdish literature. Includes many samples of Kurdish poetry.

540 Rasul, 'Izz al-Din Mustafa. "Muqadima li-Dirasat al-Fulklur al-Kurdi." [An introduction to the study of Kurdish folklore] *al-Turath al-Sha'bi* 2 (December 1969): 51-55.

541 Rasul, 'Izz al-Din Mustafa. *al-Lughah al-Adabiyah al-Kurdiyah al-Muwahadah*. [Unified Kurdish literary language] Baghdad: s.n., 1971.

542 Rasul, 'Izz al-Din Mustafa. *Dirasah fi Adab al-Fulklur al-Kurdi*. Baghdad: al-Jamhuriyah al-'Iraqiyah, Wizarat al-Thaqafah wa-al-I'lam, Dar al-Thaqafah wa-al-Nashr al-Kurdiyah, 1987. 208 p.

Topics discussed include: Kurdish short story; oral histories; epic literature; types of epics; proverbs, maxims, and popular sayings; songs; allegories, anecdotes, jokes, and puzzles.

543 Sandi, Badr-Khan 'Abd Allah al-. *Tabi'at al-Mujtama' al-Kurdi fi Adabih*. [Discusses the nature and characteristics of Kurdish society as reflected in Kurds' literature] Kirkuk: Matba'at al-Baladiyah, 1959. 118 p.

544 Wurdi, Muhammad Tawfiq. *Bahth wa-Dirasah 'an al-Fulklur al-Kurdi*. [A study on Kurdish folklore] Baghdad: Matba'at al-Za'im, 1962. 32 p.

See also items: 3, 4, 16, 19, 21, 23, 26, 370, 377, 734

EPICS, LEGENDS, STORIES, TALES

545   'Arif, Husayn. "Ashkal al-Tiknik al-Haditha fi al-Qissa al-Kurdiyah: 1970 wa-ma-Ba'diha." [Modern technical forms of the Kurdish novel from 1970 onward] *al-Aqlam* 19 (February-March 1984): 123-135.

546   Bayazid, Mela Mahmoud. "Mem et Zin." [Mem û Zîn] In *Les Kurdes par-dela l'exode*. Edited by Halkawt Hakim, pp. 232-247. Paris: L'Harmattan, 1992.

547   Blau, Joyce. "Trois textes de folklore kurde." *Correspondance d'Orient: Etudes* 7 (1965): 29-50.

548   Blau, Joyce (tr.). *Contes kurdes*. Paris: Conseil International de la Langue Française, 1986. 167 p.: ill. [Fleuve et flame] Translated from Kurdish. Includes bibliographical references.

549   Bozarslan, Emin. "Three Short Stories." ["How Tobacco Became Straw;" "Meyro;" and "The Lighter."] *The International Journal of Kurdish Studies* 7, no. 1-2 (1994): 71-82.

550   Cardeur, Aha le. "Conte populaire." [Popular stories] In *Les Kurdes par-dela l'exode*. Edited by Halkawt Hakim, pp. 248-254. Paris: L'Harmattan, 1992.

551   Celil, Ordikhan; Celil, Celile. *Kurdische Märchen*. [Kurdish tales] Frankfurt am Main: Insel, 1993. 364 p. [In German]

A collection of folktales and stories made in all the Kurdish-inhabited areas from the former Soviet states in 1954 to Kurdistan in Turkey, Syria, and Iraq in 1982. Over 125 stories are translated into German.

552   Chyet, Michael L. "A Version of the Kurdish Romance *Mem u Zin* with English Translation and Commentary: Papers in Honour of Prof. Dr. David Neil MacKenzie on Occasion of His 65th Birthday on April 8th, 1991." In *Corolla Iranica*. Edited by Ronald E. Emmerick and Dieter Weber, pp. 27-48. Frankfurt [Germany]: Peter Lang, 1991.

553   Chyet, Michael L. *"And a Thornbush Sprang up between them": Studies on "Mem u Zin," a Kurdish Romance*. Ph.D., University of California at Berkeley, 1991. Two volumes. 1013 p.

This study is based on a corpus of eighteen oral versions of the Kurdish romance *Mem u Zin*, a tragic love story reminiscent of Romeo and Juliet who is very widespread in Northern Kurdistan. All eighteen versions, which constitute the appendix, have been translated into English, complete with notes explaining cultural concepts and linguistic niceties. The eighteen versions of *Mem u Zin* are subjected to a series of comparative folkloristic analyses. Chapter One consists of an introduction to the Kurds, their language and folklore, together with a brief summary of the story of Mem and Zin. This is followed by a critical bibliographic survey of the literature that has been published about the oral versions of *Mem u Zin* and Ehmede Khani's literary poem by the same name, including also references for the general study of Kurdish folklore. The analysis of *Mem u Zin* begins with the second section of Chapter One, in which the proverbial nature of the romance, as seen in certain expressions that are derived from it, is investigated. Chapter Two is a consideration of the relationship between Ehmede Khani's literary poem, revered by the Kurds as their national epic, and the oral versions of *Mem u Zin*. In Chapter Three, *Mem u Zin* is assigned to a specific genre of folk narrative, the romance. Chapter Four is an endeavor to restore the performance aspect of the tellings of Mem and Zin, based on a new look at the scanty evidence at our disposal. The poetic nature and linguistic texture of the oral versions are explored in Chapter Five: Kurdish folk poetics are discussed, followed by the application of the Oral-Formulaic Theory to *Mem u Zin*. A detailed comparative study of the versions is undertaken in Chapter Six, looking both horizontally, i.e. across the versions, and vertically, discussing variation within each motif. The final chapter of the study includes an attempt to establish *oicotypes* by linking the variation of the story to their geographical distribution. This section includes a map of Kurdistan on which the versions have been plotted, as well as other important sites, such as Bayazid, the site of Ehmede Khani's tomb, and the city of Jezira Bohtan, where the main part of the story of Mem and Zin takes place. The study concludes with a few words about the future of the tradition. The accompanying bibliography includes sources for the study of Kurdish language and folk literature, as well as publications dealing with folkloristic theory both in general and as applied to Middle Eastern peoples in particular. (*DAI* 53, November 1992: 1626-A)

554   Chyet, Michael L. "Is Mem a Hero? (An Analytical Consideration of Oral Versions of '*Mem u Zin*')." *Acta Kurdica: The International Journal of Kurdish and Iranian Studies* 1 (1994): 155-176.

For all the ink that has been spilled about the Kurdish tragic love story of Mem and Zin, very little of a truly analytic nature has been written about the oral versions, other than an article by Basile Nikitine based on the Mukri version collected by Oskar Mann. The same can be said about Ehmede Xani's literary poem, which so far has only been analyzed in depth by Ferhad Shakely. In the present article, the behavior of Meme Alan—as depicted in the oral tradition—is scrutinized. (A)

555   Hassanpour, Amir. "Dimdim." In *Encyclopaedia Iranica*. Vol. 7, pp. 404-405. Costa Mesa, CA: Mazda Publishers, 1996.

Dimdim is a mountain and a fortress where an important battle between the Kurds and the Safavid army took place in the early 17th century. This entry discusses the history of the fortress and the importance of the battle of Dimdim in both Safavid historiography and the culture and history of the Kurds.

556 Ibrahim, Khalil Rashid. *Maqamat Mam wa-Zin*. [A discussion on the importance of the epic Mem û Zîn in Kurdish literature] Beirut: Dar al-Fikr al-Mu'asir, 1993.

557 Jalil, Jasim. *Butulat al-Kurd fi Malhamat Qal'at Dimdim*. [An account of one of the greatest Kurdish folkloric traditions] Translated into Arabic by Shakkur Mustafa. Revised and introduced by 'Izz al-Din Mustafa Rasul. Beirut: Dar al-Katib, 1988. 151 p. [Text in Kurdish and Arabic]

558 Kaka'i, Falak al-Din. "Qira'a fi Nusus Kurdiyah." [A review of some Kurdish literary works] *al-Nahj* (Damascus) 8, no. 2 (1991): 185-200.

559 Khani, Ahmad. *Mam wa-Zin: Qissat Hubb Nabata fi al-Ard wa-Ayna'a fi al-Sama'*. Naqalaha ila al-'Arabiyah wa-aqam bunyanaha al-qisasi Muhammad Sa'id Ramadan al-Buti. 5th ed. Beirut: Dar al-Fikr al-Mu'asir, 1982. 200 p.

560 Khani, Ahmad. *Diwan Mam wa-Zin*. [A translation and review of *Mem u Zin*] Tahqiq wa Tarjamat Jan Dust. Damascus: Asu, 1995. 444 p.

561 Khani, Ahmad. *Malhamat Mam wa-Zin: al-Tarjamah al-Kamilah*. [An Arabic translation of Mem û Zîn] Translated by Jan Dost. Bayrut: Dar al-Kunuz al-Adabiyah, 1998. 232 p. Includes bibliographical references.

562 Khani, Ahmad. *Mamé Alan: Epopée Kurde*. [A French translation of Mem û Zîn] Paris: Gallimard, 1999. 247 p.

563 Khaznadar, Marouf. "Ma'rakat Dimdim fi al-Fulklur al-Kurdi." [The place of Dimdim fortress war in Kurdish Folklore] *al-Turath al-Sha'bi* 1 (May 1970): 70-73.

564 Khurshid, Fuad Hama. "Mulahazat fi al-Riwayah al-Tarikhiyah al-Kurdiyah-Qal'at Dimdim." [A review of the historical novel, Dimdim fortress] *al-Aqlam* 19 (February-March 1984): 136-140.

565 Nikitine, Basile; Soane, E. B.. "The Tale of Suto and Tato." *Bulletin of the School of Oriental and African Studies* 3 (1923): 69-106.

566 Nikitine, Basile. "Kurdish Stories from my Collection." *Bulletin of the School of Oriental and African Studies* 4 (1926): 121-138.

567   Rashid, Nuhad 'Abd al-Sattar. "Mina al-Fulklur al-Kurdi." [Kurdish
       Folklore] *al-Turath al-Sha'bi* 5, no. 12 (1974): 97-100.

568   Rasul, 'Izz al-Din Mustafa. "al-Asatir al-Kurdiyah." [Kurdish legends] *al-
       Turath al-Sha'bi* 1 (February 1970): 69-75.

569   Rasul, 'Izz al-Din Mustafa. "al-Hikayat al-Kurdiyah." [Kurdish short
       stories] *al-Turath al-Sha'bi* 2 (October-November 1970): 40-49.

570   Rasul, 'Izz al-Din Mustafa. "Madkhal ila Dirasat al-Malhama fi al-
       Fulklur al-Kurdi." [An introduction to the study of epics in Kurdish folk-
       lore] *al-Turath al-Sha'bi* 2 (January-February 1971): 40-47.

571   Rasul, 'Izz al-Din Mustafa. "Ara' fi al-Qissa al-Kurdiyah." [Discusses the
       author's opinions in the Kurdish story] *al-Aqlam* 19 (February-March
       1984): 112-122.

572   Rushdi, Salih. *Qisas wa-Asatir fi al-Adab al-Kurdi*. [An overview of
       some Kurdish stories and legends] Beirut: s.n., 1967. 104 p.

573   Soane, Ely Bannister; Nikitine, Basile; Zangana, Yousuf; Mella, Jawad.
       The Tale of Suto and Tato. London: Kurdologia, 1988. 33, 30 p.: genea-
       logical table. [Kurdologia publications; no. 7] Texts in English, Southern
       Kurdish and Northern Kurdish. Added t.p. in Kurdish.

574   Tofiq, Mohammed; Thackston, Wheeler McIntosh. *Kurdish Folktales*.
       Brooklyn, N.Y.: The Kurdish Library, 1999. iii, 115 p. [*The Interna-
       tional Journal of Kurdish Studies*; vol. 13, no. 2] "The collection from
       which the translations were made is entitled "Chîrok i bar Âgirdân i Kur-
       dawârî (Stories from Kurdish Hearths)..." — p. iii

       In this collection, one of the first to present to the English reader a range
       of Kurdish folk tales, there are stories that revolve around clever youths
       of apparently humble origin who usually turn out to be sons of kings.
       Most of the tales are concerned, in one way or another, with justice, and
       usually-perhaps reflecting common experience over the centuries in Kur-
       distan-justice needs the intervention of some external (and often super-
       natural) agency to be done, like the skull that engenders a child in "The
       King of the East." The stories given here in translation were collected
       from a variety of people from Kifri and the Sulaimani area of Iraqi Kurdi-
       stan and transcribed in Sorani Kurdish by Mohammed Hama-Salih Tofiq.
       The collection from which the translations were made is entitled *Chfrok i
       bar Agirdtin i Kurdawarf (Stories from Kurdish Hearths),* and it contains
       twenty-four stories of varying lengths, of which eighteen are given here
       in translation. The handwritten texts in Sorani Kurdish were provided by
       the Kurdish Library in Brooklyn, and I am confident that readers will en-

joy them. It is hoped that the Kurdish texts will also be published soon. (Editor)

575   Wurdi, Muhammad Tawfiq. *Min Rawa'i' al-Adab al-Kurdi*. [An overview of some of the greatest Kurdish literary works] Baghdad: s.n., 1956.

576   Wurdi, Muhammad Tawfiq. *al-Qissa wa-al-Asatir fi al-Adab al-Kurdi*. [Discusses the place of stories and legends in Kurdish literature] Baghdad: s.n., 1956. 36 p.

577   Wurdi, Muhammad Tawfiq. *Qissa wa-Qasai'd fi al-Adab al-Kurdi al-Thawri*. [A discussion of a few patriotic stories and poems] Baghdad: s.n., 1960.

578   Wurdi, Muhammad Tawfiq. *Qisas Shi'riyah Kurdiyah Fulkluriyah*. [A discussion of Kurdish folkloric narrative poems] Baghdad: Matba'at Irshad, 1965. 48 p.

579   Wurdi, Muhammad Tawfiq. *Aqasis Sha'biyah Kurdiyah*. [Popular Kudish short stories] Najaf, Iraq: Matba'at al-Gharri, 1970. 100 p.

580   Wurdi, Muhammad Tawfiq. *Nawruz wa-Thawrat Kawa al-Haddad*. [An account of the national holiday, Nawruz] Najaf, Iraq: Matba'at al-Gharri, 1973. 22 p.

581   Wurdi, Muhammad Tawfiq. *Namazij min al-Turath al Sha'bi al-Kurdi*. [Discusses samples of popular Kurdish literary works] Najaf, Iraq: Matba'at al-Gharri, 1975. 207 p.

See also items: 154, 383, 394, 405, 411, 414, 415, 507, 521, 539, 542, 596, 600, 914, 920

LITERARY FIGURES

582   Fandi, Rashid. *Munaqashat Hawl Khani: Dirasah Naqdiyah li-Kitab Khani Sha'iran wa-Mufakiran wa-Faylasufan lil-Diktur 'Izz al-Din Mustafa Rasul*. [A literary criticism of the book *Khani the poet the thinker and the philosopher* by 'Izz al-Din Mustafa Rasul] Baghdad: Matba'at al-Jahith, 1986. 151 p.

583   Guran, 'Abd Allah. *al-Athar al-Shi'riyah al-Kamilah*. [An Arabic translation of the literary works of the 20th century Kurdish poet, Abdulla Goran]. Introduced, translated, and compiled by 'Izz al-Din Mustafá Rasul. Baghdad: Sharikat al-Ma'rifah, 1991. 488 p. Includes bibliographical references (p. 44- 46).

584 Hakim, Halkawt. "Nali, le Fondateur du Courant Traditionnel dans la Poesie Kurde." *DABIREH Edition Internationale*, no. 1 (November 1991): 130-140.

585 Hitchens, Keith. "Goran, Abdulla." In *Encyclopedia of World Literature in the 20th Century*. Vol. 2. 3rd ed., completely rev. and enl. Edited by Steven R. Serafin and others, pp. 276-277. Farmington Hills, MI: St. James Press, 1999.

Provides a brief account on the life and works of Abdulla Goran, "the outstanding Kurdish poet of the 20th century.

586 Krikavova, Adela. "Abdullah Goran, Hazhar, Ahmade Khani, Haji Kadyr Koyi, Sheikh Ahmad Malaye Jizri, Tawfiq Piramerd, and Arabe Shamo." In *Dictionary of Oriental Literatures*. Edited by Jaroslav Prêuések and others. New York: Basic Books, 1974.

This paper includes short biographies of Kurdish writers Abdullah Goran, Hazhar, Ahmade Khani, Haji Qadir Koyi, Sheikh Ahmad Malaye Jizri, Tawfiq Piramerd, and Ereb Shamo.

587 Maarof, Kamal. *La vie et l'oeuvre du poète kurde Dildar*. Paris: K. Maarof, 1989. 142 p.: ill. French and Kurdish. Includes bibliographical references (p. 125-141).

588 Maarof, Kamal. *Les lurs, le Luristan et le poète Baba Tahir Hamadanî: débuts de la littérature kurde*. Paris: K. Maarof, 1989. Includes bibliographical references (p. 96- 99).

589 Musaelian, Zhaklina. "Academician Iosif Orbeli and Kurdish Classic Literature." *Acta Kurdica: The International Journal of Kurdish and Iranian Studies* 1 (1994): 209-212.

The prominent Armenian Orientalist of the Soviet period, academician Iosif (Hovsep) Orbeli (1887-1961), became interested in the Kurds as far back as 1911 when, having just graduated from the University of St-Petersburg and having been recommended by academician Nicolai Marr, he was sent on an expedition, by the Academy of Sciences, to Western Armenia, Van and Moks to collect dialectological materials (study of the Moks vernacular of Armenian). It was here, while studying the Moks dialect of Kurdish, he wrote a Kurdish-Russian dictionary, listening to and writing down the vivid and picturesque Kurdish folklore; he evidently made much of the spiritual culture of the Kurds. (A)

590 Rasul, 'Izz al-Din Mustafa. *Ahmadi Khani Sha'iran wa-Mufakiran wa-Faylasufan wa-Mutasawifan*. [A detailed biography of Ahmad Khani,

the poet, the philosopher, and the sufi] Baghdad: Matba'at al-Hawadith, 19?. 512 p.

591   Rasul, 'Izz al-Din Mustafa. "'Abd Allah Guran." [A short biography of one of the most prolific Kurdish writers] *al-Tariq* (1964): 61-71.

592   'Umar, Haydar. *Faqi Tayran: Hayatih, Shi'rih, Qimatuhu al-Fanniyah-Dirasah*. [A study on the life, poetry, and literary importance of the Kurdish poet, Faqi Tayran] Beirut: Techno-press, 1993.

POETRY

593   Barwari, Salah (tr.). *Mukhtarat min al-Shi'r al-Kurdi al-Mu'asir*. [A selection of modern Kurdish Kurdish poems] Damascus: Matba'at al-Jahiz, 1991. 62 p.

594   Bekas, Cherko. "Poemes Kurdes d'aujourd'hui." [Today's Kurdish poems] In *Les Kurdes par-dela l'exode*. Edited by Halkawt Hakim, pp. 263-268. Paris: L'Harmattan, 1992.

595   Bekes, Cherko. *Les petits miroirs: poemes*. Translated by Kamal Maarof. Paris: L'Harmattan, 1995. 95 p.

596   Blau, Joyce. "The Poetry of Kurdistan: Language Embodies Nation Unity." *The World and I* 6, no. 8 (August 1991): 623-637.

In this paper, Blau discusses the origins of the Kurds and their oral tradition and the impact of religion and the arts, Kurdish dynasties, and Mongol invasions on such oral tradition. Blau then discusses Kurdish literary traditions and provides two early examples: "The Wine-Selling Sons of the Magi" and "Mam O Zin." She finally discusses the situation of Kurdish oral and written traditions since the early 1920s.

597   Chaliand, Gerard. "Poesie populaire kurde." [Popular Kurdish poetry] *Orient* [Paris] 4, no. 14 (1960): 111-124.

598   Chaliand, Gerard (ed. and tr.). *Poesie populaire des Turcs et des Kurdes*. [Popular poetry of the Kurds and Turks] Paris: F. Maspero, 1961. 147 p.

The second part of this work (pp. 71-143) contains an introduction to, and translations of, Kurdish poetry arranged in four sections: chants d'amour; chants epiques; chansons; and Meme Alan, epopee nationale des Kurdes.

599   Chaliand, Gerard. *Anthologie de la poesie populaire kurde*. La Tour d'Aigues: Ed. De l'Aube, 1997. 136 p.

600   Chaliand, Gerard; Lescot, Roger. *Anthologie de la poesie populaire kurde*. [Anthology of Kurdish popular poetry] Paris: Stock, 1980. 261 p. [Arabies/Islamies; 4]

The author resumes here the extracts of the Kurdish poetry presented in his *Poesie populaire des Turcs et des Kurdes* adding to it the Roger Lescot's translation of *Mame Alan*, a scholarly version of the Kurdish epic of Mem and Zin. The work is a very useful collection and good introduction to the Kurdish popular literature. (*AI* 4: 490)

601   Huart, Clement. "La priere canonique musulmane, poeme didactique en langue kurde." *Journal Asiatique* IX Serie, vol. 5 (1895): 86-109.

602   Husayn, Muhammad Salih (tr.). *Shi'r wa-Shu'ara': Mukhtarat min al-Shi'r al-Kurdi al-Qadim wa-al-Mu'asir*. [A selection of Kurdish poems] Qamishli, Syria: Manshurat Maktabat Jwan, 1991. 144 p.

603   Jandi, Haji, Urdikhan Jalil, and Jalili Jalil. *Qasa'id min al-Fulklur al-Kurdi*. [A selection of Kurdish folkloric poems] I'dad wa-Tarjamat Walatu. Beirut: Dar al-Katib, 1982. 184 p.

604   Jaziri, Malaye. "In Praise of Sharaf Khan: On Sufi Teachings." In *Qasida Poetry in Islamic Asia and Africa*. Edited by Stefan Sperl and Christopher Shackle. Vol. 2, pp. 244-251, 447-449. Leiden; New York: E.J. Brill, 1996.

605   Jouan, Yves. "*Azadi*, source commune: extraits d'un recueil de poemes encore inedits." [*Azadi*, common source: extracts of a collection of unpublished poems] In *Les Kurdes par-dela l'exode*. Edited by Halkawt Hakim, pp. 41-53. Paris: L'Harmattan, 1992.

606   Karim, D. L. *A Comparative Study of Free Verse in Arabic and Kurdish: The Literary Caress of al-Sayyab and Goran*. Ph.D., Glasgow, 1985.

607   Khaznadar, Marouf. "al-Riwaya al-Shi'riyah Layla wa-Majnun fi al-Adab al-Kurdi." [The place of the Arab poetic novel Layla wa-Majnun in Kurdish literature] *Majallat Kulliyat al-Adab - Jami'at Baghdad* 20 (1976): 205-220.

608   Khaznadar, Marouf. "al-Takhmis wa-al-Mukhammas fi al-Shi'r al-Klasiki al-Kurdi." *Majallat Kulliyat al-Adab - Jami'at Baghdad* 21 (1977): 443-458.

609   Maarof, Kamal. *al-Harakah al-Tajdidiyah fi al-Shi'r al-Kurdi al-Hadith, 1914-1965*. Stockholm: s.n., 1992. Includes bibliographical references.

610   Muhammad, Anwar Qadir. "al-Shi'r al-Kurdi al-Mu'asir." [An overview of modern Kurdish poetry] *Afaq 'Arabiyah* 8 (January 1983): 60-69.

611   Nikitine, Basile. "La poesie lyrique kurde." [Kurdish Lyric Poetry] *L'Ethnographie* nouv. ser., no. 45 (1947-1950): 39-53.

612   Schmid, Estella, and others. (eds.). *Anthology of Contemporary Kurdish Poetry*. Translated from Kurdish by Harold Pinter. London: Kurdistan Solidarity Committee/Yashar Ismail, 1994. viii, 48 p.

This work brings together eleven living poets from Kurdistan. These poets' main concern has to do with the politics of dispossession. Theirs, as Pinter writes in the foreword, has been a history of "appalling persecution." To write about this history without fear of persecution, the Kurds, including the eleven represented in the book, had first to go into exile in Europe, North America, or Australia. But there they soon came to realize that exile, itself a form of dispossession, exacts its own toll. Naturally, this double sense of dispossession has resulted in a poetry of profound pain. For Azad Dilzar, it is the pain of remembering the horrors of growing up in a city where everyone was afraid of everyone else. For Sherko Bekas, it is the pain of seeing the city of his boyhood, Halabja, being attacked by Saddam Hussein with poison gas in 1988. For M. Omar Gul, it is the pain of not being able to do anything for a Kurdistan robbed of its freedom. This narrative of pain becomes even more intense as it moves swiftly from a prison where Kurds are being tortured, to a village under bombardment, and then to a mother turned insane over the execution of a teenage son. From these individual scenes the focus suddenly shifts to all of Kurdistan, where Ferhad Shakeli laments, there is no escape from pain. But pain does not prevent these poets from seeing the Kurdish situation in a global context. Shahin B. Sorekli, having witnessed the reunification of Germany, the end of the Cold War, the attainment of independence by several former Soviet republics, finds no cause for celebration as far as his people are concerned; for the Kurds, unlike the Georgians, the Ukrainians, the Armenians, and the Slovaks, have no big powers campaigning on their behalf. So, while these peoples become recognized, receive foreign dignitaries, and raise their own flags, the Kurds continue to yearn for a flag of their own. (Sabah A. Salih/*World Literature Today* 70, no. 3, 1996: 753-754)

613   Shakely, Ferhad. "The Kurdish Qasida." In *Qasida Poetry in Islamic Asia and Africa*. Vol. 1, pp. 327-338. Edited by Stefan Sperl and Christopher Shackle. Leiden: E.J. Brill, 1996.

Although this paper concentrates on the qasidas of Malaye Jaziri, it also deals with the question of the Kurdish qasida generally. Subjects of discussion therefore include the emergence, development and topics of the Kurdish qasida, and the way that Kurdish poets used this poetic form ill their own language. This is no easy task, since Kurdish poetry has rarely been studied either by Kurdish scholars or by non-Kurds. The few existing works on Kurdish poetics are mostly in Kurdish, and they are far from comprehensive. (A)

614 Shakely, Ferhad. "Reflections of a Kurdish Poet: An Interview with Ferhad Shakely." *The International Journal of Kurdish Studies* 12, no. 1-2 (1998): 97-107.

615 Jaziri, Malaye. *al-'Iqd al-Jawhari fi Sharh Diwan al-Shaykh al-Jazri.* [A review of the poetical works of Mallai Jaziri] Sharahahu Ahmad bin al-Mulla Muhammad al-Zafanki. 2 vols. 2nd ed. Qamishli, Syria: Matba'at al-Sabah, 1987.

616 Zaza, Noureddine. *Contes et poèmes Kurdes: écrits ou recueillis*. Aosta, Italie: Editions Peuples et Créations, 1974. 60 p.: ill.

See also items: 24, 405, 412, 424, 425, 529, 530, 534, 539, 577, 578, 588, 592, 691

PROVERBS, MAXIMS, POPULAR SAYINGS

617 'Abd al-Karim, Muhammad al-Mulla. "Ma'thurat Sha'biyah Kurdiyah." [Popular Kurdish proverbs] *al-Turath al-Sha'bi* 1 (November 1969): 43-48.

618 Lescot, Roger. "Proverbes et enigmes kurdes." *Revue des Etudes Islamiques* 4 (1937): 307-351.

619 Lescot, Roger (ed.). *Textes kurdes*. Paris: Paul Geuthner, 1940. Kurdish and French. [Part I: Contes, proverbes et énigmes. Part II: Mamé Alan.]

620 Margueritte, Lucie Paul; Bedir Khan, Kamuran. *Proverbes kurdes, précédés d'une étude sur la poésie kurde*. Paris: Berger-Levrault, 1937. 171 p.

621 Noel, Edward William Charles. "The Character of the Kurds as Illustrated by their Proverbs and Popular Sayings." *Bulletin of the School of Oriental and African Studies* 1 (1920): 79-90.

A selection of well-known Kurdish sayings is made with a view to illustrating the character of the Kurds. In addition to some general sayings, others focused on topics such as marriage, women, relationship between the sexes, religion, riches and wealth, hospitality, fidelity and respect for authority, Kurd's attitude to their neighbors, and attitude towards Turks.

622   Segerer, Joelle. "La litterature kurde: quelques grandes lignes." [Kurdish literature: some great lines] In *Les Kurdes par-dela l'exode*. Edited by Halkawt Hakim, pp. 185-206. Paris: L'Harmattan, 1992.

See also items: 501, 521, 539, 542, 553

15

Music, Dance, and Songs

623   'Abd al-Karim, Muhammad al-Mulla. "Fi al-Ghina' al-Kurdi." [About Kurdish singing] *al-Turath al-Sha'bi* 2 (December 1970): 73-81.

624   Baksi, Mahmut. *The Kurdish Voice: Shivan Perwer*. Stockholm: Helin House, 1986. 106 p.: ill.

625   Blum, Robert Stephen. *Music in Contact: The Cultivation of Traditional Repertoires in Meshed, Iran*. Ph.D., University of Illinois at Urbana-Champaign, 1972. 374 p.

Musical styles cultivated in the city of Meshed (Iran) and its surrounding region include numerous genres of song with texts in Persian, Kurdish, Baluchi, and the Turkic dialects of the province of Khorasan. Several types of specialists in musical performance possess repertories which encompass strikingly diverse styles and genres. These styles are distinguishable in terms of (1) organization of sound materials; (2) social circumstances of performance; (3) social role and status attributed to participants in particular performances; (4) type and extent of verbal description applied to a performance; and (5) means used for teaching or reproducing a mode of performance. Such distinctions define the working situations which confront performers in particular roles. Over a period of time, professional performers in Meshed have elaborated styles which for a broad public represent characteristic expressions or particular social groups. Performing musicians seem, moreover, to play a significant role in articulating the relationships among different groups in Iranian society. (A)

626   Blum, [Robert] Stephen; Hassanpour, Amir. "The Morning of Freedom
         Rose Up': Kurdish Popular Song and the Exigencies of Cultural Sur-
         vival." *Popular Music* 15, no. 3 (October 1996): 325-343.

This is part of a special issue on Middle Eastern popular music in which
the writers discuss Kurdish popular music in the context of cultural survival. The topics discussed include the creation of a listening public, musical life in the Kurdish diaspora, and popular Kurdish singers, subjects,
and repertoires. They maintain that Kurdish cultural survival necessitates
visions and representations of national culture, but that these need not be
defined via oppositions such as "classical" versus "folk," nor do they
have to be, they assert, controlled through the centralized institutions of a
state bureaucracy.

627   Christensen, Dieter. "Ein Tanzlied der Hakkari-Kurden und seine Varian-
         ten." [A dance-song of the Hakkari Kurds and its variants] *Basler Archiv*
         23, no.1 (1975): 195-215. [In German.]

Discusses the variants with recourse to three recordings made in eastern
Turkey. Texts and notated examples of the variants are included. Includes
music examples

628   During, Jean. "Les dastgahs sacres des Ahl-e Haqq du Kurdistan: ap-
         proche comparative et procedes de tansformation." [The sacred dastgahs
         of the Ahl-i Haqq of Kurdistan: comparative approach and processes of
         transformation] In *Regionale Maqam-Traditionen in Geschichte und
         Gegenwart: Materialien der 2. Arbeitstagung der Study Group
         "Maqam" des International Council for Traditional Music vom 23. bis
         28. Marz in Gosen bei Berlin*. Berlin: Humboldt-U. Institut fur Musik-
         wissenschaft und Musikerziehung, 1992. p. 115-128.

Vocal and instrumental music of the Ahl-i Haqq is conducted by a cantor
who accompanies himself with a *tanbur*. Their *dastgahs* are similar to the
Persian and Azerbaijani *maqam* systems as a result of transformation.
Thirteen examples clarify the structure and application of scale contrac-
tion, chromatic motives, and modulation.

629   During, Jean. "The Sacred Music of the Ahl-i Haqq as a Means of Mysti-
         cal Transmission." In *Manifestations of Sainthood in Islam*. Edited by
         G. M. Smith and C. W. Ernst, pp. 27-41. Istanbul: Isis Press, 1993.

This paper shows that sacred music serves to mediate between the saint
and the faithful of the Ahl-i Haqq of Kurdistan. These Shi'i sectarians believe they can establish contact with the saints of old and that the Divine
Essence manifests itself in the secret meetings (jam') when "the hearts are
in harmony, and when music induces ecstasy by means of appropriate
melodies." The sama' (the Sufi ceremony, sometimes employing music

and dance) is often attached to the cult of a particular saint whose inter-
cession and *baraka* (spiritual power) the participants in the ritual seek. In
the Ahl-i Haqq tradition, the sacred melodies must not be modified, for
singing them in set form revives the state of saintly personalities who
have left traces in die music and in the world. Songs play the primary expressive role in the Ah1-i Haqq jam', and their musical modes manifest
the spiritual hierarchy which is so significant in the cult of the saints. (A)

630   Faydi, Suran. "Ta'qib 'ala al-Ughniyah al-Kurdiyah al-Mu'asirah [by
Yusif Sa'id]." *al-Turath al-Sha'bi* 3 (November 1971): 193-195.

A reply to Yusif Sa'id on his article "al-Ughniyah al-Kurdiyah al-
Mu'asira" (The Modern Kurdish Song), published in *al-Turath al-Sha'bi*,
vol. 3 (September 1971), pp. 113-120.

631   Hassan, Schehrazade Qassim. "The Long Necked Lute in Iraq." *Asian
Music* 13, no. 2 (1982): 1-18.

This paper describes the long-necked lute that is today known in only
three areas of northern Iraq and used by Kurds and Turkmens. The local
names for the instrument are given, and a number of drawings show its
form and variants.

632   Khaznadar, Marouf. *Aghani min Kurdistan*. [Songs from Kurdistan]
Baghdad: Matba'at As'ad, 1956. 64 p.

633   Mokri, Mohammad (ed. and tr.). *Kurdish Songs*. Tehran: Ketab-Khaneh
Danesh, 1951. 192 p. illus.

634   Mokri, Mohammad. "La Musique Sacree des Kurdes 'Fideles de Verite'
en Iran." [The sacred music of the Kurds 'Faithful to the Truth' in Iran] In
Encyclopedie des Musique Sacrees, vol. 1, pp. 441-453. Edited by
Jacques Porte. Paris: Editions Labergerie, 1968.

Among the Ahl-i Haqq Kurds, music is considered a functional part of the
liturgy, not a transitory worldly amusement. According to tradition, Shah-
Khoshin (10th A.D.), one of the great theophanies of the sect, had 900
musicians. The tuning (*kuk*) of stringed instruments was possible only after the appearance of Baba-Na'uth, the incarnation of God. Traditional instruments, the role and technique of the *tanbur*, composers and interpret-
ers, sacred songs, chants, hymns, and the *dastgah* are among the topics
discussed.

635   Nezan, Kendal. "Kurdish Music and Dance." *Le Monde de la
Musique/The World of Music* 21, no. 1 (1979): 19-32.

In Kurdish society, the history and the lyric poetry of the people of successive epochs are set to music and sung in order the better to pass them along to posterity. Composed mostly by women whose names remain anonymous, the music is made known throughout the country by *dengbej* (bards). Instrumental accompaniment plays a secondary role: the blur (flute), *duduk* (flute with reed mouthpiece), *zirne* (double- reed oboe), and the *tenbur* (Kurdish lute) are the principal instruments used for accompaniment. The author describes the cultural differences of the plains and the mountain peoples, and follows with an overview of the principal genres of each group: delal (epic songs of the plains); lawikesiwaran (epic songs of the mountains); kulamendilau (love songs); dilok (recreational songs); berdolavi (work songs); yezidis (religious, including Islamic, songs). The Kurdish dances are also briefly described. (A)

636   Ozturk, U; Perwer, S. "Singing of Home (Shivan Perwer talks about banned Kurdish music in Turkey)." *Index on Censorship* 27 no. 6 (November-December 1998): 124-127.

In an interview, Kurdish musician Shivan Perwer discusses why he and his songs were banned in Turkey. Perwer's songs spread the Kurdish voice in Kurdish, and so were offensive to the Turkish government.

637   Sa'id, Yusif. "al-Ughniyah al-Kurdiyah al-Mu'asirah." [A brief overview of modern Kurdish songs] *al-Turath al-Sha'bi* 3 (September 1971): 113-120.

638   Salihi, Nour-al-Din al-. *Die Musik in Kurdistan*. [Music in Kurdistan] Frankfurt am Main; New York: P. Lang, 1989. 173 p. [Europäische Hochschulschriften. Reihe XXXVI, Musikwissenschaft; Bd. 40] Includes bibliographical references (p. 171- 173). [In German]

Offers musical examples, detailed transcriptions, and analyses of contemporary musical practice among the Kurds and of the Kurdish musical tradition, substantiating the independent character of Kurdish music. An overview of Kurdish history, descriptions of various types of song and dance, and classifications of musical instruments are given.

639   Salihi, Nur al-Din al-. "Some Remarks and Investigations on the History of Kurdish Music." In *Yearbook of the Kurdish Academy 1990* (pp. 85-87). Ratingen, Germany: The Kurdish Academy, 1990.

640   Shiloah, Amnon. "Kurdish Music." In *The New Grove Dictionary of Music and Musicians*. Edited by Stanley Sadie, pp. 314-318. London: Macmillan, 1980.

Although short and not very much up-to-date, this article still provides an excellent overview on Kurdish music, particularly, Kurdish secular music and sacred and ritual music, as well as dance and musical instruments.

641   Tatsumura, Ayako. "Music and Culture of the Kurds." *Senri Ethnological Studies* 5 (1980): 75-93.

In 1975, the group (Second Scientific Research in Ethnomusicology in Iran and Turkey) made a field study of the music of the Kurds living in the Azerbaijan or Iran. Kurdish music is distinctive compared with that of other inhabitants of the region. All the songs collected in the villages have an antiphonal from which can be considered important in the Kurdish musical tradition. The songs of semi-professionals, recorded in the town, are characterized in particular by their melodic structures. The research aims at understanding the "rhythmical sense" which penetrates a culture as a whole to music as a sound phenomenon. This is a study on the music and culture of the Kurds. (A)

See also items: 24, 25, 72, 357, 518, 521

16

National, Cultural, and Ethnic Identity

Note: This chapter lists works that analyze the role of culture, elites, history, language, religion, state, tribe, and international powers in the Kurdish national movement and in the formation of Kurdish cultural/ethnic/national identity. Also included are works that discuss the differences within Kurdish society and the impact of these differences on Kurdish nationalism. For additional sources on the topic, see the cross-references listed at the end of the chapter.

642   Ahmadi, Hamid. *The Politics of Ethnic Nationalism in Iran (Kurdish, Azari, Baluchi, Identity)*. Ph.D., Carleton University, Canada. 1995. 554 p.

This thesis presents a critical study of the questions of ethnic nationalism and ethnic identity formation in order to explain the causes and the origins of the Kurdish, Azari and Baluchi nationalist movements in Iran. By a critical look at existing literature on ethnicity and nationalism, it argues that concepts such as ethnicity, tribe, ethnic groups and ethnic nationalism are contested and thus should not be considered universal, given and bearing the same meaning across time and place. By criticizing the Western and Orientalist approaches to the study of ethnicity, tribalism and ethnic nationalism in the Middle East in general and Iran in particular, it places its emphasis on the historical specificities of the cases under study rather than ahistorical and universal theories and conceptual frameworks. Following such a logic, and after a critical discussion of different theoretical frameworks on ethnicity and ethnic nationalism, this thesis argues that none of these sufficiently explain in themselves the formation of ethnic nationalist movements in the three Iranian cases. It then presents a theoretical framework in which three variables of state, elites, and international forces play key roles in the formation of ethnic identity and the politicization of linguistic, religious and racial ties, or the emergence of what social scientists call ethnic nationalism. In other words, the roots of ethnic nationalism are sought in: (1) the rise of the modern secular centralized state and its confrontation with the traditional autonomous and powerful tribal chiefs; (2) the manipulation of religio-linguistic differences and the construction of ethnic identities by political and intellectual, both ethnic and non-ethnic, elites; and (3) the promotion of ethnic identity and the support/encouragement of secular nationalist tendencies by Western Orientalists and external forces. Considering the historical experiences of the Iranian society, this theoretical framework is applied to explain the emergence of Kurdish, Azari and Baluchi nationalist tendencies and the formation of autonomist/separatist movements in these cases. Given the Iranian historical context, this study concludes that questions of ethnicity and ethnic nationalism are modern political phenomena and according to Eric Hobsbawm, "invented traditions." The existence of ethnic groups with distinct cultural and political identities are 'the states of mind,' or according to Benedict Anderson, "imagined communities." (A)

643   Antonius, Rachad. "Entre la mosaique et la vague: l'ethnicite instrumentalisee dans le Machrek arabe." [Between mosaic and wave: Instrumentalist ethnicity in the Middle East] *Cahiers de recherche sociologique* 20 (1993): 129-155.

It is proposed that ethnicity plays only a limited role in the political conflicts of the Middle East. Drawing on the examples of the Kurds in Iraq, the Palestinians in Israel, and conflicts in Lebanon, it is argued that the importance of ethnic dynamics is in defining group boundaries, rather than in cultural content. The role of nationalist and Islamic currents in ethnic identity formation is analyzed, and regional and international manipulations of ethnicity are evoked to illustrate the exploitation of ethnicity in inciting regional conflicts. (*SA* 94-00351)

644   Bille, Grete. "Societal Security—A Solution to the Kurdish Problems?" In *Contrasts and Solutions in the Middle East*. Edited by Ole Høiris and Sefa Martin Yürükel, pp. 532-552. Aarhus: Aarhus University Press, 1997.

In this paper, the concepts of societal security, ethnic identity, and the stateless nation are applied to the Kurdish problem. The author attempts to try and establish whether a solution can be found in terms of current policies: These are in line with the concept of societal security, based on the European security situation in existence following the lifting of the overlay of the cold war superpower confrontation. In the section on Kurds, *Ethnic Identity and Conflict*, definitions are offered for some of the basic concepts of the discussion. In the section on *Kurds and Kurdistan* a brief presentation of Kurdish societies is given, while in the section

Kurds and Societal Security the concept of societal security is dealt with and related to the Kurds. In the section *Kurds and Identity Budgets*, identity is explored in more depth and introduces the concept of identity budgets. In the section *Kurds, a Nation Denied*, the ambiguous position of the Kurdish society as a stateless nation is discussed, leading to the *Conclusion* in the final section on the problems at hand. (A)

645   Blau, Joyce. "Le role des cheikhs naqshbandi dans le mouvement national Kurde." [The Role of Naqshbandi Sheikhs in the Kurdish National Movement] In *Naqshbandis: Cheminements et situation actuelle d'un ordre mystique musulman. Actes de la Table Ronde de Sevres, 2-4 mai 1985*. Edited by Marc Gaborieau, Alexandre Popovic and Thierry Zarcone, pp. 371-377. Istanbul; Paris: Institut Francais d'Etudes Anatoliennes, 1990. (Varia Turcica, 18).

From the early years of the 19th century on, the Ottomans started to dissolve Kurdish principalities one after the other. The Sublime Porte executed or deported most of the Kurdish princes and heads of these principalities. Failing to fill the gap, however, the Central Government was unable to control the region which remained with no tribal chiefs. This situation led to the emergence of a new type of Kurdish leaders, namely religious leaders. Represented by the Naqshbandi and Qadiri *Sheikhs*, the Kurdish national movement was then led by these *sheikhs* whose influence was exercised independently of tribal divisions. The author here studies the political role of three Naqshbandi *Sheikh* families: the *Sheikhs* of Nehri (in the Ottoman Empire), the *Sheikhs* of Piran (in Kemalist Turkey), and the *Sheikhs* of Barzan (in modern Iraq). (*AI* 14: 650)

646   Blau, Joyce; Bruinessen, Martin van (eds.). "Islam des Kurdes." *Les annales de l'autre islam*, no. 5. Paris: INALCO, 1998. 400 p.

647   Bozarslan, Hamit. *Entre la 'Umma et le Nationalisme: l'Islam Kurde au Tournant du Siecle*. Amsterdam: Middle East Research Associates, 1992. [Occasional Paper No. 15 November 1992]

648   Bozarslan, Hamit. "Quel islam kurde aujourd'hui?" *Les Annales de l'Autre Islam*, no. 1 (pp. 121-132). Paris: ERISM, 1993.

649   Bruinessen, Martin van. "Nationalismus und religiöser Konflikt: Der kurdische Widerstand im Iran." In *Religion und Politik im Iran*. Edited by Kurt Greussing, pp. 372-409. Frankfurt am Main: Syndikat, 1981. [In German]

650   Bruinessen, Martin van. "Kurdish Tribes and the State of Iran: The Case of Simko's Revolt." In *The Conflict of Tribe and State in Iran and Af-*

ghanistan. Edited by Richard Tapper, pp. 364-400. London: St. Martin's Press, 1983.

The Kurdish tribe has often played an important role in the history of Persia and contemporary Iran. Van Bruinessen, author of *Agha, Shaikh, and State*, traces the history of the insurrection which erupted at the beginning of the 1920s by Ismail Agha (Simko), head of the powerful confederation of the Shikak tribes. Van Bruinessen presents a careful study of the evolution of the social and political organization of Kurdistan which was divided, until the beginning of the 20th century, between the Ottoman and Persian empires. With the arrival of the Europeans, the numerous Kurdish principalities, some of which were ancient and powerful, started to disintegrate, yet, at the same time, led to the emergence of Kurdish nationalism. Van Bruinessen introduces very interesting information on the development of inter-tribal relations within the Kurdish national movement. This information gives an original and convincing picture of the dynamics of the Kurdish national movement in today's Iran. This chapter is translated into Arabic, Persian, and Turkish. (Joyce Blau/*AI* 7:412)

651   Bruinessen, Martin van. "Popular Islam, Kurdish Nationalism and Rural Revolt: The Rebellion of Shaikh Said in Turkey (1925)." In *Religion and Rural Revolt*. Edited by Janos M. Bak and Gerhard Benecke, pp. 281-295. Manchester: Manchester University Press, 1984.

In this chapter, van Bruinessen suggests that the anti-Kemalist rebellion of the Kurds in 1925, few months after the Caliphate was abolished, was nationalist rather than religious, in spite of the leadership by dervish *sheikhs*. In order to end this rebellion, the Turkish government was forced to mobilize 35,000 soldiers who in two months pacified the region in a bloody bath. The leaders of the rebellion were executed, as well as other political opponents. The author did an excellent work here. His research is based on interviews held in Turkey and on Turkish and English documents; the author brings unpublished and precise information about the distorted events. It is an important piece of work on what became to be known as "the rebellion of Sheikh Sa'id of Piran." (Joyce Blau/*AI* 7: 413)

652   Bruinessen, Martin van. "Vom Osmanismus zum Separatismus: Religiose und ethnische Hintergrunde der Rebellion des Scheich Said." In *Islam und Politik in der Turkei*. Edited by Jochen Blaschke and Martin van Bruinessen, pp. 109-165. Berlin: Express Edition, 1985. [In German]

653   Bruinessen, Martin van. "The Ethnic Identity of the Kurds." In *Ethnic Groups in the Republic of Turkey*. Edited and compiled by Peter Alford Andrews with the assistance of Rudiger Benninghaus, pp. 613-621. Wiesbaden: Ludwig Reichert Verlag, 1989. (Beihefte zum Tubinger Atlas des Vorderen Orients. Reihe B. Geisteswissenschaften; Nr. 60)

The majority of the Kurds in Turkey are profoundly convinced that they belong to a distinct ethnicity different from that of the Turks and Christian minorities who live beside the Kurds. But what is this ethnic identity and what are its limits? Van Bruinessen answers these questions through a meticulous survey on the notion of Kurdish identity in Turkey. This work is a new contribution to the sociology of the Kurds from one of the best specialists in this field.

654 Bruinessen, Martin van. "Kurdish Society and the Modern State: Ethnic Nationalism Versus Nation-Building." In *Kurdistan in Search of Ethnic Identity: Papers Presented to the First Conference on Ethnicity and Ethnic Identity in the Middle East and Central Asia* [Department of Oriental Studies, University of Utrecht, June 1990] Edited by Turaj Atabaki and Margreet Dorleijn, pp. 24-51. Utrecht: Department of Oriental Studies, University of Utrecht Press, 1991. [Houtsma Foundation Publication Series, No. 1]

This article highlights the intra-Kurdish problems that have destroyed every attempt at Kurdish unity. Not only have most Kurdish movements been mirror-images of their non-Kurdish opposition, they have been distinctly colored by the nationalist politics of their states of residence; thus, Kurds of Iraq battle Turkish Kurds for political reasons that ignore the larger Kurdish question, but are driven by local political advantages. The article gives a historical overview of the Kurdish state movement through the last two centuries. Tribal loyalties and party discipline can have their confluences, but the former is driven by genealogy while the latter, by changing ideologies.

655 Bruinessen, Martin van. "Nationalisme kurde et ethnicites intra-kurdes." [Kurdish Nationalism and Intra-Kurdish Ethnicities] *Peuples Mediterraneens*, no. 68-69 (July-December 1994): 11-38.

While Kurdish nationalism has consolidated itself and awakened a wide spread awareness of common identity, differences within Kurdish society have at the same time become more divided than they were before. Iraqi Kurdistan appears to be torn between its Kurmanji-speaking northern part and the Sorani-speaking south. In Iran, the nationalist parties have always found their strongest support in the relatively urbanized, Sorani-Speaking region; during the 1980s these parties were actually fought by Kurmanji-speaking tribes from further north as well as Shi'i Kurds to their south. In Turkey, some of the speakers of the Zaza language, had always been considered, and had considered themselves as a separate people. The dividing line separating orthodox Sunni Muslims from heterodox Alevis has also become more important recently. This resurgence of new identities is perceived by Kurdish nationalists as a competitor of, and a threat to, the Kurdish national movement. But the intra-Kurdish divisions are not a remnant of the past that may gradually wither away. The narrower identities of region, language and religious community have been strengthened by the same factors that stimulated the awareness of Kurdish identity. And at least some of the divisions have become sharper precisely because of and in creation to the growth of the Kurdish movement.

656 Bruinessen, Martin van. "Introduction: The Kurds and Islam." *Les Annales de l'Autre Islam* 5 (1998): 13-35. Also published, in a slightly different version, as *The Kurds and Islam*. Tokyo: Islamic Area Studies Project, 1999. 24 p. [Islamic Area Studies Working Paper Series; 13].

657 Coyle, James John. *Nationalism in Iranian Kurdistan*. Ph.D., The George Washington University, 1993. 369 p.

This dissertation is a case study in nationalism, and the bases of legitimacy for nationalist movements. It examines the theoretical writings on nationalism, and concludes that all nationalism is based on a combination of ethnic markers and/or an ideology of self-determination. Using the Iranian Kurds as an example, It lends credence to the hypothesis that to the extent nationalism is based on ideology, the nationalist movement has a stronger ability to survive. To the extent that the movement is based on ethnicity, however, sub-national rivalries divide the movement. These rivalries can then be used by the central government to weaken the Iranian Kurds, and thus to defeat the nationalist movement. The dissertation examines six separate manifestations of Kurdish nationalism in Iran: the Ubaydallah Rebellion, the Treaty of Sevres, the Simko Rebellion, the Mahabad Republic, the Post War years, and the Islamic Revolution. In no case did the Kurds ever succeed for longer than a year in establishing an independent or autonomous Kurdistan. During the Ubaydallah and Simko Rebellions, as well as the post War years, Kurdish nationalism was based primarily on ethnicity. As a result, the Iranian Kurds were loyal to leaders of co-equal, segmentary tribes. Inter-tribal rivalries for power and position weakened the nationalist movements, making it easier for the central government to reassert their authority in Kurdistan. At the Treaty of Sevres, during the Mahabad Republic and the Islamic Revolution, nationalism was based primarily on ideology. To the extent that nationalism was identified by the Kurds' self-identification with the movement, then the nationalist movement was able to withstand the central government. This nationalism also had an ethnic element, however, which again allowed the government to exercise its tactics of divide and conquer. The findings of this case study support the hypothesis that ideology is a stronger basis of legitimacy for a nationalist movement than ethnicity. (A)

658 Dawod, Hocham. "Ethnies/Etats au Moyen-Orient: Le cas kurde." [Ethnic groups/states in the Middle East: the Kurdish case] *Peuples Mediterraneens*, no. 68-69 (July-December 1994): 39-56.

Attempts to address a perceived lack of attention given the development and role of Kurdish groups in the Middle East, generalizing their case to explore the origins of intense passions in contemporary ethnic societies, separatist/nationalist movements, the potential for resolution, and the opinions of numerous authors on the topic. Modernization, it is decided, cannot automatically transform ethnicities into anachronisms; neither are primordialist and instrumentalist paradigms considered sufficient to explain their predominance. Fredrik Barth's proposition that cultures are not entities but aggregates from which individuals can separate, and that belonging requires intense symbolic activity, is questioned in terms of its heavy reliance on personal choice. It is concluded that state borders inherited from the colonial era created ethno-territories that were once part of a unity, thus engendering dramatic difficulties; however, mass national, ethnic movements owe their existence to current sociopolitical, economic, and cultural contradictions and to the repression exercised by central governments on their national peripheries. (A)

659   Dorleijn, Margareet. "The Role of Medrese Graduates in the Present-Day Kurdish Cultural Movement in Turkey. The Case of Feqi Huseyin Sagnic." In *De Turcicis Aliisque Rebus: Commentarii Henry Hofman Dedicati*. Feestbundel voor professor emeritus H. F. Hofman ter gelegenheid van zijn vijfenzeventigste verjaardag aangeboden door vrienden en studenten, pp. 195-203. Utrecht: Institut voor Oosterse Talen en Culturen, 1992.

Since 1984 a stubborn and harsh struggle has been going on in Turkey between the Turkish military and security forces on one side and the Kurdish guerillas of the PKK *(Partiya Karkeren* Kurdistan--Workers' Party of Kurdistan), backed by a increasing part of the Kurdish population, on the other side. Since about 1989 this struggle has reached such dimensions that most Kurdish nationalists feel justified in speaking of a *de facto* civil war. Paradoxically, in particular since the spring of 1991 Kurdish ethnic and cultural identity can now be expressed and discussed more overtly than has ever been the case since the founding of the Turkish Republic. (A)

660   Dziegel, Leszek. "The Kurds Today: Between Local, Regional and National Identity." *Studia Ethnologica Croatica* 6 (1994): 105-117.

Forms of identification and loyalties of the Kurds in post-Soviet Transcaucasia are examined. Although the Kurdish-speaking inhabitants of Transcaucasia are considered by others to be a homogeneous ethnic group, they are distinguished by ethnic and religious differences. In Armenia, the Kurdish-speaking peoples were primarily Yezidis who fled from Turkey and persecution by Muslims. They lived side by side with Azerbaijani Kurdish refugees of the Muslim faith, although their cultures were different. The Armenian Kurds enjoyed relative cultural freedom and retained Kurdish forms of cultural expression, while Azerbaijani Kurds were forced to assimilate into the Turkish-speaking population of the region. The current goals of the two groups are also different: the Yezidis/Kurds wish to establish a non-Kurdish, religious ethnic community in opposition to Islam, while the Azerbaijani Kurds demand the restoration of the Kurdish autonomous region. (A)

661   Eller, Jack David. *From Culture to Ethnicity to Conflict: An Anthropological Perspective on International Ethnic Conflict*. Ann Arbor: University of Michigan Press, 1999. 360 p.

Violent conflict between states has declined over the years, but conflict between individual groups waving the banner of ethnicity has risen. When does ethnicity crowd out other identities (such as state, society, tribe, or nation) and trigger conflict? This anthropological study finds only complicated and tentative answers. Its central premise is that ethnic identity is subjective, based on beliefs about a common ancestry or shared historical past. From this assumption, Eller argues that ethnicity can be lost, discovered, or simply invented. Leaders who pursue practical and unsentimental agendas of power can easily exploit culture, myths, and historical memory. Taking as case studies Sri Lanka, Rwanda, Burundi, Bosnia, Quebec, and the Kurds, Eller successfully illustrates the diversity and nuances of ethnicity. But his lack of a more sweeping conclusion will frustrate readers searching for a general thesis on ethnicity and the sources of ethnic conflict. Eller discusses how the case of the Kurds (pp. 143-193) shows how a group's culture and history, while making them in a sense an ethnic group, may also hinder their realization of consciousness and mobilization as such.

662   Farzanfar, Ramesh. *Ethnic Groups and the State: Azaris, Kurds and Baluch of Iran*. Ph.D., Massachusetts Institute of Technology, 1992. 192 p.

This study is a historical examination of the relationship between the Iranian state and three trans-border ethnic groups inhabiting Iran, Azaris, Kurds and Baluch. A Comparative analysis demonstrates a dif-ference in the way the state has approached these groups. The Iranian state has been accommodating towards the Azaris while "carrot and stick" have been used to deal with other groups. This differential approach, however, is not a result of the transformation of the state through time. Indeed a relative continuity can be observed in the mutual perceptions and expectations. Such continuity is only explicable by observing the Iranian state and these groups in the historical context in which group encounters originated. As each group has had a different historical experience vis-à-vis the state, its relationship with the state has been different by virtue of that particular experience. Historical precedents, therefore, have had impacts on the nature of the nature of the relationships that have followed. At the same time as these groups share ethnic kin on the other side of the borders with the neighboring countries, the problem of their incorporation for the Iranian state has been linked, party, to the ties of these communities to their ethnic kin in the neighboring state and to its own relationships with those states. A Comparison of the relationships between the Iranian state and these groups within traditional and modern socio-political structures also demonstrates that modernization cannot be directly linked to ethnic conflict. It is the state that through implementation of various policies has been responsible for creation or resolution of conflict. The state, through utilization of myriad of policies ranging from coercion to co-optation of the political elite at the local level [Baluch and Kurds] and power sharing at the national level [Azaris] has been able, at times, to put a cap on ethnic aspirations. The Iranian state, however, due to its unwillingness to install democratic political institutions has not succeeded to create national cohesion. This explains the fact that the state, at different historical junctures, has resorted to force to bring the centrifugal elements within its sphere of influence. This study will also argue that although cultural and economic grievances are tangible and real, political factors are the most salient in the creation or resolution of conflict. (A)

663   Freij, Hanna. Y. "Tribal Identity and Alliance Behaviour Among Factions of the Kurdish National Movement in Iraq." *Nationalism and Ethnic Politics* 3, no. 3 (1997): 86-110.

While most of the current literature on secessionist and nationalist movements treats them as a collective whole, the author of this paper argues that these movements do not always act as a cohesive unit in their attempts to achieve their nationalist aspirations. The article demonstrates that primary loyalty to sectarian group identity within these movements impacts on their alliance behavior with the central government and foreign powers. The article integrates international relations theory and nationalism and group behavior theories and applies them to factions of the Kurdish national movement in Iraq. (A)

664   Garthwaite, Gene R. "Reimagined Internal Frontiers: Tribes and Nationalism—Bakhtiyari and Kurds." In *Russia's Muslim Frontiers*. Edited by Dale Eickelman, pp. 130-145. Bloomington, Ind.: Indiana University Press, 1993.

This paper offers a historical perspective on the development of "tribe" and national identities. It presumes the persistence of tribe and clan loyalties in two contrasting settings: Bakhtiyaris and Kurds. Among the Kurds, the role of various *sufi* leaders, together with discriminatory state policies, provided the impetus for a political organization that united rural and urban Kurds, shopkeepers, and other urban residents with tribal leaders. Garthwaite argues that the higher level of urbanization has contributed significantly to a rejection of "traditional" leaders in favor of those who

claim a national identity and the access that the Kurdish elite has had to
education since the time of Ottoman rule. The sustained repression of
Kurdish nationalist aspirations has itself provided an impetus toward nationalism.

665   Hakim, Halkawt. *La confrerie des Naqshbandis au Kurdistan au XXe
siecle*. [The Naqshbandi Order in Kurdistan in the 20th Century] Ph.D.,
Universite de Paris-Sorbonne, Paris IV, June 1983. 322 p.

This study is divided into three parts. After a long introduction discussing
the sources of the study, the author describes the historical background of
the Naqshbandi order and its rules. The second part, the more original
part, is dedicated to the history of Kurdistan in the beginning of the 19th
century, and more precisely to the history of the Baban dynasty that was
established on the border area of the Ottoman and Persian empires. At the
time when Mawlana Khalid of the powerful Kurdish tribe of Jaf was born
(1776 or 1779), the Baban were in decline. While discussing the life of
Mawlana Khalid, the author tries to separate between myth and reality.
The author insists on the social and political role of the Naqshbandi order
that established itself in Kurdistan in the beginning of the 19th century.
The last part discusses the national revolts that were lead since 1880 by
famous Naqshbandi *Sheikhs*: 'Ubaydallh of Nehri (1880-1882), Sa'id of
Piran (1925), and the movements of Sheikh Ahmad and Mulla Mustafa
Barzani since 1930 in Iraqi Kurdistan. (Joyce Blau/*AI* 7: 416)

666   Harris, George. "Whither the Kurds?" In *Global Convulsions: Race,
Ethnicity, and Nationalism at the End of the Twentieth Century*. edited
by Winston A. pp 205-223. Van Horne. Albany: State University New
York Press, 1997.

Considers the question of whether the Kurds will come into their own as a
cohesive ethnic group in the mold of many others in recent years in
Europe. Forces working against ethnic unity for the Kurds include geography, cultural and political fragmentation, and linguistic differences.
Further, Kurds represent a small minority in all of the countries in which
they reside; their situation in Iraq, Iran, and Turkey is briefly reviewed.
The movement toward independence of the Kurds in Iraq is shown to
have encouraged all Kurdish people to seek permanence to their affairs.
However, achievement of this end is bound up with the fate of the au-
thoritarian regimes in Iran and Iraq, which provides the essential uncertainty to their situation. It is concluded that changes will come for the
Kurds, but slowly, as political circumstances in their countries of residence slowly become amenable to democratic movements.

667   Houston, Chris. "Shortcut?" *New Perspectives on Turkey* 16 (Spring
1997): 1-22.

In this paper, Houston examines different responses to the Kurdish problem in the Islamic movement that reflect the continuous polarization of ethnic identity and nationalization of religious identity in Turkey. Discussing Islam's role as a state religion and its relationships to nationalism and discourse regarding the Kurds, it is argued that the movement's insensitivity to Kurdish suffering derives from the political mobilization and historical imaginations that underpin its constituting rhetoric, as seen in its discourses of self-definition and -analysis. The conflicting positions of Kurdish Muslims with regard to the source of the problem and their minimization of the importance of ethnic differences make it unlikely that there will be cooperation with the Islamist movement. However, the Kurdish problem offers the Islamist movement an opportunity, by allowing ethnicity as a counter to assimilation, to reconsider its historical context, and demonstrate Islam's justice.

668   Izady, Mehrdad R. *Roots and Evolution of Some Aspects of Kurdish Cultural Identity in Late Classical and Early Medieval Periods*. Ph.D., Columbia University, 1992. 233 p.

In this work, the author has attempted to demonstrate that a crucial portion of the religious and mythological heritage of the Middle East has its roots in the Zagros mountains where the Kurds have been the primary inhabitants in the past several thousand years. A thorough survey of modern religious texts of the followers of the native Zagrotian religion of Yazdanism is made alongside of the ancient Zoroastrian texts. The Mesopotamian, Graeco-Roman, Armenian, medieval Islamic and Aramean historical, geographical, and liturgical texts, as well as ancient artifacts of religious importance are also examined in detail to demonstrate the knowledge of this religion by the ancients, and substantiate the antiquity of many fundamental tenets and practices of this native religious and mythological heritage. This dissertation lays the ground for further investigation of one of the most enigmatic parts of the Middle Eastern civilization: the role and contribution of the Zagros cultures in general and the Kurds in particular. (A)

669   Jigalina, Olga. "Dawr al-Islam fi Tatawur al-Harakah al-Qawmiyah al-Kurdiyah fi Iran." [The role of Islam in the development of the Kurdish national movement in Iran] In *al-Islam fi Buldan al-Sharqayn al-Adna wa-al-Awsat*. pp. 155-182. Translated from Russian by Muhammad Sulayman Abbud. Damascus: Dar al-Ma'rifa, 1990.

670   Koohi-Kamali, [Fereshteh]. *Economic and Social Bases of Kurdish Nationalism in Iran*. Ph.D., Oxford, 1995.

This study examines the links between the structural changes in the Kurdish economy, and its political demands, namely Kurdish nationalism in Iran. The author argues that the transition of the nomadic/tribal society of

Kurdistan to an agrarian village society was the beginning of a process, whereby Kurds saw themselves as a community of homogeneous ethnic identity. She discusses the political movements of the Kurds in Iran to argue that the different phases of economic development of Kurdish society played a great role in determining the way Kurds saw themselves, and expressed their political demands for independence. The author divides the political history of Kurdistan in Iran, and incidentally its economic development from World War I to the present, into three periods. The first corresponds to tribal consciousness, during which the typical economic activity is herding, exchange relationships are based on barter, and social and political relationships are based, predominantly, on tribal "face-to-face" contact within the community. Simko's uprising is discussed to illustrate the political counterpart of this period. The second period corresponds to the reign of Reza Shah and his tribal policies. This is the period of national consciousness amongst the Kurdish leaders in Iran, illustrated by the establishment of the Kurdish Republic in Mahabad in 1946. The third period begins with the Shah's land reform program. The author analyzes the Kurdish participation in the 1979 revolution in Iran to illustrate the further development of Kurdish nationalist movement since the demise of the republic in 1947, and examines the differences and similarities of the two main Kurdish nationalist organizations at the eve of the 1979 revolution and later. (A)

671   Lescot, Roger. "Le Kurd Dagh et le mouvement mouroud." [Kurd Dagh and the Mouroud Movement] *Studia Kurdica* (1988): 101-125.

The author divides his study into four parts: 1) Kurd Dagh, its resources, population, and the history of its inhabitants; 2) the political conditions in Kurd Dagh; 3) the beginnings of Mouroudism in Kurd Dagh and; 4) history of Mouroudism in Kurd Dagh between 1933 and 1939. There is also an annex—a study on the tribes that live in Kurd Dagh. (Joyce Blau/*AI* 12: 539)

672   Nagel, Joane P. "The Conditions of Ethnic Separatism: The Kurds in Turkey, Iran and Iraq." *Ethnicity* 7 (September 1980): 279-297.

Outlined are four conditions necessary to the development of a separatist movement in any country: (1) inclusion of the group within a nation containing other, dominant ethnic groups; (2) unequal periphery-center economic and political relations; (3) penetration and activation of this ethnic periphery; and (4) an organized periphery that can both coordinate the movement and link it with outside support. A number of hypotheses related to these conditions are advanced and tested using the case of the Middle Eastern Kurds. Examined are Kurdish separatist movements in Turkey, Iran, and Iraq, particularly the development of a strong and widespread movement in Iraq during the period 1961-1975. These movements were found to best fit the model of separatist action outlined. Preliminary support for the hypotheses is provided. (B. Annesser/*SA* 81L: 8308)

673   Nezan, Kendal. "La Destruction de L'Identite Culturelle Kurde en Turquie." *Afrique et L'Asie Modernes*, no. 140 (Spring 1984): 51-58.

674   Olson, Robert W. *The Emergence of Kurdish Nationalism and the Sheikh Said Rebellion, 1880-1925*. Introduction by William F. Tucker. Austin: University of Texas Press, 1989. xix, 229 p.: ill. Bibliography: p. [213]-220.

The last quarter of the nineteenth century was crucial for the development of Kurdish nationalism. It coincided with the reign of Abdulhamid II (1876-1909), who emphasized Pan-Islamic policies in order to strengthen the Ottoman Empire against European and Russian imperialism. The Pan-Islamic doctrines of the Ottoman Empire enabled *sheikhs*—from Sheikh Ubaydallah of Nehri in the 1870s and 1880s to Sheikh Sa'id in the 1920s—to become the principal nationalist leaders of the Kurds. This represented a new development in Middle Eastern and Islamic history and began an important historical pattern in the Middle East long before the emergence of the religious nationalist leadership of Ayatollah Khomeini in Iran. This is one of the first works in any Western language dealing with he development of Kurdish nationalism during this period and is supported with documentation not previously utilized, principally from the Public Record Office in Great Britain. In addition, the author provides much new materials on Turkish, Armenian, Iranian, and Arab history and new insights into Turkish-Armenian relations during the most crucial era of the history of these two peoples. The book demonstrates categorically that the Kurds are most emphatically a people with a 'history' in spite of the efforts of many countries at various times to "deny" the Kurds their political and national development.

675   O'Shea, Maria T. "Kurdistan, the Mapping of a Myth." In *Kurdistan: Political and Economic Potential*. Edited by Maria T. O'Shea, pp. 1-26. London: GIBRC, SOAS, 1992.

Few people attempt to deny the existence of a discrete area known as Kurdistan, indeed there is adequate evidence that such an area has been recognized, documented and mapped by outsiders for over 100 years. All the maps the author presents share a common and definite core area, but its extent and exact borders are in doubt. The extent of that region is something, over which Kurds are unlikely to ever reach agreement with the surrounding states, especially since the 1940s adoption of a stylized map of Greater Kurdistan. There have never been reliable censuses on ethnographic bases, nor an acceptable cartographic representation of Kurdistan. An undertaking such as the latter is of course in itself a conundrum, as Kurdistan exists currently only as a cultural abstract. In the 20th

century the complex ethnographical make-up of the region has undergone
many changes, perhaps further fragmenting the Kurdish ethnos and a sizable portion of Kurdistan is presently apparently suffering an Armenian
style annihilation. Thus the need to document the changing borders of
Kurdistan, and hopefully to establish some acceptable territorial compromise for use in any future negotiations concerning the future of the Kurdish people, is greater than ever. The author dwells at some length on the
period around the end of the First World War. (A)

676   O'Shea, Maria T. "Between the Map and the Reality: Some Fundamental
       Myths of Kurdish Nationalism." *Peuples Mediterraneens*, no. 68-69
       (July-December 1994): 77-94.

       Despite the divisions of Kurdistan and the inadequacy of the national
       movement, the idea of a Greater Kurdistan is perpetuated. It is a powerful
       amalgamation of myths, facts and ambitions. This article explores the use
       of various myths in promoting Kurdish nationalism and the perpetuation
       of the notion of Greater Kurdistan both as a cultural abstraction and as a
       concrete expression. These myths relate to language and literature, to his-
       tory, dress, music, cultural traditions and the creation of symbols of na-
       tional belonging. Maps have been used to fashion the spatial expression
       of Kurdistan and in some respects to create Kurdistan. The Kurds do not
       possess a state apparatus that is able to create a common national ideol-
       ogy, but with the help of maps they have succeeded in creating an image
       of the territorial extent of Kurdistan. Such maps should not be seen a
       simple propaganda but rather as a form of discourse, representing the
       only available channel for the consolidation and propagation of ideas
       linking perceptions of Kurdistan to the nationalist aspirations of the
       Kurds.

677   Ozoglu, Adem Hakan. *Unimaginable Community: Nationalism and
       Kurdish Notables in the Late Ottoman Era*. Ph.D. The Ohio State Uni-
       versity, 1997. 192 p.

       The present study first analyzes the evolution of the perception of the
       Kurds and Kurdistan in history. Then, it focuses on the social and tribal
       dimensions of Kurdish nationalism in the late nineteenth and early twen-
       tieth century by introducing some data on the Kurdish nationalists. Based
       upon both qualitative and quantitative data, this study analyzes the social
       origins and kinship relations of Kurdish nationalist leaders, and examines
       literature written by and about the Kurds. One of the goals of this study is
       to ground the ideological/idealistic discourse of Kurdish nationalism
       firmly in the social realities of the Middle East in general and Kurdish so-
       ciety in particular. This dissertation demonstrates two significant claims.
       (1) Group identity is closely tied to territory. Although religion and lan-
       guage are significant contributors to identity formation, this study claims
       that the role of territory should not be overlooked. This study argues that

the perceived political boundaries of Kurdistan change in time, and in relation to this change the perception of group identity is always in flux. Nevertheless, also fundamental to this work is the claim that there always exists a core area in reference to which social groups, Kurds in this study, define themselves. (2) The social composition of· Kurdish nationalist leadership in the late 19th and early 20th centuries reveals important clues about the nature of Kurdish nationalism and its relations to territory. For example, the majority of Kurdish nationalist leaders originally belonged to the land-owning nobility. Their access to land came either through their traditional status as local notables or through their position as men of religion, or in some cases these categories overlapped. This study also claims that tribalism does not necessarily challenge nationalism. On the contrary, Kurdish nationalism clearly demonstrates that tribal loyalties and ties play a significant role in the service of nationalism. (A)

678   Ozoglu, Hakan [Ozoglu, Adem Hakan.]. "State-Tribe Relations: Kurdish Tribalism in the 16th- and 17th-Century Ottoman Empire." *British Journal of Middle Eastern Studies* 23, no. 1 (1996): 5-27.

This paper is primarily concerned with the following questions: how are tribes defined in terms of their relations with the states, and what would be the impact of such a relationship in shaping and reshaping tribal structures? While examining the role of the Ottoman state by defining Kurdish tribal structures in the 16th and 17th centuries, this paper demonstrates that a strong state plays a determining role in the socio-political configuration of tribes. Undoubtedly, these internal dynamics of tribes also contribute significantly to the process of tribal reformation. However, the contribution of the internal dynamics is beyond the scope of the paper. Focusing instead on the state, the author demonstrates the impact of the Ottoman administration in the new configuration of the Kurdish emirates. Thus, he shows that at the level of an emirate, a strong state exercises a greater authority than it does on the tribal level. Seen in this light, the author claims that the Ottoman state was actively involved in and primarily responsible for the process of Kurdish emirate formation. (A)

679   Rasul, Fadil. "al-Islam wa-al-Qawmiyah: Afkar Hawla Tajribat al-Sha'b al-Kurdi." [Islam and nationalism: a discussion of the Kurdish experience] *al-Hiwar* 1 (Summer 1986): 53-60.

680   Tapper, Richard. "The Tribes in Eighteenth- and Nineteenth-Century Iran." In *The Cambridge History of Iran. Vol. 7: From Nadir Shah to the Islamic Republic*. Edited by Peter Avery, Gavin Hambly, and Charles Melville, pp. 506-541, 1003-1005. Cambridge: Cambridge University Press, 1991.

This chapter gives in the first instance a general survey, based on available source materials, of the distribution of the tribes and their political history as a "problem" for the Iranian government in the 18th and 19th centuries. The second part of the chapter attempts an analysis, on the one hand, of the processes of ecological adaptation and social and economic organization which may be considered to have contributed to the "tribal problem," and, on the other, of the development of different tribal groups during the period as the product of interaction between these various kinds of processes: ecological, economic, social and political. (A)

681   Vali, Abbas. "Genese et structure du nationalisme kurde en Iran." (The Genesis and Structure of Kurdish Nationalism in Iran) *Peuples Mediterraneens*, no. 68-69 (July-December 1994): 143-164.

There is an influential body of opinion in Kurdish historical writing which traces the origins of the nationalist movement in Iranian Kurdistan to Sheikh Ubaydallah rebellion against the Ottoman Empire in the late nineteen century. This rebellion, it is contended, planted the seeds of modern nationalism in Kurdish which then developed in a cumulative process. This view of the genesis and development of Kurdish nationalism in Iranian Kurdistan is challenged. Kurdish nationalism in Iran is a modern phenomena, an outcome of the socioeconomic and cultural dislocations caused by the blighted and preserve modernity which followed the advent of the Pahlavi absolutism after the first World War. The Kurdish responses to the politics of territorial centralism and the cultural process of the construction of a uniform Iranian "national" identity pursued by the Pahlavi State, defined the discursive and non-discursive conditions of formation of the nationalist movement, culminating in the Republic of Mahabad. (A)

682   Vega, Anne. "L'identite ethnique kurde, *kurdayeti*." *Droit et Cultures* 27 (1994): 195-217.

683   White, Paul J. "Ethnic Differentiation among the Kurds: Kurmanci, Kizilbash, and Zaza." *The Journal of Arabic, Islamic, and Middle Eastern Studies* 2, no. 2 (November 1995): 67-90.

684   Wimmer, Andreas. "Stamme fur den Staat. Tribal Politik und die kurdbihe Nationalbewegung im Irak." [Tribes for the state: tribal politics and the Kurdish national movement in Iraq] *Kolner Zeitschrift Fur Soziologie Und Sozialpsychologie* 47, no. 1 (March 1995): 95-113. [In German.]

The political situation in northern Iraq serves to show that the social sciences need a more sophisticated analysis of tribes and states to replace the common view of the two as opposed and mutually exclusive forms of political organization. To this end, the relationships between tribal confederacies, central powers (e.g., emirs, sheiks, the current nationalist government), and regional state powers, 1850-present, are delineated. The transition from Islamic Messianism to Kurdish nationalism during the

1950s-1970s is traced, and the current situation is analyzed. It is concluded that tribe-state relations in northern Iraq have undergone a series of transformations and have included both cooperation and conflict. (A)

685 Yalcin-Heckmann, Lale. "Ethnic Islam and Nationalism among the Kurds in Turkey." In *Islam in Modern Turkey: Religion, Politics, and Literature in a Secular State*. Edited by Richard Tapper, pp. 102-120. London; New York: I. B. Tauris, 1991. [Published in association with the Modern Turkish Studies Programme of the Centre of Near and Middle Eastern Studies, School of Oriental and African Studies-University of London] Includes bibliographical references and index.

This chapter considers a theoretical problem and attempts a critical assessment of its various dimensions. The problem is the relation between ethnic and national identities and more universalist and religious commitments; more specifically, it concerns ethnicity, nationalism, Islam and social movements among the Kurds. In order to discuss the relevant issues in this sociological problem, the author uses field materials collected in Hakkari province, and various historical, sociological and political studies of Kurdish movements within the Ottoman and more recent political formations, namely the Turkish Republic and surrounding states. Lale first identifies unsatisfactory elements in the models that have been used to analyze Kurdish social movements, and secondly asks the relevant questions and suggests more suitable methods of answering them. The author's aim is to clarify some of the concepts and the models that have been used and to suggest further areas of research which would enable a more satisfactory understanding of ethnicity and Islam among the Kurds. The author's interest in Kurdish ethnicity and nationalism is older than her interest in Islam among Kurds. In her doctoral work, she discussed various aspects of Islam, but mostly as secondary issues. Here she reconsiders her material in the light of evaluations and impressions drawn from more recent visits to Hakkari. Lately there has been much general political discussion of 're-Islamization' in Turkey, especially as it concerns the Kurds. Sociologists and political scientists have shown an interest in this development and have been studying the new Islamic organizations and their publications. The Turkish press reports frequently on the activities of Islamic organizations and militant or secret groups in different parts of the country, and some recent publications suggest that areas with a Kurdish majority are becoming more susceptible to militant Islamic influences than other areas. The number of Islamic or fundamentalist movements which can be identified is still not clear. However, if there is sufficient evidence that such activities are strong and significant among the Kurdish people, the following question arises: is there a special and significant relation between Kurdish ethnicity and Islamic militancy or fundamentalism? If there is, at what level (village, region or wider) and from what aspect (ideology, recruitment, leadership or organization) should we analyze this relation? (A)

686   Yalda, Nariman. *Federalism and Self-Rule for Minorities: A Case Study of Iran and Kurdistan*. Ph.D., Claremont Graduate School, 1980. 199 p.

This dissertation is a study of the use of a federalist system of government to maintain the national integration of a country of many different religions, languages and cultures, with Iran and Kurdistan as a case study. The purpose of the study is to examine whether federalism is a possibly practical, modern solution to the demands and needs for self-rule by minorities in Iran, taking into account the historical background of Kurdish demands for self-rule, the historical development of Iranian government administration, and the current international context of the Iranian Kurdish situation. Federalism in three countries--Switzerland, Canada, and Yugoslavia--is examined in terms of its use in integrating minorities. Then a detailed summary of the history of government and administration in Iran is provided, with regard to elements of centralization and decentralization that have appeared and developed over the centuries. Kurdistan itself is fully described in its physical, cultural, and historical aspects. The past efforts to establish a government of self-rule in Kurdistan are thoroughly described and analyzed to find the reasons for their failure. Some theories of self-determination are considered as they relate to Kurdistan. First, the essentially Marxist-Leninist approach of the Kurdish nationalist leader Ghassemlou is analyzed and rejected for its failure to maintain national identity and placement of Kurdistan under the domination of a foreign socialist power. Second, an alternative theory of self-determination for Third World countries is put forward, one that provides for independence based on cultural identity and on Dr. Mossadegh's concept of negative political balance (that is, a refusal to accept any foreign domination, regardless of ideology). The dissertation concludes that the Iranian central government and the Kurdish nationalist groups should cooperate in a temporary pre-federalist arrangement designed to prepare both Iran and Kurdistan for the possibility of a full federalist partnership in which Kurdistan would have the appropriate self-rule within a unified Iranian nation. (A)

687   Yavuz, M. Hakan. "Search for a New Social Contract in Turkey: Fethullah Gulen, the Virtue Party, and the Kurds." *SAIS Review* 19, no. 1 (Winter 1999): 114-143.

Argues that Kemalist legacies can no longer represent civil society in Turkey. A new, more inclusive social contract must address the multicultural diversity of its society by drawing on a neo-Ottoman ethos.

See also items: 2, 6, 7, 26, 46, 47, 48, 74, 148, 170, 171, 172, 181, 310, 311, 315, 327, 329, 333, 332, 518, 523, 577, 626, 689, 694, 695, 698, 761, 762, 768, 769, 770, 771, 772, 784, 796, 809, 810, 811, 812, 829, 848, 859, 860, 867, 870, 875, 877, 884, 890, 893, 900, 901, 905, 909, 921, 927

17

National Identity and the Language Question

Note: Items listed in this chapter primarily discuss how Kurdish is regarded or perceived as an ingredient and prime symbol of the cultural and national identity among the Kurds. The items also discuss: (1) the policies of Iran, Iraq, Syria, Turkey, and the former Soviet Union towards the use of the Kurdish language; and (2) the consequences of these policies on the Kurdish people. For additional sources on the topic, see the cross-references listed at the end of the chapter.

688 Akin, Salih. "Designation d'une langue innommable dans un texte de loi: le cas du kurde dans un texte de loi turque." [Designations of an unnamable language in a legal text: the case of Kurdish in a Turkish legal text] In *Le Nom des Langues I: Les Enjeux de la Nomination des Langues*. Edited by Andree Tabouret-Keller, pp., 69-79. Leuven: Peeters, 1997.

A review of the current status of Kurdish emphasizes its dialectal diversity, the scattering of its speakers among five states and three alphabets, and its complete lack of institutional status in Turkey, Iran, and Syria, where it is officially represented as a dialect of Turkish, Persian, and Arabic respectively. The Turkish policy of negating the existence of Kurdish and the consequent taboo on mentioning it by name is exemplified in the text of a 1983 law forbidding its use. The text, presented in Turkish with a French translation, prohibits the use of languages other than Turkish as native languages or in publications or displays of any kind; the document exempts the "primary" official languages of other countries, as Kurdish has been recognized as the "second" language of the Iraqi state. The law reveals the failure of the policy of negation and the embarrassment of trying to enforce Turkish as the mother tongue of all citizens of Turkey.

689   Blau, Joyce; Suleiman, Yasir. "Language and Ethnic Identity in Kurdistan: An Historical Overview." In *Language and Identity in the Middle East and North Africa*. Edited by Yasir Suleiman, pp. 153-164. Richmond, Surrey: Curzon, 1996.

In this chapter Joyce Blau and the editor of the volume present a general overview of the long and drawn out process of deliberately making Kurdish an ingredient and prime symbol of the cultural and national identity among the Kurds. The crucial involvement of the elite in this process is highlighted, as is the contribution of the press in the nineteenth and twentieth centuries. The success of all those who participated in this process represents a huge triumph against adversity, created by the allure of more prestigious co-territorial languages of high culture and administration, national apathy on the part of the Kurds initially and the impact on Kurdish life of the political machinations of outside powers. The political division of the Kurds is highly reminiscent of that of the Berbers in North Africa, leading to further similarities with respect to identity anchored dilemmas of script choice and the dispersion of the national elite in Europe. The latter has however worked to the advantage of both communities in that it provided the intellectual and political space for a more robust articulation of the importance of the language ingredient in national identity construction. (A)

690   Hassanpour, Amir. "State Policy on the Kurdish Language: The Politics of Status Planning." *Kurdish Times* 4 (Summer-Fall 1991): 42-85.

In this article, Hassanpour examines the changes in the use of the Kurdish language since 1918 in Iraq, Iran, Turkey, Syria and the Soviet Union. He excellently surveys the policies of these states towards the use of the Kurdish language and its consequences on the Kurdish people.

691   Hassanpour, Amir. *Nationalism and Language in Kurdistan, 1918-1985*. San Francisco: Mellen Research University Press, 1992. xlii, 520 p.: ill., maps. Includes bibliographical references (p. [469]-520).

This book is originally the author's doctoral dissertation presented at the University of Illinois at Urbana-Champaign in 1989 under the title: *The Language Factor in National Development: The Standardization of the Kurdish Language, 1918-1985*. The sources of information of this work were based on various types of primary sources including written and oral material, participant observation, interviews, correspondence, and government documents. The first four chapters present general but detailed information on the Kurdish language and its dialects, the methodological and theoretical frameworks of the study, the formation of the Kurdish nation, and the background of Kurdish literary dialects. Chapter five examines state policies on Kurdish, language rights, and linguicide. In chapter six, a discussion of the selection of a dialect base in Iran, Iraq, Syria, Turkey, USSR, and the diaspora is presented. Unification of dialects is also discussed. In chapter seven, the functions of Kurdish (i.e., its use in printing, book publishing, journalism, broadcasting, education, administration, science, cinema, theater, and phonograph records) is discussed. Chapter eight deals with the codification of Kurdish—that is, its phonology, orthography, morphology, vocabulary, grammar, and literary forms (prose, poetry, and genres). Chapter nine examines the acceptance of Sorani standard. The social context of standardizations—that is, urbanization, literacy, the formation of a reading public and language planning—are discussed in chapter ten, followed by summary, findings and conclusions (chapter eleven).

692   Hassanpour, Amir. "The Internationalization of Language Conflict: The Case of Kurdish." In *Language Contact-Language Conflict*. Edited by Eran Fraenkel and Christina Kramer, pp. 107-155. New York: Peter Lang, 1993. (Studies in the Balkans and Turkey in Europe, vol. 1)

In this article Hassanpour deals with Kurdish language rights as a regional conflict and provide evidence for the systematic and increasing involvement of Western countries in Kurdish-language issues since the eighteenth century, during the expansion of capitalism. After a brief overview, Hassanpour examines the roles of Western powers, international organizations, and regional powers in more modern conflicts over the Kurdish language in Iraq and Turkey, two of the five states that rule over Kurdistan. Hassanpour argues that the internationalization process is inevitable and increasing, and indicates how it is generally shaped by the economic, political, and military interests of the parties involved in the conflict. Hassanpour concludes with an evaluation of the relationship between language policy as a specific issue and concerns over minority rights generally and definitions of genocide specifically.

693   Hassanpour, Amir. "Language Rights in the Emerging World Linguistic Order: The State, the Market and Communication Technologies." In *Language: A Right and a Resource: Approaching Linguistic Human Rights*. Edited by Miklos Kontra et al., pp. 223-241. Berlin: Central European University Press, 1999.

This chapter examines the implications of post-modernist claims about the erosion of state sovereignty in light of the struggle of the Kurds for language rights in Turkey. Turkey pursues a harsh policy of killing the Kurdish language, spoken by no less than twelve million people within this country. Writing, printing, broadcasting, and teaching in Kurdish have been harshly punished as crimes against the "indivisibility of the Turkish nation" and its "territorial integrity." In spite of the totalitarian "closure" of the Turkish state, a group of Kurds in Western Europe in the latter part of the 1990s undermined its sovereign rule by exercising the right to native tongue broadcasting and teaching via satellite television.

While this is an overlapping exercise of sovereignty, the chapter argues that the state continues to play a significant role in the regulation of linguistic and political power. (A)

694   Kreyenbroek, Philip G. "Kurdish Identity and the Language Question." In *Kurdistan in Search of Ethnic Identity: Papers Presented to the First Conference on Ethnicity and Ethnic Identity in the Middle East and Central Asia* [Department of Oriental Studies, University of Utrecht, June 1990] Edited by Turaj Atabaki and Margreet Dorleijn, pp. 52-70. Utrecht: Department of Oriental Studies, University of Utrecht Press, 1991. [Houtsma Foundation Publication Series, No. 1]

Emphasizes the individual histories of the two written dialects of Kurdish: Kurmanji (in Turkey and Syria) and Sorani (in Iraqi and Iranian Kurdistan).

695   Kreyenbroek, Philip G. "The Kurdish Language: Symbol and Reality." In *Kurdistan: Political and Economic Potential*. Edited by Maria T. O'Shea, pp. 27-35. London: GIBRC, SOAS, 1992.

This paper argues that while the Kurdish language has been extremely important as a symbol of Kurdish identity in the years since the partition of the Ottoman parts of Kurdistan, in an independent Kurdish state the realities of the language situation may well lead to tensions, so that language could become a destabilizing factor. It would seem possible, however, to overcome or indeed avoid such tensions by adopting adequate policies. In order to illustrate the first part of this argument, the history of Kurdish and the present language situation in the Kurdish-speaking areas is examined, with special reference to the development of two different standard written 'dialects'. The author argues that the recent history of these standard languages shows that their function is primarily that of a symbol, rather than a means of communication. The last part of the paper, which is more speculative and shorter, examines the role which forms of Kurdish could play in an independent Kurdish state. (A)

696   Kreyenbroek, Philip G. "On the Kurdish Language." In *The Kurds: A Contemporary Overview*. Edited by Philip G. Kreyenbroek and Stefan Sperl, pp. 68-83. London: Routledge, 1992.

A useful supplement to Amir Hassanpour's lengthy analysis presented in his doctoral dissertation (1988), and subsequently published as *Nationalism and Language in Kurdistan, 1918-1985*. Kreyenbroek briefly reviews the origin and early history of the Kurdish languages, but contrary to Hassanpour's contribution, argues that from a linguistic, or at least grammatical point of view, its two main dialects of Sorani and Kurmanji "differ as much from each other as English and German, and it would seem more appropriate to refer to them as 'languages.' While variations between the

Kurmanji-Sorani group of dialects on one hand and the Gurani-Dimili group on the other, allows for classification of the two groups as separate languages, Kreyenbroek is clearly exaggerating when he compares Sorani's variations from Kurmanji with those between English and German. Sorani and Kurmanji are mutually intelligible to a large extent (clearly not the case between English and German), and comprehension improves markedly with a few days of exposure of the speaker of one to the other. Kreyenbroek goes on to analyze at length the recent history and present position of the Kurdish language in Turkey, Iraq and Iran, with special reference to the development of written forms of Kurdish. He notes that "two different standard languages have now emerged," of which Kurmanji, is one of the very few languages in the world whose modern standard form has so evolved almost entirely in exile. This he attributes to the hostile attitude of Turkey towards the Kurdish language. (abridged, Michael Gunter/*IJKS* 8, no. 1-2, 1995: 135-136).

697 MacKenzie, David N. "The Role of the Kurdish Language in Ethnicity." In *Ethnic Groups in the Republic of Turkey*. Edited and compiled by Peter Alford Andrews with the assistance of Rudiger Benninghaus, 541-542. Wiesbaden: Ludwig Reichert Verlag, 1989. (Beihefte zum Tubinger Atlas des Vorderen Orients. Reihe B. Geisteswissenschaften; Nr. 60)

698 Monch-Bucak, Yayla. "The Kurdish Language in Turkey Between Repression and Resistance." *Plural Societies* 21, no. 1-2 (1991): 75-87.

Examined in the history and current situation of the Kurdish language in Turkey, one of four countries in which the Kurds live. Kurdish is unrelated to Turkish, and faces special challenges because of the Turkish governmental policy of rigid language purification to create pure Turkish. Beside the problem of the Turkish political policy of denying the separate linguistic identity of Kurdish are problems of multiple Kurdish dialects and lack of an independent alphabet. The Turkish media is a strong influence on daily life. Current cultural repression of the Kurds and discriminatory legal action prohibiting non-Turkish language use has bred resistance from Kurds in West European cities and production of Kurdish literary works that are brought back into Turkey by migrants. (J. Mayberry/*SA*: 92-07108)

699 Neier, Aryeh. "Language and Minorities." *Dissent* (Summer 1996): 31-35.

Examines conflicts throughout the world over the right of minorities to use their own language. Topics include the Tamils in Sri Lanka, the Kurds in Turkey, Russians in Latvia and Estonia, Albanians in Kosovo, and the English-only movement in the US.

700   Nezan, Kendal. "La culture kurde en Turquie a l'epreuve du second choc." [Kurdish Culture in Turkey Faces a Second Shock] *Studia Kurdica*, no. 5 (1988): 7-12.

In this article, Nezan argues that Turkey, one of the five countries that divide Kurdistan, practices in a systematic way a policy of deculturation to the 10 to 12 million Kurds residing in Turkish Kurdistan. Nezan, president of the Kurdish Institute of Paris, focuses on the gloomy linguistic situation of the Kurds in Turkey.

701   Phillipson, R.; Skutnabb-Kangas, T. "Colonial Language Legacies: The Prospects for Kurdish." In *Self-Determination: International Perspectives*. Edited by Donald Clark and Robert Williamson, pp. 200-213. New York: St. Martin's Press, 1996.

This paper concentrates on how the oppression of the Kurdish language is outstandingly severe, as well as on the importance of language rights for liberation. It also considers whether the language policies of many states that were formerly colonies represent an example to follow.

702   Pierse, Catherine. *Cultural and Language Rights of the Kurds: A Study of the Treatment of Minorities Under National Law in Turkey, Iraq, Iran and Syria in Light of International Human Rights Standards*. London: Kurdish Human Rights Project, 1997. 70 p.

703   Sallo, Ibrahim Khidhir. "A Sociolinguistic Study of Language Choice among Kurdish Students at Mosul University." *Adab al-Rafidayn* 16 (1986): 108-117.

Sallo studies the use of language among bilingual Kurdish and Arabic speakers at the University, and concludes that social or psychological factors rather than linguistic ones systematically determine the speaker's choice.

704   Skutnabb-Kangas, Tove; Bucak, Sertac. "Killing a Mother Tongue—How the Kurds are Deprived of Linguistic Human Rights." In *Linguistic Human Rights: Overcoming Linguistic Discrimination*. Edited by Tove Skutnabb-Kangas and Robert Phillipson, in collaboration with Mart Rannut, pp. 347-371. Berlin: M. de Gruyter, 1994.

This paper brings together some of the extensive documentation of how the Kurds in Turkey are prevented from using their mother tongue, in defiance of international covenants on human rights that Turkey is a signatory to—or, in some cases very significantly, is NOT signatory to. It also discusses some of the consequences of this for Kurdish culture and Kurdish children and adults, both in Turkish parts of Kurdistan, in Turkey proper and elsewhere. At the same time it shows how a clarification of concepts, here demonstrated by the concept of mother tongue, call help us in analyzing lack of linguistic rights and in formulating requirements which a universal declaration of linguistic human rights must fulfill. Since it is not always easy to get reliable information about the Kurdish language, the authors start with a short description of the linguistic situation. (A)

18

Population and Urban Studies

705   Baban, Jamal 'Abd al-Qadir. "al-Sulaymania min Nawahiha al-Mukhtalifa." [A study of the Kurdish city of Sulaymania] *Majallat al-Majma' al-'Ilmi al-'Iraqi, al-Hay'a al-Kurdiyah* 8 (1981): 326-417.

706   Bruinessen, Martin van. "Economic Life in Diyarbekir in the 17th Century." In *Evliya Celebi in Diyarbekir: The Relevant Section of the Seyahatname*. Edited by Martin van Bruinessen and H. E. Boeschoten, pp. 36-44. Leiden: E. J. Brill, 1988.

Discusses the decline of the long-distance trade and the rise of agriculture as the basis of Diyarbekir's economy. Also discussed is animal husbandary, crafts practiced in the city, and the urban social classes makeup of Diyarbekir.

707   Bruinessen, Martin van. "The Population of Diyarbekir: Ethnic Composition and other Demographic Data." In *Evliya Celebi in Diyarbekir: The Relevant Section of the Seyahatname*. Edited by Martin van Bruinessen and H. E. Boeschoten, pp. 29-35. Leiden: E. J. Brill, 1988.

Discusses the various linguistic and religious groups living in Diyarbekir in the 17th century and the population statistics of the city, province, and the nomads.

708   Cavanagh, Jon; Johnson, Fiona. "Earthquakes and Pre-Fabs." *The Ecologist: Journal of the Post Industrial Age* 6, no. 3 (March-April 1976): 104-106.

Describes how governments and foreign agencies failed to understand that house design is an integral part of a cultural pattern. Following the earthquake that hit the Kurdish town of Lice in eastern Turkey on September 6, 1975, survivors were forced to live in pre-fabricated houses that disrupted their traditional way of life.

709   Daponte, B. O.; Kadane, J. B.; Wolfson, L. J. "Bayesian Demography: Projecting the Iraqi Kurdish Population, 1977-1990." *Journal of the American Statistical Association* 92, no. 440 (December 1997): 1256-1267.

Projecting populations that have sparse or unreliable data, such as those of many developing countries, presents a challenge to demographers. The assumptions that they make to project data-poor populations frequently fall into the realm of "educated guesses," and the resulting projections, often regarded as forecasts, are valid only to the extent that the assumptions on which they are based reasonably represent the past or future, as the case may be. These traditional projection techniques do not incorporate a demographer's assessment of uncertainty in the assumptions. Addressing the challenges of forecasting a data-poor population, we project the Iraqi Kurdish population using a Bayesian approach. This approach incorporates a demographer's uncertainty about past and future characteristics of the population in the form of elicited prior distributions. (A)

710   Hassan, Mohammed Khalis. "Notes on Urban and Domestic Architecture of Central Kurdistan, Iraq." *The International Journal of Kurdish Studies* 9, no. 1-2 (1996): 79-94.

Describes the architectures of citadels, bazaars, mosques, baths, inns, and residences built in the major cities in Iraqi Kurdistan: Arbil, Sulaymania, Dohuk, and Khanaqin.

711   Haydari, 'Abd al-Baqi and 'Abd al-Jabbar Amin. *al-Tajdid al-Hadari li-Qal'at Arbil*. [The reconstruction of Arbil's Fortress] Mosul, Iraq: Mudiriyat al-Musil al-'Amma lil-Thaqafah wa-al-Shabab, University of Musil, 1985. 200 p.

712   Janabi, Hashim al-. *Madinat Duhuk: Dirasah fi Jughrafiyat al-Mudun*. [A geographical account on the Kurdish city of Dohuk] Baghdad: al-Mudiriyah al-'Ammah lil-Thaqafah wa-al-Shabab, 1985. 102 p.

713   Janabi, Hashim al-. *Madinat Arbil: Dirasat Jughrafiyat al-Hadar*. [A geographical account on the Kurdish city of Arbil] Mosul, Iraq: al-Mudiriyah al-'Ammah lil-Thaqafah wa-al-Shabab li-Mantaqat al-Hukm al-Zati fi Kurdistan, 1986. 213 p.

714 Jawishli, Hadi Rashid al-. *Turath Arbil al-Tarikhi*. [An account of the history of the Kurdish city of Arbil] Mosul, Iraq: Mudiriyat al-Musil al-'Ammah lil-Thaqafah wa-al-Shabab, University of Musil, 1985. 88 p.

715 Khesbak, Shakir. "The Trend of Population of Sulaimaniya Liwa: A Case Study of Kurdish Population." *Bulletin of the College of Arts - Baghdad University* 1 (June 1959): 42-64.

This is a demographic study of the province that argues that its population has been largely static because a high mortality rate counterbalanced a high fertility rate, but that the death rate can be expected to drop, leading to a population growth. The article includes many statistical tables.

716 Khesbak, Shakir. *al-'Iraq al-Shamali: Dirasah li-Nawahih al-Tabi'iyha wa-la-Bashariyah*. [A geographical and demographic study of the Kurds in northern Iraq] Baghdad: Matba'at Shafiq, 1973. 552 p.

717 Kohli, K. L.; Yehya, Shugun. "A Study of Differential Fertility in Iraq by Mohafadhas." *Die Dritte Welt* 5, no. 2-3 (1977): 291-302.

Because of inadequate registration of vital statistics in Iraq, data on the child/woman ratio (based on the 1965 census) rather than birth data are used to calculate overall fertility as well as regional differentials. These ratios indicate that fertility was highest in the north and lowest in the south, with the central region in an intermediate position (five to nine children). Diverse cultural backgrounds may be responsible for these differences. The Kurds, who live in the north, believe in early marriage for girls (within two years of reaching puberty). Other factors which account for the different fertility figures include proportion married, sex ratio, urbanization, and literacy. Significant correlations support the view that fertility is inversely associated with age at marriage and proportion never married, and is positively associated with sex ratio. Literacy was not significantly associated with fertility. Urban fertility was not always lower than rural; those provinces having higher urban fertility, as compared to rural, all lie in the southern region, where most urban population is concentrated in small towns with populations of less than 5,000. Significant differences were found only in six out of sixteen provinces of Iraq. (S. Whittle/*SA* 78J4117)

718 Leezenberg, Michiel. "The Kurds and the City." *The Journal of Kurdish Studies* 2 (1996-1997): 57-62.

Discusses the reasons for the enormous extent of urbanization in various parts of Kurdistan. Also, discusses the reasons for the lack of quality research on the Kurds in general and on Kurdish urbanism in particular. Reviews some of the papers presented at a conference convened in Sevres in September 19-21, 1996 that was organized by Joyce Blau, Martin van

Bruinessen, and Bernard Hourcade and sponsored by the Kurdish Institute, INALCO, the University of Utrecht, and CNRS. Leezenberg reaches
the conclusion that many of the papers presented at the conference came a
long way towards meeting the great need for empirical studies that are
both theoretically informed and rich in descriptive detail. Other presentations were more programmatic in character, and primarily served to indicate fruitful topics and areas for future research. Because of the opportunities it created for the informal exchange of opinion and the consolidation of a community of scholars, the conference also formed a step towards the further institutionalization of Kurdish studies. Combined, the
level of the presentations and discussions at, the Sevres conference gave
the gratifying impression that Kurdish studies are finally coming of age.

719   Muhammad, Khalil Isma'il. *Qada' Khanaqin (Dirasah fi Jughrafiyat al-
Sukkan)*. [A geographical and demographic study of the Kurds in the district of Khanaqin] Baghdad: Matba'at al-'Ani, 1977. 318 p.

720   Mutlu, Servet. "Population of Turkey by Ethnic Groups and Provinces."
New Perspectives on Turkey, no. 12 (Spring 1995): 33-60. Refined and
republished under the title "Ethnic Kurds in Turkey: A Demographic
Study," in *International Journal of Middle East Studies* 28 (November
1996): 517-541.

While there are no less than 51 ethnic groups in Turkey according to a
recent and comprehensive study, there is little that is demonstratively
known on their present numbers and spatial distribution. Even on the size
of the second largest ethnic group, the Kurds, the estimates vary between
3 to 20 million. Yet, knowledge of the sizes of ethnic groups and their
geographic location, especially of the Kurds, is of immediate public interest from the standpoint of search, design and implementation of policies
towards the solution of what has come to be called the "Kurdish or the
Southeastern problem," depending upon the protagonist's ethnic affiliation or sympathies. The objective of this paper is to make an as thorough
an analysis of the number and spatial distribution of the Kurds in Turkey
as the data permit. In addition, such a study is also of importance from the
standpoint of local politics. Recently, the Kurds seem to have been voting
in bloc for certain candidates, providing the swing vote. This has given
them, especially in the western parts of the country, a degree of importance far out of proportion to their number or to their ratio in the total
number of the electorate in a locality. Claiming to be objective, the author, however, fails to present accurate figures on the number of Kurds in
Turkey. A reason for that is his disregard of important British and French
sources.

721   Mutlu, Servet. "Ethnic Kurds in Turkey: A Demographic Study." *International Journal of Middle East Studies* 28 (November 1996): 517-541.

To assist in developing realistic policy alternatives for the ethnic Kurdish minority in Turkey, the number and geographical distribution of Kurds are estimated via analysis of census data. Presented is a mathematical estimation technique employing natural growth rates by province; ethnic group %s by province in the base year of 1965; inter-provincial migration figures; data on emigrants, returnees, and migration flows; and data on refugees into Turkey, 1985-1990. Findings show that the ethnic Kurdish population in Turkey more than doubled, 1965-1990, and now accounts for about 13% of the population, with settlements largely in the East and Southeast, but with presence also in the West. The spatial redistribution of the Kurds closes some policy options that might bring Turkey out of the tremors it is currently undergoing. An ethnically based federal state seems to be an impossibility short of two-way massive population movements: the Kurds might have to leave the western part of the country, and the non-Kurds, mainly Turks, the eastern part. An independent Kurdish state in the east would create conditions for a similar tragedy, only more severe.

722   Rujbayani, Muhammad Jamil Bandi al-. "Dinawar wa-Mashahiriha." [An account of the Kurdish city of Dinawar and its most popular figures] *Majallat al-Majma' al-'Ilmi al-'Iraqi, al-Hay'a al-Kurdiyah* 6 (1978): 543-591.

723   Rujbayani, Muhammad Jamil Bandi al-. "Band-Nijin (Mandali) fi al-Tarikh Qadiman wa-Hadithan." [A history of the Kurdish city of Band-Nijin] *Majallat al-Majma' al-'Ilmi al-'Iraqi, al-Hay'a al-Kurdiyah* 7 (1980): 305-439.

724   Shankland, David. "Integrating the Rural: Gellner and the Study of Anatolia." *Middle Eastern Studies*, 35, no. 2 (April 1999): 132-149.

Turkey in the 20th century must be understood in terms of the growing migration of people from rural to urban areas. The migration has created a new demographic order in which Sunni Turks have created towns and cities and the Alevi Turks and Kurds exist in surrounding diasporas. The Turkish population must also be understood as a more complex ethnic and religious mix than one that merely distinguishes between Turks and Kurds.

725   Shumaysani, Hasan. *Madinat Sinjar: Min al-Fath al-'Arabi al-Islami hatta al-Fath al-'Uthmani*. [A history of the Kurdish city of Sinjar in the middle ages] Beirut: Manshurat Dar al-Afaq al-Jadida, 1983. 459 p.: ills., maps. Includes bibliographical references.

726   Wayman, Richard. "Bright Lights Big City: Turkey's Crackdown on Kurdish Guerrillas Forces Kurdish Migration into Cities." *The Geographical Magazine* 70, no. 4 (April 1998): 79-82.

Focuses on the migration of Turkey's rural Kurdish population to the cities. Provides population figures in the 1990s.

727   Zaki, Muhammad Amin. *Tarikh al-Sulaymania wa-Anha'iha*. [A detailed account of the history of the Kurdish city of al-Sulaymaniya and the areas surrounding it] Translated from Kurdish by Muhammad Jamil Bandi al-Rujbayani. Baghdad: al-Nashir wa-al-Tiba'a, 1951.

See also items: 183, 691, 848, 859, 860

19
Religion in Kurdistan

GENERAL

728 Bachmann, Walter. *Kirchen und Moscheen in Armenia und Kurdistan*. Osnabrèuck: O. Zeller, 1978. 80 p., 71 p. of plates: ill., 1 map. [Wissenschaftliche Verèoffentlichung der Deutschen Orient-Gesellschaft; 25] Originally published in Berlin by Hinrichs in 1913. Includes bibliographical references. [In German]

729 Blau, Joyce. "Les relations inter-communautaires en Irak." [Intercommunal relations in Iraq] *Correspondance d'Orient Etudes* 5-6 (1964): 87-102.

Blau describes the various communities that make up the Iraqi population. These consist of Muslims such as the Sunni and Shi'i Arabs, the Sunni and Shi'i Kurds, and Turkmens, and non-Muslims such as the Yezidis, Christians (Assyrians, Uniate Chaldeans, Jacobites, Syrian Catholics, Greek Orthodox, Greek Catholics [Melkites], Armenian Orthodox, Armenian Catholics), Sabaens (or Mandeans), and Jews. Relations between these communities, especially in the 20th century, are also outlined

730 Bois, Thomas. "La religion des Kurdes." [The religion of the Kurds] *Proche Orient Chretien* [Jerusalem] 11, no. 2 (1961): 105-136.

731 Bois, Thomas. "Monasteres chretiens et temples yezidis dans le Kurdistan irakien." [Christian monasteries and Yezidi temples in Iraqi Kurdistan] *Al-Machriq* 61 (1967): 75-103.

732   Bruinessen, Martin van. "Religion in Kurdistan." *Kurdish Times* 4
       (Summer-Fall 1991): 5-27.

       In this paper, van Bruinessen analyzes the religious diversity among the
       Kurdish people. After describing each of the major Kurdish religions or
       sects (Sunnis, Shiites, Yezidis, Ahl-i Haqq, Alevis, Jews and Christians),
       he discusses the role of the Sunni mystical order in the Kurdish national
       movement, the relation between the *sheikhs* and the modern state, radical-
       ism, and religious modernism among the Kurds.

733   Bruinessen, Martin van. "Kurdish 'Ulama and their Indonesian Students."
       In *De Turcicis Aliisque Rebus Commentarii Henry Hofman Dedicati*.
       Edited by Marc Vandamme, pp. 205-227. Utrecht: M. Th. Houtsma
       Stiching, 1992. Updated version: "The Impact of Kurdish 'Ulama on
       Indonesian Islam." *Les Annales de l'Autre Islam* 5 (1998): 83-106.

       Topics of discussion include: Traces of Kurdish influence in Indonesia;
       The Kurds as cultural brokers; Ibrahim ibn Hasan al-Kurani (1615-1690);
       The Barzinji family of Shahrazur and Medina; Why are many Indone-
       sians called Kurdi? Muhammad ibn Sulaiman and his commentaries of
       Ibn Hajar; Two great Naqshbandi masters: Mawlana Khalid and Mu-
       hammad Amin al-Kurdi and; Conclusion: Why these Kurdish contacts? In
       a postscript, van Bruinessen also discusses Kurdish cultural brokerage in
       South Africa.

734   Campanile, Giuseppe. *Storia della regione del Kurdistan e delle sette di
       religione ivi esistenti*. Napoli: Fratelli Fernandes, 1818. xx, 213 p. plates.
       [In Italian]

735   Hamzeh'ee, M. Reza. "Structural and Organizational Analogies Between
       Mazdaism and Sufism and the Kurdish Religions." In *Recurrent Patterns
       in Iranian Religions: From Mazdaism to Sufism*. Proceedings of the
       Round Table Held in Bamberg (30th September – 4th October 1991). Ed-
       ited by Philippe Gignoux, pp. 29-35. Paris: Association pour
       l'Avancement des Etudes Iraniennes, 1992.

       Hamzeh'ee discusses similarities between Mazdaism, the Kurdish reli-
       gious communities of the Yezidis and Yaresan (Ahl-i Haqq), and some
       Sufi orders like the Khaksar with respect to angelology, ritual, and belief
       in metcmpsychosis. He points out that a group of Yezidis recently de-
       clared their adherence to Zoroastrianism.

736   Kreyenbroek, Philip G. "Mithra and Ahreman, Binyamin and Malak
       Tawus: Traces of an Ancient Myth in the Cosmogonies of Two Modern
       Sects." In *Recurrent Patterns in Iranian Religions: From Mazdaism to
       Sufism*. Proceedings of the Round Table Held in Bamberg (30th Septem-

ber-4th October 1991). Edited by Philippe Gignoux, pp. 57-79. Paris: Association pour l'Avancement des Etudes Iraniennes, 1992.

Seeks to trace the persistent influence of a pre-Zoroastrian cosmogonical myth related to that of the Veda in Roman Mithraism and the modern Yezidi and Ahl-i Haqq sects. Kreyenbroek postulates a popular tradition representing a pre-Zoroastrian form of Iranian religion and surviving in Western Iran.

737   Kreyenbroek, Philip G. "Religion and Religions in Kurdistan." In *Kurdish Culture and Identity*. Edited by Philip G. Kreyenbroek and Christine Allison, pp. 85-110. Atlantic Highlands, NJ: Zed Books, 1996.

While most readers will profit from Kreyenbroek's survey of Kurdish sufi orders, his assessment of the Naqshbandi order is quite possibly wrong. This order's contemplative appearance does make it appear to be characterized by a "quietist, contemplative form of practice." Evidence has emerged, however, that this order is far from apolitical, and least of all is it quietist. Van Bruinessen has shown how the Naqshbandi networks were "capable of mobilizing large numbers of men from different tribes for common action" (rebellions) in the mid-to-late nineteenth century. Between the two world wars, it seems, the Naqshbandis were the major source of civil unrest in Turkish Kurdistan. Kreyenbroek is on firmer ground when he discusses the origins and beliefs of the Yezidis, another descendant from the earlier "Indo-Iranian" cult. His account is lucid and factual; it will be of much use to those approaching this subject for the first time. Of much less value is his breathtaking claim that the Yezidis take their name from Yezid, the Sunni Muslim responsible for the killing of the Shi'a martyr Hussein at Kerbala (p. 101) is quite false. The Yezidis take their name from the Kurdish word for God—Yezdan. Nor is this the only slip-up. Elsewhere, the author gives credibility to the Sunni claim that the Muslim term sayyed (in Turkish seyyit, or seyyid) is applicable to Alevis, as well. Much care is needed here. Alevis deny there is any concurrence between this term and their own term seyt; some Dersim (Tunceli) Alevis even assert that this false confluence is all part of a devious scheme by Kurmanji Kurds to claim their own rebellions against Ankara. Nevertheless, Kreyenbroek's piece is generally an important, readable contribution to understanding Kurdistan's frequently heterodox religious beliefs and practices. It is easy to see, after reading it, how religion in Kurdistan is very much Kurdish in character. (Paul White)

738   Leezenberg, Michiel. "Between Assimilation and Deportation: The Shabak and the Kakais in Northern Iraq." In *Syncretistic Religious Communities in the Near East: Collected Papers of the International Symposium "Alevism in Turkey and Comparable Sycretistic Religious Communities in the Near East in the Past and Present" Berlin, 14-17 April 1995*. Edited by Krisztina Kehl-Bodrogi, Barbara Kellner-Heinkele, and

Anke Otter-Beaujean, pp. 155-174. Leiden: Brill, 1997. [Studies in the history of religions, 0169-8834; v. 76]

The bewildering number and variety of religious formations in Northern Iraq have hardly received the attention they deserve. Little is known as of yet about the small pockets of heterodox groups, such as the Shabak, the Bajalan, the Sarli, the Kakais or Ahl-i Haqq, and the Yezidis, that are scattered along the fringes of Iraqi Kurdistan, stretching all the way from Tell 'Afar and Mosul over Kirkuk to Khanaqin and beyond. All of these communities have hereditary classes of religious specialists of different ranks; their laymen are associated with such religious specialists, who thus have an important role in maintaining group cohesion. In social organization, then, these groups resemble orthodox Sufi orders or tariqas; but in their religious beliefs and practices, they move far away from Islamic orthodoxy. Except for the Yezidis, who speak Kurmanci or Badinani Kurdish like their Sunni neighbors, they are also marked off by their dialect: many (though by no means all) of their members speak a variety of Gorani, or Hawrami or Macho as it is usually called by locals. The present paper deals with two of these communities, the Shabak and the Kakais, and with a third, the Sarli, which actually is a mixture of the first two. It focuses on their historical development as distinct groups, and their relation to the state, rather than on doctrinal matters. The findings presented here are provisional and limited in scope, but even as they stand, they are indicative of the dramatic influence that recent policies of the Iraqi government have had on processes of ethnic organization and self-identification. (A)

739   Ma'ayergi, Hassan A. "History of the Works of Quranic Interpretation (*tafsir*) in the Kurdish Language." *Institute of Muslim Minority Affairs, Journal* 7 (1986): 268-274.

740   Moosa, Matti. *Extremist Shiites: The Ghulat Sects*. Syracuse, NY: Syracuse University Press, 1988.

This book is a comprehensive study of the cultural aspects of the different Ghulat (extremist Shiites) sects in the Middle East. The extremism of these sects is essentially religious, and should not be confused with the religio-political radicalism of the Shiite regime in Iran and its antagonism to the West. The extremist Shiites discussed in this book are peaceful people, and, except for the Nusayris (or Alwaites) of Syria, they do not seem to be political activists or to have assumed political power. Members of these sects live in an area extending from western Iran to Iraq, Syria, and Turkey. According to the author, they are known by different names but share common religious beliefs, the most fundamental being that the Imam Ali, the blood cousin and son-in-law of the Prophet of Islam, is God. In Iran, these sects are called Ahl-i-Haqq (truth-worshippers), or Ali-Ilahis (defiers of Ali): in Iraq they are called Shabak, Bajwan, Sarliyya, Kaka'iya, and Ibrahimiya. In Syria they are known as Nusayris (Alawis), and in Turkey, as Bektashis, Qizilbash (Alevis), Takhtajis, and Cepnis. They are of different ethnic origins and speak different languages, mainly Turkish, Persian, Kurdish, and Arabic. The main objective of this book is to study the religious, social, political, and cultural life and institutions of these extremist Shiite sects, scattered over several Islamic countries of the Middle East. It focuses on the varying pagan and Christian elements—especially the Armenian Christian elements—of the beliefs and practices of the Qizilbash Kurds of the upper Euphrates valley.

741 Poladian, Arshak. "The Islamization of the Kurds (7th-10th Centuries AD)." *Acta Kurdica: The International Journal of Kurdish and Iranian Studies* 1 (1994): 21-26.

According to the author, despite a series of publications dedicated to the problems of religion among the Kurds, there is still no thorough idea of the religious situation among the Kurds before Islam, hence the purpose of this paper.

742 Rahman, Abdul. *Folk Religion of the Kurds*. Altadena, CA: Friends of the Kurds, Zwemer Institute, 1988. 60 p.: ill. Includes bibliographical references.

743 Staley, Allen W. "The Kurds of Iraq: An Historical, Cultural and Religious Study." *Military Chaplain's Review* (July 1992): 37-43.

The following study is an introduction to the Kurds: their background, their society, and their religion/culture. Specific emphasis is given to the Kurds in Iraq. The last section of the paper presents some practical things to remember in dealing with the Kurdish people.

See also items: 1, 2, 4, 7, 9, 19, 21, 23, 24, 25, 26, 27, 28, 117, 217, 336, 357, 359, 596, 628, 635, 642, 645, 646, 647, 648, 649, 651, 652, 659, 665, 667, 668, 669, 679, 685, 707, 826, 829, 833, 893, 904, 905

AHL-I HAQQ

744 Algar, Hamid; Morris, James W.; During, Jean. "Elahi, Hajj Nur 'Ali." In *Encyclopaedia Iranica*. Vol. 8, pp. 297-299. Costa Mesa, CA: Mazda Publishers, 1998.

Describes the life, teachings, and music of Hajj Nur Ali Elahi, the innovative and charismatic leader of one branch of the Ahl-i Haqq and author of several texts on its teachings. Includes bibliographies.

745   'Azzawi, 'Abbas al-. *al-Kaka'iya fi al-Ta'rikh: Yabhathu fi Hazihi al-Nihlah wa-Mu'taqadiha.* [An overview of the history of the Kaka'is and their religion] Baghdad: Sharikat al-Tijara wa-al-Tiba'a al-Mahduda, 1949. 146 p.: ill.

746   Bruinessen, Martin van. "When Haji Bektash Still Bore the Name of Sultan Sahak: Notes on the Ahl-i Haqq of the Guran District." In *Bektachiyya: études sur l'ordre mystique des Bektachis et les groupes relevant de Hadji Bektach.* Edited by Alexandre Popovic & Gilles Veinstein, pp. 117-138. Istanbul: Éditions Isis, 1995.

747   Edmonds, Cecil John. "The Beliefs and Practices of the Ahl-i Haqq of Iraq." *Iran* 7 (1969): 89-106.

In his book, *Kurds, Turks and Arabs*, Edmonds gave some account of the Kaka'is, as the Ahl-i Haqq are generally called in Iraq. At that time he limited his discussion of this sect to its history, organization and geographical distribution of its members, avoiding as far as possible all mention of their esoteric beliefs and secret ceremonies. After a detailed account of these beliefs and practices (albeit with some playing down of their heterodoxy) has been published in Tehran by a leader of the community in north Persia (referring to Haji Nur 'Ali Shah Elahi and the article by Weightman), Edmonds decided to present his notes that he obtained at first hand from Kaka'i sources. These are: (a) a small pamphlet, or *Tazkara,* written in 1933 especially for him, in old Turkish, by an educated and intelligent Kaka'i who had formerly served in the Ottoman Civil Service; and (b) careful and detailed records preserved in his diaries of many conversations with a dozen or more adepts, supported by several poems in the Gorani dialect. The new material has been set out under nine main headings, each divided into two parts: (a) the *Tazkara,* and (b) personal information. The nine headings are: (1) fundamental beliefs; (2) the Caliphate and the status of Ali; (3) Sultan Ishaq and the three Heptads; (4) religious observances: prayer, alms, fasting, and pilgrimage; (5) the communal supper; (6) affiliation; (7) the brotherhood of the hereafter; (8) marriage and divorce; and (9) other beliefs and observances.

748   Elâhi, Nur 'Ali. *L'ésotérisme kurde: aperçus sur le secret gnostique des fidèles de vérité.* Edited by Mohammad Mokri. Paris: A. Michel, 1966. 242 p. Includes bibliographical references.

749   Halm, H. "Ahl-e Haqq." In *Encyclopaedia Iranica.* Vol. 1, pp. 635-637. London: Routledge & Kegan Paul, 1982.

Provides a brief overview of the sect and the geographical distribution of its adherents. Includes a long list of bibliographic sources.

750   Hamzeh'ee, M. Reza. *The Yaresan: A Sociological, Historical, and Re-ligio-Historical Study of a Kurdish Community*. Berlin: Klaus Schwarz Verlag, 1990. 308, 11 p. (Islamkundliche Untersuchungen; Bd. 138). Includes bibliographical references (p. 280-302) and index.

Yaresan and Ahl-i Haqq are the names of an important Kurdish community concentrated in South Kurdistan. In this work, which is the first general study of this community, attempts are made to draw an overall picture of the community and present some outlines for future research. The study focuses on three basic questions regarding the community: who the people are, their origins, and the factors that contributed to the survival of the community. This study consists of nine chapters. The first is devoted to methodological explanations. The remaining eight are divided into three groups, each of which aims at answering one of the questions mentioned above. Chapters Two through Seven are devoted to the introduction of the Yaresan, mainly to answer the first question. Chapters Eight and Nine are meant to answer the other two questions. Chapter Eight looks for an answer regarding the origin of the community. The main problem here lies in the lack of any historical reports about the community. This is mainly due to the complete secrecy in which the Yaresan have always lived. Therefore the attempt is made to reach an answer with the help of Yaresan traditions and a sociological investigation. In chapter Nine, the author tries to find some explanation for the survival of the Yaresan, the answer of the third (and last) question.

751   Ivanow, Wladimir (ed. and tr.). *The Truth-Worshippers of Kurdistan*. [Ahl-i Haqq texts edited in the original Persian and analysed by W. Ivanow.] Leiden: E. J. Brill, 1953. xiv, 246, 202 p.: maps. [The Ismaili Society series, A, no. 7]

Ivanow, formerly Assistant Keeper of the Asiatic Museum of the Russian Academy of Sciences in St. Petersburgh, provides a detailed background of the sect, including its origins, history, subdivisions, and habitat. After a section on the works cited in the book, Ivanow discusses the beliefs of the sect, their worship, the contents of the texts under study, and criticisims, emendations, and corrections of the texts.

752   'Izawi, 'Abbas al-. *al-Kaka'iyah fi al-Tarikh*. [An overview of the history of the Kaka'i religion] Baghdad: Sharikat al-Tijara wa-al-Tiba'a al-Mahduda, 1949. 146 p.

753   Mir-Hosseini, Ziba. "Inner Truth and Outer History: The Two Worlds of the Ahl-i Haqq of Kurdistan." *International Journal of Middle East Studies* (1994): 267-285.

A principal belief of the Ahl-i Haqq, an esoteric sect centered in Iranian Kurdistan, is that the Divine Essence has successive manifestations in human form. The Ahl-i Haqq religious universe comprises two distinct yet interrelated worlds: the inner world (*alam-i batin*) and the outer world (*alam-i zahir*), each with its own order and its own rules. We as ordinary human beings are aware of the order of the outer world, but our life is governed by the rules of the inner world, where our ultimate destiny lies. This article analyzes the events surrounding one of the last manifestations of the Divine Essence, one of those rare moments in which a passage is made between the two worlds, and explores the ways in which these two worlds interact, as perceived by the believers and as reflected in the developments within the sect.

754   Mir-Hosseini, Ziba. "Redefining the Truth: Ahl-i Haqq and the Islamic Republic." *British Journal of Middle Eastern Studies* 21, 2 (1995): 211-228.

This article traces the roots of a recent split among the followers of an esoteric Shi'a sect known to outsiders as Ahl-i Haqq (literally, the Followers of Truth)—popularly known as 'Ali-Ilahi (defiers of 'Ali). The seeds of the rift were sown three generations ago in a leadership struggle in a village in southern Kurdistan, but the sect's followers divided into two opposing camps only with the onset of the Islamic Republic in Iran. In mapping the split, this article focuses on the diversity and particularly the esoteric side of Shi'a Islam.

755   Mir-Hosseini, Ziba. "Faith, Ritual and Culture among the Ahl-i Haqq." In *Kurdish Culture and Identity*. Edited by Philip G. Kreyenbroek and Christine Allison, pp. 111-134. Atlantic Highlands, NJ: Zed Books, 1996.

This chapter aims to sketch the present conditions of the Ahl-i Haqq, as the author encountered them in Kermanshah in 1992. In doing so, the author tries to impart something of the subtlety of their esoteric universe and the harshness of their current experience of the outside world. Before that, the author gives a brief account on the history and mythology of the sect.

756   Mir-Hosseini, Ziba. "Breaking the Seal: The New Face of the Ahl-i Haqq." In *Syncretistic Religious Communities in the Near East: Collected Papers of the International Symposium "Alevism in Turkey and Comparable Sycretistic Religious Communities in the Near East in the Past and Present" Berlin, 14-17 April 1995*. Edited by Krisztina Kehl-Bodrogi, Barbara Kellner-Heinkele, and Anke Otter-Beaujean, pp. 175-194. Leiden: Brill, 1997. [Studies in the history of religions, 0169-8834; v. 76]

The Ahl-i Haqq are an esoteric sect, commonly reckoned by outsiders as being among the Shi'a gholat, those who 'exaggerate' in their veneration of 'Ali, the first Shi'a Imam. Long regarded as heretics by their Shi'a and

Sunni neighbors, followers of the sect kept their beliefs and practices clandestine: they regarded their faith as a secret, that 'sealed' the lips of those who knew it. There was no published account of the sect's dogmas and practices by an insider until Nur 'Ali Elahi, an Ahl-i Haqq spiritual leader, published *Borhan ol-Haqq* (The Proof of Ultimate Truth) in 1963. This paper tells the story of this 'breaking of the seal'. It is also the story of the reformist movement in the sect, which began early this century when Nur 'Ali's father, Haj Ne'mat, unified the sect's diverse traditions and constructed an 'authentic' history. In this paper the author is primarily concerned with the reformists, and how their leaders, through their publications in the course of three generations, have transformed the sect's sacred narrative.' The author examines these publications in the context, first, of internal rivalries within the sect, and secondly, of changes in the outside world, notably the wider Iranian society. Developments among the Ahl-i Haqq may clearly be viewed in the light of the historical diversity in Shi'a Islam, but they are also an example of how its less orthodox manifestations have responded to new assertions of Islamic identity or 're-Islamization' following the 1979 Revolution in Iran, as well as an instance of how the printed word inevitably transforms the centuries-old isolation and secrecy of an esoteric sect. At the same time, examination of additions, omissions and changes which these publications have undergone in successive editions, reveals something of how the reformists have sought both to refine external understandings of the sect and to respond to internal opposition to their reforms. (A)

757   Mokri, Mohammad. "Etude d'un titre de propriete du debut du XVIe siecle provenant du Kurdistan (notes d'ethnographie et d'histoire)." *Journal Asiatique* 251 (1963): 229-256.

758   Mokri, Mohammad. *La grande assemblee des fideles de verite an tribunal sur le mont Zagros en Iran: Dawra-y diwana-gawra: livre secret et ihedit en gourani ancien, texte critique traduction, introduction et commentaires avec des notes linguistiques et glossaire*. Paris: Librairie Klincksieck, 1977. 393 p. [Étude dhérésiologie islamique et de thèmes mythico-religieux iraniens Textes et études religieux, linguistiques et ethnographiques; no. 6] Added t.p. and text in Gourani. Includes bibliographical references and index.

759   Roux, Jean-Paul. "Les Fideles de Verite et les croyances religieuses des Turcs." *Revue de l'Histoire des Religions*, no. 1 (July-September 1969): 61-95.

760   Weightman, S. C. R. "The Significance of *Kitab Burhan ul-Haqq*." *Iran* 2 (1964): 83-103.

See also items: 21, 24, 25, 628, 629, 634, 732, 735, 736, 738, 740

ALEVIS AND ZAZAS

761   Bruinessen, Martin van. "Kurds, Turks and the Alevi Revival in Turkey."
       Middle East Report 26 (July-September 1996): 7-10.

This article describes the resurgence of the political culture and identity
of the Alevis and their relationship to the government and to the Kurds.
This conservative religious and ultra-nationalist bloc is not interested in
cultural and religious pluralism and rejects compromises with Kurds and
Alevis alike. In its efforts to create a monolithic state and society, this
bloc constitutes the most divisive force in Turkey today.

762   Bruinessen, Martin van. "'Aslini Inkar Eden Haramzadedir!' The Debate
       on the Ethnic Identity of the Kurdish Alevis." In *Syncretistic Religious
       Communities in the Near East: Collected Papers of the International
       Symposium "Alevism in Turkey and Comparable Sycretistic Religious
       Communities in the Near East in the Past and Present" Berlin, 14-17
       April 1995*. Edited by Krisztina Kehl-Bodrogi, Barbara Kellner-Heinkele,
       and Anke Otter-Beaujean, pp. 1-23. Leiden: Brill, 1997. [Studies in the
       history of religions, 0169-8834; v. 76]

The existence of Kurdish- and Zaza-speaking Alevi tribes, who almost
exclusively use Turkish as their ritual language, and many of which even
have Turkish tribal names, is a fact that has exercised the explanatory
imagination of many authors. Both Turkish and Kurdish nationalists have
had some difficulty in coming to terms with the ambiguous identity of
these groups, and have attempted to explain embarrassing details away.
Naive attempts to prove that Kurdish and Zaza are essentially Turkish
languages have not been given up, and have after 1980 even received a
new impetus. Kurds, on the other hand, have emphasized the Iranian element in the religion of the Alevis and suggested that even the Turkish
Alevis must originally have received their religion from the Kurds. Several articulate members of the tribes concerned, appealing to alleged old
oral traditions in their support, have added their own interpretations, often
all too clearly inspired by political expediency. The tribes have never had
a single, unambiguous position *vis-a-vis* the Kurdish nationalist movement and the Turkish Republic. The conflicting appeals of these two national entities (and of such lesser would-be nations as the Zaza or the
Alevi nation) to the loyalties of the Kurdish Alevis have torn these communities apart. The conflict has thus far culminated in the Turkish military operations in Tunceli and western Bingol in the autumn of 1994,
which were continued through 1995. Topics discussed include: a short
overview of the Kurdish Alevis; their origins; heterodox Kurds in pre-
and early Ottoman history; shifting views of self; and Zaza, Alevi and
Dersimi as deliberately embraced ethnic identities. Concludes that it is
unlikely that the question of the origins of the Kurdish Alevis will ever be

unambiguously and convincingly answered, however; however, the debate is likely to continue. (A)

763 Bruinessen, Martin van. "The Shabak: A Kizilbash Community in Iraqi Kurdistan." *Les Annales de l'Autre Islam* 5 (1998): 185-196.

764 Bumke, Peter J. "Kizilbas-Kurden in Dersim (Tunceli, Turkei): Marginalitat und Haresie." [Kizilbas Kurds in Dersim] *Anthropos* 74, no. 3-4, (1979): 530-548. [In German]

765 Bumke, Peter J. "The Kurdish Alevis: Boundaries and Perceptions." In *Ethnic Groups in the Republic of Turkey*. Edited and compiled by Peter Alford Andrews with the assistance of Rudiger Benninghaus, 510-518. Wiesbaden: Ludwig Reichert Verlag, 1989. (Beihefte zum Tubinger Atlas des Vorderen Orients. Reihe B. Geisteswissenschaften; Nr. 60)

Discusses European perception of the Kurdish Alevis and their social incorporation. Also discusses Alevi practices and tenets from both orthodox and non-orthodox views.

766 Cumont, Franz. "Kizilbash." In *Encyclopaedia of Religion and Ethics*. Vol. 7, pp. 744-745. Edited by James Hastings. New York: Charles Scibner's Sons, 1926.

After providing a historical, geographical, and socio-religio background of the sect, the author discusses three superimposed stratifications in the religion of the Kizilbash: old paganism, influence of Christianity, and Islamic affiliation. This is one of the earliest articles to be published on the Alevi Kurds. A more comprehensive paper, and one based on a field trip, was published by Melville Chater in *The National Geographic Magazine* (October 1928), pp. 485-504 under the title: "The Kizilbash Clans of Kurdistan."

767 Jacobson, C. M. "The Alevi Religion." In *Kurdish Culture: A Cross-Cultural Guide*. Written by Denise L. Sweetnam, 209-217. Bonn: Verlag fur Kultur und Wissenschaft, 1994.

768 Kehl-Bodrogi, Krisztina. "Rediscovering the Alevi Community in Turkey: Myth of History and Collective Identity." *Orient* 34, no. 2 (1993): 267-282. [In German.]

The term Alevi refers to a widespread heretical religious community in Turkey. Endogamy and esotery are main characteristics of the group. Outlawed by society due to their political and religious opposition against the Ottomans, the Alevis survived in the peripheral regions of the Empire. The republican transformation of Turkey brought for the Alevis a chance to participate in the affairs of the majority and thus led to dramatic changes for the community itself. The migration of the Alevis to the towns in the late 1950s put an end to their centuries-old geographic marginality. In the following 20 years the community has undergone a process of secularization. As a result of the political and social transformations in Turkey which followed the military coup d'etat in 1980, the idea of Alevi community gained importance again. In the last few years, a revitalization of community structures can be observed whereby the Alevi religion once more figures as boundary marker against the major society. The essay analyses the central characteristics of this development against the background of the foregoing destruction of the community. It reflects upon the conflicts of interests resulting from the new situation such as a new ethnic differentiation between Turkish and Kurdish Alevi. (A)

769   Kehl-Bodrogi, Krisztina. "Kurds, Turks, or a People in their Own Right? Competing Collective Identities among the Zazas." *The Muslim World* 89, no. 3-4 (July-October 1999): 439-454.

By examining the shifting categories of collective identity among Zaza migrants in Europe, the author attempts to illustrate how, under changing socio-political conditions and supported by modern ideologies, traditional we-group boundaries are undermined and new ones develop. The ongoing politics of identity among the Zazas provides an example of the multiplicity of options available for the construction of we-group identities, including those based on nationality. This examination also provides the reader with a unique opportunity to closely observe attempts to create a new nation. Discusses topics such as who are the Zazas, the problem of the ethnic identity of the Zazas, Zazas in the discourse of Turkish and Kurdish nationalism, shifting categories of collective identity among the Zaza Alevis, Zazas in the European diaspora, Zaza nationalism, and Alevi-Zaza nationalism.

770   Kieser, Hans Lukas. "L'Alevisme Kurde." [Kurdish Alevism] *Peuples Mediterraneens*, no. 68-69 (July-December 1994): 57-76.

Kurdish Alevism is a religious and cultural identity, a minority in many respects, which not only nourishes itself on a heterodox Sufism, but maintains elements from pre-Islamic eastern Turkey. Its Islamic credo is fragile; in Dersim, Alevis used to share pilgrimages and marriages with the neighboring Armenians. They were contesting all power and doctrines of the State; they did it with the Turkish Republic. The spirit of openness and expectation and the absence of rigid dogmas made them capable of adapting to new situations without questioning their Alevity; this still holds true for the European immigrants. Consciousness of their identity was not erased in spite of the almost complete disappearance of the organized and ritualistic make-up formerly entertained by the deed.

771 Seufert, Gunter. "Between Religion and Ethnicity: A Kurdish-Alevi Tribe in Globalizing Istanbul." In *Space, Culture and Power: New Identities in Globalizing Cities*. Edited by Ayse Öncü and Petra Weyland, pp. 157-176. London; Atlantic Highlands, NJ.: Zed Books, 1997. [Papers from a workshop held at Bogaziçi University, Istanbul, in 1994.]

The author begins by describing the chain migration of the Kockiri tribe to Istanbul starting in the 1960s, and its subsequent integration into the economy of the city. In its broad outline, this is a story which parallels the experiences of various other immigrant groups arriving in Istanbul in the 1960s and 1970s. Next, the author turns to the Alevi religious affiliation of the Kockiri and discusses how this predominantly religious identity, which served to legitimate the traditional caste-like tribal order, is currently being transformed into a chiefly ethno-political identity among the younger generation, namely that of Kurdish leftist. In the concluding part, the author argues that this shift of identity is related to the rediscovery of one's own culture through the grid of modern values and global discourses. (A)

772 Vinogradov, Amal. "Ethnicity, Cultural Discontinuity and Power Brokers in Northern Iraq: The Case of the Shabak." *American Ethnologist* 1, no. 1 (February 1974): 207-218.

An anthropological study of some aspects of the social organization of a Kurdish-speaking Shi'i sect in northern Iraq.

See also items: 380, 392, 395, 403, 409, 418, 419, 428, 478, 655, 683, 724, 732, 737, 738, 740, 860

CHRISTIANS AND CHRISTIAN MISSIONARIES

773 Badger, George Percy. *The Nestorians and their Rituals* [with the narrative of a mission to Mesopotamia and Coordistan in 1842-1844 and of a late visit to those countries in 1850; also, researches into the present condition of the Syrian Jacobites, papal Syrians, and Chaldeans, and an inquiry into the religious tenets of the Yezeedees]. London: Darf Publishers Limited, 1987. 2 v.: ill., maps. Originally published in 1852 in London by Joseph Masters. Reprinted in 1969 by Gregg International Pub. (Farnborough, England).

An account by a Catholic missionary of his work in the Mosul area in the mid-19th century, and description of the local Christians. Volume two consists of the texts and liturgy of the Assyrians/Chaldeans/Nestorians.

774   Blincoe, Robert. *Ethnic Realities and the Church: Lessons from Kurdistan, a History of Mission Work, 1668-1990*. Foreword by Ralph D. Winter. Pasadena, CA: Presbyterian Center for Mission Studies, 1998. 265 p.

Originally a thesis from Fuller Theological Seminary, School of World Mission under the title: *Missions in Kurdistan, 1668-1990, with Missiological Considerations*. Missionaries of Christ's church, both eastern and western, have yet to communicate the gospel in ways that result in Kurds gathering into viable, indigenous churches. Protestants have been active in Kurdistan since the 1840s and Catholics for three centuries, to say nothing of the historical churches of the East. This study reviews the record of the Protestant and, to a lesser extent, Catholic missions. The study purports to show that the Protestant strategy of assisting the historical churches in Kurdistan, with the stated hope that a revived Eastern Church would evangelize its Kurdish neighbors, has failed to plant a viable indigenous church among the Kurds. The results of this study suggest areas of change needed by western Christians involved in evangelism among Kurds.

775   Chevalier, Michel. *Les montagnards chretiens du Hakkari et du Kurdistan septentrional*. [The Mountain Christians of Hakkari and Northern Kurdistan] Paris: Departement de Geographie de l'Universite de Paris-Sorbonne, 1985.

Chevalier's book is a descriptive reconstruction of the Nestorian community up to the beginning of World War I. It is a lucid, straightforward account of a human population in a specific political and ecological context. It is about the Christian tribes in Kurdistan. Chevalier makes good use of the travel and missionary accounts available, especially the unpublished journals of the French Dominican priest and linguist, Jacques Rhetore (1841-1921), who lived in the area for 20 years. Beginning with a review of the different theories about the origin of the Nestorians (who are Monophysite Christians), Chevalier proceeds to a discussion of their economic, social, and political life. Chevalier describes their contacts with the Kurds, particularly with the Kurdish feudality, as well as with other non-Muslim groups. Even though Chevalier's book stops short of the full story of the Nestorian-Assyrians, it nonetheless provides a valuable contribution to the study of the Middle Eastern "ethnic mosaic." (abridged, Amal Rassam/*MEJ* 42, Summer 1988: 491-492)

776   Dodd, Edward M. "By the Grace of the Kurds." *The Moslem World* 10 (May 1920): 420-425.

This is a description of the rescue of six hundred Assyrians and Armenians, mostly women and children, in June 1919. While these refugees were in the mission grounds at Urmia, an inter-Moslem row between the Kurds and the Persians broke out, resulting in the siege of the city by the Kurds, and an insane butchery of some of the Christians by the Persians.

777   Grant, Asahel. "Asia: Kurdistan." In *Great Missionaries: A Series of Biographies*. Compiled by Andrew Thomson. London: T. Nelson and Sons, 1862.

778   Husry, Khaldun S. "The Assyrian Affair of 1933 (I) & (II)." *International Journal of Middle East Studies* [Great Britain] 5, no. 2 (1974): 161-176 and no. 3 (1974): 344-360.

Part I examines the circumstances of the Assyrian Christians in Iraq and their mentality which led to tensions between the Assyrians and the Iraqis and culminated in the 1933 massacre in Simel. Part II concludes the study of the massacre of the Assyrian Christians in the village of Simel in 1933. It discusses the consequences and various interpretations of the events. The work is based on archival material, especially from the British Foreign Office, and secondary sources.

779   Ishow, Habib. "Araden ou le 'Jardin du paradis': La Terre et les hommes dans un village chaldeen du nord de l'Irak." [Araden, or "The Garden of Paradise": Land and People in a Chaldean Village of Northern Iraq] *Etudes rurales* 76 (October-December 1979): 97-112.

Described is the Assyro-Chaldean village of Araden in northern Iraq. The inhabitants are Christian, their culture and language, Chaldean. Families tend to be patriarchal and form three groups, two of which are in constant conflict, with the third serving a negotiational role. The families have solid social structures. Araden is a rural democracy, since important decisions are made collectively by the men of the village. Collective work is a prominent form of the labor that supplies the needs of the population. The civil war (1961-1975), in which Kurds were opposed to the Baghdad government, had a devastating effect upon Araden and its people. Described is the agricultural potential of the region and the difficult conditions faced by persons there since the civil war. (*SA* 82M: 0335)

780   Joseph, John. *The Nestorians and Their Muslim Neighbors: A Study of Western Influence on Their Relations*. Princeton, NJ: Princeton University Press, 1961. xv, 281 p. (Princeton Oriental Studies, 20). Bibliography: p. 239-269.

This work is divided into two parts: part one covers the 19th century and part two, the 20th century. Between them, the author charts the political impact of Western interference on the relations of the local communities of Nestorians (also sometimes called Assyrians or Chaldeans) with the Muslim majority among whom they lived in northern Iraq. He also explains the background to the tragedy of the massacres in 1933.

781   Joseph, John. *Muslim-Christian Relations and Inter-Christian Rivalries in the Middle East: The Case of the Jacobites in an Age of Transition*. Albany, NY: State University of New York Press, 1983. 240 p.: map. Includes bibliographical references.

This work is a useful modern history of the Syrian Orthodox (Jacobite) and Syrian Catholic Christians, concentrating on their social and political developments since the early 19th century, when the Eastern Christian Churches emerged from several centuries of isolation. Jacobites and Syrian Catholics were victims in the repression of the Kurds in 1925 and many, like the Armenians before them, fled to French-ruled Syria, settling mainly in the Jezire but also in Aleppo, Hama and Homs. Tension later rose in the Jezire following the signing of the Franco-Syrian Treaty of 1936, the Christians feared their own repression in an independent Syria and demanded autonomy. The Christians supported the Kurdish revolt in the Jezire in 1937. Tension between Muslims and Christians in the area subsided from the 1950s with the development of the region's agricultural economy. The author also outlines the development of the Christian community in Syria up to the 1970s.

782   Levi, A. "Frontieres ethniques, frontieres nationales ou: comment peut-on etre Nestorien parmi les Kurdes dans le 'Royaume arabe d'Irak'?" [How to be a Nestorian among the Kurds in the Arab Kingdom of Iraq?] *L'Ethnographie* 91, no. 2 (1995): 5-6, 61-75.

783   Lohre, N. J. "The Highlanders of Kurdistan." *The Moslem World* 10 (1920): 282-286.

Provides a general description of Kurdistan, its geography, population and history. Discusses Kurds' modes of living and their personal characteristics, language, and religion. Particular emphasis is given to missionary activities in late 19th and early 20th centuries Kurdistan.

784   Kreyenbroek, Philip G. "The Lawij of Mor Basilios Shim'un: A Kurdish Christian Text in Syriac Script." *The Journal of Kurdish Studies* 1 (1995): 29-53.

At a time when the Kurds in Turkey and Iraq are facing considerable hardships and indeed serious threats, it may seem frivolous to devote time, energy and space to the study of Christian hymn in Kurdish, composed in the 18th century and preserved in Syriac script. However, recognition of Kurdish identity—and thus of language and culture—is perhaps the one aim which all Kurds involved in the struggle against oppression have in common; the author hopes that this study will help their cause, albeit indirectly, by illustrating the richness and complexity of Kurdish literature. The version of the text on which this paper is based was published as a part of a pamphlet in Syriac entitled Kafô d-Habôbê ('A handful of flowers'), which was produced for the Seminary of the Monastary of Môr Gabriel, Tûr 'Abdîn. It is attributed to Môr Basîliôs Shim'ûn Maphrian of Tûr 'Abdîn, who was born in 1695 C.E. and killed in 1740 by powerful Kurd, 'Abdul Agha (Macuch 1976: 26). Macuch gives an impressive list of Môr Shim'ûn's writings in Syriac and Arabic, but makes no mention of the present work. (A)

785 Rooy, Slivio van. "Christianity in Kurdistan." *The Star of the East* 23 (July 1962): 10-14.

786 Stead, Blanche Wilson. "Kurdistan for Christ." *The Moslem World*. 10 (1920): 241-250.

Discusses the socioeconomic life of the Kurds in rural areas including: bread-making, milking and cheese making, wool weaving and cloth making, animal raising and other agricultural activities. Also discussed is the relationship between the family and the tribe and religion in Kurdistan with particular emphasis on Christianity and the missionaries.

787 Yacoub, Joseph. "Les Assyro-Chaldeens: une minorite en voie d'emergence?" *Etudes Internationale* 21 (June 1990): 341-373.

Discusses history and current situation of the Assyrian minority in Turkey, Iraq, and Iran, who are predominantly Christians of Semitic ethnic group speaking Modern Aramaic dialects and inhabiting areas in Kurdistan and adjacent regions.

788 Yacoub, Joseph. "The Assyrian Community in Turkey." In *Contrasts and Solutions in the Middle East*. Edited by Ole Høiris and Sefa Martin Yürükel, pp. 323-340. Aarhus: Aarhus University Press, 1997.

Discusses this forgotten people, their assimilation and loss of culture. There numbers in Turkey dropped from almost half a million at the turn of the century to no more than 5,000 presently. They live primarily in four villages in the Hakkari area and Tur Abdin. Describes their history and the causes of their sufferings--Turkish, Kurdish, and Persian intolerance, the aridity of the land, the harshness of life, and the oppression of the Kurdish Aghas and the consequences of the Kurdish rebellions.

789 Yousif, Ephrem-Isa. *Parfums d'enfance a Sanate: Un village chretien au Kurdistan irakien*. Paris: L'Harmattan, 1993. 139 p.

This story takes us to a Christian village lost in the mountains of Iraqi Kurdistan during the 1950s. It gives us a colored vision of the Assyro-Chaldean life, people, family, marriage, death, women, and traditions. The narrator, Yousif, a sensitive and enthusiastic small boy, is endowed with a rich memory. He considers himself the heir of a very ancient history and the guardian of the Aramean language that Christ spoke. He tells us his joys and his sorrows, his wonders before nature, and his childhood dreams.

See also items: 4, 64, 123, 130, 131, 137, 140, 151, 155, 163, 264, 265, 313, 653, 728, 729, 731, 732, 740, 766, 813, 914

SUFI ORDERS

790   'Azzawi, 'Abbas al-. "Mawlana Khalid al-Naqshbandi." [A biography of Khalid al-Naqshbandi, a Kurdish client of the Naqshbandi sufi order] *Majallat al-Majma' al-'Ilmi al-Kurdi* 1, no. 1 (1973): 696-729.

791   Bruinessen, Martin van. "Religious Life in Diyarbekir: Religious Learning and the Role of the Tariqats." In *Evliya Celebi in Diyarbekir*. Edited by Martin van Bruinessen and H. E. Boeschoten, pp. 45-52. Leiden: E. J. Brill, 1988.

Discusses the eight medreses of Diyarbekir mentioned by Evliya, the place of the Hanafi and Shafi'i mazhabs in Diyarbekir, and the tariqats.

792   Bruinessen, Martin van. "The Naqshbandi Order in 17th Century Kurdistan." In *Naqshbandis: Cheminements et situation actuelle d'un ordre mystique musulman. Acte de la Table Ronde de Sevres, 2-4 mai 1985*. Edited by Marc Gaborieau, Alexandre Popovic and Thierry Zarcone, pp. 337-360. Istanbul; Paris: Institut Francais d'Etudes Anatoliennes, 1990. (Varia Turcica, 18).

The political and social importance of the Naqshbandi *Sheikhs* in the 19th and 20th centuries is well known both in Kurdistan and other parts of the Middle East. In this study, van Bruinessen, and in contrast to what many has dated back the history of the Naqshbandi order to the 19th century, argues that the Naqshbandiya was present in Kurdistan continuously since the 17th century. This is an important piece of work that uncovers, among other things, the history of the Kurds in 17th century Ottoman Empire. (abridged, Joyce Blau/*AI* 14: 680)

793   Bruinessen, Martin van. "Sûfîs and Sultâns in Southeast Asia and Kurdistan: A Comparative Survey." *Studia Islamika* (Jakarta) 3, no.3 (1996): 1-20. French version: "Les soufis et le pouvoir temporel." In *Les voies d'Allah: les ordres mystiques dans le monde musulman des origines à aujourd'hui*. Edited by Alexandre Popovic and Gilles Veinstein, pp. 242-253. Paris: Fayard, 1996.

794   Hourani, Albert. "Shaikh Khalid and the Naqshbandi Order." In *Islamic Philosophy and the Classical Tradition*. Edited by M. Stern, Albert Hourani, and Vivian Brown, pp. 89-103. Oxford: Oxford University Press, 1972.

795   'Izawi, 'Abbas al-. "Khulafa' Mawlana Khalid." [An account of the successors of Khalid al-Naqshbandi] *Majallat al-Majma' al-'Ilmi al-Kurdi* 2, no. 2 (1974): 182-222.

796   Singer, Andre. "The Dervishes of Kurdistan." *Asian Affairs* [Great Britain] 61 (June 1974): 179-182.

Traces the history of the Qadiri Dervishes of Kurdistan. Their devout Sunni Muslims follow the teaching and descendants of Sheikh Abd al-Qadir Gilani, a Persian who established himself in Baghdad in 12th century. Their worship and rituals consist of repetitive and rhythmic chanting and swaying, and on special occasions these activities end in the eating of glass, playing with poisonous snakes, and thrusting skewers and swords into their bodies. These actions are viewed as demonstrations of faith in God and their leaders, and serves as proof of righteousness since the participants suffer no pain or injury. The more extreme acts are undertaken only by the poorer dervishes to gain status in a society where they have none on an economic or political level. These activities account for the survival of Kurdish identity despite invasions by powerful neighboring nations. Based on a field study in the village of Baiveh in Iran. (S. H. Frank/*HA*: 22B-2171)

797   Mélikoff, Irène. *Hadji Bektach: un mythe et ses avatars: genèse et évolution du soufisme populaire en Turquie*. Leiden: E. J. Brill, 1998. xxvi, 317 p.: ill. [Islamic history and civilization. Studies and texts, v. 20] Includes bibliographical references (p. [290]-304) and index.

See also items: 7, 10, 11, 604, 629, 645, 651, 657, 664, 665, 674, 681, 733, 735, 736, 737, 738, 770, 857, 859, 867, 887, 893, 897, 904, 919

YEZIDIS

798   Abovian, Khachatur. "Die Kurden und Jesiden." *Acta Kurdica: The International Journal of Kurdish and Iranian Studies* 1 (1994): 181-206. [In German.]

799   Ahmed, Sami Said. "A Study of the Yazidis: An Introduction." *The Iliff Review* 30, no. 3 (Fall 1973): 37-48.

800   Bois, Thomas. "Les Yezidis: Essai historique et sociologique sur leur origine religieuse." [The Yezidis: historical and sociological essay on their religious origin] *Al-Machriq* 55 (1961): 109-128; 190-242.

801   Cherchi, Maecello; Platz, Stephanie; Tuite, Kevin. "Yezidis." In *Encyclopedia of World Cultures, Volume VI: Russia and Eurasia/ China*. Edited by Paul Friedrich and Norma Diamond, pp. 407-411. Boston, MA: G. K. Hall and Co., 1994.

Topics discussed include: Orientation (identification, location and demography), History and Cultural Relations, Settlements, Economy, Kinship, Marriage and Family, Sociopolitical Organization, and Religion and Expressive Culture of the Yezidi Kurds of the former Soviet Union.

802   Colpe, Carsten. "Konsens, Diskretion, Rivalitat: Aus der Ethnohistorie von Kurden und Yeziden." In *Ethnizitat, Nationalismus, Religion und Politik in Kurdistan*. Edited by Carsten Borck, Eva Savelsberg, and Siamend Hajo, pp. 279-300. Mèunster: Lit, 1997. [In German]

803   Damluji, Siddiq al-. *al-Yazidiyah*. [An overview of the Yezidi religion] Mosul, Iraq: Matba'at al-Ittihad, 1949.

804   Edmonds, Cecil John. *Pilgrimage to Lalish*. London: Royal Asiatic Society, 1967. xii, 88 p.: ill., map.

Lalish in Iraqi Kurdistan is the shrine of Sheikh 'Adi, the traditional founder of the Yezidi sect, long though mistakenly known to the West as devil worshippers. Other travelers—Layard and Gertrude Bell, for instance—discuss their experiences with the Yezidis, however, Edmonds does not quote from any of them. He has set down only what he saw with his eyes and heard at first hand. Nevertheless his is the nearest approach to a systematic account of Yezidi beliefs and practices, in so far as they can be disclosed to an outsider.

805   Empson, Ralph H. W. *The Cult of the Peacock Angel: A Short Account of the Yezidi Tribes of Kurdistan*. Commentary by Sir Richard Carnac Temple. London: H. F. & G. Witherby, 1928. 235 p.

Describes the ancient faith of the Yezidi tribes of Iraq and traces the origin of these people and their rites and customs. The work also examines the history of their faith, beliefs, orders, saints and holy books. These people are the worshippers of Melak Taus 'The Peacock Angel', and are also known as devil worshippers. The author links this tribe with the Zoroastrians because of the many common characteristics of the two peoples. There is a long commentary by Sir Richard Carnac Temple, which in fact constitutes a second part to the book.

806 Frayha, Anis. *New Yezidi Texts from Beled Sinjar, 'Iraq*. Baltimore, MD: s.n., 1946. 26 p.

Reprinted from the *Journal of the American Oriental Society*, vol. 66, pp. 18-43. In his preface Henry Field tells us that these Yezidi texts were purchased privately by him when leader of the Field Museum Anthropological Expedition to Near East near Beled Sinjar, the copier, who had both Arabic and Kurdish, having access to the original documents, two of which were on paper and one on gazelle skin. Dr. Anis Frayha, in his introduction, classifies the texts, which comprise the *Kitab al-Jalwah* and the *Mishaf Resh*, poems ascribed to Shaikh 'Adi, stories about Shaikh 'Adi and other Yezidi notabilities, genealogies and proclamations. It is worth mentioning that the legends of creation given in the Mishaf Resh differ considerably from the oral tradition of the people. As for the translation of the two first books, the reviewer suggests that comparisons should be made with other sources such as Layard's *Nineveh and Babylon* and Badger's *Nestorians and their Rituals*. (E. S. Drower: 103)

807 Fuccaro, Nelida. "A 17th Century Travel Account on the Yazidis: Implications for a Socio-Religious History." *Annali dell'Instituto Universitario Orientale di Napoli* 53, no. 3 (1993): 241-253.

808 Fuccaro, Nelida. *Aspects of the Social and Political History of the Yazidi Enclave of Jabal Sinjar (Iraq) Under the British Mandate, 1919-1932*. Ph.D., Durham, 1994.

This thesis focuses on various aspects of the social and political history of the Yezidi Kurds of Jabal Sinjar (Iraq) during the British mandate. When relevant to the history of mandatory Sinjar it also deals with the neighboring Yezidi community of Iraqi Shaikhan. Chapters I and II are primarily concerned with the society and economy of Jabal Sinjar in the period under consideration with particular emphasis on the socio-economic and political organization of the Yezidi tribes settled in the area. They also provide a general historical perspective of the socio-economic development of the region. Chapter III discusses the late Ottoman period in detail with a view to defining community-state relations and the development of Yezidi inter-tribal affairs in Jabal Sinjar. Chapters IV and V examine the history of the Yezidi Mountain in the years of the British mandate when the emerging structures of the Iraqi state had significant repercussions on Sinjari society, especially on the attitude of a number of Yezidi tribal leaders. These developments are analyzed primarily in the context of the policies implemented in the northern Jazireh by the British and Iraqi administrations and by the French mandatory authorities who controlled its Syrian section. Particular emphasis is placed on the dispute between Great Britain and France concerning the delimitation of the Syro-Iraqi border in the Sinjar area that affected relations between the Yezidis, the British mandatory administration and the Iraqi authorities. Chapter VI gives an account of the Sinjari Yezidis' quest for autonomy that became increasingly associated with the Assyro-Chaldean autonomist movement in the last years of the mandate.

809 Fuccaro, Nelida. "Ethnicity, State Formation, and Conscription in Post-colonial Iraq: The Case of the Yazidi Kurds of Jabal Sinjar." *International Journal of Middle East Studies* 29, no. 4 (November 1997): 559-580.

Based on a conference paper which appeared in the Proceedings of the Annual Conference of the British Society for Middle Eastern Studies, 1994, University of Manchester, pp. 190-211 (Manchester: University of Manchester, 1994) under the title: "The Effects of the Application of the 1934 Iraqi Conscription Law on the Yezidi Community of Jabal Sinjar." Fuccaro discusses the effect of conscription on the Yezidi Kurds of Jabal Sinjar in northwestern Iraq, in order to explore the significant part played by ethnicity during the initial stages of Iraqi national development following independence from British Mandatory control in 1932. She also discusses state and society in monarchical Iraq; the issue of conscription, which was introduced in 1934; religion and identity among the Kurdish tribes of Jabal Sinjar; the enforcement of conscription in Jabal Sinjar, which lay at the root of a number of disturbances that took place in the region between 1935 and 1940; relations between Syria and Iraq and the involvement of France in Yezidi affairs; and how land policies in Sinjar affected the antagonism between the Yezidi tribes and the Iraqi Shammar bedouin.

810 Fuccaro, Nelida. "Die Kurden Syriens: Anfange der nationalen Mobilis-ierung unter franzosischen Herrschaft." In *Ethnizitat, Nationalismus, Religion und Politik in Kurdistan*. Edited by Carsten Borck, Eva Savels-berg, and Siamend Hajo, pp. 301-326. Mèunster: Lit, 1997. [In German.]

811 Fuccaro, Nelida. *The Other Kurds: Yazidis in Colonial Iraq*. London: I.B. Tauris, 1999. xiii, 230 p. [Library of Modern Middle East Studies, v.14.]

Although the Yezidi Kurds are the second largest non-Muslim commu-nity in northern Iraq, the stigma of religious difference (for which they became known as devil worshipers), their physical seclusion in moun-tainous areas, and their closely knit tribal organization, have accentuated their isolation for centuries. This book offers the first account of a fasci-nating and complex tribal society. Fuccaro is not so much concerned with their syncretistic religious beliefs, long the focus of Yezidi studies, as with their attempts to accommodate the state in the late Ottoman and Brit-ish mandate periods. She analyzes the construction of communal identi-ties within several overlapping frames of reference: tribal, religious, and socioeconomic. The complex relationship between colonialism and the development of ethnic consciousness is at the center of her study. The author argues that the tension between two authorities, the British colonial administration and the Iraqi government, encouraged among Yezidis (and others) local solidarities and a continuity with the past, thereby contributing to the political instability that marked post-independence Iraq. Fuccaro looks at community/state relations primarily from the Kurdish perspective and highlights new trends of intertribal mobilization, changes in the Yezidi power structure, and the emergence of new inter-communal identities.

812   Fuccaro, Nelida. "Communalism and the State in Iraq: The Yazidi Kurds, c.1869-1940." *Middle Eastern Studies* 35, no. 2 (April 1999): 1-26.

Focuses on the tribal, religious and ethnic identities of the Yezidis in Iraq, during the 1869-1940 period.

813   Guest, John S. *Survival among the Kurds: A History of the Yezidis*. London; New York: Kegan Paul International, 1993. xvii, 324 p. [44] p. of plates.

This is a revised, expanded, and updated edition of *The Yezidis* published by Kegan Paul International in 1987. It has been revised and reissued due to popular demand arising from worldwide interest in the Kurdish people, of whom the Yezidis are a long established religious group. The history of the Yezidi community and their place in the annals of the Kurdish people goes back 900 years—even longer if their antecedents are traced back through antiquity. This narrative—which describes the origin of their religion, their discovery by Western travelers and missionaries in the nineteenth century, their traumatic recent history and present condition—fills an important niche in the history of the Near East. The 200,000 members of the Yezidi community live today in the northern parts of Iraq and Syria, in eastern Turkey, in Germany and in the former Soviet republics of Armenia and Georgia. They possess their own religion, quite distinct from Islam, which most other Kurds profess, and from the Christian and Jewish faith. The Yezidis believe that Lucifer, the fallen angel, has been forgiven by God and reinstated as chief angel. Their faith, like their history, is characterized by dignity and survival in the face of great odds. After examining the antecedents of the Yezidis, the life of Sheikh 'Adi who is venerated as the prophet of the Yezidi religion, and the Yezidi religions itself, the work describes early encounters between the Yezidis and the outside world and the close friendship forged in the 1840s between Yezidi leaders and the British archaeologist Sir Henry Layard. The British ambassador Sir Stratford Canning helped them to obtain civil rights, and a hitherto unpublished letter of thanks from the Yezidi leaders appears as an appendix. Chapters also deal with Sultan Abdulhamid's cruel but vain efforts to force the Yezidis to embrace Islam, leading to the emergence of Mayan Khatun, a strong-willed Yezidi princess who ruled the community from 1913 to 1958. An epilogue reviews the present status of the Yezidi community, based on recent contacts with their political and religious leaders. The author paid three visits to Armenia in 1992, enabling him to bring the history of the Yezidis in Transcaucasia up to date. He also visited the United Nations security zone in northern Iraq in 1991 and 1992. A new appendix presents a recent outline of Yezidi religious doctrine set forth by contemporary Yezidi religious leaders.

814   Hasani, Abd al-Razzaq al-. *al-Yazidiyyun fi Hadirihim wa-Madihim*. [A history of the Yezidis] 6th ed. Baghdad: Dar al-Katib al-Jadid, 1974. 187 p.: ills. Includes bibliographical references.

815   Kizilhan, Ilhan. *Die Yeziden: eine anthropologische und sozialpsychologische Studie uber die kurdische Gemeinschaft*. Frankfurt, Germany: Verlag Medico International, 1997. 283 p. Includes bibliographical references (p. 272-283) and ills. [In German.]

816   Kleinert, C. "Eine Minderheit in der Turkei: die Yezidi." *Zeitschrift fur Yurkeistudien* 6, no. 2 (1993): 223-234. [In German]

817   Kreyenbroek, Philip G. *Yezidism: Its Background, Observances, and Textual Tradition*. Lewiston [NY]: E. Mellen Press, 1995.
Kreyenbroek's book is a welcome contribution to the study of the religion of Yezidi Kurds, which has been long neglected. A useful reference work on the community, it is descriptive, informative, carefully researched and clearly laid out. It constitutes an essential reference for undertaking further studies on Yezidism. Moreover, it is particularly useful for scholars and students interested in religious syncretism, doctrinal dissidence and orality as linked to the transmission of religious tradition in Kurdistan, and more generally in the Middle East. The book includes two main sections. Part one deals with Yezidism as a religious system with particular emphasis on earlier perceptions of the community, its beliefs, rituals and social organization. Part two includes texts from current Yezidi oral tradition gathered by the author in the Shaykhan district of northern Iraq, which has been the religious center of the community for centuries. (Nelida Fuccaro/*BJMES* 26, no. 1, 1999: 104-105)

818   Marie, (Pere) Anastase. "Le decouverte recente des deux livres sacres des Yezidis." *Anthropos* 6 (1911): 1-39.

819   Sulaiman, Khidir. "al-Akrad al-Yazidiyyin." [A brief account on the Yezidi Kurds] *al-Turath al-Sha'bi* 5, no. 10 (1974): 49-60.

820   Vangent, A. "The Yezidi Struggle to Survive." *Swiss Review of World Affairs* 6 (June 1993): 20-21.

In the portion of northern Iraq controlled by the Kurds, the Yezidis have experienced a brief cultural renaissance even though the Baghdad government has forced the community's highest priest to leave and Saddam Hussein's army has razed many Yezidi villages. As Islamic fundamentalism grows among the Kurds, the Yezidis increasingly fear a renewal of persecution.

821   Wahby, Taufiq. *The Remnants of Mithraism in Hatra and Iraqi Kurdistan, and Its Traces in Yazidism: the Yazidis Are not Devil-Worshippers*. London: T. Wahby, 1962. 52 p. Includes bibliographical references.

See also items: 130, 131, 140, 155, 265, 331, 346, 394, 446, 517, 518, 519, 635, 660, 728, 729, 731, 732, 735, 736, 737, 738, 835

ZOROASTRIANISM

822   Boyce, Mary. *A History of Zoroastrianism*. 3 vols. Leiden: E. J. Brill, 1975, 1982, 1989. Includes bibliographies and indexes.

A work of three well-written books on the history of Zoroastrianism, the old religion of the Kurds. The author has written these volumes after she periodically lived for several months among Zoroastrian villagers in Iran in the 1970s and 1980s. Volume I provides a background history to the various pagan cults and their gods, the prehistoric period of the faith and Zoroaster (628?-?551 BC) and his teachings. This volume has been reproduced, with corrections, in 1996. Volume II discusses the period during which Zoroaster was known to be in Iran and the spread of Zoroastrianism, with reference to the historic achievements and religious beliefs of Cyrus the Great (550-530 BC) and the following rulers of Persia to Darius III (336-331 BC). The second volume is a more systematic and uniform study. Volume III treats Zoroastrianism under Macedonian and Roman rule.

823   Gurani, 'Ali Saydu al-. "Zaradasht wa-al-Zaradashtiyah." [An overview of Zoroaster and Zoroastrianism] *Majallat al-Majma' al-'Ilmi al-Kurdi* 3, no. 3 (1975): 577-594.

See also items: 668, 735, 736, 805

20
Sociology

824 'Aqrawi, Hashim Taha. *al-Usus al-Ijtima'iyah wa-al-Nafsiyah lil-Qaba'il al-Kurdiyah*. [The social and psychological structure of Kurdish tribes] Kirkuk, Iraq: Matba'at al-Baladiyah, 1971. 160 p.

825 Barth, Frederik. *Principles of Social Organization in Southern Kurdistan*. Oslo: Brodrene Jorgensen boktrykkeri, 1953. 146 p. illus., maps. [Universitetets etnografiske museum bulletin ; no. 7] Bibliography: p. 145-146.

826 Bierbrauer, Gunter. "Reactions to Violation of Normative Standards: A Cross-Cultural Analysis of Shame and Guilt." *International Journal of Psychology/Journal International de Psychologie* 27 (April 1992): 181-193.

Compares responses to violations of legal, religious, and traditional norms given by individuals from three cultures (37 native German men, 28 Kurdish men from Turkey, and 41 Arab men from Lebanon; the latter two groups were asylum seekers living in Germany an average of 21 months). Because the native Germans demonstrated more individualistic orientations than the other groups, it was hypothesized that the Kurds and Lebanese would respond to normative violations with more shame and that Germans would respond with more guilt. Interview data reveal, however, that the individuals from the collectivistic cultures responded to transgressions with both more shame and more guilt than did those from the more individualistic culture. The influence of religious beliefs on these findings is considered.

827   Bierbrauer, Gunter. "Toward an Understanding of Legal Culture: Variations in Individualism and Collectivism Between Kurds, Lebanese, and Germans." *Law and Society Review* 28, no. 2 (1994): 243-264.

Legal culture is a society derived product encompassing interrelated concepts as legitimacy and acceptance of authorities, preferences for and beliefs about dispute arrangements, and authorities' use of discretionary power. This study investigated five attributes of legal culture by comparing subjective notions of law and the legal system of respondents from Turkey (Kurds), Lebanon, and Germany. Our samples fell into two distinct groups on cultural orientation: the German group showed a distinct individualistic orientation; the two others group (Kurds and Lebanese) showed a relative collectivistic orientation. The findings suggest a substantial variety of legal preferences and practices between the two orientations. Collectivistic groups had a greater preference for abiding by the norms of tradition and religion and were less willing to let state law regulate in-group disputes; individualistic respondents showed a clear preference for formal procedures guidelines. The study suggests that legal norms prevailing in Western societies may be inconsequential to people socialized in other cultures. Implications of diverse conceptions of law expectations, and legitimacy for various cultural groups in multiethnic and plural societies are discussed.

828   Bois, Thomas. "La vie sociale des Kurdes." [The social life of the Kurds] *Al-Machriq* 56 (1962): 597-661.

829   Bois, Thomas. "Kurdish Society." In *Encyclopedia of Islam*. New ed. Vol. 5, 470-479. Leiden, E. J. Brill, 1986.

Topics discussed: (A) The Fundamental Structures of Kurdish Society: 1) The Kurdish family; 2) Tribal organization: (a) listings of the Kurdish tribes, (b) the Kurdish tribe and its components, (c) the chief of the tribe, his obligations, his responsibilities and his compensations and; 3) The economic structures: (a) Kurdish nomadism and (b) the Kurdish peasantry; (B) The Religious Aspect and; (C) Customs and Social Tradition: 1) Dress; 2) Marriage and burial customs; 3) Festivals and seasonal rites; 4) Dances and music and; 5) Games, sports and hunting.

830   Jawishli, Hadi Rashid al-. *al-Hayat al-Ijtima'iyah fi Kurdistan*. [An overview of social life in Kurdistan] Baghdad: Matba't Dar al-Jahiz, 1970. 160 p.

831   Kahn, Margaret. *Children of the Jinn: In Search of the Kurds and their Country*. New York: Seaview Press, 1980. xiv, 302 p.

Different from other peoples of the Middle East, the Kurds are devout Sunni Muslims whose women, garbed in brilliantly colored clothes, go unveiled. They are fierce defenders of Kurdish independence, but kind and hospitable hosts and neighbors. Traveling to Iranian Kurdistan in 1974 to study the Kurdish language, Kahn and her husband took jobs teaching English in Rezaiyeh, a northwestern city. Since Kurdish was officially outlawed in Iran, Kahn's task turned into a frustrating maze of false leads and suspicious silences as she attempted to make contact with the Kurds. Slowly breaking through the barriers of language, custom, and politics, Kahn "discovered" Kurdistan and a people clinging firmly to their heritage as well as their undying dream of independence. Unlike the Turks and Persians of Rezaiyeh, the women of Kurdistan warmly welcomed the author. Their rainbow-hued dresses shone among the four black chadors of other Muslim women and their earthy humor contrasted with the primes of urban Iranian women. One of the few Western women to write about the Kurds, Kahn provides a fascinating look at the role of women as members of *harems* and as food providers in subsistence-level villages. Through anecdotes, history, and original insights, Kahn paints a vivid portrait of the Kurds from their historical origins to the contemporary conflicts inherent in technology, feminism, and urban life. *Children of the Jinn* explains how a persecuted, indomitable people survive in one of the most volatile regions of the word.

832   Khasbak, Shakir. "Mumayyazat al-Hayat al-Qabaliyah al-Kurdiyah." *Majallat Kulliyat al-Adab - Jami'at Baghdad* 2 (February 1960): 126-133.

Argues that the distinguishing features of Kurdish tribal life are limited to three major characteristics: leadership, fighting, and tribal responsibilities.

833   Masters, William Murray. *Rowanduz: A Kurdish Administrative and Mercantile Center*. Ph.D., University of Michigan, 1954. 367 p.

This study has two purposes, the first of which is an analysis and interpretation of the culture of Rowanduz, a Kurdish administrative and mercantile town of northern Iraq. The second purpose of this study is the delineation of the impact of the modern state on the structure of the society of the town and the district within which it lies. The materials were obtained from seven weeks' intensive investigation in the summer of 1951. An analysis and interpretation of the culture of Rowanduz are presented in six areas of discussion: 1) the administrative center; 2) the mercantile center; 3) house, dress, and diet; 4) the society; 5) the family; and 6) religious life. The population of the town numbers about 5000 and is basically made up of merchants, craftsmen, laborers, and servants. The town dominates a large district of agricultural villages both as a center of government administration and as one of commerce. Detailed description of the aspects of life pertinent to the areas of discussion are given. The most important focus of investigation, connected with the second object of the study, is found to be the society of the town. The conclusions implement the two purposes of the study. 1) Kurdish culture, as represented in Rowanduz, is discovered to be strongly regulated by Islam and to have many general similarities to that of Islamic peoples elsewhere, in spite of numerous peculiarities. 2) The impact of the modern state is changing the structure of Kurdish society and threatens to eliminate the native aristocracy by replacing it with the government elite. The Kurdish chieftains have reacted to this with a series of revolts, while many of the commoners are being absorbed into the new order, particularly in towns like Rowanduz. Popular understanding of the reaction, as well as of the transformation of the commoners into a body of citizenry, is obscured by a nationalistic ideology directed against the rulers (who belong to other ethnic groups) of the Kurds. (*DA* 14: 581)

834   Mokri, Mohammad. "Le mariage chez les kurdes." [Marriage among the Kurds] *L'Ethnographie* N.S. 56 (1962): 42-68.

835   Lamb, Harold. "Mountain Tribes of Iran and Iraq." *The National Geographic Magazine* (March 1946): 385-408.

Topics covered include physical anthropology, ethnology of the Bakhtiaris, Lurs, Kurds in the Sulaymania area as well as Yezidi Kurds.

836   Rudolph, Wolfgang. "Einige Hypothetische Ausfuhrungen Zur Kultur Der Kurden." [Some hypothetical remarks on the culture of the Kurds] *Sociologus* 9, no. 2 (1959): 150-161. [In German]

837   Rudolph, Wolfgang. "Grundzuege Sozialer Organisation Bei Den Westiranischen Kurden." [Principles of social organization among the Kurds of western Iran] *Sociologus* 17, no. 1 (1967): 19-38. [In German]

838   Sharif, 'Abd al-Sattar Tahir. *al-Mujtama' al-Kurdi: Dirasah Ijtima'iyah Thaqafiyah Siyasiyah*. [A social, cultural, and political study of the Kurds] Baghdad: Dar al-'Iraq, 1981. 87 p.

839   Sharif, 'Abd al-Sattar Tahir. *al-Jam'iyat wa-al-Munazzamat wa-al-Ahzab al-Kurdiyah fi Nisf Qarn, 1908-1958*. Baghdad: Sharikat al-Ma'rifah lil-Nashr wa-al-Tawzi' al-Mahduda, 1989. 346 p.: ill. Includes bibliographical references (p. 291-293).

A historical survey of Kurdish political parties and social and cultural organizations established in Turkey, Iran, Iraq, and Syria.

840   Vasil'eva, Eugenia. "The Social Aspect of Genealogical Descent among the Kurds." *Acta Kurdica: The International Journal of Kurdish and Iranian Studies* 1 (1994): 73-76.

Argues that among the Kurds, social prestige is most influenced by gene-alogy rather than education, wealth, and other socio-economic indicators.

841 Vega, Anne. "Tradition et modernite au Kurdistan et en diaspora." [Tradition and Modernity in Kurdistan and its Diaspora] *Peuples Mediterraneens*, no. 68-69 (July-December 1994): 107-142.

Field research regarding traditional Kurdish views and strategies of par-enthood and matrimony is drawn on to describe an extended family in Beytushebab (Turkish Kurdistan), with diaspora members in Turkey and Syria, and immigrants in France. The strength of tribal relations is proven remarkably strong. Alliances by marriage (between cousins, tribal mem-bers, and same religious sect members), matrimonial transactions (e.g., bride price), and parenting terminology are compared to their equivalents in Turkish and Arabic societies. Beliefs regarding maternity and women's roles in Kurdistan and the Paris region are compared as well, showing splits from the traditional in the process of change; immigrant women miss the sociability of the area of origin, but are drawn to the individual liberty of the new culture.

842 Wolfram, Eberhard. "Nomads and Farmers in Southeastern Turkey: Prob-lems of Settlement." *Oriens* 6 (1953): 32-49. [In German]

843 Yalcin-Heckmann, Lale. "Kurdish Tribal Organisation and Local Political Processes." In *Turkish State, Turkish Society*. Edited by Andrew Finkel and Nukhet Sirman, pp. 289-312. London: Routledge, 1990.

This paper intends to look at the assumptions sociologists and political scientists have made about Kurdish and Eastern Turkish tribal organi-zation and to assess them in view of data collected from Hakkari in Southeast Turkey, a province that is generally described as 'tribal' and 'backward.' The paper also looks at the historical and economic basis of Hakkari's tribes and their history. Tribes in the region are said to have ex-isted for many centuries and different forms of autonomous or semi-autonomous tribal structures have long been recorded. The historical background is outlined here in terms of continuities and discontinuities in political structures, which includes the pattern of tribal alliances. Part of Hakkari's peculiar historical legacy may be accounted for by its physical environment (high mountains, narrow valleys, well-protected settlements with little and poor-quality land) and its geopolitical as a buffer zone be-tween various states. From the evaluation of the past and a comparison of the social and political organization of the present, the paper proceeds to discuss tribal ideology as it is constituted by inter-and intra-tribal rela-tions, the type and nature of leadership and authority, and more specifi-cally, the meaning, acquisition and maintenance of *agalik* (being an *aga*) as an institution. Finally, the author looks at local concepts of political machinery, the state and the region.

See also items: 1, 3, 4, 6, 7, 9, 10, 19, 23, 24, 26, 50, 71, 114, 117, 140, 142, 143, 145, 154, 160, 168, 170, 171, 172, 173, 181, 183, 229, 231, 315, 320, 325, 326, 327, 339, 343, 348, 351, 354, 364, 517, 642, 644, 650, 654, 663, 670, 677, 678, 680, 681, 698, 706, 742, 772, 775, 786, 805, 811, 812, 815, 817, 848, 850, 851, 853, 854, 855, 856, 860, 861, 863, 872, 877, 888, 890, 893, 904, 910, 920, 924, 926, and the chapter on Anthropology.

21

Women

844   Begikhani, Nazand. "La femme kurde face a la montee islamiste." *Cahiers de l'Orient* 47 (1997): 43-53.

845   Brooks, Geraldene. *Nine Parts of Desire: The Hidden World of Islamic Women*. New York: Anchor Books, 1995. 239 p.

The author discusses the lives of Muslim women in various parts of the world. "Some, like the female soldier in the army of the United Arab Emirates and the female politician in Kurdistan, are remolding Islamic tradition. Others, like the belly dancer in Cairo who accepted forced retirement... bow to a traditional interpretation of Islam. And still others, like the teacher in a school run by an Islamic fundamentalists organization in Gaza, find in Islam a vehicle of rebellion against existing political authority."

846   Bruinessen, Martin van. "Matriarchy in Kurdistan? Women Rulers in Kurdish History." *The International Journal of Kurdish Studies* 6, nos. 1-2 (Fall 1993): 25-39.

Kurdish society is known as a male-dominated society, and it has been for all of its known history. Throughout Kurdish history we find, however, instances of women reaching high position and becoming the political, in some cases even military, leaders of their communities. It is hard to find comparable cases among the Kurds' most important neighbors, the Turks, Arabs, and Persians. These recurrent instances of rule by women are interesting enough in their own right, but they also raise a number of questions about the nature of Kurdish society and the position of women in it. Various conflicting interpretations of the phenomenon of rule by women is discussed briefly in this article. The main purpose of the article is to describe the best documented cases of women who became rulers or played other "manly" roles in Kurdistan.

847   Fuad, Tania. "National Liberation. Women's Liberation." *Freedom Review* 26 (September-October 1995): 31-33.

Kurdish women are often considered to be more liberated than other Middle Eastern women. In this article, the author questions whether Kurdish women are truly liberated and discusses the role of women in the two major political parties, the Patriotic Union of Kurdistan and the Kurdish Democratic Party.

848   Galletti, Mirella. "La donna curda e il suo ruolo nella lotta di liberazione." [Kurdish Women and their Role in the Liberation Struggle]. *Inchiesta* 21, no. 93 (July-September 1991): 9-12. [In Italian.]

Kurdish women articulate diverse roles as mothers, life companions, political leaders, and militants in traditional, nomadic society. Compared to their Arab counterparts, Kurdish women enjoy the freedom to choose their mates and live in a monogamous marriage. They are faithful companions who often assume leadership of the tribe upon the death of tribal chief husbands. Militant women active in the Kurdish nationalist movement since the 1920s include Hafsa Khan, Adila Xatum, Marguerite Georges, and Layla Wasem. The roster of the Kurdistan Patriotic Union in the 1980s lists 70+ female warriors. It is noted that detribalization, urbanization, and schooling have contributed to create a more nuclear family and less cross-cousin, endogenous marriages. (A)

849   Gearing, Julian. "The Ones Left Behind." *The Middle East* [London], no. 218 (December 1992): 43-45.

Kurdish women are burdened with the enormous responsibility of looking after the children without their menfolk's assistance. An estimated 180,0000 lives have been lost since Saddam Hussein waged war on the Kurdish people. Life without a husband, brother or father has become normal among them, although some women are still not used to it. In an attempt to further demoralize the rebellious Kurdish men, rape is being carried out by the Iraqi army. Despite the numerous setbacks, the women have managed to remain resilient and optimistic.

850   Hacettepe University, Institute of Population Studies. *Fertility Trends, Women's Status, and Reproductive Expectations in Turkey: Results of Further Analysis of the 1993 Turkish Demographic and Health Survey*. Ankara, Turkey: Hacettepe University, Institute of Population Studies, 1997. v, 127 p.: ill. Funding was provided by the U.S. Agency for International Development (USAID).

This report summarizes additional findings of the further analysis for the 1993 Turkish Demographic and Health Survey (item 224).

851   Hansen, Henny Harald. *Daughters of Allah: Among Moslem Women in Kurdistan*. Translated from Danish by Reginald Spink. London: George Allen and Unwin, 1960. 191 p.: ill.

Hansen describes her work as a travel book by an ethnographer who visited the area due to be flooded by the Dokan dam in 1957 and carried out research in the surrounding Kurdish villages. It is an account of her work and the life of the local people written for the general reader. A more formal account of her ethnographic research was published as *The Kurdish Woman's Life: Field Research in a Muslim Society, Iraq*. In addition to the initial advantage of being a woman, Mrs. Hansen has brought to this study of Kurdish society the special qualifications of a trained scientific investigator and a warm-hearted mother and grandmother. Having shared as she did in the daily round of her hosts, she is able to give us detailed and accurate accounts of such things as: the arrangement and furnishing of the ladies' apartments; feminine attire, jewelry and make-up; the customs and observances connected with birth, with marriage (at all stages from the negotiations for an engagement through the contract, preparing the trousseau, decking the bride and escorting her to her new home, the merry-making and the arranging of the bridal chamber, to consummation), and with death; superstitions; the polygamous household; shopping and dress making; at-homes; cooking, meals, washing-day and other domestic chores; the care, or rather the shocking ignorance about the care, of children; and much more besides. There is a short description of dancing by men but, curiously, no mention of the mixed *rashbalak*, when women Join the line. (C. J. Edmonds)

852   Hansen, Henny Harald. *The Kurdish Woman's Life: Field Research in a Muslim Society, Iraq*. Copenhagen: The National Museum, 1961. xii, 213 p.: ill., maps, diagrs., plans, tables. (Copenhagen. Nationalmuseet. Nationalmuseets skrifter. Etnografisk raekke, 7) Bibliography: p. [198]-203.

853   Jawishli, Samia al-. "al-Wad' al-Ijtima'i lil-Mar'a al-Kurdiyah fi al-'Iraq." [A brief overview of the social conditions of Kurdish women in Iraq] *al-Thaqafah al-Jadidah* 36 (February 1989): 59-64.

854   Kohler, Gesa; Nogga-Weinell, Dorothea. *Azade: vom Uberleben kurdischer Frauen*. Aufl. Bremen: Edition CON, 1984. 152 p.: ill. (Sudwind Bericht.) [In German.]

855   Kordi, Gohar. *An Iranian Odyssey*. London: Serpent's Tail, 1991. 141 p.

This is an account of the author's life. Born in a Kurdish village, Kordi lost her eyesight as the result of an illness at age four.... After moving to Tehran, her family put her in the streets to beg. From a neighbor's empty house, Kordi put in a phone call to a radio talk show, which ultimately led to her acceptance at the only blind school in the country.

856   Kurdistan Solidarity Committee. *Resistance: Women in Kurdistan*. London: Kurdistan Solidarity Committee: Kurdistan Information Centre, 1995. 62 p.: ill.

857   Mojab, Shehrzad. *Women in Politics and War: The Case of Kurdistan*. [Working Paper # 145, September 1987] Michigan State University. 18 p.

In Kurdistan as in other traditional societies, politics and war have been exclusively male domains, though in recent decades, the national struggle for establishing a Kurdish state and achieving autonomy has made female participation in political and military action possible. This paper examines the sexual division of labor in Kurdish society and female participation in four movements: Shaikh Mahmud's revolt (1918-1924, Iraq), the Kurdish Republic (1946, Iran), the autonomist wars in Iraq (1961-1975), and Iran (1979-1985). Some findings include: women activists are mostly urban and literate; the extent of their participation is related to the ideological and political line of the leadership of these movements. (A)

858   Mojab, Shehrzad. "Crossing the Boundaries of Nationalism, Patriarchy, and Eurocentrism: The Struggle for a Kurdish Women's Studies Network." *Canadian Woman Studies* 17, no. 2 (Spring 1997): 68-72.

This article examines the state of feminist practice and scholarship of the Kurds.

859   Mojab, Shahrzad (ed.). *Women of a Non-State Nation: The Kurds*. Costa Mesa, CA: Mazda Publishers, 2000. xii, 295p. Includes bibliography.

This book is the first scholarly work on feminism and nationalism in the context of one of the most persistent nationalist movements of the twentieth century Kurdish nationalism. While a considerable volume of the literature on the Kurds deals with their nationalism, the place of women in this nationalist movement has rarely been studied. The relationship between nationalism and feminism is quite complex and conflictive. While some progress has recently been made in theorizing the relationships, there is a dearth of empirical studies of the topic. The contributors to this book examine aspects of Kurdish women's lives in light of current theoretical debates. For the first time, the contributors apply gender critique to the understanding of the nationalism of the world's largest non-state nation, the Kurds. The book introduces a gender dimension into the growing literature on Kurdish nationalism. The diversity of Kurdish women's lives and experiences, from their membership in the parliament to military activism to mothering is documented. At the same time, it provides extensive evidence and analysis, which questions the widely accepted claim that Kurdish women enjoy more freedom compared with their Arab, Turkish and Persian sisters. Many of the topics in the book have never been addressed in Kurdish studies, for instance, gender and self-determination, women and Sufism, feminism and nationalism, and women and health choices. The editor's introductory chapter is the first survey of Kurdish women's studies, and provides a critical overview of the state of research, and examines theoretical and methodological issues as well as the politics and political economy of research on the women of a non-state nation. Chapters include: Shahrzad Mojab, "The Solitude of the Stateless: Kurdish Women at the Margins of Feminist Knowledge;" Janet Klein, "The Natural Resources of the Nation: Women in Kurdish Nationalist Discourse of the Late Ottoman Period;" Rohat Alakom, "Kurdish Women's Movement in Constantinople;" Shahrzad Mojab, Women and Nationalism in the Kurdish Republic of 1946;" Martin van Bruinessen, "From Adela Khanum to Leyla Zana: Women as Political Leaders;" Heidi Wedel, "Kurdish Migrant Women in Istanbul: Community and the Resources for Political Participation of Marginalized Social Group;" Susan McDonald, "Kurdish Women and Self-determination: A Feminist Approach to International Law;" Maria O'Shea, "Medic, Mystic or Magic? Women's Health Choices in a Kurdish Town;" Christine Allison, "Folklore and Fantasy: The Portrayal of Women in Kurdish Oral Tradition;" Mirella Galletti, "Western Images of the Woman's Role in Kurdish Society;" Annabelle Bottcher, "Portraits of Kurdish Women in Contemporary Sufism;" and Amir Hassanpour, "The (Re)production of Patriarchy in the Kurdish Language."

860   Wedel, Heidi. "Binnenmigration und ethnische Identitat: Kurdinnen in turkischen Metropolen." [Internal migration and ethnic identity: Kurdish women in Turkish metropolises] *Orient* 37, no.3 (September 1996): 437-452. [In German.]

According to Turkish allegations, more than half of the Kurdish population of the Turkish Republic has migrated to the west. By migration and intermixture of the Kurds with the Turkish populace the so-called Kurdish problem would dissolve in the melting pot of the metropolises. However, the results of the author's field research in two squatter areas in Istanbul show that even families who migrated 15-20 years ago are economically, socially, culturally, and politically only partially integrated into the city. Because of the sexual division of labor, squatter women suffer even more than men from the lack of infrastructure and social institutions in the neighborhoods and are widely excluded from the public and the political arena. They are conscious of the oppression or discrimination they are exposed to as Alevis and Kurds, but their dominant ethnic identity changes in the course of time and varies according to the conditions of their neighborhood. Their critical attitude towards the governing parties is rarely transformed into collective action or support for the Kurdish movement. However, in view of the Turkish-Kurdish conflict and the aggravation of the situation by forced migration it can be expected that ethnic tensions will intensify in the Western metropolises. Migration does not solve the "Kurdish problem," but diversifies it. (A)

861 Yalcin-Heckmann, Lale. "Gender Roles and Female Strategies among the Nomadic and Semi-Nomadic Kurdish Tribes of Turkey." In *Women in Modern Turkish Society: A Reader*. Edited by Sirin Tekeli, pp. 219-231. London: Zed Books, 1995.

Recent feminist debates on the specific nature and particularities of patriarchy have led social-scientific inquiries to focus on the power of women in different social systems; where this female power stems from and how it articulates itself. In this article the author does not deal with the definition(s) of patriarchy, nor with concepts such as oppression or male hegemony. Her concern here is to present an example from the Kurdish tribal women, and hence contribute to the discussion on the power of women in a specific historical and socio-cultural setting. She states that the social status of the women we are concerned with here is marked by two factors: the tribal setting and the semi-nomadic or nomadic mode of production. By tribe and tribal structures the author is not referring to an evolutionist framework of society: the term tribe is not to be understood as a primitive form of social organization, nor the tribal system as a historical survivor of some earlier political system. The author uses the term tribe here in the sense that has been defined and used within the anthropology of the Middle East. In this sense, a tribe consists of people who believe themselves to be kin to one another, who hold collective rights and duties with one another, and who share a moral code of tribal honor, righteousness and solidarity. In the Middle East almost all tribes share an ideology of patrilineal descent which influences inheritance and property relations, residence after marriage, extended families and household structure. For instance, as studies of tribes in Turkey by previous studies show, women are denied the right to inherit land on the grounds of 'tribal custom'. Immovable property like fields, houses and gardens, as well as movable property such as animals, are usually not inherited by women. Their rights, and the possibilities of controlling and managing these means of production, are limited indeed. When tribal rules and traditions are combined with semi-nomadic or nomadic modes of life, the exclusion of women from property rights seems to become stricter and more widespread. (A)

862 Yusuf, Muhammad Khayr Ramadan. *al-Mar'a al-Kurdiyah fi al-Tarikh al- Islami: Tarajim li-Amirat Kurdiyat wa-Muhaddithat 'Alimat*. Beirut: Dar al-Qadiri, 1992. 89 p. Includes bibliographical references (p. 84- 87).

863 Zana, Leyla. *Writings from Prison*. Watertown, MA: Blue Crane Books, 1999. xxvii, 114 p.: map. [Human rights & democracy] Texts translated from Kurdish and Turkish by Kendal Nezan and from French by Harriet Lutzky. Includes bibliographical references (p. 112-114).

See also items: 4, 9, 17, 22, 23, 24, 26, 32, 46, 48, 154, 224, 358, 517, 518, 621, 717, 747, 801, 829, 831, 834, 841, and the chapter on Sociology.

22

Miscellaneous

Note: Items listed in this chapter are primarily history and politics literature. They are included in this book because of their quality and/or unique contributions to several aspects of Kurdish culture and society, including but not limited to: anthropology, biography, communication, culture, demography, economy, education, ethnicity, folklore, health conditions, language, literature, religion, and social life and customs.

864   Ahmad, Kamal Madhar. *Kurdistan During the First World War*. Translated from Arabic by Ali Maher Ibrahim. Foreword by Akram Jaff. London: Saqi Books, 1994. 234 p.: map. Translated from Kurdish by Muhammad Mulla Karim. Baghdad: Kurdish Academy Press, 1977. Includes bibliography and index.

865   Ali, Othman. *British Policy and the Kurdish Question in 'Iraq, 1918-1932*. Ph.D., University of Toronto, 1993. 529 p.

After World War I, in common with other minorities in the former Ottoman Empire, the Kurds wished to form their own nation-state, a sentiment which Britain did much to encourage. Yet, Britain also manipulated Kurdish separatist tendencies in ways calculated to strengthen her hold over Iraq as a viable and united country and hence did much to prevent the formation of a Kurdish state. This dissertation will investigate why Great Britain pursued this seemingly contradictory policy. It will examine this many-faceted question in the light of newly available archival sources. The thesis is primarily concerned with the local and regional factors which shaped Britain's policy in Kurdistan. From 1918 to 1923, Britain's Kurdish policy was indecisive, inarticulate and provisional. This was due mainly to rapid developments in the Kurdish regions of Iraq, Turkey and Iran. The lack of a peace treaty between Turkey and Britain as a mandatory power in Iraq, also contributed to the uncertainty in Britain's policy in Iraqi Kurdistan. With the signing of the Treaty of Lausanne in 1923 Britain's policy in Kurdistan began to develop. This policy aimed at reconciling Kurdish national aspirations with Britain's desire to strengthen Iran, Iraq and Turkey in order to prevent Bolshevik Russia's southward advance to the Gulf. (A)

866   'Ani, Khalid 'Abd al-Mun'im al-. *The Encyclopedia of Modern Iraq*. Baghdad: Arab Encyclopedia Publishing House, 1977. 3 vols.: ill. English and Arabic. Added t.-p.: *Mausu'at al-'Iraq al-Hadith*.

867   Arfa, Hassan. *The Kurds: A Historical and Political Study*. London: Oxford University Press, 1966. xi, 178 p., [8] p. of plates. Bibliography: p. 161-163.

Most of the books about the Middle East were written by people who come from outside that region. It was refreshing, therefore, to find a first-rate, scholarly and yet readable book about the Kurds written by a Persian who, as a general of the Iranian army and Chief of Staff from 1944 to 1956, conducted many of the military operations against the Kurds. The whole book, in its exposition of the history of this people, their ethnic and cultural identity and their will to national expression, constitutes a glowing declaration of the reality and validity of Kurdish nationalism. The book is divided into five chapters, the first a short history, the second, third and fourth an account of the Kurds in Turkey (focusing on the revolt of Sheikh Sa'id, Ihsan Nuri Pasha and the Jelali, Sayid Reza Dersimi, and the Turkish government's policy towards the Kurds), Iran (focusing on Simko's revolt, the revolt in Kordestan province, Hama Rashid's revolt, and Mahabad Republic), and Iraq (focusing on Sheikh Mahmud Barzinji, Sheikh Ahmad Barzani, and Mulla Mustafa Barzani). The fifth chapter and weakest is a conclusion. Here and there an authority might argue about factual details, but General Arfa's integrity as a military man is a powerful argument in support of his version of the facts, often drawn from personal experience or information available to members of his family. Much new information never collected in a book is contained in these chapters, particularly regarding military operations. On political matters he is weaker. He obviously found difficulty in reconciling the fact that Mulla Mustafa Barzani, the leader of the Kurdish national movement in Iraq, is a conservative if not reactionary personality, with the mixture of support he received from western liberals, leftists and eastern European communists. (Dana Adams Schmidt/*Asian Affairs* 54, February 1967: 78-79)

868   Aristova, T. F. "The Kurds in Persia." *Central Asian Review* 7, no. 2 (1959): 175-201.

The present article consists of selections from Soviet material on the Kurds which has appeared during 1957-1958. Attention has been concentrated on those passages that contain material not apparently easily available elsewhere. Such passages have been translated in full. This has meant more attention to specific information about Kurdish tribes, recent political history, and modern Kurdish writing.

869   'Azzawi, 'Abbas al-. *'Asha'ir al-'Iraq*. 4 vols. [Volume 2: Kurdish Tribes.] Baghdad: Matba'at al-Ma'arif, 1947. 272 p. Includes bibliographical references.

870   Barkey, Henri J.; Fuller, Graham E. *Turkey's Kurdish Question*. Lanham, MD: Rowman & Littlefield Publishers, 1998. xix, 239 p. Includes bibliographical references and index.

871   Basri, Mir. *A'lam al-Kurd*. [Biographies of famous Kurdish persons] London: Riad al-Rayyis lil-Kutub wa-al-Nashr, 1991. 311 p. Includes bibliographical references and indexes.

872   Batatu, Hanna. *The Old Social Classes and the Revolutionary Movements of Iraq: A Study of Iraq's Old Landed and Commercial Classes and of Its Communists, Ba'thists, and Free Officers*. Princeton, N.J.: Princeton University Press, 1978.

This is the most important study of the social structure of Iraq as inherited from the days of Ottoman rule to the rise of political parties (especially the Communist Party) and movements and their impact on domestic politics. This work is divided into three books: Book one, The Old Social Classes, contains two sections: *Introduction* and *The main classes and status groups*. Book two, The Communists from the Beginnings of Their Movement to the Fifties, contains: *Beginnings in the Arab East*; *Beginnings in Iraq*; *Causes*; *Fahd and the Party (1941-1949)*; *The Party in the years 1949-1955, or the period of the ascendancy of the Kurds in the Party*. Book three contains: *The Communists, the Ba'thists, and the Free Officers from the Fifties to the Pressent*. The Appendixes give documents, supplementary information about early Bolshevik activities, and tables of families and tribes.

873   Blau, Joyce. "Vie et oeuvre de Thomas Bois: 1900-1975." *The Journal of Kurdish Studies* 1 (1995): 85-96.

874   Blaum, Paul. "A History of the Kurdish Marwanid Dynasty. Part I & II."*International Journal of Kurdish Studies* 5 (Spring-Fall 1992): 54-68; 6 (Fall 1993): 40-65.

875   Bozarslan, Hamit. *La question kurde: Etats et minoritbes au Moyen-Orient*. Paris: Presses de sciences politiques, 1997. 383 p.: maps. Based

chiefly on the author's thesis (Institut d'etudes politiques de Paris, 1994).
Includes bibliographical references (p. [373]-376) and index.

876   Bruinessen, Martin van. "The Ottoman Conquest of Diyarbekir and the
Administrative Organisation of the Province in the 16th and 17th
Centuries." In *Evliya Celebi in Diyarbekir: The Relevant Section of the
Seyahatname*. Edited by Martin van Bruinessen and H. E. Boeschoten,
pp. 13-28. Leiden: E. J. Brill, 1988.

Discusses the role of the great Kurdish statesman and scholar Mulla Idris
Bitlisi in the incorporation of Diyarbekir into the Ottoman Empire, the
administrative division of Diyarbekir and the privileges of the Kurdish
rulers, the autonomous sanjaqs in the 17th century, and the position of the
nomadic tribes in the administrative system.

877   Bruinessen, Martin van. "Genocide in Kurdistan?: The Suppression of the
Dersim Rebellion in Turkey (1937-1938) and the Chemical War Against
the Iraqi Kurds (1988)." In *Genocide: Conceptual and Historical Dimensions*. Edited by George J. Andreopoulos, pp. 141-170. Philadelphia,
PA.: University of Pennsylvania Press, 1994.

In this paper, van Bruinessen discusses two earlier massacres in Kurdistan
that have by some been called genocide. Both took place in the course of
the suppression of Kurdish rebellions, the first in Turkey, in 1937-1938,
the other in 1988 in Iraq, where Saddam Hussein bombed his disobedient
Kurdish subjects with chemical warheads. Both massacres are borderline
cases; while there are those who argue that they constitute genocide by
the terms of the 1948 Convention, others (including, hesitantly, the author) are reluctant to use that term. Van Bruinessen argues that it will be
hard, on the one hand, to prove that in these two cases the state intended
to destroy, in whole or in part, [the Kurds] as such. On the other hand,
these were not simply punitive actions carried out against armed insur-
gents. In fact, these massacres were only the tip of the iceberg and have to
be understood within the context of the two regimes' overall policies toward the Kurds. These policies amount to variant forms of *ethnocide*—in
the case of Turkey, deliberate destruction of Kurdish ethnic identity by
forced assimilation, and in Iraq destruction of Kurdish social structure
and its socioeconomic base. Both regimes presented these policies as fundamentally benevolent forms of engineered modernization, in the Turkish
case even as a civilizing mission.

878   Bruinessen, Martin van. "Genocide of the Kurds." In *The Widening Circle of Genocide*. Edited by Israel W. Charny; with a foreword by Irving
Louis Horowitz, pp. 165-191. New Brunswick, NJ: Transaction Publishers, 1994. (Genocide; 3)

In this paper, van Bruinessen has assembled an important chapter about past and recent massacres and genocide of the Kurdish people in what appears to be a pattern of unending persecution and destruction through most of the twentieth century that continues to this very day. The Kurds have the distinction also of being the subjects of genocide by several governments, including the Turks, Iraqis, Iranians and Soviets. This work is a long-needed introduction for Western scholars to a case history of persecution of a substantial people, who number about 30 million strong in this world today, and whose outcome has not even yet been determined.

879   Chaliand, Gerard. *The Kurdish Tragedy*. Translated from the French by Philip Black. London: Zed Books in association with UNRISD, 1994. viii, 120 p.: maps. Translation of *Le malheur kurde*. Includes bibliographical references and index. Paris: Editions du Seuil, 1992).

An internationally acknowledged authority on guerrilla wars and resistance movements, Chaliand, a French-Armenian scholar, was commissioned by the United Nations to report on the situation of the Kurds following the Gulf War. Chaliand's book serves as an excellent introduction to the Kurdish issue. It provides a history of the Kurdish communities from their foundation, covering their eventual incorporation into the Ottoman Empire during the 15th century, the great Kurdish revolts of the 19th century, and the crucial period following the First World War. Chaliand, then, documents the precarious situation of the Kurds in recent times, culminating in the tragic exodus of Kurdish refugees fleeing from Saddam Hussein's brutal repression to a dubious welcome in Turkey. He also deals with the situation in the UN-protected 'safe havens,' where the Kurds have achieved a degree of autonomy in the teeth of the opposition of all the surrounding regimes. The political situation of the Kurds in contemporary Iran, Iraq, Syria, and Turkey is analyzed and the position of the multifarious Kurdish political groups, the legislation affecting Kurdish life, and the role of the Kurds in recent Middle Eastern confrontations are examined. Chaliand's portrayal of the Kurdish political parties and their often conflicting aspirations offers insights that even the specialist reader will find of great relevance. There are also appendices containing UN Security Council Resolution 688 which "condemns the repression of the Iraqi civilian population in many parts of Iraq, including most recently in Kurdish populated areas," the resolution adopted by the European Parliament which "strongly condemns the attempted genocide against the Kurds by Saddam Hussein's regime," a list of "villages bombarded with chemical weapons by the Iraqi air force," and a historical chronology which largely covers events in the twentieth century.

880   Cohen, Aharon. "Emir Dr. Kamuran Ali Bedir-Khan: An Outstanding Kurdish Intellectual." *New Outlook* 22 (May-June 1979): 29-32.

881   Diakonoff, I. M. "Elam." In *The Cambridge History of Iran, Vol. 2: The Median and Achaemenian Periods*. Edited by Ilya Gershevitch, pp. 1-24. Cambridge, England: Cambridge University Press, 1985.

Elam is the biblical name for the region that was later called Khuzestan, and is the land in which a level of urban civilization emerged before any other region of present-day Iran. The author covers the history of Elam from the earliest times to the 6th century BC, as well as its cultural, geographical and archaeological significance.

882   Diakonoff, I. M. "Media." In *The Cambridge History of Iran, Vol. 2: The Median and Achaemenian Periods*. Edited by Ilya Gershevitch, pp. 36-148. Cambridge, England: Cambridge University Press, 1985.

The subject of the author's study is Media where the Kurds and other Aryan tribes established their largest empire in the 6th century BC. This paper deals with that region's population structure, and dating as far back as the end of the 23rd century BC. The main topics of discussion in this paper are: Iranian-speaking tribes; the emergence of urbanization at the end of the 9th century BC; the neighboring countries and their advances into Median territory; the rise of the Median kingdom in ca. 673-672 BC, and its campaigns; the society, culture and religion of Media; and, finally, the fall of the Median empire to the Persians in the 6th century.

883   Dziegiel, Leszek. "Kurdistan as a Subject of Research." In *In Search of Paradigm*. Edited by Anna Zambrzycka-Kunachowicz; translated from Polish by Krzysztof Kwasniewicz, pp. 235-253. Cracow: Wydawnictwo Platan, 1992.

Portrays the history, development, and future of research on the Kurds.

884   Eagleton, William. *The Kurdish Republic of 1946*. London: Oxford University Press, 1963. 142 p.: ill. Issued under the auspices of the Royal Institute of International Affairs.

Available in Arabic, French, and Turkish, this book is an account of the Kurdish Republic based primarily on interviews and field observations. It is the only full-length work dealing with the ephemeral Kurdish Republic of Mahabad in Iranian Kurdistan. The author, a U.S. foreign officer and later ambassador in Syria, reports on the rise and fall of the Republic, pointing out the role of the Soviet Union and relating the episode to the larger problem of Kurdish nationalism.

885   Farouk-Sluglett, Marion; Sluglett, Peter. *Iraq Since 1958: From Revolution to Dictatorship*. London; New York: KPI, 1987. xvii, 332 p. Bibliography: p. [269]-323.

The history politics of Iraq and the context which had given rise to Saddam Hussein's violent Ba'thist regime were barely understood. This highly praised book is the first to explore the emergence of modern Iraq from its foundation in 1920 to the August 1990 invasion of Kuwait. It covers the period from the revolution in 1958, concentrating particularly on Saddam Hussein's rise to power and his consolidation as leader. It is the only political history of modern Iraq now available to provide a critical analysis of the Ba'thist regime which has ruled since 1968. The authors also explore the role and decline of the Iraqi Communist Party, the shifting policies towards the Kurds and Shi'is, the nationalization of oil and Iraq's relations within its neighbors. The authors also provide a stimulating analysis of the economy over the last three decades. Concerning the Kurds, the authors treat them largely in this book; they focus on the gains that the Kurds had achieved under Qassim's rule (1958-1961) and lost under the Arab nationalist and Ba'thist regimes. (Joyce Blau/*AI* 13:234)

886   Gache, Paul. "Les Kurdes." [The Kurds] *Revue de psychologie des peuples* 17, no. 1 (1962): 23-54; no. 2 (1962): 191-220.

887   Ghareeb, Edmund. *The Kurdish Question in Iraq*. Syracuse, NY: Syracuse University Press, 1981. x, 223 p.: map. (Contemporary Issues in the Middle East). Includes bibliographical references and index.

In this book, originally the author's doctoral dissertation (Georgetown University, 1979), Ghareeb examines the history of the Kurdish issue in Iran and Turkey and then concentrates on Iraq, chronicling the Iraqi Ba'th government's attempts since 1968 to achieve a political understanding with the Kurds concerning their status in Northern Iraq. The failure of both sides to reach agreement contributed to widespread Kurdish armed rebellion that was encouraged by covert Iranian, American, and Israeli assistance. Drawing upon extensive personal interviews with pro-and anti-Ba'th Kurdish leaders, including Mulla Mustafa Barzani and members of his family, Iraqi government and Ba'th party officials, and U.S. government officials, Ghareeb discusses in detail the positions of the Ba'th and Kurdish leaders and the factors which led to the failure of negotiations between them and, ultimately, to the collapse of the Kurdish rebellion itself.

888   Ghassemlou, Abdul Rahman. "Kurdistan in Iran." In *A People Without a Country: The Kurds and Kurdistan*. Edited by Gerard Chaliand; translated from French by Michael Pallis; foreword by David McDowall, pp. 95-121. London: Zed Books Ltd., 1993.

Includes a discussion on the geography, demography, religion, language and literature, education, health, economic conditions, the tribe and its development, and social structure of the Kurds and Kurdistan in Iran.

Also included is a discussion on cultural oppression and changes in the Kurdish society through 1980.

889 Hajjaj, al-Sa'id Rizq. *al-Akrad wa-al-Arman fi al-'Asr al-Hamidi*. Cairo: Matba'at al-Amanah, 1991. 148 p. Includes bibliographical references (p. 141- 145).

Provides a general background of the Kurds and their relations with the Armenians during Sultan Hamid II rule. The author blames the Armenians themselves for most of the deaths inflicted on them by the Ottomans with the help of the Kurds. The author also blames the Armenians for damaging the chances of creating a Kurdish state in the disintegrated empire. Particular emphasis is paid on Armenian massacres and violence against the Kurds and Turks.

890 Howell, Wilson Nathaniel, Jr. *The Soviet Union and the Kurds: A Study of National Minority Problems in Soviet Policy*. Ph.D., University of Virginia, 1965. 689 p.

This study attempts for the first time to describe systematically and analyze critically the attitude and policies of the Soviet Union toward the Kurds. Such an attempt involves analysis of the underpinning of the Kurdish problem as it concerns principally three Middle Eastern states (Iran, Iraq and Turkey), the interests of the West in the area, and the evolution of the Soviet policy toward the Kurdish minority problem both within and outside the Soviet Union. The fundamental thesis or this study is that the Soviet Union strives to manipulate the Kurdish problem which is primarily influenced by indigenous geographic, ethnic and historical-political factors and forces. The approach to this study is essentially interdisciplinary, utilizing historical and sociological as well as political data. The study draws upon primary as well as secondary sources, mainly in English, French and Russian, and involves documentary research, personal correspondence and interviews. The study is divided into two parts. Part one, containing three chapters seeks to discuss the Kurdish problem by dealing with the geographic concept of "Kurdistan," the Kurdish demography and social organization, and nationalism. Part two, divided into four chapters, attempts to analyze policy statements and actions of the Soviet Union aimed at exploiting the Kurdish problem toward the achievement of its objectives in the Middle East, by identifying the mainsprings of the Soviet attitude, by analyzing the Soviet Kurdish diplomacy clandestine operations and propaganda, and by discussing the role of the communists in Soviet Kurdish strategy. A few of the basic findings of this study may be cited here. One, the Kurdish problem cannot be attributed to Soviet intrigues alone, although Moscow has frequently sought to exacerbate its effects. Two, the Kurdish problem offers clear opportunities for any great power including the Soviet Union, to seek to later the prevailing status quo in the Middle East, if doing so should accord with its interest.

Three, analysis of the Soviet Kurdish policy does not reveal the existence of a master pain for exploiting the Kurdish problem. In fact, Soviet policy-makers have often had difficulty in harnessing the discontent of in depended-minded Kurdish nationalists to Soviet objectives. Four, the Soviet government has sought to manipulate the Kurdish problem against Middle Eastern states and the West since the late 1920s. Five, the attempt to maximize Soviet interests in the Middle East has been increasingly apparent since 1945, particularly as evidenced by Soviet policy toward the Kurdish revolution in Iraq since 1961. (A)

891   Imset, Ismet G. *The PKK: A Report on Separatist Violence in Turkey (1973-1992)*. Ankara: Turkish Daily News, 1992. iv, 450 p. (Turkish Daily News Publications; 1). Includes bibliographical references.

Ismet G. Imset, a Turkish journalist, is one of the most knowledgeable writers on the PKK. Despite its massive size, the present work is basically a compilation of many of Imset's earlier reports and articles, printed in the Ankara's English-language weekly *Briefing* and *The Turkish Daily News* since 1988. Even though by necessity he has relied heavily on Turkish intelligence sources for much of his information, the work is one of the best treatments of PKK in print. Although reflecting the views of the Turkish side of the issue, the author tries to be fair in treating the Kurdish side as well. It is thus a required reading for anyone who wants to begin understanding the Kurdish situation in Turkey in general, and PKK's early activities in particular. Imset's analysis begins with a chronological history of the PKK's early years from 1973 to the formal establishment of the party on November 27, 1978 under Abdullah Ocalan and the Turkish military coup on September 12,1980. These first chapters also contain a great deal of detailed data on the early years from 1973 to 1986, such as the initial camps and alliances, as well as the party structure and activities. Imset also analyzes the "village guards" system of local pro-government militia created by the government beginning in 1985 and argues that it was a successor to the Hamidiya regiments of the 1890s. One of Imset's most valuable discussions is his structural analysis of the PKK. Additional chapters analyze Ocalan's "guerrilla's handbook," PKK financing, internal PKK divisions and executions, foreign and domestic PKK relations, and recent events in the 1990s, including the return to power of Suleiman Demirel. Imset notes that PKK finances consist of voluntary donations, taxation, protection money, small and medium business investments, robberies, and narcotics. Seven appendices then conclude the lengthy analysis.

892   Izady, Mehrdad (ed.). *The Republic of Kurdistan: Fifty Years Later*. Published as a special issue of *The International Journal of Kurdish Studies* 11, nos. 1-2 (1997): 1-240.

Commemorating the 50th anniversary of the declaration of the Republic of Kurdistan at Mahabad, this issue included contributions from: Ali Homam Ghazi (the son of President Ghazi Muhammad), Ibrahim Ahmed (a senior Kurdish politician), the late General Mullah Mustafa Barzani (a translation of speech delivered in Baku on January 19, 1948), Massoud Barzani (the General Secretary of the KDP in Iraq), Helene Ghassemlou (the wife of the late Dr. Abdul Rahman Ghassemlou), Abdullah Hassanzadeh (the First Secretary of the KDP in Iran), Mahmud Osman, William Eagleton (a former member of the US Foreign Service in the Middle East, Olga Jigalina, and Mikhail S. Lazarev. Borhanedin Yassin's paper (pp. 115-240), titled "A History of the Republic of Kurdistan" is originally part of his doctoral dissertation.

893 Jwaideh, Wadie. *The Kurdish Nationalist Movement: Its Origins and Development*. Ph.D., Syracuse University, 1960. 924 p.

The aim of this study is to give an account to the origins and development of the Kurdish nationalist movement from the early part of the nineteenth century to the present. Two chapters are devoted to the geography, history, religion, literature and social organization of the Kurds, and are designed to provide the necessary background against which the study is presented. The study proper begins with an account of the suppression of the semi-autonomous Kurdish principalities as part of a comprehensive scheme for the reorganization of the Ottoman Empire. This is followed by a chapter on Sheikh Ubaydallah, the precursor and model of a new type of Kurdish national leader. His ideas and political activities are dealt with at some length. An account of his rebellion in Turkey and his invasion of Persia is given in detail. The Young Turk Revolution and Kurdish-Turkish relations form the subject of the following chapter. In the following chapter, the Kurdish policy of Russia, Turkey's historical antagonist, is examined. The fortunes of the Kurds during the First World War are then described. The Postwar period is treated in four chapters. The first of these deals with the situation in Turkey, Persia, and Syria, while the next three are devoted to the complex situation in Iraqi Kurdistan. The growth of Kurdish nationalist activities is examined at length in all four chapters, and the causes of Kurdish rebellions against the new British rulers in Iraq are discussed in detail. Next the Kurdish rebellion of Sheikh Sa'id of Piran, of Agri Dagh and of Dersim in Turkey are dealt with, and the revolutionary activities of *Khoyboun*, the Kurdish nationalist organization, are reviewed. The Barzani rebellions of 1931-1932 and 1943-1945 are discussed in two separate chapters. The new leftist tendencies of Kurdish nationalists which came to light during the later rebellion are analyzed. The rise and fall of the Kurdish Republic of Mahabad is the subject of another chapter. Two significant developments, the increasing importance of leftist elements in Kurdish nationalism and the open support given by the Soviet Union to the Mahabad regime are covered. The final chapter deals with the new extremist tendencies in Kurdish nationalism, Soviet support, the attitude of the Kurds toward the governments of the countries which they inhabit and toward the Western powers allied with these governments. It also deals with the ceaseless efforts of the Kurds to gain the support of world opinion and to induce the United Nations to intervene in their favor. (A)

894 Marouf Khaznadar. *Tarikh al-Istishraq wa-al-Dirasat al-'Arabiyah wa-al-Kurdiyah fi al-Mathaf al-Asiawi wa-Ma'had al-Dirasat al-Sharqiyah fi Liningrad, 1818-1968*. [History of Orientalism and Arab and Kurdish studies in the Asiatic Museum and the Institute of Oriental Studies in Leningrad, 1818-1968] Baghdad: Jami'at Baghdad, 1980. 384 p. Includes bibliographical references and indexes.

895 Kinnane, Derk. *The Kurds and Kurdistan*. London: Oxford University Press, 1964. 85 p.: map. Issued under the auspices of the Institute of Race Relations). Includes bibliographical references.

Kinnane first became interested in the Kurds and the Kurdish question while in Iraq as a lecturer at Baghdad University. He tells that his direct experience of Kurdistan is small. But, using his sources with care and discrimination, he has written a workmanlike "introduction to a nation which, despite its distinct culture and millions of people, has yet to achieve a durable government of its own." The scene is set by chapters, all of course drastically condensed, on the "Country and People," "Society," and "History" (from the earliest times to the Treaty of Lausanne in 1923). These are followed by short accounts of conditions under the "Turkish Republic," in "Iraq between the Wars," and in "Persia," and by brief references to the small minorities in Syria and the Caucasian Republics. In the last and longest chapter, "The Present War in Iraq," the author traces the causes of the outbreak and the ups and downs of the fighting from the first clashes in July 1961 to the cease-fire announced by President Arif and Mulla Mustafa Barzani on February 10, 1964. (abridged, C. J. Edmonds/*Asian Affairs* 52, January 1965: 64)

896 Kissinger, Henry. *Years of Renewal*. New York: Simon & Schuster, 1999. 1151 p.: ill., maps. Includes bibliographical references (p. 1081-1120) and index.

In this second draft of history, Kissinger details the 1974 to 1977 years of his service under Gerlad Ford's Administration. The book works on two levels. One is a detailed account on specific foreign policies, including but not limited to the Kurdish question (Chapter title: "Tragedy of the Kurds."). The other is Kissinger's reflections on the larger meaning and historical contexts of the policies.

897 Korn, David A. "The Last Years of Mustafa Barzani." *Middle East Quarterly* 1 (March 1994): 12-27.

898   Kutschera, Chris. "A Voice from Behind the Bars." *The Middle East*
[London], no. 256 (May 1996): 40-41.

Mehdi Zana believes that his more than 15 years in prison has made a
writer out of him. By the mid-1990s, he had published five books. His
most lengthy account is on his 1980 imprisonment, a story of a descent
into hell on earth. He describes the prison conditions and the tortures that
he and his fellow inmates had been subjected to, from the totalitarian
state's de rigueur electric shock to the genitals to the seldom-practiced
immersion in shit. Leyla, his wife, who is as politicized as he, is now in
prison.

899   Kutschera, Chris. *Le défi kurde, ou, Le rêve fou de l'indépendance*.
Paris: Bayard éditions, 1997. 352 p., [12] p. of plates: ill. Includes bibliographical references (p. [349]-350).

With the majority of the Kurdish population divided among four principal
countries, the modern history of the Kurds seems to be an endless saga of
cross-border betrayals by their own kinsmen and allies, manipulations by
powerful states, and above all of hardship, death and destruction. The
veteran French journalist Chris Kutschera's new book covers the contemporary story of all these betrayals, manipulations and rebellions, as well
as the tragic mistakes made by real and purported leaders of the Kurds.
This is a highly readable account of events starting with the debacle of the
Kurdish insurrection in Iraq following the 1975 Algiers Accord between
the shah of Iran, Muhammad Reza Pahlavi, and the then Iraqi strongman,
Saddam Husayn. The book, which is divided into three sections that discuss the Kurdish experience in Iran, Iraq and Turkey, sets out to give a
vivid description of the events that have made their mark on contemporary Kurdish history: the 1979 Iranian Revolution and the ensuing ill-
fated revolt in Iranian Kurdistan, the Iran-Iraq War (1980-88), the 1991
creation of the autonomous region in northern Iraq and its near demise in
September 1996, the 1988 gassing of Halabja, and the rise of the many
Kurdish groups, including the Kurdistan Workers' Party (PKK), in Turkey. Of the three accounts, the Iraqi one is the strongest and most rivet-
ing. It reflects the author's rich knowledge of the events, terrain and personalities involved. (Henri J. Barkey/*MEJ*, 52, 1998: 130-131)

900   Laizer, Sheri. *Martyrs, Traitors, and Patriots: Kurdistan After the Gulf
War*. Atlantic Highlands, NJ: Zed Books, 1996. xiii, 224 p.: maps. Includes bibliographical references (p. [215]-217) and index.

What has happened to the Kurds since their great uprising against Saddam and the tragic exodus to the safe havens? What factors condition the
course of the continuing guerrilla war in Kurdistan? What policies have
Turkey, Iraq and Iran pursued to deal with the Kurdish people, the largest
ethnic group devoid of nationhood in the world? Can the Kurds establish

their own distinct political identity, on a par with their cultural distinct-
iveness, or are they condemned to endless internecine conflict and tribal
rivalries? These questions are answered in depth in this book. Informed
by frequent visits to the frontline areas, Laizer provides the reader with a
clear analysis of Kurdish *realpolitik*, focusing on the political practices of
the PKK and the other major Kurdish groups. The issues facing the Turkish parliament and army, the long term strategies pursued by Iran and
Iraq, and the evolution of Kurdish democratic institutions is brought to
the fore. Chapters include: the Kurdish uprising—March 1991; Kurdish
realpolitik and the failed uprising; summer of the safe haven, 1991; wait-
ing in the cold—winter 1991-1992; the fraternal war—autumn 1992; the
dirty war in Turkey—21 March 1993; death by a thousand cuts; the war
of the colours—1994-5; Turkey: only a military solution, 1994-1995; and
Kurdish women: identity and purpose.

901 Major, Marc R. "No Friends but the Mountains: A Simulation on Kurdistan." *Social Education* 60, no. 3 (March 1996): C1-8.

Presents a simulation that focuses on Kurdish nationalism and the struggle for autonomy and independence from the states that rule over Kurdish
lands. Students assume the roles of either one of the countries directly involved or the governing body of the United Nations. Includes extensive
background material.

902 Mardukh, Abdollah [Abd-allah]. *Contribution a l'etude de l'histoire des
Kurdes sous la dynastie Ardalan du XVIeme siecle au XIXeme siecle*.
[A Contribution to the Study of Kurdish History Under the Ardalan Dy-
nasty from the 16th to the 19th Century.] Ph.D., Universite de Paris III-
Sorbonne-Nouvelle, 1988. 434 p.

The author studies the history of Ardalan dynasty since its foundation in
the 12th century until its collapse during the second half of the 19th century. The principality of Ardalan is considered one of the most ancient
and most prestigious Kurdish principalities, and was the most important
one in the Persian empire. The author has consulted all the available
sources on the subject. He has made access to manuscripts of great value
that he uses very skillfully. (Joyce Blau/*AI* 12:545)

903 Mardukh, Abd-allah. "Aux sources de l'historiographie kurde." *Studia
Iranica* 21, no. 1 (1992): 103-118.

904 McDowall, David. *The Kurds*. 7th ed. London: Minority Rights Group,
1996. 44 p. Includes bibliographical references (p. 43).

This revised and updated seventh edition was published in December
1996. Sections include: Introduction: the land of the Kurds; Kurdish society (demography, health, language, religion, sufisim); Historical back-

ground to 1920; The Kurds in Turkey; The Kurds in Iran; The Kurds in Iraq; Road to genocide, 1976-88; Uprising and self-rule 1990-6; Iraqi Kurdistan: an international cockpit; The challenge of relief and rehabilitation; The Kurds in Syria and elsewhere (USSR, Lebanon, and Europe); Recommendations.

905 McDowall, David. *A Modern History of the Kurds*. London: I. B. Tauris, 1996. 451 p.

In this book, the first comprehensive history of the Kurds from the nineteenth century to the present day, McDowall examines the interplay of old and new aspects of the struggle, the importance of local rivalries within Kurdish society, the enduring authority of certain forms of leadership and the failure of modern states to respond to the challenge of Kurdish nationalism. In his informative introduction on Kurdish identity and social formation, McDowall describes the internal linguistic, political, religious and tribal divisions that have contributed to a lack of Kurdish cohesion in past and recent times. He divides the remainder of his work into five sections. Section one covers Kurdish history from the seventh century to 1918, focusing on Ottoman Kurdistan and Iranian Kurdistan under Qajar rule. Section two discusses the political incorporation of various parts of Kurdistan into the post World War I emerging states of Turkey, Iraq and Iran. Section three focuses on Kurdish nationalism in Iran, with a chapter devoted to the short-lived Mahabad Republic. Sections four and five deal with Kurdish ethnonationalism in Iraq and Turkey. The last chapter discusses the Kurdish Workers Party (PKK) and its impact on Kurdish identity in Turkey. McDowall blames the continuing influence of tribally organized traditional society for many of the problems the Kurds have faced in building a real national movement. Certainly the Kurds' own internal divisions have been much exploited by their enemies, and McDowall's own historical narrative displays the consequences vividly.

906 Minorsky, Vladimir F. *Studies in Caucasian History: I. New Light on the Shaddadis of Ganja; II. The Shaddadis of Ani; III. Prehistory of Saladin*. London: Taylor's Foreign Press, 1953. 178 p. (Cambridge Oriental Series, no. 6). The Arabic text of the chapter on the Shaddadis is from *Munnajjim-Bashi's Duwal al-Islam*. 18 p.

The master of mediaeval Persian history provides a fascinating monograph on a little known period of Trans-Caucasian history; that is, the dynasty of the Shaddadis who ruled in the towns of Ganja and Ani during the eleventh and twelfth centuries. The core of the work, chapter two, is the Arabic text and translation of the chapter on the Shaddadids from the book *Jami' al-duwal*. The third and final chapter is concerned with the family from which came Saladin; for Saladin, like the Shaddadids, was a Kurd with family origins in Trans-Caucasia. The mass of details concerning the various Georgian, Armenian, Greek, and Muslim (Arab, Kurd, Persian, and Turkish) princes or commanders who march across the pages is at times confusing, but Minorsky has done a great service in putting order into the confusion. Minorsky's study also throws light on the Turkish conquest of Anatolia and on the Ayyubid dynasty, the most famous member of which was Saladin. (Richard N. Frye: 301-303)

907   Minorsky, Vladimir. "Kurds and Kurdistan: Origins and Pre-Islamic History Up to 1920." In *Encyclopedia of Islam*. New ed. Vol. V, 447-464. Leiden: E. J. Brill, 1986.

Discusses the origins of the Kurds and their history from pre-Islamic times up to 1920. Provides detailed accounts of the major Kurdish tribes and leaders throughout that period of time.

908   More, Christiane. *Les Kurdes aujourd'hui: mouvement national et partis politiques*. [The Kurds Today: National Movement and Political Parties] Paris: L'Harmattan, c1984. 310 p.: maps. Bibliography: p. 292-293. Includes index.

This book is divided into three parts. In the first part, More outlines the history of the Kurdish question and of the Kurdish national movement, and gives a clear and ample general survey of the Kurdish people. In parts two and three, More studies, with as much precision as possible, the history of Kurdish political parties and organizations in each of the countries that divide Kurdistan, namely Turkey, Iran, Iraq, and Syria. In these parts, More explains the reasons behind the foundation of these parties in Kurdistan and their representation abroad, and defines their ideologies and their programs. (Joyce Blau/*AI* 8:374)

909   Muftuler-Bac, Meltem. "Addressing Kurdish Separatism in Turkey." In *Theory and Practice in Ethnic Conflict Management: Theorizing Success and Failure*, 103-119. Edited by Marc Howard Ross and Jay Rothman. Houndmills, Basingstoke, Hampshire: Macmillan Press, 1999. [Ethnic and Intercommunity Conflict Series]

Describes the conflict over Kurdish "separatism" in Turkey and offers an account of the mainstream Turkish Union of Chamber of Commerce's initiative to collect basic demographic and public opinion data on the Kurds as a strategy for both getting the issue of Kurdish needs and aspirations on the agenda and for reassuring the Turkish majority that the radical and sometimes violent PKK did not represent the views of most Kurds. The chapter first describes the background of the Kurdish "conflict" and then discusses the initiative's organization, goals, and underlying strategy. The major objectives were: (1) to highlight the distinction between the PKK and the Kurdish community as a whole; (2) to assess the extent, and ways in which, the Kurdish community desires to be apart

of the Turkish state, that is, independent Kurdish state, federation, autonomy, legal reforms; and (3) to generate a greater public awareness of the
Kurdish community's needs and interests. The author then considers the
question of what constituted success in the initiative and reflects on its
implication for the "Eastern Question."

910   Nezan, Kendal. "Kurdistan in Turkey." In *A People Without a Country:*
      The Kurds and Kurdistan. Edited by Gerard Chaliand; translated from
      French by Michael Pallis; foreword by David McDowall, pp. 38-94. Lon-
      don: Zed Books Ltd., 1993.

      Includes a discussion on the geography, demography, education, culture,
      religion, health, and economic and social structures of the Kurds and
      Kurdistan in Turkey. Also included is a discussion on cultural oppression
      and changes in the Kurdish society through 1980.

911   Nezan, Kendal. "The Kurds Under the Ottoman Empire." In *A People*
      Without a Country: The Kurds and Kurdistan. Edited by Gerard Cha-
      liand; translated from French by Michael Pallis; foreword by David
      McDowall, pp. 11-37. London: Zed Books Ltd., 1993.

      Includes information on various Kurdish tribes and leaders and their role
      in the Kurdish national movement. Also includes a discussion on the first
      Kurdish national organizations.

912   Perry, John R. *Karim Khan Zand: A History of Iran, 1747-1779*. Chi-
      cago: University of Chicago Press, 1979. [Publications of the Center for
      Middle Eastern Studies, No. 12] xi, 340 p.

      Karim Khan Zand, the founder of the Kurdish Zand dynasty and the *de
      facto* ruler of the greater part of Persia in the third quarter of the 18th cen-
      tury. Having no claim to the title of *shah*, he instead, assumed, that of
      wakil, "regent lieutenant," and placed on the vacant throne of Persia a Sa-
      favid boy of eight, whom he styled Ismail III. This book is divided into
      three parts. Part I of the book deals essentially with the 1747-1763 power
      struggles and high level bloodletting while Part II narrows to the years of
      1763-1779 of Karim Khan's "consolidation and expansion" of the Zan-
      dian state. Part III, refreshingly and humanely, touches on some of the
      major economic, social and diplomatic aspects of Zand rule. Finally, the
      reader is treated to an excellent discourse of historiographical insights in
      the appendix as well as to a lengthy and thorough bibliography.

913   Randal, Jonathan C. *After Such Knowledge, What Forgiveness?: My
      Encounters with Kurdistan*. New York: Farrar, Straus and Giroux, 1997.
      356 p.: maps. Includes bibliographical references (p. [343]-345) and in-
      dex.

An American reporter who has covered the Kurds for more than a decade, Randal has interviewed many Kurdish political leaders. He provides much historical information, however, Randal's best chapters are about U.S. involvement in Kurdistan. He shows in persuasive insider detail how Nixon, Kissinger and the Shah of Iran betrayed a Kurdish uprising against Saddam Hussein in 1975; how Bush, Baker and feckless diplomats both "suckered" the Kurds into rebellion after the Gulf War and waffled on aiding them; and how the Clinton Administration might have brokered a settlement in northern Iraq in 1996 instead of allowing a civil war and then airlifting thousands of friendly Kurds to Guam. Randal's chapter on Turkey records how the United States has in recent years skirted its own laws restricting arms sales to human rights abusers and made Turkey "the biggest single importer of American military hardware," much of it used against Kurds inside Turkey and in the so-called safe haven of northern Iraq. "After such knowledge," Randal refuses "forgiveness" to U.S. governments that have contributed to the Kurds' historical repression and present plight.

914 Rasooli, Jay M.; Allen, Cady H. *The Life Story of Dr. Sa'eed of Iran*. Pasadena, CA: William Carey Library, 1983. An Arabic translation was published in 1970 by Jam'iyat Dar Kalimat Allah (Beirut: Dar Kalimat Allah).

First published in 1957, this is a thrilling story of a Kurdish doctor: his acceptance as a mullah and teacher by his own people, his struggles in turning from Islam to Christianity, his banishment from his home on a winter night, his flight from his native city, the persecutions he faced as a Muslim apostate, his refusal of an offer from the Shah to become court physician so that he might minister to all classes of people, and his outstanding service both as Christian physician and evangelist to the people of Iran—princes and peasants, notables and nomads. All this adds up to a fabulous tale, more absorbing than fiction or a mystery, yet all of it is true.

915 Reid, James J. "Hakkari Clan and Society: Kurdistan, 1502-1656." *The Journal of Kurdish Studies* 2 (1996-1997): 13-30.

Provides a brief history of the Hakkari clan, peoples, and tribes of the Hakkari district, and ideals and conventions of the clan.

916 Roosevelt, Archie, Jr. *For Lust of Knowing: Memoirs of an Intelligence Officer*. 1st ed. Boston: Little, Brown, 1988. xiv, 500 p., [16] p. of plates: ill. Includes index.

The period of World War II and its immediate aftermath was a time of discovery for many Americans of the world of Islam, of the intractable problems of the Middle East, and of the resistance of the colonial powers to the idealistic American drive for colonial independence. Archie Roosevelt's book tells the first-hand story of one man's discovery of these realities. The book is the story of political discovery, a memoir by a member of a prominent American family, succinct summaries of history, and a sophisticated travelogue. Through it run the threads of a personal romance and of the experiences of an intelligence officer. In writing the book, Roosevelt had the benefit of notes, letters, and diaries that he wrote over many years. His quotes from these contemporary sources provide vivid pictures of conditions of life and the personalities of the regions he visited, including Abdul Aziz Ibn Saud, his Syrian counselor Sheikh Yusuf Yasin, Habib Bourguiba, shah of Iran, and a host of Kurdish, Arab, and Iranian figures. Roosevelt discusses his experiences with the Kurds, particularly on Mahabad on pp. 248-288. (abridged, David D. Newsom/ *MEJ* 42, Autumn 1988: 700-701)

917   Saeedpour, Vera Beaudin (ed.). *The Legacy of Saladin*. New York: The Kurdish Library, 1999. Being volume 13, no. 1 of *The International Journal of Kurdish Studies*.

This issue of the journal is dedicated to the legacy of this most illustrious of Kurds. Egyptian scholar Fahmy Hafez sets the stage for the era of Saladin in his introduction to the Crusades. A portrait of Saladin's character as drawn by chronicler Baha' ad-Din ibn Shaddad is reprinted from a translation by the late Francesco Gabrielli. Cambridge University scholar M. C. Lyons assesses Saladin's life and legend based largely on early European source material. A third article taken from sources in the Kurdish Library deals with the debate surrounding Saladin's legacy and the rather remarkable accolades he has received even from critics. Of particular interest is the influence on Saladin of his Kurdish heritage. The original biographers are of little help on this score. To complicate matters, today many Kurds dismiss their ancestor as yet another failed Kurdish leader who placed the interests of non-Kurds above those of his own people. They credit this founder of the Ayyubid Empire with its loss, convinced that had he been more ethnocentric, Kurds would have been ruling the Middle East today. Research conducted by R. Stephen Humphreys on the origins of the Ayyubid confederacy, which we have reprinted from his book on the dynasty, tells a different story. This is also true in the extended article by Paul A. Blaum, which begins with his successors and ends with the demise of Ayyubid reign. Complete bibliographic details are as follows: Fahmy Hafez: "The Crusades and the Era of Saladin," pp. 1-14; Francessco, Gabrielli: "Saladin's Character," pp. 15-32; M. C. Lyons: "Saladin: Life and Legend," pp. 33-42; Vera Beaudin Saeedpour: "The Legacy of Saladin," pp. 43-62; R. Stephen Humphreys: "The Origins of the Ayyubid Confederacy," 63-104; Paul A. Blaum: "Eagles in the Sun: The Ayyubids after Saladin," pp. 105-180.

918 Safrastian, Arshak. *The Kurds and Kurdistan*. London: Harvill Press, 1948. 106 p.: ill.

The main content of the book is an able and well-balanced summary of Kurdish history over the last 3,000 years. The author is erudite and cautious in his use of materials, but the reader needs to remember that it is really only during the last fifty years or so that the Kurds as a whole have moved out of the realm of legend into the arena of power politics. The change has not been a happy one. Safrastian concedes that the real troubles of the Kurds only began with the collapse of the Ottoman Empire. Under the Sublime Porte, four-fifths of the Kurdish "nation" were to be subjects of one administration, however unjust and incompetent. After the failure of the Treaty of Sevres in 1923, the Kurds found their country partitioned among no less than five national authorities, all deeply suspicious of each other's ultimate political intentions. (abridged, Edmund R. Leach/*Asian Affairs* 36, January 1949: 94)

919 Schmidt, Dana Adams. *Journey among Brave Men*. Foreword by William O. Douglas. Boston: Little, Brown, 1964. xiv, 298 p.: ill., maps. An Arabic translation was published in 1972 by Dar al-Tali'a (Beirut).

This book is written by an American journalist who made trips "behind the lines" to interview Mulla Mustafa and other Kurdish leaders. Schmidt, then of *The New York Times*, visited the Mulla in August 1962 and twice again in 1963. He was able in Iraq to inspect military installations, observe some military action and talk with responsible party leaders. The author provides rather personal accounts of his hardships getting into and out of Kurdistan, as well as evaluations of Mulla Mustafa Barzani and other leaders. Schmidt presents a sympathetic yet balanced account of the Kurds' struggle. He portrays Barzani as a popular, almost legendary hero who has succeeded in uniting all Kurdistan, an effective politician and military strategist, a sincere person and disposed to distrust the communists in spite of his sojourn in the USSR. The Kurds' goal is local autonomy within an Iraqi republic; that is, economic, governmental and social matters in Kurdistan would be administered by the Kurds, with Baghdad responsible for foreign affairs and national defense. Each succeeding regime in Baghdad has begun with promises of support for Kurdish claims, yet the Arabs have to date made no real concession to the Kurds. Schmidt sees eventual Kurdish victory; they desire now only an autonomous Kurdistan within an Iraqi federation and will not demand a Greater Kurdistan unless driven to it by Iraqi intransigence and un-realism. He concludes that the U.S. should support Kurdish desires, which are just, by applying gentle pressure on Baghdad to make it see reason and by assuring Turkey and Iran of U.S. basic commitment to CENTO. Otherwise the Kurds may become desperate, unreasonable and dangerous. Includes varying amounts of historical and cultural background. (abridged, Ernest N. McCarus/*MEJ* 20, Winter 1966: 116-117)

920 Semo, Ereb (Shamilov, Arab). *Sivane Kurd/Le berger kurde, Kurdifransizi/Kurde-francais*. [The Kurdish Shepherd, Kurdish-French] Translated into French and Kurdish by Basile Nikitine and Noureddine Zaza, respectively. Paris: Institut kurde de Paris, 1989. 325 p.

This autobiographic tale romanced by Ereb Semo (1897-1978) was published for the first time in 1935 in Erivan by the State Publishing House under the title *Sivane Karmatsa*. The work was soon widely distributed and then translated and published in Russian. Basile Nikitine made the French translation that served as a base for Noureddine Zaza's Kurdo-Latin alphabet version that appeared in Beirut in 1947 under the title *Sivane Kurd u Kurden Alagoz*. In 1958, Ereb Semo wrote a new version of the tale, this time in the Cyrillic alphabet under the title *Berbang* (*The Dawn*). The present edition is a bilingual (Kurdish-French) translation of the original version. The Kurdish text is Zaza's translation whereas the French text is Nikitine's. This work, which interests both the anthropologists and sociologists, portrays the social and economic conditions of the Kurds in the 20th century and describes some cultural aspects of the Kurdish society, emphasizing on those of the nomads. In 1988, an Arabic version was published by Matba'at al-Sabah (Damascus); it was translated by Tawfiq al-Husayni and titled: *al-Ra'i al-Kurdi*. Al-Husayni also translated *Sivane Kurd u Kurden Alagoz* into Arabic (Damascus: Matba'at al-Sabah, 1990).

921 Sluglett, Peter. *Britain in Iraq, 1914-1932*. London: Ithaca Press for the Middle East Centre, St. Antony's College, Oxford, 1976. [13], 360 p.: 2 maps. (St. Antony's Middle East Monographs; no. 4). Bibliography: p. 332-347. Includes indexes.

The book traces in two parts the origins and development of the system of British control imposed on Iraq from the beginning of World War I to the end of the British mandate in 1932. Part I gives a general historical and political sketch of the entire period. Part II, together with two significant appendices, treats in more detail the specific administrative and military policies that were pursued by the British in order to secure control over Iraq and promote British imperial interests there. The essay on tribal, educational and defense policies in Part II for example, serve to amplify and illuminate themes which would fit very awkwardly into a chronological study, yet they are crucial for an understanding of the extent of British influence in Iraq. (abridged, G. Neal Lendenmann/ *MEJ* 31, Spring 1977: 213)

922 Vanly, Ismet Chériff. *Le Kurdistan irakien: Entite nationale. Etude de la Revolution de 1961*. [Iraqi Kurdistan: National Entity. A Study of the Revolution of 1961.] Neuchatel: Editions de la Baconniere, 1970. 419 p. (Histoire et Societe D'aujourd'hui)

Vanly's book tells the tale of the latest and longest of the fights in the 1960s. The book is primarily a political history of the Kurdish side of things in the decade since major fighting broke out in 1961. It quotes extensively from Kurdish documents relating to internal administrative affairs, to party matters and to dealings between Baghdad and the Kurds. Included also are a dozen important texts (translated from Kurdish) as appendices. In sum, this is a valuable book, basically fair despite its author's commitment to the Kurdish cause, and an important contribution to understanding the reasons why these tough mountain men have hung together for ten years against larger and better armed forces, determined to secure a measure of autonomy for themselves.

923   Vanly, Ismet Chériff. "Kurdistan in Iraq." In *A People without a Country: The Kurds and Kurdistan*. Edited by Gerard Chaliand; translated from French by Michael Pallis; foreword by David McDowall, pp. 139-193. London: Zed Books Ltd., 1993.

Includes a discussion on the geographic and demographic features of the Kurds and Kurdistan in Iraq. Also included is a discussion on discrimination and economic exploitation in Kurdistan.

924   White, Paul J. "Citizenship under the Ottomans and Kemalists: How the [Turkish] Kurds Were Excluded." *Citizenship Studies* 3, no. 1 (February 1999): 71-102.

This article examines the relevance of concepts of citizenship as tools for analyzing and comprehending minorities in ethnically complex societies. Taking the Kurds of Turkey as a case study, this article traces the evolution of civil society from the Ottoman Empire through to the modern Turkish state, using a human rights-based definition of citizenship. The changed situation of the Kurds is shown in each epoch and appropriate conclusions are drawn. The complex diversity of the Kurds is also noted. An assessment is made of the applicability of what could be called Weberian and neo-Weberian concepts of citizenship.

925   Williams, Gwyn. *Eastern Turkey: A Guide and History*. London: Faber and Faber, 1972. 255 p.: illus. Bibliography: p. 247-250.

926   Xenophon. *The Persian Expedition*. Edited by E. V. Rieu. Translated by Rex Warner. Harmondsworth, Middlesex, England: Penguin Books, 1949. 309 p.

An excellent record of one of the most famous marches in history, during the early 4th century B.C., in which the author took part by joining Cyrus's army of Greek mercenaries. While narrating the long march into Persia through the mountains of Kurdistan, and the tedious return to Greece, the author presents a genuine picture of the social life in general.

927   Yassin, Borhanedin A. *Vision or Reality? The Kurds in the Policy of the Great Powers, 1941-1947*. Lund, Sweden: Lund University Press, 1995. 246 p.: maps. Includes bibliographical references (p. 230-242) and index.

Originally the author's dissertation, Yassin analyzes Kurdish nationalism, with particular emphasis on the Kurds in Iran, by examining a variety of factors, some within the Kurdish community itself, others lying outside of it, i.e., in the policy of the states where the Kurds reside, and in the wider international arena (especially regarding British and Russian interventions). In this study the Kurdish people are linked to major developments in the period 1941-1947, with particular emphasis on the policy of the Great Powers vis-avis the Kurds. The establishment and demise of the Kurdish Republic of Mahabad is discussed in detail. Many primary sources are used in this study.

928   Zaki, Muhammad Amin. *Mashahir al-Kurd wa-Kurdistan fi al-Dawr al-Islami*. [Biographies of famous Kurdish persons from the rise of Muhammad to the late days of the Ottoman Empire] Vol. 1. Translated from Kurdish by Sanha Amin Zaki. Baghdad: s.n., 1945. 276 p.

929   Zaki, Muhammad Amin. *Mashahir al-Kurd wa-Kurdistan fi al-Dawr al-Islami*. [Biographies of famous Kurdish persons from the rise of Muhammad to the late days of the Ottoman Empire] Vol. 2. Translated from Kurdish by Muhammad 'Ali 'Awni. Cairo: Matba'at al-Sa'ada, 1947. 250 p.

930   Zana, Mehdi. *Prison no. 5: Eleven Years in Turkish Jails*. Watertown, MA: Blue Crane Books, 1997. [Human rights & democracy] Text translated by André Vauquelin.

Zana, a Kurdish activist, describes his awakening to the idea of rights for the Kurds and his sufferings in prison as a result of his activism. He also describes the region of his birth near the city of Diyarbekir where he was once mayor, and cites the Muslim hero Saladin, who was a Kurd.

931   Zaza, Noureddine. *Ma vie de Kurde, ou, le cri du peuple kurde*. [My Life as a Kurd or the Cry of the Kurdish People] Lausanne: P.-M. Favre, 1982. 266 p., [16] p. of plates: ill. (Collection "Des causes et des hommes.")

This work is an itinerary of the Kurdish writer and Dr. Noureddine Zaza since his childhood in the Ottoman and Kemalist Turkey, through Syria, Iraq, Lebanon and Switzerland, and once again through Syria, Lebanon, and Turkey ending in Switzerland where he spent the rest of his life as a Swiss citizen. An affectionate account that permits one to grasp, through Zaza's difficult route, the tragedy of the Kurdish people nowadays. (Dominique Ferrandini/*AI* 5:681)

Appendix: Kurdish World Wide Web Resources

The list given here is limited to sites of independent non-profit Kurdish organizations. These sites, however, include many links to other sources. A listing of all Kurdish political parties' sites that are available on the Internet can be found in these same sites and at the following address: http://www.politicalresources.net/kurdistan.htm.

AKA Kurdistan (http://www.akakurdistan.com)
This site provides the opportunity to build a collective memory with a people who have no national archive. The site actually continues the work begun by Susan Meiselas in *Kurdistan: In the Shadow of History* (Random House, 1997). The book's stunning collection of old photographs are included here, and visitors are invited to add photos and stories that help tell and preserve the Kurds' history.

The American Kurdish Information Network (http://www.kurdistan.org)
AKIN is a non-profit, tax-exempt organization established in 1993 to serve the information needs of the United States relative to the Kurds. AKIN collects, translates, and disseminates information about the Kurds. It provides the latest news on the situation in Kurdistan; exposes human rights violation and repression against the Kurdish people; and informs the public about the political and cultural developments in Kurdistan. AKIN aims to disseminate information to the press and media; to solicit the support of human rights organizations; to secure the interest of Congress, political leaders, and other democratic and progressive forces; to publish documents, reports, and books related to the politics and culture of Kurdistan; and to provide information and give advice to journalists, representatives, and human rights activists intending to visit the

region. AKIN publications include press releases and newsletters; reports from government officials, lawyers, and human rights organizations concerning human rights abuses in Kurdistan. It also has information on prisons and some heart-wrenching photos of Kurdish oppression in Iraq, Turkey and Iran.

Institut Kurde de Paris (http://www.institutkurde.org/homea.htm)

After ten years of activity in the form of a non-profit organization, the Institute became a Foundation of recognized public benefit by a decree signed by the French Prime Minister on March 2nd 1993. It is run by a 15 Board of Directors, two of which are representatives of the French Ministries of Culture and of the Interior. This Board is renewed every three years. The Institute enjoys the support of many western intellectuals and organizations, often in the form of sponsoring its activities. It maintains the largest Kurdish library in the western world. At present, the Institute possesses over 6,500 monographs on the Kurds, in 23 languages, several tens of thousands of writings, collections of periodicals and newspapers, photos, videos as well as an archive of sounds and musical recordings. The library is open to public and is heavily used by voluntary associations, the media, and institutional bodies in France and the European Union. The Institute also reprints older publications and serves as a publishing house, primarily for publications in Kurdish. News from major papers of the world and the Middle East and an extensive list of Kurdish sites are also provided on the Institute's web site.

The International Kurdish Women's Studies Network
(http://www.oise.utoronto.ca/projects/kwnet/eframeset.htm)

The Network was formed in the fall of 1996. It started as a response to a growing need for opening a space for Kurdish women in international debates on women's studies, and promoting gender justice among the Kurdish communities in the diaspora and the Middle East. The Network was founded by a number of Kurdish and non-Kurdish women activists and researchers. Currently it has an international body with individual and organizational membership from Europe, North America, and the Middle East. It provides a forum for exchange of experience and knowledge among those who are interested in and work for improving the lives of Kurdish women. The Network's aims are to act as a liaison for community-based, institution-based, academic and independent researchers and activists in all parts of Kurdistan and in the diaspora, to assist those engaged in Kurdish women's studies and activism in all regions of Kurdistan and in the diaspora, and to promote women's rights and gender equality in Kurdistan. The site is available in English and German.

Kurdish Academic Network
(http://www.zyworld.com/kan_kurd/home.htm)

KAN is a non-political voluntary organization established by academics in the United Kingdom to support education at all levels in Iraqi Kurdistan. This site provides a brief background on the Kurdish people, the geographical area of Iraqi Kurdistan and its existing education system. It also highlights the needs of education and the role of KAN in meeting those needs. The site has a news section and provides links to universities in Iraqi Kurdistan.

Kurdish Human Rights Project (http://www.khrp.org/)
KHRP is an independent, non-political project founded and based in Britain. It is a registered charity that is committed to the protection of the human rights of all persons within the Kurdish regions, irrespective of race, religion, sex, political persuasion or other belief or opinion. Its supporters include both Kurdish and non-Kurdish people. KHRP Press Releases provide human rights lawyers, activists, politicians and journalists with the latest breaking news on developments in the Kurdish region and in particular on cases that KHRP is assisting. Press releases since 1994 are available online. Site includes KHRP activities and publications, as well as links to an extensive list of human rights organizations, governmental bodies, and Kurdish organizations.

MED-TV (http://www.med-tv.be/med/)
MED-TV is a satellite channel broadcasting to Kurdish communities all over Europe, the Middle East and North Africa. It is the only international television station to offer a complete schedule of Kurdish-language programming, to a potential audience of 35 million Kurds across the globe, and aims to assist in the development of the cultural identity of the Kurdish people and the Kurdish language, celebrating the rich cultural diversities within.

Washington Kurdish Institute (http://myweb.clark.net/kurd/)
WKI is a non-profit, nonpartisan, research and educational organization whose motto is "For Kurdish People Worldwide." WKI amplifies informed, independent perspectives of issues which affect Kurds and bear directly on regional stability and U.S. national interests. The Advisory Committee includes prominent scholars, human rights practitioners, Middle East and foreign policy experts, and Kurds from around the world. Highlights include the WKI online newsletter, "*Zagros,*" a gallery of Kurdish artwork, bibliography on Kurdish and related issues, the Voice of America (VOA) Kurdish programming schedule, and links to human rights resources. Users may contact the webmaster to subscribe to an excellent mailing list to receive daily news coverage via email (e.g., from Reuters, Turkish Daily News, International Herald Tribune).

Name Index

Title Index

Subject Index

About the Compilers

LOKMAN I. MEHO is a Ph.D. candidate at the School of Information and Library Science, University of North Carolina, Chapel Hill. He is the author of two earlier bibliographies, *The Kurds and Kurdistan: A Selective and Annotated Bibliography* (Greenwood, 1997) and *Libraries and Information in the Arab World: An Annotated Bibliography* (Greenwood, 1999), and is working on a documentary history of the Kurdish question in U.S. government publications.

KELLY L. MAGLAUGHLIN is a Ph.D. student at the School of Information and Library Science, University of North Carolina, Chapel Hill.